ILLINOIS
BIOGRAPHICAL
DICTIONARY
2008–2009 EDITION

ILLINOIS
BIOGRAPHICAL
DICTIONARY
2008–2009 EDITION

VOLUME

2

K-Z

State History Publications, LLC
P.O. Box 510
Hamburg, MI 48139 U.S.A.

ISBN 978-1878592-60-6

Editorial Staff:

Caryn Hannan: *Researcher/Writer/Editor*

B.A. in English Literature – Hope International University, Fullerton, CA

Jennifer L. Herman: *Researcher/Writer/Editor*

B.A. in American Studies – Pitzer College, Claremont, CA

Biography Writers and Editors:

Bryan Dye, Mel Ewald, Gloria Genel-Gonzalez, Lyla J. Lawry,
Carol Malin, Lori Forte Miller, Cladia Naber, Rebecca Mordue,
Joe Posner, Russell Schaffer, Pat Tatum, William Turner

Table of Contents

Volume Two

K

KANE, ELIAS KENT

(1794-1835) Senator from Illinois; Senate Years of Service: 1825-1835; born in New York City on June 7, 1794; attended the public schools; graduated from Yale College in 1813; studied law; admitted to the bar and commenced practice in Nashville, Tenn.; moved to Kaskaskia, Ill., in 1814; appointed judge of the Territory of Illinois; delegate to the first State constitutional convention in 1818; unsuccessful candidate for election in 1820 to the Seventeenth Congress; first secretary of State of Illinois 1820-1824; member, State

Elias Kent Kane

house of representatives 1824; elected to the United States Senate in 1824; reelected in 1831 and served from March 4, 1825, until his death in Washington, D.C., December 12, 1835; chairman, Committee to Audit and Control the Contingent Expenses (Nineteenth through Twenty-first Congresses), Committee on Private Land Claims (Twenty-first through Twenty-third Congresses), Committee on Public Lands (Twenty-second Congress); interment in the family cemetery on the old Kane farm, near Fort Gage, Ill.

KEANE, JAMES JOHN

(1857-1929) — Roman Catholic prelate, was born August 26, 1857, in Joliet, Illinois, one of the five children of John and Margaret (O'Connor) Keane, Irish emigrants. His parents soon moved to a frontier farm near Rochester, Minnesota, and sent Keane to St. John's Seminary in Collegeville, Minnesota, and to the College of St. Francis Xavier in New York City. Deciding to enter the priesthood, Keane was assigned to the Grand Seminary at Montreal, Canada, where he completed his theological studies under the Sulpicians, and was ordained by Archbishop E.C. Fabre on December 23, 1882. He served as a curate at St. Mary's and as pastor of St. Joseph's Church in St. Paul, Minnesota, from 1882 to 1885.

Transferred to St. Thomas College as instructor and bursar, Keane was appointed rector in 1888 by Archbishop Ireland. In 1892, he was given the rectorship of the Church of the Immaculate Conception, the leading parish of Minneapolis, where he won the love of his congregation as a forceful preacher, as a democratic, candid man, and as a builder. Influenced by his archbishop, he played a leading citizen's part in civic affairs, and no small share in the beginning of the Basilica of St. Mary's can be ascribed to his skill as a collector. He was selected as the third bishop of Cheyenne, Wyoming.

Consecrated at the St. Paul Cathedral by Archbishop Ireland, on October 28, 1902, Keane commenced the arduous labors of the missionary bishop of a huge, sparsely settled area with 7,000 scattered communicants and only a few priests. Wyoming grew slowly, but under his rule, the number of Catholic communicants almost doubled, missions gave way to churches, new stations were established, and funds were gathered for the erection of St. Mary's Cathedral. On August 11, 1911, Keane was translated to the archiepiscopal See of Dubuque, a compact, prosperous diocese. Again, he proved an invigorating leader of priests and people rather than a ruler. Liberal in his views, he lived as simply as a curate and despite ill health carried the burdens of his office. He fostered the *Catholic Tribune Weekly*, founded in 1899, and the *Daily American Tribune*, founded in 1920; established a diocesan organ, *The Witness*, in 1921; built about thirteen churches; reorganized Columbia College, collecting an endowment of a million dollars and erecting nine halls; and created a diocesan bureau of missions and a bureau of education in the hope of standardizing the eight academies and a hundred parochial schools; supported Clarke College for women; established St. Therese's Home for Foundlings; and displayed unusual interest in the charitable institutions and the eleven hospitals with which the diocese was provided.

In 1920, Keane was a member of the Peace Commission on Ireland; and in 1926, he was a speaker at the eleventh annual meeting on the World Alliance for International Friendship, held in Pittsburgh, Pennsylvania. He was made an assistant at the pontifical throne in connection with the celebration of his Episcopal jubilee. Long in unstable health, he died suddenly on August 2, 1929, of apoplexy and was buried from St. Raphael's Cathedral in Mount Olivet Cemetery.

KEEFE, DANIEL JOSEPH

(1852-1929) — Labor leader, industrial arbitrator, and U.S. commissioner general of immigration, was born on September 27, 1852, at Willowsprings, Illinois, near Chicago, the son of John and Catherine Keefe. When he was ten, his mother died, and shortly afterward, he left school with a fourth-grade education. At twelve, he began driving for his father, who was a teamster in Chicago, but two years later his father's death left him to make his own way. At age eighteen, he was a lumber handler and longshoreman. Later, he contracted with shipping companies to furnish men, largely recent immigrants, to load and unload vessels, and in 1882 was elected president of the Lumber Unloaders' Association.

When the National (now International) Longshoremen's Association was formed in 1892, he promptly became the dominant figure in that organization, serving as its president, except for three years, from 1893 until 1908. Keefe was also, from 1897 to 1901, a member of the Illinois State Board of Arbitration. Like a brother who became a capitalist, Keefe was a shrewd business man who knew how to deal successfully with employers and under his leadership the longshoremen developed a system of cooperative contracts, taken directly by the union for specific pieces of work, which soon became general on the Great Lakes. He favored an industrial rather than a craft form of organization, and he built up a powerful industrial federation, which claimed, in 1905, approximately one hundred thousand members, and included all workers connected with water transportation except seamen. He took an active part in the organization and early history of the National Civic Federation, and was intimately associated with the development of Roosevelt's plan for the use of his Nobel Peace Prize money to establish the Foundation for the Promotion of Industrial Peace.

Keefe was also a member of the executive council of the American Federation of Labor from 1903 to 1908, first as seventh and later as sixth vice-president. But when, in 1908, the federation came out for William Jennings Bryan for president, Keefe, who had previously always voted with the Republican Party on national issues, campaigned for William H. Taft. On December 1, 1908, President Theodore Roosevelt appointed him commissioner general of immigration. In that office, he soon found himself merely an instrument for the administration of an act that he considered entirely inadequate as interpreted by the solicitor of the Department of Commerce and Labor. In defense against criticisms of his administration by former associates in the labor movement, he could only recommend in his annual reports methods of strengthening the law — recommendations which fell with Taft's veto of the bill imposing a literacy test. Shortly after leaving office on May 31, 1913, he made a tour of parts of Asia and Europe studying labor conditions and organizations. During World War I, he was a conciliation commissioner for the U.S. Department of Labor, and from August 1921 until his retirement in April 1925, he was engaged in the prevention and settlement of labor disputes for the U.S. Shipping Board Merchant Fleet Corporation. His last years were spent at Elmhurst, Illinois, a suburb of Chicago, where he died on January 2, 1929.

In 1878 he married Ellen E. Conners and in 1904, after her death, married Emma L. Walker, who died in 1925.

KELLY, EDWARD JOSEPH

(1876-1950) — Political boss and mayor of Chicago, was born on May 1, 1876, to Stephen and Helen (Lang) Kelly. His father, who worked as a city fireman and then as a policeman, found it difficult to support his ever-growing family, so Kelly began selling newspapers at the age of nine, left school at twelve, and over the next five years, worked at odd jobs. While watching a crew at work on the Columbian Exposition of 1893, he was inspired to become an engineer. He got a job as an axman with the Sanitary District of Chicago, the political authority controlling the city's sewage and water systems. To make up for his educational deficiencies, Kelly enrolled in night classes at the Chicago Athenaeum, a school specializing in mathematics, and later studied engineering. He rose in the sanitary district up to chief engineer (1920).

During this time, mismanagement, payroll padding, and reckless spending was running rampant through the local government offices. In 1930, Kelly and nine other sanitary-district officials were named in a federal indictment charging conspiracy to defraud the district of five million dollars. The indictment against Kelly was revoked for lack of evidence, but was later cited for underpayment of income taxes between 1919 and 1929, a claim that he settled for $105,000. Meanwhile, he was cementing his relationship with Patrick A. Nash, a leader in the local Democratic Party and an affluent sewer contractor. Kelly's political connections won him a post on Chicago's South Park Board in 1922. He initiated projects to beautify the city's lakefront, oversaw construction of the Shedd Aquarium and Adler Planetarium, and cooperated with the philanthropist Julius Rosenwald in establishing Chicago's Museum of Science and Industry.

When Mayor Anton J. Cermak was killed in 1933, Nash, as

chairman of the Cook County Democratic Central Committee, ordered a subservient city council to appoint Kelly to serve out Cermak's term. Kelly remained the city's chief executive for fourteen years, winning the 1935, 1939, and 1943 elections. Meanwhile, he and Nash built one of the nation's strongest political organizations through firm control of some 40,000-patronage jobs.

Chicago was virtually bankrupt when Kelly first took office, and millions of dollars in delinquent taxes and unpaid bills. Through federal public works projects and the mortgaging of land owned by the Board of Education, he restored the city's financial health. He pushed through innumerable physical improvements, from the widening of State Street, to the building of the first section of a subway system; he also developed the city's fire department into one of the nation's most efficient. He was a firm exponent of public housing, and he insisted on a policy of nondiscrimination. He established the Chicago Recovery Administration and the Keep Chicago Ahead Committee, which worked for the development of business and industry; he initiated "Drama of Chicago on Parade," a series of civic pageants; and secured one hundred million dollars for a superhighway program. During World War II, he established a group of servicemen's centers that made Chicago noted for its hospitality. On the national scene, Kelly was the Democratic national committeeman, and in 1940, he spearheaded President Franklin Roosevelt's third-term campaign.

For all the material improvements, Kelly's mayoral years were speckled with scandal. Chicago's civil service system was manipulated to reward political underlings and their relatives. Despite sporadic cleanup campaigns, the streets and alleys remained the dirtiest in the world. In addition, the school system was under constant fire, principally from the National Education Association.

Such adverse publicity, coupled with local Democratic losses in the 1946 elections, prompted party leaders to choose a new mayoral candidate in 1947. Kelly, after completing his term, retired from active politics. In the last three years of his life, he headed an engineering consulting firm and devoted much time to raising money for a new building for Chicago's Mercy Hospital.

Kelly was married twice: on March 20, 1910, to Mary Edmunda Roche, who died in 1918; and on January 25, 1922, to Margaret Ellen Kirk. The only child by the first marriage died at the age of fourteen. With his second wife, Kelly adopted three children. Kelly died on October 20, 1950, of a heart attack in Chicago.

KELSEY, RAYNER WICKERSHAM

(1879-1934) — Quaker minister, historian, and teacher, was born on January 29, 1879, in Western Springs, Cook County, Illinois, the youngest of the five children of Asa and Sarah (Atwater) Kelsey, who had four sons and one daughter. His ancestry can be traced to William Kelsey, who emigrated from England to Cambridge, Massachusetts, about 1630, and in 1636, joined the followers of Thomas Hooker in the founding of Hartford, Connecticut. His mother was active in the ministry and the daughter of two well-known ministers of the New York Yearly Meeting, Mead and Huldah (Hoag) Atwater.

His childhood was spent in Western Springs, where he attended the public schools. He graduated from Earlham College, Richmond, Indiana, in 1900. On February 23, 1901, he married Naomi Harrison Binford of Greenfield, Indiana. Their only son, Rayner Wilfred, was born in 1910. From 1900 to 1904, he gave instruction in German and public speaking in Pacific College, Oregon, and from 1904 to 1906, he taught in the same fields in Whittier College, California. In 1909, he received the degree of doctor of philosophy from the University of California, his thesis being *The United States Consulate in California* (1910). In 1909, he was appointed instructor in history in Haverford College, becoming professor in 1911, and curator of the Haverford Collection of Quakeriana in 1922, the most important source for Quaker research in America.

Kelsey was distinguished as a teacher and had a profound influence not only on those in his classes, but also on the entire student body. One of his major interests throughout his life was the just treatment and promotion of the welfare of Native Americans. He was a member and later chairman of the Associated Executive Committee of Friends on Indian Affairs. In 1917, he published *Friends and the Indians*. He wrote the *Centennial History of Moses Brown School* (1919), a school in Providence, Rhode Island. He was also the author of a valuable series of handbooks of citizenship.

He was president of the association of History Teachers of the Middle States and Maryland (1921-1922); a life member of the American Historical Association and of the Historical Society of Pennsylvania; and was president of Friends' Historical Association, 1913-1915. For ten years (1922-1932), Kelsey was editor of the *Bulletin of Friends' Historical Association*. He contributed numerous articles to the *Dictionary of American Biography*, the most important of which were those on William Penn and Isaac Sharpless. From 1925 until his death, he was one of the seven trustees of the Proportional Representation League.

He was a recorded minister of the Society of Friends. He made a large contribution to the historical knowledge of the Quakers, but at the same time he was a living and significant transmitter of the Quaker message and way of life. He died from a heart attack on October 29, 1934, in Haverford, Pennsylvania.

KEMPFF, LOUIS

(1841-1920) — Naval officer, was born on October 11, 1841, near Belleville, Illinois, the son of Friedrich and Henrietta Kempff. He entered the Naval Academy in 1857, was detached in April 1861, and was ordered to the *Vandalia* on the Charleston blockade. After taking a captured schooner to New York he was sent to the *Wabash*, took part in the attack on the forts at Port Royal, and commanded a howitzer in the boat attacks on Port Royal Ferry and Fernandina, Florida, all before he was warranted as a midshipman in 1862.

In that year, he was sent to the *Susquehanna*, was present at the recapture of Norfolk, West Virginia, and engaged in blockade duty off Mobile, Alabama. In 1863, he served on the gunboat *Sonoma* off the Sabine River and in the next year was on the *Connecticut* off Wilmington, Delaware. The close of the war found him on the gunboat *Suwanee* in the Pacific, the region in which, except for a short period at the War College, he served the rest of his career. This service involved duty as executive officer on the *Portsmouth*, *Independence*, *Mohican*, *Saranac*, and *California*, various posts at the Mare Island Navy Yard, and command of the *Alert* (1881-1882), of the *Adams* (1885-1888), and of the *Monterey* (1893-1895).

In 1899, Kempff was made a rear admiral and assigned to duty as second in command of the Asiatic Squadron. In 1900, he was the senior American naval officer off Taku, where an international fleet was assembled to protect the lives of foreigners in northern China. Under his orders, sailors and marines were landed, but when the other foreign admirals demanded that the Chinese surrender the Taku forts, Kempff declined to join in the demand, fearing that the Boxers would seize them and thus be able to interrupt communication with Tien Tsin and Peking. His decision was based on his belief that the Chinese imperial authorities had not as yet committed any act of war and was in accordance with his instructions from Washington and the general policy of the United States toward China.. Kempff cooperated with the other foreign commanders in later operations and was commended by the Navy Department for his refusal to join in the attack on the forts. When he returned to the United

States, the Chinese minister, Wu Ting Fang, gave him a complimentary banquet in San Francisco, California.

After this cruise, Kempff served as commandant of the Pacific Naval District until he was retired in 1903. He died on July 29, 1920, in Santa Barbara, California, and was buried there. In 1873, at Fair Oaks, California, he had married Cornelia Reese, adopted daughter of Thomas H. Selby. His wife survived him.

Keokuk

KEOKUK

(1780-1848) — Native American Indian chief of the Sauk (Sac) and Fox tribes, also known as Keokock and "Watchful Fox." Born at the village of Saukenuk on the Rock River in what is now Illinois, Keokuk was probably part French. His rise to power was largely the result of his capitulation to the American government and his skills as an orator.

Since he was not born to a ruling family, Keokuk first assumed a subordinate roll at the Sauk council. Later, as tribal guest-keeper, he became the official host of the tribe. His election as war chief followed an emotional speech he delivered to tribal council urging them to defend their lands during the War of 1812. This was the last time he ever urged resistance to the Americans.

As Native American agents and the military played upon Keokuk's ambition with gifts and prestige, Keokuk's importance grew in the eyes of the tribe. Many Sauk, however, favored resistance and followed Black Hawk, chief of the rival Thunder clan. During the War of 1812, Black Hawk and his warriors came to the aid of the British against the Americans on the Canadian frontier. While Black Hawk fought the Americans to the North, Keokuk remained behind with the main body of the tribe and assumed an important seat on the Sauk council.

Although this successful bid for power intensified the rivalry between Keokuk and Black Hawk, they did work together on at least one occasion. In 1823, they tried to convince the government to retain the traditional tribal villages that sat on land the government had taken earlier in the century. Keokuk traveled to Washington, D.C., to argue their case, but the question of the villages was not solved.

While Keokuk was in Washington, the government sponsored a tour of the eastern United States for him. The tour convinced Keokuk more than ever that resisting the advance of white settlers was futile. He returned to the Sauk with stories of the white settlements to the east as further proof that his position of capitulation to the government was the only course. Black Hawk remained unconvinced and sought unsuccessfully to organize against white expansion. Later, in 1831, the federal government put the tribal villages, which Keokuk had sought to save, up for sale.

As American settlers moved closer to the ancient tribal lands along the Rock River, Keokuk urged the Sauk to be patient. When hostilities broke out further north between the American settlers and the Winnebago, Keokuk kept his people friendly to the Americans. In the late 1820s, Keokuk urged the Sauk and the Fox to comply with the government's demand that they move westward, abandoning their ancestral homelands to the influx of settlers. Black Hawk retained a following, however, and in 1832, led a band of Sauk up the Rock River country to lead a united Sauk-Fox force against the Illinois Militia and their allies. Keokuk warned the American agent at Rock Island of Black Hawk's intentions, and Black Hawk was defeated. During the negotiations that followed, the American government appointed Keokuk chief of the Sauk-Fox and gave him the responsibility of administrating the money that the government paid for the Sauk lands. In addition, Keokuk's faction was awarded land on the Iowa River.

In 1837, he again journeyed east to debate Sioux representatives over land in what is now Iowa. He won his case for the Sauk-Fox in Iowa. However, a few years later, Keokuk complied with government demands, turning over the reservation in Iowa to the American government and moving his tribe to Kansas in 1845.

By that time Keokuk was out of favor with the federal government, for he had lost any influence he had with the Sauk, and he was, therefore, of no use to the authorities. Keokuk was poisoned in June 1848 at the Sauk Agency in Franklin County, Kansas. Little is known about either of Keokuk's two wives, Emma and Hannie. He had one son with Hannie, Moses Keokuk, who succeeded his father as chief.

Otto Kerner, Jr.

KERNER, OTTO, JR.

(1908-1976) — Thirty-fifth governor of Illinois, (1961-1968) was born in Chicago, Illinois, the son of Rose B. Chmelik and Otto Kerner. His father was a lawyer and served as judge of the Cook County Circuit Court and the U. S. State Court of Appeals.

Kerner received his degree from Brown University, and after a year's study at Cambridge University, England, began studying law at Northwestern University in Evanston. He was admitted to the state bar in 1934, and joined a law firm, where he dealt with corporate legal questions. During World War II, he joined the U. S. Army and rose to the rank of Major General within ten years (1936-1946).

Kerner began his political career in 1947, when he was appointed U. S. District Attorney for the Northern District of Illinois. Meanwhile, he was also a member of Chicago Bar Association committees on constitutional amendment, criminal law, and war activities. From 1950 to 1953, he was a member of the Chicago Crime Prevention Council, which may have led to his candidacy for Cook County Judge, where he served from 1954 until taking office as governor of the state in 1961.

In the first months of his gubernatorial term, Kerner approved raises in the state sales and corporate taxes to pay for his unprecedented three billion dollar budget. He also supported passage of a fair employment practices law, a consumer credit law, and a new criminal code. Although he faced opposition by party lines in both houses of the state legislature, most of his bills were passed. In 1964, Kerner was reelected to a second term, but he resigned to become a judge in the U. S. Court of Appeals in Chicago in 1968.

His judicial term proved less successful than his governorship, as he was indicted and convicted of bribery, conspiracy, income tax evasion, mail fraud, and perjury charges while on the bench. He went to jail after resigning in 1974 from his judgeship. He was paroled after one year.

Kerner died in his hometown in 1976, and was buried at Arlington National Cemetery.

KILEY, RICHARD PAUL

(1922-1999) — Musical and dramatic actor, was born on March 31, 1922, in Chicago, Illinois. His first acting experience was in the high school production of *The Mikado*. Kiley studied at Loyola University for a few months, but then accepted a scholarship to the Barnum Dramatic School. He stayed there a year, and then entered the U.S. Navy during World War II, serving as a gunnery instructor in Florida.

At war's end, Kiley returned to Chicago and began working on several radio soap operas such as *Ma Perkins*. He moved to New York and got a role in a production of *The Trojan Women*. He secured a job as understudy for the Stanley Kowalski role in the touring company of *A Streetcar Named Desire*. When lead actor, Anthony Quinn, left the show, Kiley took over the top spot.

In 1953, Kiley made his Broadway debut in the role of Joey Percival in a revival of George Bernard Shaw's *Misalliance*, a production that was a major success, both critically and commercially. In December of that year, Kiley appeared on Broadway in the musical *Kismet*.

Kiley began appearing in several television roles, making a name for himself on such shows as the *Robert Montgomery Show*, *Playhouse 90*, *Omnibus*, *Studio One*, and *Kraft Television Theatre*. Kiley began working in films in the 1950s, appearing in such movies as *The Mob*, 1950; *The Sniper*, 1951; *Eight Iron Men*, 1952; and *Pickup on South Street*, 1954. In 1955, he appeared in the controversial film, *Blackboard Jungle*.

The actor returned to the stage in 1954, in the off-Broadway production, *Sing Me No Lullaby*. The play, which dealt with issue of McCarthyism, caused Kiley to lose some work for several months afterward. In 1960, Kiley appeared in *Redhead*, and he won his first Tony Award for his work in that production. In 1960, Kiley played the lead role of Brig Anderson in *Advise and Consent*, a play based on the Pulitzer Prize-winning book by Allen Drury.

In 1965, Kiley starred in what would become his most famous role, that of Miguel de Cervantes/Don Quixote in *Man of La Mancha*. Kiley received several honors for this work, including a second Tony Award, the Drama League Award, and the Drama Critics Poll.

A busy actor in every media, Kiley appeared in the popular

mini-series *Thorn Birds*, for which he won an Emmy and a Golden Globe award, as well as *Do You Remember Love?*, *A Year in the Life* (receiving his second Emmy, 1988), and *Absolute Strangers*. Kiley won both an Emmy Award and a Golden Globe for the 1990s hit shows *A Year In The Life*, and the offbeat *Picket Fences*, his reoccurring role earning him an Emmy Award. For his work in the mini series *The Thorn Birds*, Kiley was also honored with Best Supporting Actor Golden Globe and Emmy Awards.

Kiley died March 5, 1999, at his home after battling a rare bone marrow disease. His second wife, Patricia Ferrier Kiley and his six children from his marriage to the late Mary Bell Wood survived him.

KILGALLEN, DOROTHY MAE

(1913-1965) — Newspaperwoman and television and radio personality, was born on July 3, 1913, in Chicago, Illinois, the daughter of James Lawrence Kilgallen, a newspaperman, and Mary Jane ("Mae") Ahern. Her family lived in Laramie, Wyoming, and Indianapolis, Indiana, before returning to Chicago when she was six. They moved to Brooklyn, New York, in 1923. Kilgallen attended public school and graduated from Erasmus Hall High School in Brooklyn in 1930. Following her freshman year (1930-1931) at the College of New Rochelle, she took a summer job at William Randolph Hearst's *New York Evening Journal*. By the time she was twenty, Kilgallen had a by-line familiar to *Journal* readers.

Murders became her specialty. After covering the trial of Bruno Richard Hauptmann, the convicted kidnapper of the son of Charles Lindbergh, Kilgallen, raced around the world in 1936 on commercial airlines in a contest with two other reporters. She came in second, taking twenty-four days, but "finished first in acclaim and publicity" and instantly became a celebrity.

Sent to Hollywood, California, to capitalize on her new renown, Kilgallen collaborated on a screenplay, *Fly Away Baby* (1937), based on her recent race, wrote a gossip column, played a bit part in the film *Sinner Take All* (1936), but failed to impress the movie kingdom. When she was called back to New York in 1937, she concentrated on social occasions and began participating in news events. While single-handedly covering the coronation of George VI for her paper, Kilgallen became for her readers part of the ceremony. In 1938, she took over the syndicated gossip column "The Voice of Broadway," in the *Journal American* (the two papers had merged in July 1937).

On April 6, 1940, she married Richard Tompkins Kollmar, an

actor whose ancestor, Daniel D. Tompkins, had been governor of New York and vice-president of the United States. In 1945, they began "Breakfast with Dorothy and Dick," a radio program in which they detailed their glamorous lives, criticized small-town America, preached right-of-canter political views, and praised their sponsors' products. Their three children often joined them on this popular show, which continued until 1963.

In 1950, Kilgallen became the "most visible and celebrated journalist of her time" when the Columbia Broadcasting System picked her for "What's My Line?," a television program on which panelists guessed the occupations of guests. She remained on the show the rest of her life. While helping it capture ten million weekly viewers, she doubled (raising to 146 by 1965) the number of newspapers carrying her "Voice of Broadway" column.

After covering Jack Ruby's trial for murdering Lee Harvey Oswald, President John F. Kennedy's assassin, Kilgallen published Ruby's Warren Commission testimony a month before it was made public. Although the *Dallas Times-Herald* shared this scoop with her, she, as usual, got most of the publicity.

Kilgallen died on November 8, 1965, in her Manhattan home from a combination of barbiturates and alcohol.

KINGSBURY, ALBERT

(1862-1943) — Mechanical engineer, was born on December 23, 1862, in Goose Lake, near Morris, Illinois, to Lester Wayne and Eliza Emeline (Fosdick) Kingsbury. The family moved to Cuyahoga Falls, Ohio, where Albert completed high school in 1880. He attended Buchtel College (later the University of Akron) for a year, then left to become an apprentice machinist. Three years later, Kingsbury enrolled in the mechanical engineering course at Ohio State University.

Forced by lack of funds to withdraw near the end of his second year, he worked two more years as a machinist, and then in 1887, entered Cornell University. There, under the direction of Robert H. Thurston, he conducted a series of tests on Pennsylvania Railroad bearings that marked the beginning of his career in lubrication and bearing design. The tests revealed anomalies that accepted theories of friction could not explain, and Kingsbury was not then acquainted with the empirical and analytical work in lubrication that had been done in England, culminating in 1886 in the fundamental theoretical paper of Osborne Reynolds.

Following his graduation in 1889 with the degree of mechanical engineer, Kingsbury accepted appointment as instructor in mechanical engineering and physics at New Hampshire College (later the University of New Hampshire), where he remained until 1899. For several years, Kingsbury did experimental work on friction in screw threads, particularly threads used in an action similar to that of a jack screw, which exerts a large end thrust. While testing screw threads with a torsion-compression machine, he noticed the phenomenon of air as a lubricant. When he presented the paper before the navy's Bureau of Steam Engineering in Washington, D.C., in 1896, a listener called his attention to Osborne Reynolds's work.

Reynolds's observation led Kingsbury directly to the invention of his segmental end-thrust bearing. In 1898, he made the initial trials of a bearing consisting of a series of flat polygonal metal tilting pads, pivoted on radial supports and arranged symmetrically about the bearing axis. They proved entirely successful: his bearing maintained full lubrication under thrust pressure from ten to a hundred times greater than those in conventional thrust bearings. Kingsbury received a patent for his bearing in 1910.

In 1899, Kingsbury was appointed professor of applied mechanics at Worcester Polytechnic Institute in Massachusetts. Four years later, he accepted a position with the Westinghouse Electric & Manufacturing Company in Pittsburgh, Pennsylvania. In 1912, at Kingsbury's expense, the company built the first large commercial Kingsbury bearing for the Pennsylvania Water & Power Company's hydroelectric plant at McCall's Ferry (Holtwood) on the Susquehanna River. The success of that installation led to general acceptance of the bearing for stationary hydroelectric turbines and generators. The U.S. Navy adopted his bearing for use on propeller shafts in 1917. Kingsbury opened a shop in Philadelphia, Pennsylvania, to produce the bearing. After the war, he expanded the Philadelphia shop, and in 1924, incorporated the Kingsbury Machine Works, of which he was president until his death.

For his thrust bearing and his experimental work in lubrication, Kingsbury was awarded the Elliott Cresson Medal of the Franklin Institute (1923), the John Scott Medal of the City of Philadelphia (1931), and the gold medal of the American Society of Mechanical Engineers (1931). In his last years, he made his home in Greenwich, Connecticut. On July 25, 1893, at Stamford Connecticut, he married Alison Mason; they had five daughters. He died of a cerebral thrombosis on July 28, 1943, at Greenwich Hospital and was buried in Greenwood Cemetery,

Brooklyn, New York.

KINZIE, JOHN

(1763-1828) — Fur-trader on the site of Chicago, was born December 3, 1763 at Quebec. His father, John McKenzie, had come thither as a surgeon with the British army and had there married Anne, the widow of William Haliburton, an army chaplain. When McKenzie died soon after their son was born, Anne McKenzie took as her third husband William Forsyth, who moved to Detroit, Michigan and there opened the first tavern.

Young John, who changed his name to Kinzie, left home early and learned the trade of silversmith, from which he received the Native American name, "Shaw-nee-aw-kee," the Silver Man. When about eighteen, he began trading with tribes on the Maumee River, at Fort Wayne, then on the site of Defiance, Ohio. Here he lived with Margaret McKenzie, an Indian captive, whose legal marriage to him has been often asserted and as often denied. In 1795 she found her own family and went home to Virginia. The next year Kinzie moved to St. Joseph River, where in 1798 he brought his bride, Eleanor (Little) McKillip, whose first husband Daniel McKillip, an officer in the British militia, had fallen at Wayne's battle of 1794. The Kinzies moved in 1804 to the mouth of the Chicago River, a site Kinzie had visited and traded on years earlier, where in 1803 Fort Dearborn had been built. Here business prospered and three of their four children were born.

In 1812 Kinzie had a quarrel with Jean Lalime, a French trader, whom he killed, supposedly in self-defense. In the massacre of Fort Dearborn troops in August of that year, friendly Native Americans saved Kinzie and his family. They retreated first to St. Joseph and then to Detroit, where Kinzie, suspected of American sympathies, was arrested by the British and for some time imprisoned. He never recovered from the effects of the war either in his property or person.

In 1816 he returned to Chicago and lived there until his death on January 6, 1828. In 1821 he aided the commissioners who came to make a tribal treaty, and in 1825 was commissioned justice of the peace. He was remembered as a kindly, pleasant man, devoted to his family, shrewd at trade, and always popular with his Native American customers.

KIRKLAND, JOSEPH

(1830-1894) — Author, was born in Geneva, New York, on January 7, 1830. He was educated at home by his mother. In 1835, the family

Joseph Kirkland

immigrated to Michigan, where, in 1846, the father died. Ten years later, Joseph Kirkland took up a permanent residence in Chicago and engaged in the coal-mining business. In 1861, he enlisted in the U.S. Army as second lieutenant, Company C, 12th Illinois Infantry. Later he became aide-de-camp to General McClellan and served under him in the West Virginia Campaign.

Resigning from his regiment, he was appointed aide-de-camp on the general's staff (with the rank of captain in the regular service), in the reorganization of the army of the Potomac. During the siege of Yorktown he was transferred (at his own request) to the staff of General Fitz John Porter, when he gained his majority. He took an active part in the battles of Hanover Court House, Mechanicsville, Gaines's Mill, Malvern Hill, the "Seven Days' fight," and Antietam. Upon General Porter's retirement he resigned his commission and returned to citizen's life.

In the commercial disaster that followed the great fire of Chicago, Major Kirkland failed in business. After settling with his creditors he took office (1875) in the internal revenue service, during which occupation he read law, and in 1880, after fifty years of age, was admitted to the bar. He at once formed a partnership with Mark Bangs, ex-judge of the Circuit Court, and pursued a long and successful practice. In the midst of his legal career, Major Kirkland carried out a goal long dormant in his mind—the writing of a novel of western rural life. "Zury, the Meanest Man in Spring County," was published in 1885, by Houghton, Mifflin & Company, and immediately gained a marked and unusual acceptance at the hands of reviewers and the public. Following this, at an interval of forty-five years, the path marked out by his mother in her "New Home," he found that his life work was shaping itself in the way he would have been happy, during his career, to foresee. He, therefore, gradually dropped his law practice and devoted himself to literature.

Zury was followed (1887) by *The McVeys*, and (1889) *The*

Captain of Company K, a war novel, which took first prize in the competition (anonymous) in which the Detroit *Free Press* offered $1,600, $900, and $500, for the three best stories submitted. Later it was published in book form by the Dibble Publishing Company of Chicago and had a large sale. Major Kirkland also wrote "The Story of Chicago," a short history of the Chicago massacre of 1812, and several short stories and bits of verse.

In 1863, he was married to Theodosia Burr Wilkinson, of Syracuse, New York, daughter of John Wilkinson, one of the founders of that city. They had four children. Major Kirkland died at his home in Chicago, April 29, 1894.

KIRKMAN, MARSHALL MONROE

(1842-1921) — Railroad executive and author, was born on July 10, 1842, on a farm in Morgan County, Illinois, the son of Thomas and Catherine (Sweet) Kirkman. After receiving only the most elementary schooling he entered the employ of the Chicago & North Western Railroad Company in 1856 as a messenger boy on the Chicago-Oshkosh line. He continued with the company until his retirement in 1910, at which time he held the office of vice-president in charge of receipts and disbursements. He was therefore connected with the road from almost the beginning of its history.

Personally, Kirkman was precise and meticulous, both in appearance and utterance. His primary interest was railroad finance, particularly the accounting of operating receipts and expenditures. He held the position of auditor of freight accounts as early as 1861, and by 1881 had been promoted to the rank of comptroller of the entire line. This latter office he retained until his retirement, although the name was twice changed prior to 1910. He was active in advocating the simplification and standardization of railroad accounting, and many of his published works were written with that end in view. He was instrumental in the formation of the Association of American Railway Accounting Officers in 1888, and was the first president of that body. Kirkman was chairman of a committee of railway accounting officers that worked with representatives of the Interstate Commerce Commission to obtain a greater uniformity in railroad accounting. The most important contribution of Kirkman, however, was his numerous publications. Starting in 1877, he published many pamphlets and books touching all phases of the railroad business, but emphasizing the financial. Among them he included treatises on interstate commerce, railway disbursements, railway revenue, baggage car traffic, railway service, track accounts, maintenance of railways, rates, legislation, and the handling of supplies.

His most pretentious work was *The Science of Railways* (twelve volumes, 1894). Also of considerable value was his *Classical Portfolio of Primitive Carriers* (1895). After 1900, his published works were all historical novels, except for *A History of Alexander the Great* (1913). Possibly the change was due in part to his contact with the World's Columbian Exposition at Chicago in 1893, for he was one of its early sponsors and served for two years on the committee of transportation. His first novel, *The Romance of Gilbert Holmes* (1900), dealt with a boy prodigy who knew all of the important men who lived in Illinois during the 1830s and 1840s — men who survived numerous wrecks, attacks, murders, explosions and other harrowing experiences with unblemished character and unshaken nerves. Kirkman's later fiction dealt entirely with the life and times of Alexander the Great, which he described in five novels, two of which he later revised and republished under different titles. His fiction was in no sense excellent, but it was better done than might have been expected in view of his temperament and background. His wife was Fannie Lincoln, by whom he had two children. He died on April 18, 1921, in Chicago, Illinois.

KOCH, FRED CONRAD

(1876-1948) — Biochemist, was born on May 16, 1876, in Chicago, Illinois, the son of Frederick Koch and Louise Henrietta (Fischer) Koch. The Koch family, moved to Elmhurst, Illinois in 1882, where Koch received his primary education. He graduated from Oak Park High School and received his B.S. and M.S. in chemistry from the University of Illinois in 1899 and 1900 respectively.

His next two years were spent as an instructor in chemistry at the University of Illinois. On August 20, 1901, Koch married Bertha Ethel Zink. He then took a research chemist position with Armour and Company in Chicago. In 1909, he won a graduate fellowship at the University of Chicago in the department of physiological chemistry. He received the Ph.D. in 1912.

The next twenty-nine years were spent on the staff of the University of Chicago. Koch's first wife died in 1918, and four years later, on September 7, 1922, he married Elizabeth Miller, also a biochemist. In 1926, after having served as acting chairman since 1919, Koch was elected chairman of the department of physiological chemistry and pharmacology and served in that capacity until his retirement in 1941. Upon retirement he was named Frank P. Hixon distinguished service professor emeritus and thereupon, took a position with Armour and Company as director of biochemical research.

Koch's research covered the areas of internal secretions, including hormones, vitamins, and quantitative analytical methods. His laboratory is best known for its work on the male hormone testosterone. In collaboration with Lemuel C. McGee and others, Koch successfully extracted the hormone from the lipid (fatty) fraction of bulls' testicles, and injected small quantities of the extract into capons, which caused accentuation of secondary sex characteristics, notably growth of the comb. Koch and Thomas F. Gallagher made comb growth the basis for bioassay of testicular hormone preparations.

Later, Koch developed methods for the extraction of male hormones from human urine. This work eventually led to the isolation and synthesis of androsterone by Adolf Butenandt at Danzig in 1931, and later of testosterone and other male hormones. Other researchers on secretions involved work on secretion and other gastrointestinal hormones, thyroid and pituitary hormones, and on the activation of pepsin, rennin, and trypsinogen. He also worked on blood chemistry and, with his second wife, was the first to observe the conversion of heat-treated cholesterol to provitamin D in 1925.

Koch is also credited with several inventions of laboratory equipment, the best known of which is the Koch pipette. Among his other apparatus were a stopcock pipette with reservoir, a modified van Slyke apparatus for determination of amino nitrogen, and a microburette. In addition to numerous research papers, he was the author of a manual, *Practical Methods in Biochemistry* (1934); its fifth edition (1948) was co-authored by a departmental colleague, Martin E. Hanke.

In his later years, Koch built a summer home at Ephraim, Wisconsin. He received numerous honors, and in 1930, Koch was the American delegate to the Second International Congress for Sex Research in London, and was also a delegate to the Pan American Congress on Endocrinology in Montevideo in 1941. Koch was editor of *Archives of Biochemistry*, and in 1936, became a member of the committee on endocrinology, National Research Council. After his retirement in 1941, Koch continued his research projects at Armour and Company. In 1946, he suffered a stroke that weakened him, and later, aggravated by pneumonia, led to his death on January 26, 1948. He was buried in Chicago, Illinois.

KOHLSAAT, HERMAN HENRY

(1853-1924) — Restauranteur and editor, the son of immigrants, Reimer and Sarah (Hall) Kohlsaat, was identified with Galena, Illinois, in his youth, although he had been born at Albion. With little formal education, he undertook his living in Chicago, Illinois, and was very successful. He married at the age Mabel E. Blake, daughter of E. Nelson Blake, the president of the Chicago Board of Trade in 1880. Before he was forty, he had bestowed upon his adopted town, Galena, a striking statue of General Ulysses Grant, and a Thomas Nast's painting of General Robert E. Lee's surrender.

Kohlsaat's fortune came from his interest in a wholesale baking concern, in which he had first worked as an errand boy and drummer, and from a chain of low-price lunchrooms in Chicago. He was a devoted Republican, going to the convention of 1888 as an alternate, and bringing to the party the support of the *Daily Inter-Ocean*, of which he was part owner from 1891 until May 3, 1894. He was a devoted Chicagoan, too, using his journal for the advancement of the interests of the world's fair of 1893. And he had now become a devoted admirer of William McKinley. After the sale of his interest in the *Inter-Ocean*, Kohlsaat took the first vacation of his life. On April 21, 1895, Kohlsaat appeared as editor and publisher of the *Chicago Times-Herald*, converting it immediately into an independent journal devoted to a protective tariff and the gold standard. On March 28, 1901, he renamed it the *Chicago Record-Herald*, having bought the *Chicago Record* from Victor Lawson. The *Chicago Evening Post*, which had been part of the *Times-Herald* property, he released in 1901 to John C. Schaffer.

As the aggressive antagonist of free silver, Kohlsaat increased his prominence among western Republicans. He pressed upon McKinley the necessity for an emphatic stand upon gold, and he was with Mark Hanna in the pre-convention conferences of 1896, when the leaders agreed that the Democrats should be met squarely upon this issue. For several years after 1902, he took a vacation from journalism, interesting himself in Chicago real estate; but he was back in the editorial chair of the *Record-Herald* from January 1, 1910, until September 7, 1911, directing that journal alongside the *Chicago Tribune* in the fight to unseat William Lorimer as senator from Illinois. A little later, he had a year with the *Inter-Ocean* again, before James Keeley merged it and the *Record-Herald* into the *Chicago Herald*, which first bore the new name on June 14, 1914. His death came suddenly on October 17, 1924, in Washington,

D.C., where he had gone on the invitation of Judge K.M. Landis to see the World Series. His two daughters survived him.

KORNER, GUSTAV PHILIPP

(1809-1896) — Jurist, statesman, and historian, the son of Bernhard and Marie Magdelena (Kampfe) Korner, was born in the free city of Frankfurt-am-Main where his father, an ardent German patriot, was a bookseller and dealer in works of art. Gustav received his early instruction in the model school Musterschule of Frankfurt, Germany, and continued his preparation in the gymnasium. In 1828, he entered the University of Jena, East Germany, to study jurisprudence. Here, he joined Burschenschaft, the patriotic student society that aimed at the unity and freedom of Germany. Continuing his studies at the universities of Munich and Heidelberg, where he received his doctorate, he returned to Frankfurt where he practiced law.

He took part in the revolutionary movements that had broken out in many parts of Germany. In the Frankfurt revolt of 1833, Korner was wounded, fled to France, where he joined some friends who were about to sail for the United States. They arrived in New York on June 17, 1833, and settled in St. Louis, Missouri. Korner and his party were, however, disappointed when they discovered that the state allowed slavery. They therefore decided to settle in St. Clair County, Illinois, where a number of their relatives and friends lived. On June 17, 1836, Korner married Sophie Engelmann, with whose family he had come to the United States.

To become acquainted with American law and to improve his English, Korner took a law course at Transylvania University at Lexington, Kentucky. Returning to Belleville, Illinois, he soon found himself drawn into politics. In 1845, he was appointed justice of the Illinois Supreme Court, a post that he held until 1850. Korner refused the renomination for the position. In 1852, he was elected lieutenant governor, which office he occupied until 1856.

In the meantime, Korner took part in the growing antislavery movement, and he joined the new Republican Party, and encouraged his fellow Germans to do the same. He took over some of the Abraham Lincoln's law cases at Springfield, Illinois, and was consulted occasionally on important matters. In 1862, Lincoln, appointed him minister to Spain. His chief task in this position was to counteract English and French attempts to bring about a joint recognition of the Confederacy, and to cultivate the traditional friendly relations with Spain.

Korner succeeded remarkably well.

After his return from Spain in 1864, he took little or no interest in active politics for a number of years. When the corruption of the Grant administration was growing more and more intolerable, however, he joined the Liberal Republican movement. Again in 1876, he asserted his political independence, as well as his steadfast devotion to the principles of the liberal movement by advocating the candidacy of Samuel Tilden against Rutherford B. Hayes. Disappointed by the course of events following the election of 1876, he retired from his former active participation in politics and devoted the remaining years of his life almost exclusively to literary work. It was then, that he wrote his valuable historical study, entitled *Das Deutsche Elemen in den Vereinigten Stoaten von Nordamerika* (1880). His object was "to show how strongly and to what extent the arrival of the Germans in large numbers since 1818 had influenced this country politically and socially."

Korner also wrote an autobiography at the suggestion of his children. It was finished shortly before his death in 1896.

KROC, RAYMOND ALBERT "RAY,"

(1902-1984) — Restauranteur, originator of McDonald's hamburger chain corporation; philanthropist, and author, was born on October 5, 1902, in Oak Park, Illinois, on October 5, 1902. He dropped out of high school in his sophomore year, and at the age of fifteen, he lied about his age to join the Red Cross ambulance corps during World War I. When the war ended, he returned to high school for a short time, but left once again to pursue a career as a jazz pianist.

After getting married, Kroc found the life of a musician too hard to maintain and went to work as a salesman for the Lily-Tulip Cup Company. A few months later, he became involved in the music field once again when he was asked to serve as the musical director for a new Chicago radio station, WGES. Since most of the programming was live, it was Kroc's responsibility to arrange and play some of the music, as well as hire other musicians and singers.

Kroc stayed with the station for a year and a half, then moved to Florida to take advantage of the burgeoning land boom by working in real estate; however, the bottom fell out of the real estate market, and by the end of 1926, Kroc was completely broke. That experience remained fresh in his mind many years later.

After returning to his salesman job at Lily-Tulip, Kroc was impressed by a new invention he had seen, a milkshake machine that could mix several of the drinks at once. Seeing its potential, he started his own small business in order to become the exclusive distributor of the machine. It was this product that led him to the McDonald brothers.

Richard and Maurice McDonald ran a small, but highly successful, restaurant in San Bernardino, California, that had a very basic menu — hamburgers, French fries, and milkshakes. Their eatery was so popular it was literally always packed with teenagers and adults. Kroc initially connected with the brothers after he discovered that they used eight of the milkshake machines at their establishment, more than any other restaurant. With a businessman's instinct, Kroc made a deal with the brothers in which he would establish a chain of restaurants using their simplified method, and give them a small percentage. In April 1955, in the Chicago suburb of Des Plaines, Illinois, Kroc opened the very first McDonald's franchise.

Several more franchises began to spring up, and seeing that this was going to be a successful venture, Kroc sold his small business in order to devote all of his time to his new business. In 1961, Kroc bought the McDonald brothers' share of the business, and by 1972, the two-thousanth franchise had been established. By the early 1970s, a McDonald's could be found in every state, as well as in countries throughout the world including Canada, Japan, Australia, and several in Europe.

In his later years, Kroc involved himself in various philanthropic interests. He established the Kroc Foundation in 1969, and in the mid-1970s, his McDonald's corporation joined with several professional athletic teams to support construction of a series of Ronald McDonald houses that were located near children's hospitals, which gave families a place to stay when a child was seriously ill. For five years (1974-1979), Kroc was the owner of the San Diego Padres baseball team. He also wrote a book about his success, entitled *Grinding it Out: the Making of McDonald's*. Kroc was married to Jane Dobbins. He died in San Diego, California, on January 14, 1984.

L

LA SALLE, RENÉ-ROBERT CAVELIER, SIEUR DE

(1849-1932) — French explorer, born René-Robert Cavelier on November 22, 1643, in Rouen, France, to Jean Cavelier and Catherine Geeset Cavelier. Little is known about his childhood, but he did receive some education from Jesuits and was continuing school to become a priest when he abandoned this idea and moved to New France (Canada). Shortly before he left France, he added "Sieur de La Salle," the name of his family's estate, to his name in order to sound more like nobility.

Around 1666, La Salle moved to New France, settling along the St. Lawrence River near present-day Montreal in southern Québec. As a trader, he came into contact with different Indian tribes, learning much from them about the surrounding wilderness. He was intrigued by the possibility of a river flowing to California from where he could then sail to China. La Salle ventured out on his own, exploring the territory below Lake Ontario and Lake Erie; he reached Ohio in 1669-1670.

La Salle and the French Canadian governor the Count de Frontenac shared a vision of increasing France's stronghold in the New World. From 1672-82, the two of them attempted to expand France's control in the New World in all aspects: military, land, and trade. Their strategies were not accepted by all of the other immigrants to the New World. In particular, French merchants, the Jesuits, the Dutch, and the English objected to La Salle's plans.

In 1674, La Salle went to France, following the construction of the French Fort Frontenac near Lake Ontario. The king gave La Salle the fort and surrounding land. La Salle was also given the rank of esquire. He returned to New France and built the *Griffon*, a commercial sailing vessel that he hoped would cover the costs of the construction of the new forts. La Salle hoped to establish more French forts throughout the West; he made another trip to France, in 1677, to secure royal approval for his plan. La Salle

Rene-Robert Cavelier La Salle

407

returned with the king's permission to build forts, and another explorer, Henri de Tonty (Tonti), to help him.

On August 7, 1679, La Salle, de Tonty, and a party of Frenchmen and Indians set out on their westward journey onboard the *Griffon*. The ship's maiden voyage brought them safely to Lake Michigan. La Salle, de Tonty, and all but six of the crew disembarked and began exploring Illinois. The ship headed up to Green Bay, Wisconsin, to collect furs. On its return trip, the ship vanished, probably somewhere off the coast of Michigan.

La Salle and de Tonty, constructed Fort Crevecoeur along the Illinois River, near present-day city of Peoria in Illinois. They waited for the *Griffin* to return for them, and when it failed to arrive, La Salle returned to Québec on foot, leaving de Tonty at the fort. La Salle crossed through northern Indiana, where he built a few other forts along the St. Joseph River in 1680. He then proceeded across the Lower Peninsula of Michigan, before reaching Montreal.

A mutiny occurred at Fort Crevecoeur and de Tonty fled. La Salle went to help him, finding de Tonty at Mackinaw. They then headed toward the Mississippi River, where they explored the northern section of the river before sailing down it to the Gulf of Mexico. La Salle proclaimed the entire Mississippi River Basin for France in April 1682 and named it Louisiana in honor of the French king Louis XIV.

On his return from the mouth of Mississippi, La Salle built Fort St. Louis on Starved Rock, overlooking Illinois River near Ottawa. He organized a colony made up of local Indians and asked Québec for help mainting it. His political enemies were in power in New France, forcing La Salle to return to France and appeal directly to the king.

While in France, La Salle devised a plan to build a fort at the mouth of the Mississippi River to fortify France's position there, and then invade part of Mexico, which was then owned by Spain, France's enemy. La Salle set sail for the Gulf of Mexico in 1684 with two hundred Frenchmen. His course was miscalculated, and in February 1685, La Salle ended up off the coast of Matagorda Bay, Texas, hundreds of miles from his destination. Believing he was close to his destination, he and his crew disembarked and searched for other French posts. While still in Texas, a mutiny occurred and La Salle was murdered by his crew in March 1687.

LARDNER, JOHN ABBOTT

(1912-1960) — Journalist, was born May 4, 1912, in Chicago, Illinois, the son of the writer Ringgold (Ring) Wilmer Lardner and Ellis Abbott. Both parents came from prosperous small-town Midwest families. When John was four, the Lardners moved to Greenwich, Connecticut, and soon thereafter to Great Neck, Long Island. John attended private school in Great Neck and then Phillips Academy at Andover, Massachusetts. While still a boy, he had demonstrated the interest in sports and the wit that would mark his later writing. A family friend and neighbor, the columnist Franklin P. Adams, published in his column the ten-year-old's first printed work, which was about sports.

Lardner entered Harvard College in 1929. He remained only a year before leaving for Paris, where he studied briefly at the Sorbonne and then spent a few months working on the European edition of the *New York Herald Tribune*. When he returned to New York in 1931, he found a job as a reporter with the *Herald Tribune*. For the next two-and-a-half years, he wrote general news stories for the city desk and reviewed books on sports for the Sunday book section. Lardner left the *Herald Tribune* to concentrate on sports by writing a syndicated column for the North American Newspaper Alliance (NANA), a position he held until 1948.

On September 14, 1938. Lardner married Hazel Cannan Hairston, a reporter. To support his family, which eventually included three children, he began writing sports articles for magazines. In 1939, he took on a column for *Newsweek* called "Sport Week." When World War II broke out in Europe, Lardner requested a foreign assignment. Two months after Pearl Harbor, *Newsweek* sent him overseas as a war correspondent; his column, "Lardner Goes to the Wars," appeared throughout the war datelined Australia, the South Pacific, North Africa, Italy, and finally Iwo Jima and Okinawa. At the same time, he also wrote stories for newspapers syndicated by NANA and longer magazine articles for the *Saturday Evening Post* and the *New Yorker*, which were published in book form as *Southwest Passage: The Yanks in the Pacific* (1943). The Lardner sons seemed to share a family characteristic of bravery. After World War II, Lardner's work was so much in demand, that in 1948, he dropped his syndicated sports column and began writing exclusively for magazines. Although sports remained a special love, his interests were diverse. Lardner's articles ranged from the war, to a history of drinking in America, on which he was working when he died. Twenty magazines published his material during the postwar years, and it also appeared in three collected sets of essays: *It Beats Working* (1947),

White Hopes and Other Tigers (1951), and *Strong Cigars and Lovely Women* (1951). In 1952, Lardner initiated a feature page in *Look* called "John Lardner's New York," which gave him the scope to write on varied subjects, although most of the articles discussed the theater. A bout with tuberculosis forced him to drop this new venture by the end of the year. At that point, Lardner changed his *Newsweek* column from "Sport Week" to "Lardner's Week," therefore enabling him to extend the range of his interests. In 1958, when he began to fear a loss of mobility due to an advancing case of multiple sclerosis, he decided to concentrate on television criticism in a new *New Yorker* column called "The Air."

By the late 1950s, Lardner had achieved a considerable reputation. He suffered a fatal heart attack on March 24, 1960, while writing an appreciation of Adams, who had died the day before.

LASKER, ALBERT DAVIS

(1880-1952) — Advertising executive, considered the father of modern advertising, and philanthropist, was born on May 1, 1880, in Freiburg, Germany, the son of American parents Morris Lasker and Nettie Heidenheimer Davis. When Lasker was six weeks old, the family moved back to Texas. At twelve, he started his own weekly newspaper, the *Galveston Free Press*, and the next year, worked for the *Galveston Morning News*. After graduating from high school in Galveston, Texas, he then worked for papers in New Orleans and Dallas. In 1898, his father, opposed to a profession in journalism, arranged for Lasker to work at the advertising agency of Lord & Thomas in Chicago, Illinois.

Beginning as an office assistant, then moving up to a top salesman position, Lasker became general manager and a full partner of the firm in 1903, buying out Lord's share of the business. In 1910, he was the sole owner. Throughout the years, he built the company into the leading advertisement company in the nation, and broke the mold of traditional advertising. He developed the use of advertisement copy as a means to sell products instead of just provide information. To develop and promote talented copywriters, Lasker created in house copywriting classes, and gave unprecedented salaries. He was also one of the first to use radio as an advertising medium, sponsoring such programs as the Metropolitan Opera, radio dramas, and broadcast football games. He retired in 1938, and sold the company to his three vice presidents (Emerson Foote, Fairfax Cone, and Don Belding) in 1942, with the stipulation that they rename the company. It was renamed Foote, Cone & Belding.

While still in the advertising business, Lasker was involved with politics and professional baseball. He was in charge of Warren G. Harding's publicity on his successful presidential campaign, and Harding appointed him chairman of the U.S. Shipping Board in 1920. He served for two years. In baseball, he owned stock in the Chicago Cubs, and was instrumental in orchestrating the creation of the office of baseball commissioner.

In his later years, he supported medical research, establishing the Albert and Mary Lasker Foundation. The foundation recognizes discoveries in clinical research, and awards a number of financial grants each year for continued research.

Lasker was married three times: to Flora Warner in 1902, who died in 1936; to Doris Kenyon in 1938, which ended in divorce one year later; and finally to Mary Woodward Reinhardt in 1940. He had three children from his first marriage, and died on May 30, 1952.

LATHROP, JULIA CLIFFORD

(1858-1932) — Social worker, was born on June 29, 1858, in Rockford, Illinois, the daughter of William and Adeline (Potter) Lathrop, and the eldest in a well-to-do family of five children. Her father, a lawyer, served as a member of the Illinois legislature, and later, 1877-1879, in Congress.

Lathrop attended the local high school and spent a year at the seminary, then entered Vassar College, where she graduated in 1880. Following her graduation, she worked as her father's secretary and acquired a good knowledge of law from him and her brother. She associated herself with Jane Addams and the Hull-House, where she went to live in 1890.

In 1892, Governor John P. Altgeld appointed her the first woman member of the Illinois Board of Public Charities, a position in which she served until 1909. She began a thorough study of the best methods of public care for persons in state institutions. She went to Europe around the turn of the century to study the extra-mural care of mental patients, and the working of the epileptic colonies. She was an early advocate of extra-mural care of the insane and believed that the population of institutions could be greatly reduced under intelligent, competent planning and supervision.

Lathrop was an early supporter of the new mental hygiene movement, and became a member of the board of the National Committee for Mental Hygiene, which was organized in 1909. During this period, she also took an active part with Graham Taylor in organizing the Chicago Institute of Social Science. This school, which was later called the Chicago School of Civics and Philanthropy, became the School of Social Service Administration of the University of Chicago in 1920. She served as an active trustee from 1907 to 1920, and was also a lecturer and, for a short time, a director of the research department of the school.

Other activities included her help in framing, in 1899, the first juvenile court law in the world, and she was one of the group that organized a juvenile court committee in Chicago. Her work in this connection is described in *The Child, the Clinic and the Court* (1925), to which she contributed "The Background of the Juvenile Court in Illinois." Later, Lathrop was largely responsible for planning the Juvenile Psychopathic Institute, the first mental hygiene clinic for children. In 1911, she supported the first mothers' pension act. Her experience in caring for the victims of the Cherry Mine disaster in Illinois in 1909 led to a state investigation of mining and other dangerous occupations. She was also an active member of the board of the Immigrants' Protective League in Chicago.

In 1912, President William H. Taft appointed her chief of the new federal Children's Bureau, the first woman to become head of a statutory federal bureau with appointment by the president confirmed by the Senate. She began her work with investigations of infant mortality. Out of these studies came the bureau's crusade for uniform birth registration under federal supervision. Studies of child labor, juvenile courts, mothers' pensions, illegitimacy, feebleminded children, rural child welfare, and recreation followed.

Following her resigned from the bureau in 1921, Lathrop lectured frequently on various public questions and engaged in numerous services. She then helped bring some of the European child-welfare leaders to the United States for the series of "Children's Year" conferences. In 1922, she was appointed by the secretary of labor as a member of the committee to investigate conditions in the overcrowded immigration station at Ellis Island.

Lathrop was a pioneer suffragette, and she was active in the League of Women Voters. In 1922, she became president of the Illinois league and she was influential in the national league. She was an active member of the National Conference of Charities and Correction (after 1917 the National Conference of Social Work). From 1925 to 1931, she was an assessor for the Child Welfare Committee of the League of Nations. Lathrop died in 1932.

LAWSON, VICTOR FREEMONT

(1850-1925) — Journalist, was born on September 9, 1850, in Chicago, Illinois, the son of Iver and Melinda (Nordvig) Lawson. Both parents were Norwegian, the father having been born in Norway, his mother in Illinois. Lawson had been educated in the Chicago public schools and at Phillips Academy at Andover, Massachusetts. Poor health put an end to further study. His father died in 1873, and Lawson returned to Chicago to take charge of his father's estate. Lawson inherited an interest in the daily *Skandinaven*, which his father and others had established.

In 1876, Lawson bought the *Chicago Daily News*. He retained Melville E. Stone as editor and later took him into partnership. Under the efficient management of Lawson, the *Daily News* made rapid progress. In 1878 He died in 1873 the *Evening Post* was taken over with its Associated Press franchise. In 1881 He died in 1873 a morning edition was brought out which later became the *Chicago Record* and eventually the *Record-Herald*, when it was merged with the *Times-Herald*. The *Record-Herald* ceased publication in 1914 because of Lawson's reluctance to be connected with a paper publishing on Sunday. He had assumed editorial duties upon Stone's retirement in 1888.

Lawson took up the cause of the Associated Press, which was rivaled by the United Press, a news service organized on a commercialized rather than a cooperative basis. As president of the organization from 1894 to 1900, his former partner, Melville E. Stone, at this time manager of the Associated Press, supported him. He remained as director from 1893 until his death. In 1898, he turned his attention to the development of a foreign news service. The Spanish-American War had shown the need of an unbiased handling of foreign news affecting American interest. Up to this time, correspondents representing the British or other foreign papers supplied cable news received by American newspapers. At the close of the war, Lawson placed his own correspondents in the leading European capitals and in Asia. The example of the *Daily News* was widely followed by other papers and press associations. Another of Lawson's pioneering activities was his strong advocacy of postal savings banks. Both by financial assistance and the use of his publishing organization, he consolidated support for the bill, which was finally passed in 1910.

The independent policy of the *Daily News* in politics and in civic reform made the paper a powerful influence in Chicago. He gave generously to support a system of free lectures in public-school halls, to found a fresh air sanitarium, to maintain "better government associations," to support the YMCA, to endow the Chicago Theological Seminary, and to provide homes for the symphony orchestras, and for leading clubs of which he was a member. He was a lifetime member of the New England Congregational Church of Chicago, and it was in connection with his work in the church that he met Jessie S. Bradley, daughter of W.H. Bradley of Chicago, whom he married in 1880. It was she who guided much of his humanitarian work for the relief of the poor, particularly African Americans. She died in 1914. Lawson died on August 19, 1925.

John Doyle Lee

LEE, JOHN DOYLE

(1812-1877) — Mormon elder, notorious for his part in the Mountain Meadows Massacre, was born on September 23, 1812, in Kaskaskia, Randolph County, Illinois. At the age of eight, he was left an orphan among relatives. He had little formal schooling. At nineteen, he saw action in the Black Hawk War. After his marriage on July 24, 1833, to Agathe Ann Woolsey, he settled in Fayette County, Illinois. Upon hearing of Mormonism from missionaries, he traveled to Missouri to investigate the new sect and remained there a convert. He was soon zealous in the new church and as a member of the Mormon military organization took part in several skirmishes with the Missourians.

At Nauvoo, Illinois, he rose rapidly in favor with the Mormon leaders, holding important municipal and ecclesiastical offices. He twice (1839 and 1841) served as missionary. He reports a number of prophetic dreams and visions, which assisted him in his conversion of others. In 1843, he became a Mason. Like many other Mormons, he spent the spring of 1844 in near-by states supporting Joseph Smith's campaign for the presidency of the United States. After the Smith's assassination, Lee returned to Nauvoo where he soon transferred his loyalty to Brigham Young.

In 1845-1846, Lee accepted the Mormon practice of polygamy

and added seven more wives to his household. Altogether, he had eighteen wives who bore him sixty-four children. Upon moving to Utah, he was active in colonizing outlying sections and finally settled in southern Utah not far from the Mountain Meadows. He was a fanatical mystic about his religion. Like many other Mormons, he was highly aroused during the summer of 1857 over the impending invasion of Utah by federal troops under General Albert Sidney Johnston, and over the rumors that a company of emigrants en route from Arkansas to California was robbing Mormon settlements. Early in September 1857, a band of Native American warriors and Mormons massacred this company at Mountain Meadows.

The first attempt (1859) to indict the leaders in the crime was unsuccessful. Finally in 1875, Lee and others were brought to trial. Lee's first trial ended in a disagreement of the mixed jury of eight Mormons and four non-Mormons. At the second trial (1876), Lee was found guilty of murder in the first degree and sentenced to be shot. After the Utah Supreme Court upheld the original judgment, he was executed on March 23, 1877, on the spot where the massacre had taken place nearly twenty years before.

LEIBER, FRITZ

(1882-1949) — Actor and theatrical producer, was born on January 31, 1882, in Chicago, Illinois, the fifth of the six children of Albrecht Leiber and Meta (von Klett) Leiber. Fritz Chicago's Lake View High School. While still in high school, he attended a performance of Richard Mansfield's, which turned his interests to the stage. On March 30, 1902, he made his professional debut, and followed on April 6, 1902, with his first Shakespearean role as Cinna in *Julius Caesar*, both at Chicago's Dearborn Theatre. Soon after, he signed with a Chicago stock company, the People's Theatre. During the next two years, he appeared in the more than thirty roles.

In April 1904, Leiber joined Ben Greet's Woodland Players. Hired initially as a "utility" actor, he eventually assumed more important roles. In December 1907, he joined Julia Marlowe for a season as her leading juvenile. Producer William A. Brady then signed him to a three-year contract with Robert Mantell's company. From 1908 until 1915, he played second leads exclusively for Mantell, whose popularity in large cities across the United States enabled Leiber to be introduced as a significant classical actor. When Mantell disbanded his company in 1915 to go to Hollywood, Leiber tested himself in nonclassical roles. His brief

415

appearances that season in Edward Locke's melodrama *The Revolt* and Belasco's romantic *Van der Decken* were critical failures.

His few later attempts to break from Shakespeare, as in E. Holmes Hinkley's *High Tide* (1925) and Paul Green's *The Field God* (1927), also received poor notices. After his film debut in *Primitive Call* (1916), in which he played an American Indian, he rejoined Mantell. He wanted to play leads, and Mantell, aware of Leiber's box-office appeal, agreed to star him in Hamlet, supported by Mantell's company. Leiber opened in New York on December 18, 1918, to mixed reviews. Mantell then continued to alternate both Hamlet and Romeo with him, but critics encouraged Leiber to play on his own. On November 8, 1920, he opened his own company in Chicago with a two-week repertory of *Richard III*, *Romeo and Juliet*, *The Merchant of Venice*, *Hamlet*, and *Macbeth*. These became staples in the Leiber repertoire; in future years, he added *Julius Caesar*, *King Lear*, and *The Taming of the Shrew*.

In 1929, the Chicago Civic Shakespeare Society, founded by Midwest industrial and cultural leaders headed by the utilities magnate Harley L. Clarke, invited him to form a resident repertory company at the Civic Theatre. It opened on November 11, 1929, and then moved to New York City for a limited engagement. Although successful, the Great Depression and competing motion pictures proved to be more powerful. The Chicago Civic Shakespeare Society folded after the 1931-1932 season. Leiber resumed touring with his own company, but by 1935, abandoned the road for the financial security of films. He made about thirty-six movies from 1935 to 1949.

Leiber suffered a heart attack in 1943 and died of a coronary occlusion on October 14, 1949, in Pacific Palisades, California. He married Virginia Bronson on March 9, 1910. They had one child, Fritz Leiber, Jr., a science fiction writer.

LEITER, JOSEPH

(1868-1932) — Capitalist, only son of Levi Zeigler Leiter and Mary Theresa (Carver) Leiter, was born on December 4, 1868, in Chicago, Illinois. He was educated at St. Paul's School, Concord, New Hampshire, and at Harvard University, where he received an A.B. in 1891. After leaving Harvard, his father gave him a million dollars and the agency of his real-estate holdings. Leiter managed this trust with fair ability from 1892 to 1898. Meanwhile, he did some speculating in wheat, and at length conceived the project of cornering the entire American wheat market. He was twenty-eight years old and had under his control about thirty million dollars' worth of his father's property when he began buying wheat in April 1897 at seventy-three cents a bushel. The price remained low that summer, rising through the autumn, as Leiter and some minor associates bought steadily, and early in December reached $1.09, which brought floods of wheat into Chicago from the prairie states. Philip D. Armour, who months before had sold a quantity of wheat "short" to Leiter for December delivery, chartered a fleet of Great Lakes vessels, and using ice-breakers, brought 2,000,000 bushels from Duluth. Wheat stocks in Chicago rose from 5,000,000 to 9,000,000 bushels in the last two weeks of December, and Leiter took nearly all of it.

The storage and insurance costs for carrying it were $4,450 a day. Between February 1 and June 1, 10,000,000 bushels more came in. At one time the price momentarily reached $1.85. Leiter owned 18,000,000 bushels of actual wheat and 22,000,000 bushels in futures. The price sagged in the spring of 1898 and on June 10 reached $1.03. That day the Department of Agriculture predicted a record-breaking crop for the year; within three days the price had dropped to eighty-five cents and Leiter's corner was broken. Estimates as to his losses range from six to ten millions. His father assumed some of the obligations, but Joseph Leiter failed to pay in full and was suspended from the Board of Trade. Litigation over the matter continued for years afterward. His father took the management of the realty away from his son, but upon his death in 1904, Joseph became trustee and manager of the thirty-million-dollar estate, which included the Washington, D. C., Gas Company and the rich Zeigler coal properties in southern Illinois.

Leiter became president of the Zeigler Coal Company and the Chicago, Zeigler & Gulf Railway. He was also a director in many public utilities. He merged three street railways in. His career was notable for the litigation against him. A suit brought in 1922 by former associates for $680,000 alleged to be due on notes, he escaped from by pleading that the debts were outlawed by the statute of limitation in Illinois before the suits were brought. Shortly after this, his sister and the daughters of another sister, brought suit to oust him as trustee of his father's estate, alleging mismanagement; but after eight years of litigation, Leiter was again victor.

He died on April 11, 1932, at his Chicago home of a complication of pneumonia and heart disease. He had married, on June 10, 1908, Juliette Williams of Washington; two of their four children survived him.

LENZ, SIDNEY SAMUEL

(1873-1960) — Authority on contract bridge, was born July 12, 1873, in a suburb of Chicago, Illinois, the son of John J. and Joanna L. Lenz. The family moved to New York City in 1888. Sometime before his twenty-first birthday, Lenz returned to the Midwest. A combination of enterprise and good luck made him successful in business, and he soon became owner of a lumber mill and paper-box factory in Wisconsin. At the age of thirty-one, he announced his retirement, intending to devote the rest of his life to his athletic and intellectual interests.

Lenz first turned his attention to sports: table tennis, golf, and especially bowling. In 1909, he bowled an average of 240 over twenty consecutive games. About this time, whist (a card game) fascinated him, and a year later, was a member of the team that won the Hamilton Trophy, representing the most important championship of the American Whist League.

He began to take up auction bridge, and in 1924, he led a team from the Knickerbocker Whist Club of New York to victory in the first "All America" trophy competition, sponsored by the American Whist League. This team maintained its reputation as the best in the country throughout the period when auction bridge was popular. Lenz's greatest successes, however, came in pairs events, of which he won a great many during his career.

From the early 1920s on, he published a large number of articles in bridge magazines and general periodicals, including instructional pieces, humorous essays, verse parodies, and fiction, with and without bridge themes. He was the first bridge columnist of the *New York Times*, beginning in 1923. He also wrote for the humor magazine *Judge*, of which he was part owner. His most important book, *Lenz on Bridge* (1926), was an immediate success as much for the informality of its tone as for its clarity of exposition and technical excellence.

By the time contract bridge began its rise to popularity in the late 1920s, Lenz was firmly established as one of the foremost experts at all forms of the game. This circumstance brought him to the front rank of the battle against the growing empire of Ely Culbertson, who attempted to dominate the new game. Some of them, including Lenz, formed Bridge Headquarters and promulgated a system of bidding, in which Lenz's ideas were prominent. Culbertson and his wife challenged the combined forces of Bridge Headquarters to a match. Lenz, in partnership with Oswald Jacoby, was selected to represent the Headquarters side.

The match, often called the Bridge Battle of the Century, began

418

on December 7, 1931, at the Hotel Chatham in New York. The Culbertsons, with a margin of 8,970 points, won the match on January 8, 1932. Lenz had opposed them throughout whist with a second partner, Commander Winfield Liggett, after a dispute over a bid had caused Jacoby to withdraw.

Although Lenz continued to appear in bridge competitions for a few years afterward, the result of the match, and the acrimony attending it, diminished his taste for play. He remained a revered member of the bridge community, in his later years often acting as an honorary referee at major matches. He continued to play privately until his death. Lenz, who never married, died on April 12, 1960, in New York City.

LEWIS, DEAN DeWITT
(1874-1941) — Surgeon, was born on August 11, 1874, in Kewanee, Illinois, the only child of Lyman Wright Lewis, a merchant, and Virginia Winifred (Cully) Lewis. His paternal grandfather was a Baptist minister. Lewis attended Lake Forest College, Illinois, graduating with an A.B. in 1895. He then entered the College of Physicians and Surgeons in New York City, but transferred the next year to Rush Medical College in Chicago, where he received an M.D. in 1899. After a year's internship at Chicago's Cook County Hospital, Lewis returned to Rush Medical College (which had become affiliated with the University of Chicago) as assistant in anatomy. There, he became interested in the process of vital staining of tissues and used it to demonstrate the microscopic changes and proliferation of the chromophile cells that take place in the anterior lobe of the pituitary gland in a patient suffering from acromegaly. In 1903, after spending six months working in Leipzig, Germany, with the renowned anatomist Werner Spalteholz, he was advanced to instructor.

Two years later, Lewis moved to the department of surgery. In addition to giving popular courses in surgical anatomy and operative surgery, he carried on a large private practice and served as attending surgeon at the Presbyterian Hospital in Chicago. In 1917, following America's entry into World War I, Lewis was commissioned as a major in the Army Medical Corps and organized Base Hospital 13 from the staff of the Presbyterian Hospital. He took the unit to France in May 1918, and subsequently headed several evacuation hospitals that specialized in reconstructive and neurological surgery. After his discharge in 1919, with the rank of lieutenant colonel, he received the Distinguished Service Medal for his work in saving lives among the wounded combat troops.

It is said that in the five years after 1920, Lewis was offered every major vacant surgical chair in the country. In January 1925, he became professor of surgery at the University of Illinois, but six months later, he moved to Baltimore, Maryland, to fill the post formerly held by William S. Halsted as professor of surgery at the Johns Hopkins University School of Medicine and surgeon-in-chief of Johns Hopkins Hospital. He retained this post until illness forced his retirement in 1939.

Lewis' publications include *A Laboratory Manual of Human Anatomy* (1904), written with Lewellys F. Barker. He also published a large number of papers dealing with the ductless glands; methods of transplanting nerve and bone; reconstructive surgery; acromegaly; the role of sex hormones in tumor growth; and ethylene as an anesthetic. Lewis was one of the founders and the first editor (1920-1940) of the *Archives of Surgery*, a journal designed to give young surgeons a place to report their investigative work. He also edited the *International Surgical Digest* (1926-1941) , and the widely used eleven-volume set, *Practice of Surgery* (1932).

On November 26, 1903, Lewis married Pearl Miller of St. Anthony, Idaho. She died in 1926, and on December 26, 1927, he married Norene Kinney of Girard, Ohio. They had three children. In 1938, on one of his many lecture trips, Lewis suffered a cerebrovascular disturbance from which he never fully recovered. He died on October 9, 1941, at his home in Baltimore, Maryland, and was buried in New Cathedral Cemetery.

LEWIS, JAMES HAMILTON

(1863-1939) Representative from Washington and Senator from Illinois; Senate Years of Service: 1913-1919; 1931-1939; born in Danville, Pittsylvania County, Va., May 18, 1863; moved with his parents to Augusta, Ga., in 1866; attended Houghton school in that city and the University of Virginia at Charlottesville; studied law in Savannah, Ga.; admitted to the bar in 1882; moved to the Territory of Washington in 1885 and commenced the practice of law in Seattle; member, Washington Territorial legislature 1887-1888; elected as a Democrat to the Fifty-fifth Congress (March 4, 1897-March 3, 1899); unsuccessful candidate in 1898 for reelection; served during the Spanish-American War as inspector general with rank of colonel in Puerto Rico; unsuccessful Democratic candidate for United States Senator in 1899; moved to Chicago, Ill. in 1903 and resumed the practice of law; corporation counsel for Chicago 1905-1907; unsuccessful candidate for

Governor in 1908; elected as a Democrat to the United States Senate and served from March 26, 1913, to March 3, 1919; unsuccessful candidate for reelection in 1918; Democratic whip 1913-1919; chairman, Committee on Expenditures in the Department of State (Sixty-fourth and Sixty-fifth Congresses); unsuccessful Democratic candidate for Governor of Illinois in 1920; practiced international law; again elected as a Democrat to the United States Senate in 1930; reelected in 1936 and served from March 4, 1931, until his death in Washington, D.C., April 9, 1939; Democratic whip

James Hamilton Lewis

1933-1939; chairman, Committee on Expenditures in Executive Departments (Seventy-third through Seventy-sixth Congresses); funeral services were held in the Chamber of the United States Senate; original interment in the Abbey Mausoleum, adjoining Arlington National Cemetery, Arlington, Va.; remains removed and reinterred in unknown location.

LILLIE, GORDON WILLIAM, "PAWNEE BILL,"

(1860-1942) — Frontiersman and Wild West showman, was born on February 14, 1860, to Susan Ann (Conant) Lillie and Newton Wesley Lillie in Bloomingdale, Illinois, where his father had a mill. Lillie attended the local school and worked in the mill in the evenings and on Saturdays. He was greatly interested in tales of cowboys, buffalo, and wild game on the Native American Territory frontier. In 1874, while he was in high school, fire destroyed his father's mill, and the family moved to Kansas and resettled near the town of Wellington. There, Lillie made frequent visits to nearby Native American encampments, where he became acquainted with the Pawnees.

Longing for adventure, Lillie left home at the age of fifteen intending to become a cowboy, but in Wichita, Kansas, became involved in a gunfight in which he was forced to kill his opponent. After being acquitted, he rode on to visit his Pawnee friends, now removed to the

Indian Territory, and stayed nearly a year, working in the Pawnee rock quarry and the government sawmill. During the next five years, he spent some time in the Cherokee Outlet (later part of Oklahoma) and the Texas Panhandle; held a government job as schoolteacher and interpreter at the Pawnee Agency; and worked as a cattle rancher.

In 1883, Buffalo Bill Cody was organizing a new version of his traveling Wild West show and wished to include a group of Pawnees. The federal commissioner gave his consent as long as Lillie traveled with them as interpreter and protector, and consequently, Lillie gained his nickname of "Pawnee Bill." At a performance given in Philadelphia, Pennsylvania, that first summer, he met May Manning; they were married on August 31, 1886. In 1888, he launched his own show, "Pawnee Bill's Historic Wild West."

Returning to Wichita, Lillie took an active role in the Kansas "boomer" movement, seeking to open the unassigned lands of neighboring Native American Territory (later Oklahoma) to white settlers. He organized the Pawnee Bill Oklahoma Colonization Company, and when the land was officially opened on April 22, 1889, he led a group of 3,200 colonists in their run to stake claims. He led a similar group at the opening of the Cherokee Outlet in 1893.

Meanwhile in 1890, Lillie had revived his Wild West show, which now became one of the best-paying circus properties in the United States. For nearly twenty years, he toured the United States and Canada, giving performances. In 1894, he took his show to the international exposition at Antwerp, Belgium, and later toured in Holland and France. Lillie agreed to a merger with Buffalo Bill's show in 1909, but Cody was erratic in his business methods and the combination lasted only four years, after which the company was disbanded.

Lillie retired to Oklahoma, where he had acquired a 2,000-acre ranch near Pawnee, and for the rest of his life, he devoted himself to the interests of the state he had helped to open. He joined the national effort to save the buffalo from extinction and maintained a large herd on his estate, and helped in the establishment of an 8,000-acre tract in the Wichita Mountains as a national game preserve. He established on his ranch an Old Town and Tribal Trading Post that recaptured the romance of pioneer days and attracted many visitors.

In September 1936, Lillie and his wife were injured in an automobile crash. She died three days later. Although Lillie survived for several years, he never fully recovered, and on February 3, 1942, he died at his ranch home. He was buried at Highland Cemetery in Pawnee,

Kansas.

LINCOLN, ABRAHAM

(1809-1865) — sixteenth president of the United States, was born in Hardin County, Kentucky, February 12; the son of Thomas and Nancy (Hanks) Lincoln. Abraham Lincoln's early education from books was fitful and scanty ; schools were infrequent on the wild frontier. In 1816 the Lincoln family moved to Spencer County, Indiana, where they built and lived in a log cabin, where Mrs. Lincoln died October 5, 1818, at the age of thirty-five. In the autumn of the following year Thomas Lincoln married Mrs. Sally

Abraham Lincoln

Johnston. She was a woman of some mental ability and great kindness of heart; her influence over the boy was great and beneficent. Aided by her, Abraham secured the reading of the few books to be found in the settlement, and became noted as a hungry reader. As he grew older he took to making impromptu speeches among the neighbors on any topic that chanced to be under discussion. His first glimpse of the world was afforded in the spring of 1828, when, in company with a son of one of the traders of Gentryville, Indiana, he embarked on a flatboat loaded with produce and floated down the creeks and rivers to New Orleans, 1,800 miles distant, where the cargo and craft were disposed of, and the young voyagers made their way homeward.

His family moved once more, in 1830, this time to Illinois, where they built another log cabin, near Decatur, Macon Co. After helping his father to build the cabin, split rails, and fence and plough fifteen acres of land, Abraham Lincoln struck out for himself, hiring himself to any who needed manual labor. His father finally settled in Goose Nest Prairie, Illinois, where he died in 1851 at the age of seventy-three. His son cared for him up to his final years.

In the spring of 1831 Abraham Lincoln, accompanied by his cousin, John Hanks, took a flatboat, produce-laden, to New Orleans, for one Denton Offutt, a country trader, and on his return was engaged by Offutt to take charge of a small trading store in New Salem, Illinois. He took an active interest in politics, was noted as a graphic and humorous story-teller, and was regarded as one of the oracles of the neighborhood. His unflinching honesty gained him the title of "Honest Abe Lincoln." Resolving to run for the legislature, he issued a circular dated March 9, 1832, appealing to his friends and neighbors to vote for him. Before the election came on, Indian disturbances broke out in the north part of the state, and Black Hawk, the chief of the Sacs, headed a formidable war party. Lincoln joined a party of volunteers and marched to the scene of hostilities. The conflict was soon over, and Lincoln returned to New Salem, ten days before the election. He was defeated, but he received nearly every vote of his own town. He was a Whig in politics, and was an ardent admirer of Henry Clay, then the great leader.

Once more he made an essay in trading, and bought on credit, after the fashion of the time, a small country store and contents, associating with himself, at sundry times, partners in business. The venture was a losing one, and the principal occupation of Lincoln during this period was that of diligent study and the reading of everything on which he could lay hands, newspapers and old political pamphlets chiefly. He studied law and surveying, and in 1833 he began work as a land-surveyor, a vocation which in that region then gave one frequent employment. In that year, too, he was appointed postmaster of New Salem, an unimportant office, which he valued only because it gave him an opportunity to read the newspapers of its patrons.

He was again a candidate for the legislature in 1834, was elected at the head of the poll, there being three other candidates in the field. He was now twenty-five years of age, manly, independent, well-poised and thoroughly informed in all public matters. In the legislature his commanding height attracted attention, but he took very small part in the active duties of legislation, contenting himself with observation and study of all that passed. Next year, when he was again returned to the legislature, he participated actively in the affairs of the house, and distinguished himself by an unavailing protest against the "Black Laws" of the state, which forbade the entrance of free persons of color into Illinois, and by his support of the bill to remove the seat of government from Vandalia to Springfield.

In 1837 Lincoln removed to Springfield, the new capital of the state, and established himself very modestly in the business of a lawyer. In this practice he remained until his election to the presidency in 1860. His first partner in business was John T. Stuart, in 1837; this partnership was changed four years later, when he associated himself with Stephen T.

Logan. In 1843 the law partnership of Abraham Lincoln and William H. Herndon was formed ; this firm was not dissolved until the death of Lincoln in 1865. During the "Tippecanoe and Tyler too" campaign of 1840, when the country was deeply stirred by the presidential candidacy of Gen. William Henry Harrison, Lincoln threw himself into the canvass, and was one of the electors on the Whig ticket. He was highly elated by the triumph of Harrison and the Whig party, and he distinguished himself by his fearless opposition to the party that had, up to that time, been dominant in the country.

About this time he suffered a great disappointment in the death of a beautiful young lady, Ann Rutledge, to whom he was attached, and this grief made upon his temperament a lifelong impression. In November, 1842 he married Mary Todd of Kentucky. Miss Todd was visiting relations in Springfield, when circumstances brought her into intimate friendly contact with Lincoln. He was not gradually acquiring a profitable law practice, and the days of grinding poverty, long endured without complaint, were passing away.

In 1846, after several disappointments, he was given the Whig nomination to Congress from the Sanagamon district, and was elected over his Democratic opponent, Peter Cartwright, by a majority of 1,611, polling an unexpectedly large vote. During the preceding winter Texas had been admitted to the Union, and the bitterness with which the Whigs opposed this step, and the measures that grew out of it, was shared by Lincoln, who made good use of arguments against these matters on the canvass, and subsequently during his term in Congress. Among the members of the House of Representatives with Lincoln were John Quincy Adams, Robert C. Winthrop, Alexander H. Stephens, Robert Toombs and Andrew Johnson. In the Senate were Daniel Webster, Lewis Cass, John C. Calhoun, Jefferson Davis and Stephen A. Douglas.

Lincoln in Congress opposed the war with Mexico, but voted consistently for rewards to the soldiers who fought in it. He served only one term in Congress, and did not leave any marked impression in the annals of that body. He voted with the men who favored the formation of the new territories of California and New Mexico without slavery, and he introduced a bill to abolish slavery in the District of Columbia, providing for the emancipation of slaves there by governmental purchase. He was not a candidate for reelection, and was succeeded by his intimate friend, Edward D. Baker. Gen. Zachary Taylor having been elected president of the United States, Lincoln applied for the office of commissioner of the general land office, but was offered, in lieu thereof, the governorship of the territory of Oregon. He declined, and returned to his practice of law in Springfield.

The eldest son of Abraham and Mary Lincoln, Robert Todd, was born August 1, 1843; the second, Edward Baker, was born March 10, 1846, and died in infancy; the third, William Wallace, was born December 21, 1850, and died during his father's first year in the presidential office; Thomas, the youngest son, was born April 4, 1853, and surviving his father, dying at the age of nineteen years. As a lawyer, Lincoln was now engaged in several celebrated cases. One of these was that of the negro girl, Nancy, in which the question of the legality of slavery in the Northwestern territory, of which Illinois formed a part, was involved. Another, in which the seizure of a free negro from Illinois by the authorities of New Orleans was opposed, was also undertaken and conducted by him. In both these causes Lincoln succeeded. In 1850 there were many premonitions of the coming of the storm which the long-continued agitation of the slavery question had induced. Lincoln was a close but generally silent observer of the signs of the times. In 1854 the virtual repeal of the Missouri Compromise measures, in which Stephen A. Douglas took a leading part, aroused the Northern and free states to excited debate. The passage of the Kansas-Nebraska bill, by which those two territories were organized, with the question of the legality of slavery left open to be settled by a popular vote, was the signal for a great outburst of feeling against the institution of slavery in the non-slaveholding states.

In October of that year Lincoln and Douglas met in debate at the great annual State Fair held in Springfield, Illinois, and Lincoln made his first famous speech on the question that from then on began to engross the minds of the people. Lincoln opposed the repeal of the Missouri Compromise, and Douglas defended it. A few days later the two men met again at Peoria, Illinois, and the debate was renewed, amidst great popular excitement. On both occasions Lincoln's speeches evoked much enthusiasm by the closeness of their logic and their perspicacity. His public speeches from this time forth were regarded throughout the western states as the most remarkable of the time.

In 1856 the first Republican National Convention was held in Philadelphia. John C. Fremont was nominated for president of the United States and William L. Dayton for vice-president. Abraham Lincoln received 110 votes for the second place on the ticket. James Buchanan and John C. Breckenridge were nominated by the democratic party. Lincoln was a candidate for presidential elector on the Republican ticket of Illinois, and took an active part in the canvass, speaking from one end of the state to the other almost continually throughout the campaign. The Democratic candidates were elected, Buchanan receiving 174 electoral votes against 114 cast for Fremont. Maryland cast her eight electoral votes for Fillmore and Donelson, the Whig candidates.

In 1848, Douglas's term in the Senate drawing to a close, Lincoln was put forward as a competitor for the place. The two men accordingly agreed on a joint canvass of the state, the members of the Illinois legislature then to be elected being charged with the duty of choosing a senator. The contest between Lincoln and Douglas that year was memorable and significant. The debates attracted the attention of the entire country. In their course the slavery question in all its bearings, but more especially with reference to its introduction into territory previously regarded as free, was debated with great force and minuteness on both sides. The total vote of the state was in favor of Lincoln, but as some of the hold-over members of the legislature were friendly to Douglas, and the districting of the state was also in his favor, he was chosen senator by a small majority.

At the Republican Convention, held in Decatur, Illinois, in May, 1859, Lincoln was declared to be the candidate of his state for the presidential nomination of 1860. This was the first public demonstration in his favor as a national candidate. At that convention several rails from the Lincoln farm in Macon County were exhibited as the handiwork of Abraham Lincoln, and the title of "the rail-splitter" was given him. In the autumn of that year, Lincoln made political speeches in Ohio and Kentucky, arousing great enthusiasm wherever he appeared. In February, 1860, he accepted an invitation to speak in New York, and, for the first time in his life, he visited the Atlantic states. He spoke in the Coper Union Hall, New York, and his oration, which was a discussion of the great question of the day, created a profound impression throughout the country. It gave him at once a national reputation as a political speaker.

The Democratic National Convention assembled in Charleston, South Carolina, April 23, 1860, to nominate candidates for president and vice-president. The slavery issue divided the body, so that the pro-slavery delegates finally withdrew, and organized a separate convention in Richmond, Virginia, where John C. Breckinridge was nominated. The remaining delegates adjourned to Baltimore, where they nominated Stephen A. Douglas. Meanwhile the Whigs and a few other conservatives met in Baltimore and nominated John Bell, of Tennessee. The Republican National Convention assembled in Chicago, Illinois, June 17,

1860, and nominated Abraham Lincoln for president. Hannibal Hamlin, of Maine, was nominated for vice-president. The electoral canvass that year was one of the most intense excitement. It was universally conceded that the question of the extension or the confinement of slavery to its present limits was to be determined by the result of this election. Douglas was the only one of the four presidential candidates who took the field to speak in his own behalf.

Lincoln was elected, having received 180 electoral votes; Breckinridge had seventy-two votes; Douglas twelve, and Bell thirty-nine. The popular vote was distributed as follows: Lincoln, 1,866,452; Breckinridge, 847,953; Douglas, 1,375,157; Bell, 590,631. As soon as the result of the election was known, the members of President Buchanan's cabinet who were in favor of a secession of the slave states began to make preparations for that event. The army, which mustered only 16,000 men, was scattered through the southern states, and the small navy was dispersed. United States arms had been already ordered to points in the Southern states, and active steps had been taken by the more rebellious of those states toward a formal severance of the ties that bound them to the Union. Their attitude was one of armed expectancy. The cabinet of President Buchanan was torn by the conflicting views of its members, some of them being in favor of resolutely confronting the danger of secession, and others opposing any action whatever. The Federal forts in Charleston Harbor, South Carolina, being threatened by the secessionists, Lewis Cass advised reinforcement; he resigned when his advice was disregarded at the instance of his associates. Jeremiah S. Black, Attorney-General, gave an opinion that the states could not be coerced into remaining in the Union, and shortly a general disruption of the cabinet ensued.

Southern senators and representatives now began to leave Washington for their homes, declaring that they could no longer remain in the councils of the nation. Formal ordinances of secession were passed by the states in rebellion. South Carolina adopted its ordinance of secession December 20, 1860; Mississippi, January 9, 1861; Florida, January 10th; Alabama, January 11th; Georgia, January 19, 1861; Louisiana, January 26th, and Texas February 1st. Representatives of the seceding states met at Montgomery, February 4, 1861, and organized a provisional government, generally resembling in form that of the United States; Jefferson Davis, of Mississippi, was chosen president, and Alexander H. Stephens, of Georgia, vice-president. Davis assumed an aggressive tone in his public speeches, and, while on his way to take the reins of government of the new Confederacy, he said: "We will carry the war where it is easy to advance, where food for the sword and the torch awaits our armies in the densely populated cities."

Lincoln remained at his home in Springfield, Illinois, making no speeches. He broke this silence for the first time when, on February 11, 1861, he bade his friends and neighbors farewell, as he took the railway train for Washington. In that simple address he said, among other things: "I go to assume a task more difficult than that which has devolved upon any other man since the days of Washington. He never would have succeeded except for the aid of divine Providence, upon which he at all times relied. I feel that I cannot succeed without the same divine blessing which sustained him; and on the same Almighty Being I place my reliance for support." On the way to Washington the president-elect was received with great popular enthusiasm, and was frequently called from his railway carriage to speak to the people. He learned of a plot to take his life while passing through Baltimore, and, by the advice of trusty friends, the movements of the party were changed, in order to disconcert the conspirators. Speaking at Independence Hall, Philadelphia, February 22nd, during these trying hours, he referred to the fundamental principle propounded in the Declaration of Independence, and said: "If this country cannot be saved without giving up that principle, I was about to say I would rather be assassinated on the spot than surrender it."

Lincoln was inaugurated president of the United States at noon, March 4, 1861, in front of the national capitol, Washington. His inaugural address was an earnest and plaintive appeal for peace and union. At the same time he took care to say that the union of the states is perpetual, and that to the best of his ability he would "take care that the laws of the Union be faithfully executed in all the states." He closed with these memorable words: "The mystic chords of memory, stretching from every battlefield and patriot grave to every living heart and hearthstone all over this broad land, will yet swell the chorus of the Union, when touched again, as surely they will be, by the better angels of our nature." In the South, and in such communities of the North as sympathized with the cause of rebellion, the speech was received with coldness, and in many instances with jeers and derision.

Lincoln's cabinet, then announced, was as follows: Secretary of State, William H. Seware; Secretary of War, Simon Cameron; Secretary of the Treasury, Salmon P. Chase; Secretary of the Navy, Gideon Welles ; Post-master General, Montgomery Blair; Secretary of the Interior, Caleb B. Smith; Attorney-General, Edward Bates. Of this group, Seward,

Chase, Bates and Cameron had been candidates for the nomination of president at the convention at which Lincoln was nominated. Some of the new president's friends were troubled by the selection of these prominent and ambitious men as his counselors. Subsequently it was found, when attempts were made to subordinate him to his cabinet, that he was the sole interior spirit of his administration. Of these cabinet ministers only Secretaries Seward and Welles remained in office during the remainder of Lincoln's lifetime. Secretary Chase resigned his place in 1864, and was succeeded by William Pitt Fessenden, of Maine, who resigned after a short term, and was succeeded by Hugh McCullough in March, 1865. Simon Cameron resigned at the close of 1861, and was succeeded by Edwin M. Stanton. Secretary Smith resigned his office to accept a judicial post in 1862, and was succeeded by John P. Usher. Attorney General Bates retired from office in 1864, and was succeeded by James Speed, of Kentucky, and Montgomery Blair about the same time resigned the office of post-master general, and was succeeded by Ex-Gov. William Dennison, of Ohio.

The Confederate Congress, on March 11, 1861, passed a bill providing for the organization of an army. No notice was taken of this insurrectionary measure, which, it had been expected, would be regarded as a casus belli by the Federal authorities. Next, two commissioners, Messrs. Forsythe and Crawford, were sent to Washington to negotiate a treaty with the government of the United States, the assumption being that the new Confederacy was a foreign power. Lincoln refused to receive the commissioners, and sent them a copy of his inaugural address. Secretary Seward served upon them, however, a formal notice that they could have no official recognition from the United States government. Meantime, the determination of the president to send aid to the beleaguered Federal garrison Charleston Harbor, then collected in Fort Sumter, was made public. The people of South Carolina, impatient for the war to begin, threatened to fire upon Fort Sumter, and to attack any vessel that might bring aid. Every device to induce the president to commit "an overt act of war" was resorted to in vain. While he waited for the rebels to fire the first gun, there was much impatience manifested in the loyal Northern states at what was considered the sluggishness of the administration.

On April 12, 1861, Gen. Beauregard, commanding the rebel forces at Charleston, sent a demand to Major Anderson, in command of Fort Sumter, to surrender. He refused to surrender, but he subsequently agreed to evacuate the fort April 15th, unless he received instructions to the contrary, or provisions for sustenance, before that date. After due warning, Beauregard opened fire on the fort early in the morning of April 12th, and, after feeble defense, the famishing garrison of sixty-five men was forced to surrender, and the United States flag fell on the walls of Sumter. The war had begun. The effect of this overt act of the Confederates was instant and inflammatory all through the North. Patriotic meetings were held, men were ready to volunteer for the war, state authorities began to arm and equip troops, and a general note of preparation now sounded through the loyal states.

The president called a special session of Congress at the national capital for July 4, 1861. In a proclamation dated Apr. 15, 1861, the president asked for 75,000 men. This was responded to in the North with enthusiasm, and in the South with cries of derision. In the states bordering on the confederacy, where the great battles of the war were afterward fought, this call was received with coldness. Patriotic excitement ran high all over the North, and for a time nothing was thought of but the war for the sake of the Union. One of the first regiments to march to the defense of the national capital, menaced on all sides and distracted with interior conspiracies, was the 6th Massachusetts. It was fired upon in the streets of Baltimore. This act inflamed the loyal North still more, and the excitement became intense. The governor of Maryland, alarmed by this collision, implored the president to invoke the mediation of the British minister at Washington. Lincoln referred the governor to the Secretary of State, who declared that "no domestic contention should be referred to any foreign arbitrament, least of all to that of a European monarchy.

Gen. B. F. Butler surprised the people of Baltimore by seizing Federal Hill, a fortified position commanding the city, and troops thereafter marched unmolested through the city on their way to Washington. On the 19th of April the president issued his proclamation declaring the ports of Texas, Louisiana, Mississippi, Alabama, Georgia, Florida and South Carolina in a state of blockade, and closed to commerce. One week later, North Carolina and Virginia, having also passed ordinances of secession, were added to this list. Another call for troops was made, thirty-nine regiments of infantry and one of cavalry being asked for; and, the maximum force of the regular army was increased to 22,714 men; and 18,000 volunteer seamen were called for.

An embassy from the state of Virginia having been sent to the president while the ordinance of secession was under consideration, Lincoln, in reply to application for his intentions, again referred to his inaugural address, and added: "As I then and therein said, the power confided to me will be used to hold, occupy and possess property and places belonging to the government, and to collect duties and imports; but beyond what is necessary for these objects, there will be no invasion, no using of force against or among the people anywhere." Furthermore, he intimated that it might be necessary to withdraw the United States mail service from the states in which disorder prevailed. He did not threaten to collect duties and imports by force, but he would employ force to retake the public property of the government, wherever that had been seized.

By a vote of eighty-eight to fifty-five the ordinance of secession was adopted in Virginia, and the capital of the state now became the seat of the confederate government. Meanwhile, the Confederates had taken possession of Harper's Ferry, Virginia, and the arsenal and munitions of war at that point, and of the navy-yard near Norfolk, Va., with the stores and vessels there accumulated. These seizures gave them much additional war material. The hostile camps on the northern border of Virginia were drawing nearer to each other as both increased in numbers and efficiency. When Congress assembled in July, Confederate flags on the Virginia heights opposite Washington could be seen from the top of the capitol. The first serious engagement was that on the line of Bull Run Creek ending on July 21, 1861. The Confederate forces, under Gen. Joseph E. Johnston, numbered about 18,000, and those under Gen. Irvin McDowell, the Union commander, were 17,676. The result was a defeat for the Union forces and a panic-stricken retreat upon Washington.

The effect of the disaster on Lincoln and on the country was depressing; but the people soon rallied, and indignation took the place of mortifying regret. Volunteering was resumed with vigor. Two naval and military expeditions were successful, and Fort Hatteras, North Carolina, and Port Royal, South Carolina, surrendered to the Union forces. Gen. McClellan had also cleared the Confederates from that part of Virginia which lies west of the Blue Ridge, afterward erected into the state of West Virginia. Congress responded to the call of the president for more men and money by voting $500,000,000 for war purposes, and authorizing him to call for 500,000 men. Great excitement was created throughout the country when James M. Mason and John Slidell, Confederate emissaries to European courts, were taken, November 8, 1861, from the British packet-ship Trent, at sea, by Captain Wilkes, commanding the U. S. steamer San Jacinto. The event was the cause of much congratulation with the people, and cabinet ministers and Congress openly approved of the seizure.

Lincoln was disturbed by this, and decided that the envoys should be given up to the demand of the British government. In the face of popular indignation, he remained firm, and the envoys were released. Eventually, the wisdom and the justice of this course were generally admitted. In July, 1861, General McClellan was assigned to the command of the army of the Potomac, and Gen. Fremont to that of the department of the West, with headquarters at St. Louis. Radical differences on the subject of slavery at once began to appear in the orders of these two generals. Lincoln was greatly embarrassed and disturbed when Fremont, August 31st, issued a proclamation confiscating the property of Confederates within his lines, and emancipating their slaves. Congress had passed a bill to confiscate property used for insurrectionary military purposes, and slaves had been declared "contraband of war." The president wrote privately to Fremont, advising him to modify his orders. Fremont refused to make these modifications, and Lincoln, in an order dated September 11, 1861, did so modify his orders. Fremont refused to make these modifications, and Lincoln, in an order dated September 11, 1861, did so modify Fremont's proclamation.

During May of the following year Gen. David Hunter, commanding the department of the South, with headquarters at Hilton Head, South Carolina, issued an order resembling Fremont's: it was instantly revoked by the president. Lincoln was sticking to his determination to save the Union, if possible, without meddling with the question of slavery; and while none doubted his hostility to slavery, it was difficult for many to understand why he did not strike it in its vulnerable parts whenever he had an opportunity. The controversy arising out of the disposition of captured slaves by the army of the Potomac (which was usually a recognition of the rights of the slave-holders), and out of the orders of Hunter and McClellan, was very bitter in the North, and many who had supported Lincoln's administration complained that his policy was "pro- slavery."

March 6, 1862, the president sent to Congress a message in which he intimated very distinctly that if the war ended then, or very soon, slavery would probably remain intact; but it should continue, and if gradual and compensated emancipation were not accepted, then slavery would be destroyed by the operations of the war. Congress adopted a resolution approving the policy outlined by the president; but the border state representatives, although invited by the president to a free conference with him on the subject, kept aloof from the matter. Congress had not passed a bill to abolish slavery in the District of Columbia. It was signed by Lincoln, who, in 1849, had introduced a bill for that purpose.

During the summer of 1862 the proposition of arming the freed negroes was begun; it was opposed by many conservative people, but was warmly advocated by Lincoln, who said: "Why should they do anything for us if we do nothing for them? It they stake their lives for us, they must be prompted by the strongest of motives, even the promise of freedom. And the promise, being made, must be kept."

The law authorizing the arming of the ex-slaves, accordingly, contained a clause giving freedom to all slaves who served in the Union army, and to their families as well. During the summer military operations lagged, and much complaining was made of the sluggish movements of the army of the Potomac under Gen. McClellan. This impatience found expression in a letter to the president, written by Horace Greeley and published in the New York Tribune, in which the writer severely arraigned the president for his alleged inactivity and lack of vigor in dealing with the slavery question. Lincoln wrote a letter in reply, in the course of which he said: "If I could save the Union without freeing any slave I would do it; if I could save it by freeing all the slaves, I would do it; and if I could do it by freeing some and leaving others alone, I would also do that. What I do about slavery and the colored race, I do because I believe it helps to save this Union; and what I forbear I forbear because I do not believe that it would help to save the Union." This appeared to settle for a long time the position of Lincoln on the slavery question.

The Confederate army, under Gen. Robert E. Lee, invaded Maryland, crossing the Potomac in September, 1862. At that time Lincoln had under consideration a proclamation freeing all slaves within the jurisdiction of the United States government, or thereafter to be brought under it. In the imminence of the danger then apparent, he resolved that if success should crown the Union arms, he would issue that proclamation. The battle of South Mountain was fought on September 14th, and that of Antietam on the 17th; the Confederates were defeated on both fields, and retreated in great disorder. The proclamation of emancipation was issued September 22nd, declaring freedom to all slaves in bondage on American soil. This proclamation electrified the nation and greatly excited the people of other countries. January 1, 1863, the president issued a supplementary proclamation, in which the terms of the previous document were reaffirmed, and the parts of states exempted from the operation of emancipation were named. These portions were inconsiderable, and the action of congress in abolishing slavery throughout the entire territory of the United States made an end of slavery in the Republic.

Lincoln's general plan for the conduct of the war, formulated after anxious consultation with his most trusted advisers, was as follows: To blockade the entire coast-line of the Confederate states, to acquire military occupation of the border states, so as to protect Union men and repel invasion; to clear the Mississippi of obstructions, thus dividing the Confederacy and relieving the West, which was deprived of its natural outlet to the sea; to destroy the Confederate army between Richmond and Washington, and to capture the Confederate capital. This vast plan had been formed in the mind of Lincoln by the necessities of the situation. Gen. Scott, who held the highest command in the army of the United States, had asked to be relieved from active duty and placed on the retired list. His request was granted.

General George B. McClellan was now in supreme command. Lincoln's immediate anxiety was for the speedy opening of the Mississippi River. In pursuance of his program, General U.S. Grant, then rising in popular esteem, attacked and destroyed Belmont, a military depot of the confederates in Mississippi. General Garfield defeated Humphrey Marshall at Middle Creek, Kentucky, and General George H. Thomas defeated General Zollikoffer and Crittenden at Mill Spring. This was followed up by the capture of Fort Henry on the Tennessee, and Fort Donelson on the Cumberland River. These streams, emptying into the Ohio River, were very necessary to promote military operations against the confederates in the southwestern states.

On April 6, 1862 the great battle of Shiloh, or Pittsburg Landing was fought in which the carnage on both sides was very great. The defeated Confederates retreated to their fortified line at Corinth, Mississippi, where they were attacked by General H. W. Halleck, and again compelled to retreat, leaving behind them a large accumulation of military stores. By the end of May, 1862, Missouri, Arkansas, Kentucky and Tennessee were virtually free from Confederate domination.

That part of the program which required the blockade and occupation of Atlantic ports of the seceded states was not overlooked. During much of March and April, 1862, Roaoke Island, North Carolina, was captured. Next fell Newbern, North Carolina, and Fort Macon and Fort Pulaski on the same coast. In the spring of 1862 an expedition under Gen. B.F. Butler landed at Ship Island, in the Gulf of Mexico, about midway between New Orleans and Mobile. A fleet of armed vessels under Adm. Farragut soon after arrived, and on the 17th of April Farragut appeared below the fort that guarded the approaches to the city of New Orleans. After some skirmishing, Farragut's fleet passed the forts, destroying the fleet above, and ascended the Mississippi and appeared before the city of New Orleans, to the amazement of its people.

Baton rouge, the capital of Louisiana, next fell, and the surrender of Natchez, May 12, 1862, opened the Mississippi as far north as Vicksburg, which with its fortifications resisted the free navigation of the Mississippi River. McClellan meanwhile remained inactive before Washington, and popular discontent was constantly making itself manifest in consequence of his alleged tardiness, many people insisting that the government had failed to supply his necessary wants.

Lincoln was in frequent consultation with McClellan and the other generals gathered at the capital. During the latter part of January, 1862, Lincoln issued an order specially intended to direct the movements of the army of the Potomac, in which among other things, the army was commanded to seize upon the occupy a point on the railroad southwest of Manassas Junction. Details of this movement were to be left to the judgment of the general commanding. To this McClellan demurred, and in a long letter to the secretary of war detailed his objections and submitted a plan of his own. A council of war, to consist of twelve general officers, was finally called, and it was decided that McClellan's plan should be adopted. Information of these debates having reached the Confederate generals, their forces withdrew from Manassas to the lower side of the Rappahannock, thereby rendering both plans useless.

By this time two weeks had elapsed since the president's order directing a general advance of all the armies had been issued. After the enemy abandoned his line at Manassas, McClellan moved forward for a day or two, but soon after returned to his entrenched position at Alexandria, on the Potomac near Washington. On the 11th of March, 1862, General McClellan was relieved from command of other departments of military activity and was placed in sole and immediate command of the army of the Potomac. A new base of operations was now established at Fortress Monroe at the entrance of Chesapeake Bay; but meanwhile a fight between the ironclad Merrimac and the Federal Monitor had taken place near Fortress Monroe, and the ironclad had been beaten back to Norfolk.

McClellan's immediate field of operations was on the peninsula formed by the York and James Rivers. The enemy were behind a line of entrenchments that stretched across the peninsula, the key of the situation being at Yorktown on this line. Again there were unaccountable delays, and on the 3rd of April the president ordered the Secretary of War to direct that the army of the Potomac should begin active operations; but McClellan demurred, and informed the president by letter on the 5th of April that he was sure that the enemy in front of him and behind formidable works was in great force. He required more men. Lincoln was confident that McClellan exaggerated the strength of the force in front of him, and he ordered Secretary Stanton to hurry forward everything that McClellan seemed to think necessary to insure the safety of an advance.

The line held by the Confederate forces was about thirteen miles long. Much of the force behind that line was scattered in the defense of points in the rear. In answer to McClellan's call for more troops, the president yielded and sent him Gen. Franklin's division, which had been retained to defend the line between Richmond and Washington. On the 13th of April McClellan's army, according to official reports, had 130,378 men, of which 112,392 were effective. About this time McCllellan called for Parrott guns, to the consternation of the president, who wrote him on the 1st of May: "Your call for Parrott guns from Washington alarms me, chiefly because it argues indefinite procrastination. Is anything to be done?" Nothing was done, and on the 25th Lincoln telegraphed McClellan: "I think the time is near at hand when you must either attack Richmond or give up the job and come to the defense of Washington."

Meanwhile, the confederates, disconcerted by the accumulation of Federal troops, abandoned their line across the peninsula and retreated up to their second line of works. On the 21st of June McClellan wrote to the president asking permission to address him on the subject of "The present state of military affairs throughout the whole country." The president replied: "If it would not divert your time and attention from the army under your command, I should be glad to her your views on the present state of military affairs throughout the whole country."

The greater part of June, 1862, was spent by the army under McClellan, in fighting, advancing, retreating, and in various maneuvers. At one time a portion of the troops was within four miles of Richmond without meeting any considerable force of the enemy. On the 27th of June McClellan announced his intention to retreat to the James River, and in a letter to the Secretary of War said: "If I save this army, I tell you plainly I owe you no thanks, nor to any one at Washington. You have done your best to destroy this army." Lincoln was greatly disturbed by the temper of this dispatch.

The army, harassed by the Confederate forces hanging on its

rear, retreated to Malvern hill, and the campaign of the peninsula was over. By this time it was generally understood that General McClellan would b the presidential candidate at the next election of that portion of the Democratic Party which was dissatisfied with the conduct of the ever and with the emancipation measures then under contemplation. In order to see for himself the condition of the army, the President visited the headquarters of Gen. McClellan at Harrison's Landing on the 7th of July. He examined the rosters of the troops and scrutinized the reports of the chiefs of divisions, and gave it as his judgment that the army should be recalled to Washington, and in this conclusion he was supported by the corps commanders; but to this McClellan was opposed. He required Burnside's army, then operating in North Carolina, and with this large reinforcement he thought he might achieve success. Lincoln found that McClellan had 160,000 men, and on his return to Washington he wrote to him reminding him of this fact and calling attention to the additional fact that while he, Lincoln, was in the army with McClellan he found only 86,000 effective men on duty. In reply, McClellan said that 38,250 men were "absent by authority." Lincoln, feeling the necessity of a military adviser who should be near him in Washington and always readily accessible, called to the capital Gen. Henry W. Halleck, who on the 11th of July was given the rank and title of general-in- chief.

About this time General John Pope, whose successes in the valley of the Mississippi had given him fame, was called to the command of a new military organization of three army corps, commanded by Gens. Fremont, Banks and McDowell. These were known as the army of Virginia. On September 22, 1862, a conference of the governors of loyal states was assembled at Altoona to determine on the best means of supporting the president in carrying on the war. They issued an address, assuring the president of the readiness of the states to respond to calls for more troops and to support vigorous war measures. Thereupon the president issued a call for 300,000 men. Pope's army, 38,000 strong, was employed to defend Washington, against which point Lee was now advancing with a large force.

It was expected that McClellan would make a bold attack on Richmond from his position on the James, Lee's attention being directed toward Pope. This was not done, and the army of the Potomac was ordered to the line of the Potomac River to support Pope; but McClellan, repeatedly ordered to make haste, delayed, and several weeks elapsed before he showed any indications of moving. Finally, on the 23rd of August, he sailed from Fortress Monroe, arriving at Alexandria on the

Potomac on the 27th, nearly one month after receiving his orders. Meanwhile, Pope was being driven toward Washington, assailed in turn by the confederate forces under Jackson, Longstreet and Lee. Pope was forced back on Washington. Disaster and defeat, divided councils in the cabinet, virulent and heated debates in Congress, agitated the country. Lincoln alone remained patient.

The army of the Potomac was reorganized and McClellan soon had under him not only that force, but the remnants of Pope's army of Virginia and the men brought from North Carolina by General Burnside. To these were added other reinforcements from new levies, making the force under McClellan the largest that had been massed together in one army-more than 200,000, all told. On the 15th of September Harper's Ferry was surrendered to the confederate forces. Lee, advancing into Maryland, brought on another battle, which was fought at Antietam September 17th. The Confederates were defeated, and were obliged to retreat across the Potomac. McClellan failed to follow up his victory, and Lincoln on the 6th of October, 1862, through Gen. Halleck, directed McClellan to "cross the Potomac and give battle to the enemy or drive him south." McClellan declined to obey.

On the 10th of October Gen. J.E.B. Stuart crossed the Potomac, going as far north as Chambersburg, Pennsylvania, made the entire circuit of McClellan's army, and re-crossed in to Virginia. Finally, on the 5th of November, 1862, just one month after the order to cross had been issued, the army did cross the Potomac, but it was too late. General McClellan was relieved from command of the army on the 5th of November, and his military career was ended. He was succeeded by General A. E. Burnside, a graduate of the U. S. Military Academy, who, until the outbreak of the war, had been engaged in civil pursuits. At the outset there was a disagreement between Burnside, Halleck and Lincoln as to the best line of attack upon the Confederate forces. The result of many consultations was, that the route through Fredericksburg, on the Rappahannock, should be adopted. Owing to delays, Lee was able to seize and fortify the heights above the city of Fredericksburg, and Burnside was speedily confronted by a concentrated army. An attack was made in the face of many difficulties on the 15th of December, 1862. The assault failed with great disaster, and the year closed in gloom.

In the West, Buell had been driven back in Kentucky, and the Confederate forces had re-entered that state and a provisional Confederate government had been organized at Frankfort, the capital of the state. The cities of Louisville, Kentucky, and Cincinnati, Ohio, were threatened, and it was found necessary to fortify them. At the end of September the combined Federal forces under General Sherman and McClernand made a vigorous but unsuccessful assault on the defenses of Vicksburg. Lincoln was now besieged on the one hand with demands for the reinstatement of McClellan, and on the other with importunities for an armistice during which negotiations for a settlement might be carried on. The press of the North was often bitter in its criticisms of the administration. In the army there were mutterings of discontent, and many of the elder officers openly expressed their belief that nothing but the reinstatement of McClellan could lead to victory. On the 26th of January, 1863, Gen. Joseph Hooker was placed in command of the army of the Potomac. The army was soon in good fighting condition, and the rosters, examined by the president during a visit to the army headquarters in April, 1863, showed 216,718 men on the rolls, of which 16,000 were on detached service; 136,720 were on active duty, 1,771 absent without authority, 26,000 sick, and the actual effective force was 146,000 which number could be increased at any time to 169,000 by calling in the men from outlying stations. Early in May Hooker's offensive movement began against the Confederate forces lying south of the Rappahannock. The battle of Chancellorsville terminated that campaign, and on May 6 the president received a dispatch from Gen. Hooker's chief of staff, announcing that the army of the Potomac had re-crossed the Rappahannock and was camped on its old ground. This disaster deeply agitated the country, and the President immediately visited headquarters, accompanied by Gen. Halleck.

Soon after this, a law authorizing the conscription of citizens for fighting was enacted, and under the provision of the constitution permitting it, the president suspended the privileges of the writ of habeas corpus, by which the citizen deprived of his liberty could appeal to the courts for an examination in his case. Under the same authority the president proclaimed martial law. These acts, severely criticized at the time, were justified by the "war powers" of the president of the United States under the Constitution. Another important act was the authorizing of the enlistment of negro troops. The arming of the ex-slaves was the cause of much popular discontent both North and South. From first to last, the number of negro troops enlisted in the war was 178,975.

Financial measures also occupied the attention of Congress, and the Secretary of the Treasury was authorized to borrow money to carry on the war. The total amount which he was given leave to raise on the obligations of the government of the United States was $900,000,000.

Bonds were issued to bear fixed rates of interest, and, to meet the pressing necessities of the times, he was authorized to issue $100,000,000 in treasury notes. The finances of the country were in a disordered condition. Gold and silver had disappeared from circulation, and the small change needed in every-day transactions of the people was now in small paper notes. In the western states popular discontent had resulted in the formation of secret societies for the propagation of sedition doctrines and the discouragement of the war.

In July, 1863, Vicksburg fell, thus opening the Mississippi River, the operations being conducted under command of General Grant. In the early days of that month the battle of Gettysburg was fought in which the troops under Gen. Lee, who had invaded the state of Pennsylvania, were given back. The Federal troops were commanded by General Meade. The effective force under Meade in his three days' battle at Gettysburg was from 82,000 to 84,000 men, with 300 pieces of artillery. Lee's effective force was 80,000 men, with 250 guns. The total of killed, wounded and missing in this fight was about 46,000 men, each side having suffered equally. Twenty generals were lost by the Federal army, six being killed. The Confederates lost seventeen generals, three being killed, thirteen wounded and one taken prisoner. On July 4, 1863, Lincoln issued an announcement to the people of the United States, giving the result of the battle of Gettysburg, and concluding with these words: "The President especially desires that on this day He whose will, not ours, should ever more be done, be everywhere remembered and reverenced with profoundest gratitude."

There was great joy throughout the loyal states. The president was serenaded at the White House, and appearing to the crowd said, among other things: "I do most sincerely thank God for the occasion of this call." On November 19, 1863, the battle-field of Gettysburg was dedicated as a burying-place for the remains of those who had given their lives on that now historic ground. The principal speech was delivered by Edward Everett, of Massachusetts, but the brief address of the president on that occasion has now passed into the literature of the world as one of its great masterpieces.

The year closed auspiciously, Grant being in command of a large force stationed in the military division of the Mississippi, with headquarters at Louisville, Kentucky General George H. Thomas was in command of the departments of the Ohio and Cumberland. Hooker, Sheridan and Sherman were subordinate commanders under Grant. The battles of Mission Ridge, Lookout Mountain and Chattanooga were

Federal successes, and the confederates were expelled from Tennessee. Burnside, besieged in Knoxville, was relieved by Sherman, and the Confederate army under Longstreet was driven back into Virginia.

The session of Congress during the winter of 1863-64 was largely occupied by political measures, a presidential campaign now coming on. Some of the Republican leaders were apposed to Lincoln's renomination, considering that he was not sufficiently radical in his measures. As a rule these persons favored the nomination of Chase, the Secretary of the Treasury, and others expressed a preference for General Fremont, whose career in Missouri had excited their sympathies. Lincoln remained silent regarding his political desires. The only expression of his opinion in reference to the political situation was found in his famous saying, "I don't believe it is wise to swap horses while crossing a stream." One of the most important military events of that winter was the appointment of General Grant to the post of lieutenant-general of the army, that rank having been created by act of Congress with the understanding that it was to be conferred upon him. On February 22, 1864, the act was approved, and Gen. Grant was nominated to the post. He was confirmed March 2nd.

General Sherman was assigned to the command of the military division of the Mississippi, succeeding Grant, who, in an order dated March 17, 1864, took command of all the armies of the United States, with headquarters in the field. From this time all of the armies in the West and in the East acted in concert, and the enemy was pressed on all sides. General Grant made his headquarters with the army of the Potomac, on the banks of the Rapidan, and the campaign against the confederate capital at Richmond opened in May, Meade in command of the army of the Potomac, reinforced by the ninth corps under Burnside. The army moved at midnight on the 3rd of the month. On the 5th and 6th were fought the bloody battles of the Wilderness. On the 11th Grant telegraphed to Lincoln: "Our losses have been heavy, as well as those of the enemy, and I propose to fight it out on this line if it takes all summer."

On July 22, 1864, Atlanta fell into the hands of Sherman, and Hood, hoping to drive Sherman to the northward, moved against the Tennessee country once more, passing to the right of Atlanta. The Federal forces under Thomas and Schofield fell upon Hood, who was ignominiously put to flight, and after a two days' fight his army was virtually destroyed. Gen. B.F. Butler took possession of Cit Point, on the James River, where Grant established a base of supplies. Gen. Hunter was sent to clear the Valley of the Shenandoah, but was compelled to retire, and the confederate forces under Early pressed on toward Washington from the valley, entered Maryland and threatened the national capital. A great panic prevailed in that city for several days, but two army corps, dispatched by General Grant saved the capital, and the invading force withdrew. Later in the year Gen. Sheridan cleared the Shenandoah Valley, and by the end of September that region was free once more from Confederate forces.

The Republican National Convention was held in Baltimore, June 8, 1864. Lincoln was renominated for the presidency, and Andrew Johnson was nominated for vice-president. In August of that year the Democratic National Convention assembled in Chicago, and Gen. McClellan was nominated for the presidency, and George H. Pendleton, of Ohio for the vice-presidency.

Rumors of negotiations on the part of the confederates looking toward a return of peace now grew more frequent. Clement C. Clay, of Alabama, and Jacob Thompson, of Mississippi, appeared on the Canadian border and put themselves in communication with Horace Greeley, who wrote to Lincoln July 7, 1864, asking for a safe conduct for these emissaries in order that they might go to Washington and discuss terms of peace. To this Lincoln replied in writing: "If you can find any person anywhere professing to have authority from Jefferson Davis, in writing, embracing the restoration of the Union and the abandonment of slavery, whatever else it embraces, say to him he may come to me with you." some correspondence ensued, and Mr. Greeley went to Niagara Falls to hold an interview with the Confederate emissaries. It soon became apparent that these agents had no authority to treat for peace on the part of the Richmond government, and the incident passed away.

The losses of war required fresh levies of troops, and a call was now issued for 500,000 men. If the required number should not appear buy September 5, 1864, then a draft must be ordered. The presidential election came on in November, 1864, resulting in an overwhelming majority for Lincoln. Every state that voted that year declared for Lincoln and his policy, excepting the states of Delaware, Kentucky and New Jersey. The total number of votes cast in all the states was 4,015,902, of which Lincoln had a clear majority of 411,428. Lincoln had 212 of the 233 electoral votes, and McClellan had twenty-one electoral votes. There was renewed talk about peace and compromise during the winter of 1864-65. Francis P. Blair, Sr., a private citizen, was furnished with a safe-conduct signed by the president, and went to Richmond, saw

Jefferson Davis, and returned to Washington with a letter addressed to him by the president of the confederacy, the contents of which he was authorized to communicate to Lincoln. In that document Davis expressed his willingness "to enter into conference with a view to secure peace in the two countries." Lincoln replied to Mr. Blair in a note in which he stated that he was willing to treat on terms with a view to securing peace to the people of "our common country."

This correspondence, although it did not result in any official conference, did bring to Hampton Roads, Virginia, Alexander H. Stephens, R.M.T. Hunter and John A Campbell, who were received on board a steamer anchored in the roadstead of Fortress Monroe, by President Lincoln and Secretary Seward. The purpose of the Confederate agents was to secure an armistice, but Lincoln turned a deaf ear to all suggestions of this sort, and while the matter was yet pending wrote to Gen. Grant, saying: "Let nothing that is transpiring change, hinder or delay your military movements or plans." The president and secretary returned to Washington, and it was seen that the Hampton roads conference resulted in nothing but defeat of the confederate attempt to procure a cessation of hostilities.

The second inauguration of Lincoln took place March 4, 1865. In his inaugural address the President briefly reviewed the political and military situation of the country, and closed with these memorable words: "With malice toward none, with charity for all, with firmness in the right as God gives us to see right, let us finish the work we are in, to bind up the nation's wounds, to care for him who shall have borne the battle, and for his widow and his orphans, and to do all which may achieve and cherish a just and lasting peace among ourselves and with all nations."

The spring of 1865 opened with bright prospects for a speedy ending of the rebellion. General Sherman's march to the Atlantic sea-coast from Atlanta had split the Confederacy. His subsequent movements in the Carolinas compelled the abandonment of Charleston. The capture of Fort Fisher, North Carolina, by Gen Terry, closed the last Atlantic port against possible supplies from abroad. The scattered remnants of the Confederate army now rallied around Gen. Lee for the defense of Richmond, and on March 27th a conference between Lincoln, Grant and Sherman was held on board a steamer lying on the James River, near Grant's headquarters. At that conference final and decisive measures of the campaign were decided. Closely followed by Grant, Sheridan now drew a line completely around the army of Virginia, under General Lee.

The Confederate lines were everywhere drawn in, their forces operating to the north of the James being now joined with the main army.

On Sunday morning, Apr. 2nd, the bells of Richmond sounded the knell of the rebellion, and Jefferson Davis, seeing that all was lost, fled southward, but was subsequently captured and sent a prisoner to Fortress Monroe. On Monday morning, April 3rd, the flag of the Union was hoisted over the building in Richmond which had been occupied by the confederate Congress. Lincoln was at City Point waiting for the final result of these movements. He entered the fallen capital of the Confederacy soon after its downfall. Here he was met by General Grant, who announced that one more battle might be fought. The president returned to Washington, and on April 7, 1865, Grant opened with Gen. Lee the correspondence which resulted in the surrender of the army of northern Virginia, April 9th, in the village of Appomattox Court- House, Virginia. Great rejoicing took place all over the North, and on the night of Apr. 10th the city of Washington and many other cities throughout the country were illuminated. On April 11th the city was again illuminated by the government, and a great official celebration took place.

The war was over. At noon, April 14, 1865, the President's cabinet held a meeting, at which Gen. Grant was present. That evening the president, Mrs. Lincoln, Clara Harris and Maj. Rathbone, of the U. S. Army, occupied a box near the stage in Ford's Theater, Washington. John Wilkes Booth, an actor, who had conspired with certain other persons to take the president's life on the first convenient occasion, approached the box from the rear, and at half-past ten o'clock in the evening, while all persons were absorbed in the play, crept up in the rear of the president, and, holding a pistol within a few inches of the base of the brain, fired. The ball entered the brain and Lincoln fell forward, insensible. Booth escaped from the theater in the confusion which followed. The President was carried to a house on the opposite side of the street, where he lingered between life and death through the hours of the night. At twenty-two minutes past seven o'clock on the morning of April 15, 1865, Lincoln died. Andrew Johnson, the vice-president, now succeeded to the presidency by virtue of his office, and was sworn in during the morning. Lincoln's body was finally laid to rest in Oak Ridge Cemetery, near Springfield, Illinois, where a monument was subsequently erected.

LINCOLN, MARY TODD

(1818-1882) — First lady and wife of President Abraham Lincoln, was

Mary Todd Lincoln

born in Lexington, Kentucky, on December 12, 1818, to well-to-do slave-holding family. Her father, Robert S. Todd, belonged to a family of pioneers foremost in the development of the commonwealth of Kentucky. Mary Todd, who spent most of her childhood at the home of an aunt, was well educated and cultured.

At the age of twenty-one, while visiting a married sister in Springfield, Illinois, she met Abraham Lincoln, a rising lawyer, and after a short engagement they were married on November 4, 1842. They settled in Springfield Illinois, and she gave birth to her first of four children, Robert Todd Lincoln. Her other three sons were born between 1846 and 1853, but they died at age four, eleven, and eighteen. The deaths of her children greatly affected Mary Todd, and she was reputed to have hysterical outbursts throughout the remainder of her life.

In 1846, her husband was elected to the U.S. Congress. The family moved to the national capital, where Mary Todd hoped to be accepted into the Washington social life. Her husband served one term, and then they returned to Illinois, where he resumed his law practice. He continued to be involved with politics, campaigning for his party's candidates. In 1856, Abraham Lincoln became a member of the Republican Party, and two years later, he again ran for senator, but was unsuccessful. In 1860, the Republican convention in Chicago, Illinois, nominated her husband for president of the United States. He won the election, and the Lincoln family moved into the White House.

On March 9, 1860, Mary Todd gave her first public reception, assisted by her sisters and nieces. She presided at the gloomiest period in the history of the capital. Her husband was bowed down by national cares; her family was devoted to the cause of the South, while her hopes, with those of her husband and children, were with the North. Unable to cope with these critical issues, Mary Todd soon found herself the target of malice, detraction, and lies. She gave weekly receptions at a time when the state of the country made the gaiety that she preferred out of keeping with the position she occupied, and the death of their son, Willie, shed a gloom over the private life of both parents.

Nonetheless, during the whole of her occupancy of the White House, Mary Todd was unremitting in her care of the sick soldiers in the hospitals of Washington, D.C. She spent the summer of 1864 at the seaside. After her husband's reelection in the fall, the receptions of the season were renewed with a promise of unusual gaiety. After the inauguration, Mary Todd felt that brighter days were in store, and when the surrender of Confederate General Robert E. Lee on April 9, 1865, was announced, she shared in the happy excitement that filled the White House and the city.

On April 14, 1865, Mary Todd, her husband, Clara Harris and her fiancé Major Henry R. Rathbone, went to a play at Ford's Theater. At approximately 10:30 pm, one of the actors, John Wilkes Booth, entered the box where the four were seated, and shot President Lincoln. He was rushed to a lodging house across the street, and lingered through the night. The president died the next morning. Mary Todd never fully recovered from her husband's death. After a severe illness, she returned with her two boys to Springfield, where she was further afflicted by the death of Thomas, the youngest boy.

In 1868, with a mind somewhat unbalanced and broken health, she sought rest in travel. Congress had already paid her the amount of the president's salary for one year, and in 1870, voted her an annual pension of $3,000, afterward increased to $5,000. Still later an additional gift of $15,000 was presented to her by Congress to insure comfort in her old age. In 1880, she returned from travels to various countries, her mind still impaired, and spent her last days with her only remaining son in Chicago.

Mary Todd Lincoln died of a stroke on July 16, 1882, and was laid to rest by the side of her husband and children in Springfield, Illinois.

LINCOLN, ROBERT TODD

(1843-1926) — Secretary of war and minister to England, devoted most of his life to private and personal affairs, and sedulously avoided the appearance of capitalizing the reputation of his father. Born in Springfield, Illinois, on August 1, 1843, he was the eldest and the only surviving child of Mary (Todd) Lincoln and Abraham Lincoln. During his childhood, his father rose from insignificance to national importance, and every effort was made to give to Robert Lincoln the educational advantages that Abraham was conscious of having missed. He attended the Springfield schools, and then Phillips Exeter Academy in New

Robert Todd Lincoln

Hampshire. He was sent on to Harvard in the fall of 1859. During the Civil War, he stayed in college because his father did not want him to join the military. After graduating in 1864, he spent four months in the Harvard Law School, but left when he was given an appointment on the staff of General Ulysses S. Grant.

He married Mary Harlan, the daughter of Senator James Harlan of Iowa, on September 24, 1868. Of the three children of this marriage, two daughters survived him.

On leaving the army, Robert Lincoln studied law in Chicago, Illinois, and was admitted to the bar in 1867. He gained profitable clients among the railroad and corporate interests, and his name appears as a charter member of the Chicago Bar Association (1874). He went to the state Republican convention in 1880, at the head of a Grant delegation from Chicago, and was in close sympathy with the effort of Senator John Logan to procure a third term for Grant. Logan repaid him, when he had himself accepted defeat and had switched his allegiance to James Garfield, by inducing Garfield to summon Robert Lincoln to the War Department. He became secretary of war, and had an uneventful term of office. He supported Chester Arthur for renomination in 1884 to the disappointment of Logan. He resumed the practice of law in 1885, but was recalled to public service in 1889 by President Benjamin Harrison who sent him to London, England, as minister.

For nearly twenty years after his return from England, Robert Lincoln continued in his work as counsel for great business interests, and in his semi-seclusion upon which he would permit no intrusion. Among his chief clients was the Pullman Company; and when the founder of this company, George M. Pullman, died in 1897, he became first its acting executive and then its president. After the Pullman strike of 1894, and the use of the injunction in connection with this it became common for radicals to compare adversely his apparent lack of interest in the common man and his father's humanity in the emancipation of the slaves, but he paid no attention to the criticisms. In 1911, he was forced to resign the presidency on account of his health, though he retained a connection with the company as chairman of the board of directors.

In 1912, Robert Lincoln moved to Washington, D.C. He remained almost unknown as he advanced in years. He had acquired a summer home, "Hildene," at Manchester, New Hampshire. His father's papers, which Hay and Nicolay had worked over in the 1880s, remained in his possession until near the end of his life when he deposited them in the Library of Congress to be sealed for twenty-one years after his death. Robert Todd Lincoln died on July 26, 1926, in Manchester, New Hampshire.

LINDBERG, CONRAD EMIL

(1852-1930) — Lutheran clergyman, was born in Jonkoping, Sweden, where he received his early schooling in the Gymnasium. At eighteen he began to preach, and in 1871, with the aid of friends, he came to the United States to study at Augustana College and Theological Seminary, then located at Paxton, Illinois. In two years he completed the theological course, but being too young to be ordained he continued his studies at Mount Airy Lutheran Theological Seminary, Philadelphia, Pennsylvania, where he remained until 1876.

In 1874 he was ordained to the Lutheran ministry by the Augustana Synod, and while under its charge he also managed to study at the University of Pennsylvania. In 1879 he was called to the Gustavus Adolphus Church in New York City, where for eleven years he served as pastor and as president of the New York Conference of the Augustana Synod. In 1890 he was called to be professor of systematic theology at the Augustana College and Theological Seminary, which had been moved to Rock Island, Illinois. From 1901 to 1910 he was vice-president, and from 1920 until his death, dean of the institution. He was also vice-president of the Augustana Synod (1899-1907), and a member of the Augustana Synod Home and Foreign Mission Board (1899-1913). In 1901 he was made knight of the Royal Order of the North Star by the king of Sweden and in 1924, commander of the Royal Order of Vasa.

He was a diligent student throughout his whole life, and the fact that he was a bachelor rendered it possible for him to adhere closely to a fixed schedule of devotions and study; his whole life, as well as his theology, was pervaded by a spirit of deep mysticism and reverence. Although at different times, he taught in practically every theological field, his chief work was done in dogmatics and apologetics. In 1898 he published *Encheiridion I Dogmatik Jamte Dogmhistoriska Anmarkninger*. This was later expanded into a larger book, *Christian Dogmatics and Notes on the History of Dogma*, which in 1922 was issued in an English translation by Reverend C. E. Hoffsten. It was adopted as a textbook in Lutheran theological seminaries both in America and Europe, and attained a position of established authority. In 1928 a revised edition appeared.

In the field of apologetics, he wrote *Apologetics, or a System of Christian Evidence* (1917, 1926). Unlike Lutheran theologians who have come to America in their maturity, Lindberg apparently had no fear of issuing his works in the English language. Besides these major productions, he also wrote a number of smaller books, and articles and reviews in church magazines. He was chief editor of the *Augustana Theological Quarterly* from 1900 to 1902, and after his retirement from the editorship, due to other pressing duties, he still continued to contribute to the publication. He died on August 2, 1930, just as he had finished his last book, *Beacon Lights of Prophecy in the Fatter Days*, issued posthumously in 1930.

LINDSAY, (NICHOLAS) VACHEL

(1879-1931) — Poet, was born on November 10, 1879, in Springfield, Illinois, the son of Vachel Thomas Lindsay and Catharine (Frazee) Lindsay. His paternal ancestry was Kentuckian, his maternal Virginian, and on both sides it was Scotch. His father, one of the pioneer settlers in the Springfield region, was a physician; his mother possessed some literary talent and was an ardent member of the Christian church. Their son early developed the combined interest in religion, poetry, and art, which was to dominate his entire life.

After graduation from the local high school in 1897, he attended Hiram College in Ohio for three years with the thought of entering the ministry. This aim was then abandoned for the study of art, pursued under difficulties, while working in Marshall Field's wholesale department, at the Chicago Art Institute night school, 1900-1903, and later continued at the New York School of Art, 1904-1905, where he worked under William M. Chase and Robert Henri, also lecturing on art at the west side Young Men's Christian Association in the winter of 1905-1906.

Meanwhile, beginning at the age of eighteen, he had written a few intermittent poems, and, in the spring of 1906, being without funds and unable to obtain work, he started on his famous walking trip through the South, distributing a poem, "The Tree of Laughing Bells," in exchange for bed and board. After further YMCA lecturing in New York City, he drifted back to Illinois in 1908, where in the course of the winter, he appeared on YMCA programs at Springfield, and during the next two years, stumped the state on behalf of the Anti-Saloon League. In the spring of 1912, he attempted to repeat his southern adventure on a walking trip to the Pacific Coast, but he found the western ranchmen less hospitable to the claims of poetry and his journey came to a sudden end in New Mexico.

His first volume of poetry, *General William Booth Enters into Heaven and Other Poems* (1913), attracted little attention, but its successor, *The Congo and Other Poems* (1914), met with popular acclaim. The title-poem started a whole school of literature devoted to African Americans. In it, Lindsay created a new poetic music of ragtime and echolalia, a blend of speech and song, clattering but impassioned, that well expressed the hurtling energy of America. His new technique was exercised with almost equal felicity in "A Negro Sermon: Simon Legree" and "John Brown," while in the more conventional verse of "The Eagle that is Forgotten" (in honor of Governor Altgeld) and of "Abraham Lincoln Walks at Midnight" he achieved high dignity and prophetic power.

Unquestionably, Lindsay's influence counted greatly in the contemporary revival of American poetry. His literary genius, however, was short lived according to critics, who declared that his next couple works were notably uneven, labored, and artificial. In 1920, he was asked to recite his poems at Oxford University.

Lindsay's personal eccentricities, such as his habit of dining publicly with a number of huge dolls set up at his table, continued to attract local attention wherever he sojourned, but in the literary world at large, he had already become a legend rather than a living reality long before his death. He married Elizabeth Conner of Spokane, Washington on May 19, 1925. He briefly lived in Spokane, but returned to his native town of Springfield, Illinois, where he died suddenly from heart failure on December 5, 1931. There were two children, a son and a daughter.

LOGAN, JOHN ALEXANDER

(1826-1886) Representative and Senator from Illinois; Senate Years of Service: 1871-1877; 1879-1886; born in Murphysboro, Jackson County, Ill., on February 9, 1826; attended the common schools and studied law; served in the war with Mexico as a lieutenant; returned to Illinois; clerk

John Alexander Logan

of the Jackson County Court 1849; studied law; admitted to the bar in 1852, and practiced; member, Illinois house of representatives 1852-1853, 1856-1857; prosecuting attorney for the third judicial district of Illinois 1853-1857; presidential elector on the Democratic ticket in 1856; elected as a Democrat to the Thirty-sixth and Thirty-seventh Congresses and served from March 4, 1859, until April 2, 1862, when he resigned and entered the Union Army; chairman, Committee on Revisal and Unfinished Business (Thirty-sixth and Thirty-seventh Congresses); during the Civil War was commissioned brigadier general, and then major general of Volunteers, and served until 1865; elected as a Republican to the Fortieth, Forty-first, and Forty-second Congresses and served from March 4, 1867, until his resignation on March 3, 1871, at the end of the Forty-first Congress, having been elected Senator; chairman, Committee on Military Affairs (Forty-first Congress); one of the managers appointed by the House of Representatives in 1868 to conduct the impeachment proceedings against President Andrew Johnson; conceived of the idea of Memorial Day and inaugurated the observance in May 1868; elected to the United States Senate as a Republican and served from March 4, 1871, to March 3, 1877; unsuccessful candidate for reelection; chairman, Committee on Military Affairs (Forty-third and Forty-fourth Congresses); resumed the practice of law in Chicago; again elected to the United States Senate in 1879; reelected in 1885, and served from March 4, 1879, until his death; chairman, Committee on Military Affairs (Forty-seventh and Forty-eighth Congresses); unsuccessful Republican nominee for Vice President of the United States in 1884; died in Washington, D.C., December 26, 1886; lay in state in the Rotunda of the U.S. Capitol, December 30-31, 1886; interment in a tomb in the National Cemetery, Soldiers' Home, Washington, D.C.

LORIMER, WILLIAM

(1861-1934) Representative and Senator from Illinois; Senate Years of Service: 1909-1912; born in Manchester, England, April 27, 1861;

immigrated to the United States in 1866 with his parents, who settled in Michigan; moved to Chicago, Ill., in 1870; self-educated; apprenticed to the trade of sign painter at the age of ten; worked in the packing houses and for a street railroad company; ward boss and constable 1886; engaged in the real estate business and later as a builder and brick manufacturer; elected as a Republican to the Fifty-fourth, Fifty-fifth, and Fifty-sixth Congresses (March 4, 1895-March 3, 1901); unsuccessful candidate for reelection in 1900 to the Fifty-seventh Congress; elected to the Fifty-eighth and to the three succeeding

William Lorimer

Congresses and served from March 4, 1903, until his resignation, effective June 17, 1909, having been elected Senator; chairman, Committee on Expenditures in the Department of the Navy (Sixty-first Congress), Committee on Mines and Mining (Sixty-second Congress), Committee on Pacific Islands and Puerto Rico (Sixty-second Congress); presented credentials as a Senator-elect to the United States Senate for the term that had commenced March 4, 1909, and served from June 18, 1909, until July 13, 1912, when, after a Senate investigation and acrimonious debate, the Senate adopted a resolution declaring "that corrupt methods and practices were employed in his election, and that the election, therefore, was invalid"; resumed his former pursuits and was president of La Salle Street Trust & Savings Bank 1910-1915; subsequently engaged in the lumber business; died in Chicago, Ill., September 13, 1934; interment in Calvary Cemetery

LOVEJOY, ELIJAH PARISH

(1802-1837) — Newspaper editor, preacher and martyred abolitionist; he was killed while defending his newspaper against an armed mob. Elijah Parish Lovejoy was born on November 9, 1802, near Albion, Maine, the son of Daniel Lovejoy, a Congregationalist preacher and farmer, and Elizabeth Pattee. He was educated at Waterville College (now Colby) in Maine in 1826 and moved to St. Louis the following year, where he established a private school and also edited the *St. Louis Times*, an anti-Jacksonian paper. In 1832, he was influenced by a religious revival and decided to become a preacher. He studied at and graduated from Princeton Theological Seminary and in April 1833 was license to preach by the Philadelphia Presbytery. He returned to St. Louis and organized a Presbyterian Church on the city's outskirts, and began editing a religious newspaper, *The Observer*. On March 4, 1835, he married Celia Ann French, daughter of a local planter; they had two children.

Lovejoy's intense preoccupation with the emerging reform movements was evident from the beginning with his affiliation with the *Observer* and it reflected his "new school" faction of Presbyterianism. He had a particular focus on moral lapses such as blasphemy, breaking the Sabbath, and the use of tobacco and alcohol. As an evangelical protestant, he editorialized against the growing influence of Catholicism. Lovejoy greatly endangered his position by expressing his anti-slavery position and endorsing gradual emancipation of slaves. Missouri was a slave state at the time, and St. Louis in particular opposed any discussion of the subject. Leading citizens in St. Louis round his views disgusting and a number of important men signed a letter to Lovejoy, requesting he moderate his tone in his editorials. Where Lovejoy was initially in his career, mild in his disapproval of slavery, a lynching in 1835 embittered him on the topic. Lovejoy refused despite threats of violence against the Observer. Instead, he reasserted his right of free discussion of even unpopular concerns. His consistent stance on these principles earned him a place in history but led to his death.

In May 1836, Lovejoy protested the lynching of a free black man in St. Louis and chastised Judge Luke E. Lawless in his editorials for seemingly condoning the act. The night following publication of the article, a mob damaged the *Observer's* press. Lovejoy's reaction was to move to Alton, Illinois, but before his press could be unloaded there, a mob destroyed it. He would not move again trying to escape the opposition. At the time, the national abolitionist movement was sharply divided as to the use of force: whether it was morally wrong and tactically imprudent, or whether force used defensively against proslavery violence was justifiable. At first, Lovejoy was influenced by William Lloyd Garrison and was completely passive and non-resistant when harassed by angry mobs. However, after his home was raided repeatedly and his wife was driven to hysteria, he felt non-violence had failed and he placed guns in his house. The mood of Alton, Illinois was likewise changing. Upon Lovejoy's arrival, his first press was dumped into the river, but sympathetic citizens had expressed outrage at a public meeting and pledged to fund him a new press. Afterward, also at a public meeting, Lovejoy asserted he would remain "an uncompromising enemy of slavery" but the *Observer* would not function as an abolitionist newspaper. His audience interpreted this statement as a pledge to quit aggravating the slavery issue. But Lovejoy's views had shifted to a belief in outright abolitionism and that the preservation of civil rights for white Americans required the immediate end of slavery. As he moved closer to full-blown abolitionism, local opposition grew increasingly resentful. Late in August 1837, he press was destroyed by a mob a second and third time. Lovejoy and his supporters then decided to sue force to protect the press from a fourth. Following news of these events, Lovejoy became an intense object of interest among reformers.

Tension had mounted when news was released that a fourth printing press was on its way by riverboat. Each previous time a press was dumped into the river, the Ohio Anti-Slavery Society replaced them. Mobs of furious citizens expressed outrage. In October 1837, Lovejoy issued a call for formation of a state auxiliary to the American Anti-Slavery Society. Local hostility became extreme, especially from people who felt that an antislavery reputation might have a negative effect on local commercial growth. Prominent men asked Lovejoy to leave town; he refused to do so. On November 7, the new press arrived and was stored in a stone warehouse near the river, guarded by Lovejoy and sixty youths from the local area. Each was armed with the mayor's permission. After darkness had fallen, an angry crowd stormed the warehouse. There was an exchange of shots and one from the mob was killed. Lovejoy had emerged from the building trying to prevent an attacker with a torch from setting fire to the roof. When the mob defied the mayor's orders to disperse, the mayor reassured Lovejoy and his party of their right to shoot in their own defense. Several attackers fired simultaneously, mortally wounding Lovejoy. He staggered back into the warehouse. Later, both members of the attacking mob and defenders of the press were put on trial. There were no convictions.

Abolitionists hailed Lovejoy as a martyr to their cause. Even among the abolitionists, however, the sentiment was divided. The Executive of the American Anti-Slavery Society would neither endorse nor censure the actions, but rather they pledged "strictly to adhere to the pacifist principles of the society." Whatever effect, Lovejoy's death strengthened the esteem that African Americans had for white antislavery crusaders. The First Colored Presbyterian Church in New York mourned

Lovejoy and collected sixty dollars, sent to his widow with a letter of condolence. Lovejoy's persistence as an abolitionist editor ranks him among the leading defenders of a free press in American history. At the time, the Alton, Illinois, riots were used by the abolitionists to support their contention that slavery threatened the liberties of all people. To that end, Lovejoy's death great contributed to the growth of antislavery and abolitionist controversy.

LOWDEN, FRANK O.

(1861-1943) — Twenty-seventh governor of Illinois (1917-1921), was born in Sunrise, Minnesota, the son of Nancy Elizabeth Breg and Lorenzo Lowden. His father was the town blacksmith, farmer and Justice of the Peace.

In 1885, Lowden graduated from the University of Iowa. Two years later, after receiving a degree from Union College of Law, he passed the bar. Until 1906, he practiced law in Chicago, and in 1899, was given a professorship at Northwestern University School of Law.

During the Spanish American War, Lowden was a lieutenant colonel in the first Infantry of the Illinois National Guard. In 1900, and again in 1904, he was a delegate to the Republican National Committee. Although he was an unsuccessful candidate for governor in 1904 against Charles Deneen, he was elected to represent the state in Congress in 1906. In 1916, he defeated incumbent Democrat Edward Dunne for the governorship.

While he was in office, World War I began, and Lowden urged support for the president. In 1917, he pushed through the legislature a state Council of Defense to organize all the state's resources for victory in the war. Lowden also was concerned with cuts in government bureaucracy, as evidenced by his administrative reorganization, which combined 128 overlapping agencies into nine departments, saving the state over one million dollars a year. state taxes were reduced by seven million dollars by 1921, and a large state surplus remained when he left office.

Lowden also continued his predecessor's support of increased and improved roadways in the state. Although he was intent on trimming government expenditures, Lowden produced a plan by which the new highways would be financed through car license fees, and the state acquired 3,000 miles of cement roads by 1920. However, the governor slowed down construction soon afterwards, since the price of cement had risen markedly.

Lowden also supported women's suffrage while in office, urging the legislature's ratification of the nineteenth constitutional amendment, and was instrumental in the passage of anti-religious and anti-race discrimination legislation.

In 1921, after Lowden left office, he returned to his farm and estate, which he kept as a legally protected bird sanctuary. He also owned cotton plantations in Arkansas, and became known as one of Chicago's elite because of his ties with his father-in-law, George Pullman, and his view of civic reformism. In 1920, he received 300 votes for the presidential nomination at the Republican National Convention, and he declined the vice presidential nomination in 1924.

Lowden remained in private life until his death in 1943. He was married to Florence Pullman, daughter of railroad man George Pullman, in 1896.

LUCAS, SCOTT WIKE

(1892-1968) Representative and Senator from Illinois; Senate Years of Service: 1939-1951; born on a farm near Chandlerville, Cass County, Ill., February 19, 1892; attended the public schools and graduated from the law department of Illinois Wesleyan University at Bloomington in 1914; admitted to the bar in 1915 and commenced practice at Havana, Ill.; during the First World War served as an enlisted man and later as a lieutenant in the United States Army; State's attorney of Mason County 1920-

Scott Wike Lucas

1925; chairman of State Tax Commission 1933-1935; elected as a Democrat to the Seventy-fourth and Seventy-fifth Congresses (January 3, 1935-January 3, 1939); did not seek renomination, having become a candidate for Senator; elected as a Democrat to the United States Senate in 1938 and reelected in 1944 and served from January 3, 1939, to January 3, 1951; unsuccessful candidate for reelection in 1950; Democratic whip 1947-1949; majority leader 1949-1951; chairman, Committee to Audit and Control the Contingent Expense (Seventy-seventh through Seventy-ninth Congresses); engaged in the practice of law in Springfield, Ill., and Washington, D.C.; died en route to Florida at

Rocky Mount, N.C., February 22, 1968; interment in Laurel Hill Cemetery, Havana, Ill.

LUNDIE, JOHN

(1857-1931) — Engineer, inventor, son of James and Anne (Honeyman) Lundie, was born in Arbroath Scotland. After graduation from the Dundee high school in 1873, he served for four years as a pupil in the office of the harbor engineer of the Port of Dundee, where he obtained training in civil engineering. Entering the University of Edinburgh, he graduated in 1880 with the degree of Bachelor of Science.

Lundie then came to the United States, and for four years, did railroad work in Oregon and Washington, including the building of Table Rock Tunnel. Going to Chicago, Illinois, he engaged in private practice, and later took a job with the city government. In this capacity, he made the preliminary survey of the Chicago Drainage Canal and designed several bridges. In 1890, he became engineer in Chicago for the King Bridge Company of Cleveland. During the next four years , Lundie erected numerous structures including steelwork for some of the buildings of the Columbian Exposition. He then returned to private practice, laid out the first low-level drainage system for Chicago, and was connected with water-supply projects for other places.

While working in Memphis, Tennessee, he developed a method of determination of the yield of artesian wells. As a result of investigations regarding the use of electricity for the suburban travel of the Illinois Central Railroad, he adopted the principle of "rapid acceleration" and the advisability of utilizing a high percentage of weight upon the driving wheels. From this work he prepared a thesis, "The Economics of Electric Train Movement," which he presented to the University of Edinburgh, from which he received the degree of doctor of science in 1902. This thesis also established the Lundie formula for train resistance.

In 1898, Lundie was called to New York City in connection with some heavy traction problems, and soon afterward began practice there. About this time, he reported upon power handling of freight for the Central of Georgia Railroad, and in the course of his investigation, designed the first combined electric hoist and tractor (telpher). He also designed and patented the Lundie Ventilated Rheostat on November 26, 1901, now in extensive use. In addition to a wide consultation practice upon railroad electrification problems in the United States, Lundie was called to London to advise regarding the Metropolitan Underground system; and to Canada, on electric railway work. In 1904, he reported to the General Electric Company upon waterpower development and the use of electric power on the Isthmus of Panama, and at the same time directed the affairs of the Panama-American Corporation.

In 1913, Lundie designed and patented the Lundie Tie Plate on June 14, 1913, and later, a duplex rail anchor. Thereafter, these inventions and their applications took much of his time and energy, requiring eventually the formation of the Lundie Engineering Corporation, of which he was president. He was now able to give more personal time to research and technical work. In 1921, he became technical adviser to the United Central America Corporation.

Although not in the best of health during the latter part of his life, he remained active in business up to the time of his death on February 9, 1931, in New York City. In 1906, he married Iona Oakley Gorham, who died in 1925; and in 1929, Mrs. Alice Eddy Snowden, widow of Dr. Albert A. Snowden.

M

MARQUETTE, FATHER JACQUES

(1637-1675) — Explorer and missionary, was born on June 1, 1637, in Laon, France, the son of aristocrats. Like many of the youngest sons of such families, young Jacques was destined for the Church, and when he was seventeen, he joined the Jesuit order. After nine years of studying and tutoring, he finally was granted permission to travel to New France as a missionary. He had always wanted to travel, and was not satisfied with his work on the shores of Lake Superior.

Wishing to start his own mission post with Native Americans who had never seen the "black robe," Marquette joined Joliet and five voyages on an expedition to explore the Mississippi in 1673. Traveling in two birch canoes, the group floated by way of the Fox River to the Wisconsin. After seven days of paddling through marshy and shallow waters, they hit upon the "Big Water" described to them by Indians. They then traveled about 300 miles down the Mississippi, and met with a friendly village of Illinois Native Americans along the way. Tribesmen at the mouth of the Arkansas River warned them of danger further downstream, so Joliet turned the group back upstream. The Illinois Native American tribes on the way back advised them that the Illinois River was a shortcut to the Great Lakes. The group accordingly followed the advice and carried their canoes over a portage, which was the future site of Chicago, Illinois.

The trip, though a success, had depleted both Marquette's and the crew's energy, and the priest spent over a year recuperating at the Mission St. Francis in De Pere, Wisconsin. He then departed on canoe in 1674 to found a mission in Illinois and arrived at the Chicago River two months later. Having learned Native American language, he was able to preach to the Illinois for a few weeks, but illness and deprivation caused him to try to return to the mission at St. Ignace. He died on the way, in Ludington, Michigan, on May 18, 1675. Christianized Ottawa tribesmen

Father Jacques Marquette

followed after him the next year, however, and exhumed his bones for preparation according to Indian funeral customs. They took the body to the chapel at St. Ignace in 1676, where his grave was later honored with a monument.

MARQUIS, DONALD ROBERT PERRY "DON"

(1878-1937) — Humorist, poet, and dramatist, was born on July 29, 1878, in Walnut, Bureau County, Illinois, the son of James Stewart Marquis, a physician, and Virginia Elizabeth (Whitmore) Marquis. After attending the local high school, he worked for brief periods as a clerk, hay baler, railroad section hand, and schoolteacher, meanwhile contributing occasional verses to the Walnut newspaper.

In 1899, he went to Washington, D.C., where he was a student at the Corcoran School of Art, a clerk in the Census Bureau, and a reporter for the *Washington Times*. He also acted briefly with a touring stock company. In 1902 he joined the staff of the *Atlanta News* in Georgia, becoming an editorial writer on the *Atlanta Journal* two years later. There he became acquainted with Joel Chandler Harris, who made him assistant editor of his *Uncle Remus's Magazine*.

In 1909, Marquis moved to New York City, where, after working as a reporter on the *American* and the *Brooklyn Daily Eagle*, he joined the editorial staff of the *Evening Sun*. Next year, in April 1913, he began the "Sun Dial," the column he was to make famous. Most columnists used contributions, but Don Marquis wrote almost all of his himself. He peopled it with characters that delighted a numerous body of readers, in and out of New York. The two that became most popular were Archy, the lower-case cockroach, and Archy's friend Mehitabel, the rowdy queen of the alley cats, whose philosophy was "Wotthehell! *Toujours gai!*" Marquis used Archy and Mehitabel to satirize such targets as the free-verse movement and to puncture pretension and humbug generally. His "Archy" books in particular have had a lasting appeal. When the original *Archy and Mehitabel* (1927), *Archy's life of Mehitabel* (1933), and *Archy Does His Part* (1935) were republished as the *Life and Times of Archy and Mehitabel* (1950).

In 1922, Marquis left the *Evening Sun* for the *New York Tribune*, where for several years wrote a column called "The Lantern." During the years when he was writing a column six days a week he still found time and energy to write novels, plays, and numerous short stories and poetry and essays as well. His many works include: *The Almost Perfect State* (1927), *The Old Soak* (1921), *Hermione and Her Little*

Group of Serious Thinkers (1916), *Sonnets to a Red-Haired Lady* (1922), *Noah an' Jonah an' Cap'n John Smith* (1921), *Dreams and Dust* (1915), *The Old Soak* (1922), and *The Dark Hours* (1924).

His first wife, Reina Melcher, whom he had married in Atlanta on June 8, 1909, died on December 2, 1923, and their children, Robert Stuart and Barbara Theresa, died also. His second wife, the actress Marjorie (Potts) Vonnegut, whom he married on February 2, 1926, died before him. He himself was in increasingly failing health for many years, and during his long final illness he was completely incapacitated by a cerebral hemorrhage. He died on December 29, 1937.

MARTIN, EVERETT DEAN

(1880-1941) — Social psychologist and educator, was born on July 5, 1880, in Jacksonville, Illinois, the son of Buker E. and Mollie (Field) Martin. He attended Illinois College in Jacksonville (B.A. 1904), then continued his studies at the McCormick Theological Seminary in Chicago, Illinois, from which he received a diploma in 1907. Ordained that year as a Congregational minister, he held pastorates in Lombard, Illinois (1900-1908); Dixon, Illinois (1908-1910); and in Des Moines, Iowa, where he was minister of the Unitarian Church (1910-1914). He then left the ministry to devote his time to writing on social questions.

In 1916, Martin began a long association with the People's Institute, a center for adult education in New York City founded in 1897 by Charles Sprague Smith. As its principal activity, the Institute conducted an extensive series of public lectures, held at Cooper Union and known as the Cooper Union Forum. In 1917, Martin, appointed initially as a lecturer in social philosophy, was made director of the forum and assistant director of the institute itself (he became its director in 1922). From 1919 to 1922, he was also chairman of another institute committee, the National Board of Review of Motion Pictures. Beginning in 1917, Martin developed still another People's Institute undertaking, a group of classes in literature, biology, psychology, and other subjects, held in libraries, settlement houses, and elsewhere, that became known as the School of Philosophy. Funds for the Institute's program, always difficult to raise, virtually vanished during the Depression years, and in 1934, it went out of existence. At this time, Cooper Union took over the adult lecture series, establishing a Department of Social Philosophy with Martin as its head. He was president of the American Association of Adult Education in 1937.

Along with his teaching and administrative work, Martin wrote twelve books on social psychology, social philosophy, and politics. In his first and most important book, *The Behavior of Crowds* (1920), he viewed mob action as a form of mental disorder, the product of repressed impulses of individuals that the presence of others, under certain circumstances, brought to the fore. In *The Meaning of a Liberal Education* (1926), he condemned what he considered the utilitarian emphasis of contemporary schooling and advocated a humanist education as the bulwark of liberal democracy, believing that it inoculated individuals against infection by the irrational behavior of crowds, behavior that paved the way for revolution.

Martin left Cooper Union in 1938 to become professor of social philosophy at the Claremont Graduate School in Claremont, California. Three years later, at the age of sixty, he died of a heart attack on May 10, 1941, at Claremont.

In 1907, he married Esther W. Kirk of Jacksonville, Illinois, whom he divorced in 1915. They had three children: Mary, Margaret, and Elizabeth. His second marriage in 1915 to Persis E. Rowell also ended in divorce; they had one son, Everett Eastman. His third wife, Daphne Crane Drake, whom he had married in 1931, survived him.

William Ernest Mason

MASON, WILLIAM ERNEST

(1850-1921) (father of Winnifred Sprague Mason Huck) Representative and Senator from Illinois; Senate Years of Service: 1897-1903; born in Franklinville, Cattaragus County, N.Y., July 7, 1850; moved with his parents to Bentonsport, Van Buren County, Iowa, in 1858; attended the Bentonsport Academy and Birmingham College 1863-1865; taught school in Bentonsport 1866-1868, and in Des Moines, Iowa, 1868-1870; studied law; moved to Chicago, Ill., in 1872; admitted to the bar and commenced practice; member, State house of representatives 1879; member, State senate 1882-1885; elected as a

Republican to the Fiftieth and Fifty-first Congresses (March 4, 1887-March 3, 1891); unsuccessful candidate for reelection in 1890 to the Fifty-second Congress; resumed the practice of law in Chicago; elected to the United States Senate as a Republican and served from March 4, 1897, to March 3, 1903; chairman, Committee on Manufactures (Fifty-fifth and Fifty-sixth Congresses), Committee on Post Office and Post Roads (Fifty-seventh Congress); again resumed the practice of law in Chicago; elected to the Sixty-fifth, Sixty-sixth, and Sixty-seventh Congresses and served from March 4, 1917, until his death in Washington, D.C., on June 16, 1921; interment in Oakwood Cemetery, Waukegan, Ill.

MASTERS, EDGAR LEE

(1869-1950) — American poet and attorney, best known for his poems about life in the Midwest; he was born in Garnett, Kansas, the son of Hardin Wallace Masters, a lawyer, and Emma J. Dexter. His father had moved the family briefly to Kansas for his law practice, Edgar grew up in small towns of Petersburg and Lewistown, Illinois, the Midwestern "Spoon River" country he made famous later. He was educated in

Edgar Lee Masters

their public schools and spent a year in an academy school hoping to be admitted to Know College. He also worked as a newspaper printer after school. He entered Knox College for about one year before leaving to read law with his father's practice and was admitted to the Illinois bar in 1891. After a brief time as a bill collector, he formed a law partnership with Kickham Scanlan in 1893. For the next ten years, he expressed his Populist views in his essays and plays written under the pen name of Dexter Wallace. In 1898, he married Helen M. Jenkins, the daughter of a Chicago lawyer; they had three children. They separated in 1917. He remarried in 1926, to an English teacher named Ellen Coyne; they had one child

In 1903, he joined the law firm of Clarence Darrow, where for eight years he defended the indigent and poor. Many unrecognized plays and books of poems were written in these early years; then he wrote *A Book of Verses* (1898) before he gained fame with *Spoon River*

Anthology in 1915. Extramarital affairs and an argument with Darrow stirred his personal and professional life from 1908 to 1911, when he went into the practice of law on his own. Masters remained an attorney until about 1920, when he decided to devote his talents to fulltime writing. However, in 1914 Masters had begun a series of poems about his boyhood experiences in western Illinois, published under the pseudonym of Webster Ford in *Reedy's Mirror*, St. Louis. This was the beginning of *Spoon River Anthology*, one that not only made his reputation but also became one of the most popular and widely read works in all American literature at the time. Masters later recalled in "Genesis of Spoon River," (*American Mercury*, January 1933) how his interest turned to "combinations of my imagination drawn from the lives of the faithful, tender- hearted souls" that he knew in his youth. He continued publishing poetry, novels, essays, and biographies for thirty years although he never equaled the achievement of the anthology. Masters' place in twentieth-century American literature is still debated because his quantity and broad range of his productions far exceeded its quality by most critical accounts. The anthology was, however, a celebrated series of poignant and often sardonic graveside monologues that captured small town American and the midwestern values. Masters presented these poems as voices of the town graveyard occupants talking openly about their lives. In part, the book was a best seller due to its treatment of sexual behavior and misbehavior. The book remains a landmark in the literature of realism and revolt against conventional social standards that prospered in the early twentieth century.

Masters' lifelong celebration of that Midwestern region continued with *The New Spoon River* (1924) and in three dozen nostalgic, lyric poems published in various books and now collected in *The Enduring River: Edgar Lee Masters' Uncollected Spoon River Poems*, edited by Herbert K. Russell (1991). The original anthology was adapted for the stage with music added, thereby adding to the demand for the book. Other volumes of poems set on the Illinois prairies included *Songs and Satires* and *The Great Valley* (1916), *Toward the Gulf* (1918), *Starved Rock* (1919), and *The Open Sea* (1921). In *Domesday Book* (1920) and *The Fate of the Jury* (1929) he used his legal experience to create courtroom poems. His later poetry reflected his wide range of interests, including *Lichee Nuts* (1930), and his lengthy narratives, *The Serpent in the Wilderness* (1933), *Invisible Landscapes* (1935) and *The New World* (1937). During the 1920s and 1930s Masters also tried writing fiction and biography. Three novels involved growing up in

Illinois and had little success: *Mitch Miller* (1920), *Skeeters Kirby* (1923), and *Kit O'Brien* (1927). He wrote biographies such as reflecting his adulation for Vachel Lindsay, the poet; and of Walt Whitman; and controversial portrayals of Abraham Lincoln and Mark Twain. Masters saw biography as a form of revisionist history and set out to correct the prevailing misinterpretations about some of America's heroes and values. For much of his life he was an outsider, politically and socially.

In the years "Spoon River" enjoyed its greatest notoriety, Masters' personal life was not doing well. He was trying to balance both careers as lawyer and writer, and suffered a near-fatal bout of pneumonia. In 1923 he went through a bitter divorce and moved to New York, where he practiced law for several years. After he toured the country in 1925, he published *Selected Poems* (1925), a collection that received much-deserved attention for its variety. When he remarried Ellen Coyne (1926) they lived in New York though later on her teaching position required that they live apart at times. Masters retired to the Chelsea Hotel and wrote a series of biographies as well as an autobiography covering his boyhood years and his career up to 1917. *Across Spoon River: An Autobiography* (1936) was straightforward, blunt and somewhat irritable about life he saw as "scrappy and unmanageable." He described his story of many arguments, troubled personal affairs, and feelings of neglect and injustice. He regarded himself as betrayed and disillusioned in a cold, materialistic world. He did receive recognitions, but later in his life. He won *Poetry* magazine's Levinson Prize (1916), and two decades later, the Mark Twain Medal for his biography of Lindsay (1936). In 1942, both the American Academy and the National Institute of Arts and Letters awarded him its Award in Literature, and the Poetry Society of America gave him its medal. In 1944, he was granted a fellowship from the American Academy of Poets.

Reconciled with his wife Ellen, Masters moved with her to her teaching positions in North Carolina and Pennsylvania. He was retired and in ill health following a bout with pneumonia in 1943; he gradually became paralyzed. On March 5, 1950, Masters died in Melrose, Pennsylvania, near Philadelphia; he was buried in Oakland Cemetery in Petersburg, Illinois.

MATTESON, JOEL ALDRICH

(1808-1873) — Tenth governor of Illinois (1853-1857), was born in New York, the son of Elnathan and Eunice (Aldrich) Matteson, who were farmers in Jefferson County, New York. He taught school in Illinois, but in 1834, began work as a foreman on the first railroad in South Carolina. Before that, he had moved to Kendall County, Illinois, to continue farming, but sold his land and moved to Joliet in 1836, during the speculation rush that year.

His business interests in the city led Matteson to secure a contract for the Illinois and Michigan Canal in 1848, and in 1842, he was elected governor. While he was in office, a great boom in railroad building took hold in the state. The Illinois Central, the Chicago and Rock Island, Burlington and Quincy, the Alton and St. Louis, and the Chicago and Galena Union were all built during this time.

Matteson was also a proponent of growth in education within the state; in 1854, he appointed Ninian Edwards a special officer of public instruction, which helped in that expansion. His governorship didn't interfere with his business career, however, since Matteson held the presidency of the Chicago and Alton Railroad for several years, and a controlling interest in several banks.

At the end of his term, Matteson retired to private life, and he died in Chicago in 1873.

MAYER, OSCAR GOTTFRIED

(1888-1965) — Meat packer, was born on March 10, 1888, in Chicago, Illinois, the son of Oscar Ferdinand Mayer and Louise Christine Greiner. In 1883, his father established the small Chicago meat market and sausage factory that became Oscar Mayer & Company. He graduated from Robert Waller High School in Chicago in 1905, and in 1909, from Harvard, where he studied engineering methods that he later put to use in the company. He also developed broad cultural interests at Harvard and wrote for the *Harvard Advocate*. Beginning as assistant superintendent in 1909, Mayer advanced rapidly in his father's company, becoming secretary, director, and general manager in 1912. He married Elsa Stieglitz on May 10, 1913; they had four children.

From the beginning, Mayer concentrated on industrial operations, and under his leadership Oscar Mayer & Company pioneered methods of processing and packaging prepared meats that were adopted throughout the industry. By 1912, he had invented several devices, including a lard-tub washer and a casing flusher, and had introduced the packaging of sausage in cardboard cartons. He also realized that future success depended upon expansion of markets beyond the western Great Lakes area. In 1919, the company acquired a farmers' cooperative packing plant in Madison, Wisconsin, which soon became its biggest operation. Other plants were acquired after World War II in Philadelphia, Pennsylvania; Los Angeles, California; and Davenport, Iowa. In 1961, controlling interest in a Caracas, Venezuela, packinghouse was purchased.

In 1921, Mayer became vice-president in charge of operations, and in 1928, when his father retired, he succeeded him as president of the firm. At that time, the company employed 900 and had annual sales of $21.5 million. By 1955, when Mayer retired as president, the company employed 8,500 and had annual sales were $220.2 million. When supermarkets were introduced, Mayer realized that customers were distressed by the loss of the neighborhood butcher, who had advised them on meat selection. He therefore saw that the manufacturer would have to replace the butcher, and that a company's success would depend on customers' confidence in easily identified brands. In 1929, the company introduced wieners with a band around every fourth wiener, and in 1944, its engineers developed Kartridg-Pak, a machine that automatically banded wieners. The sausages were then distributed with a strong advertising campaign; "Look for the yellow band on every wiener," designed to build confidence in "a wiener with a conscience."

Other techniques developed by the company included a linker, a stripper, a tube machine, and the Slice-Pak, which vacuum-packed sliced meats in plastic. All of this equipment was manufactured by subsidiaries of Oscar Mayer & Company, and leased to other meatpacking companies.

Mayer retired as president of the firm in March 1955, but he remained chairman of the board until his death. In 1960, the company introduced a vacuum-sealed package for sausage and wieners after spending six years and $1.5 million to develop it. Such investment was possible because 85 percent of the company's stock was owned by family members and consequently more than half the profits could be plowed back into capital expansion and research. Using computerized market research, it was able to predict the demand for its products with remarkable accuracy and to pursue its "vacuum policy," which deliberately kept production slightly less than demand in order to eliminate the need to unload "distress merchandise." The company also developed local distribution centers, with refrigeration facilities sufficient to maintain an adequate inventory.

In 1956, Mayer published *A Plan for Living*, originally an address to Beloit College students. In 1959, the American Meat Institute honored him for fifty years of service to the industry in which he was one of the great pioneers. He also established and headed the Oscar Mayer Foundation, which aided many medical and educational institutions. He died on March 5, 1965 in Evanston, Illinois.

McADAMS, CLARK

(1874-1935) — Editor, and newspaper humorist, was born on January 29, 1874, near Otterville, Jersey County, Illinois, the son of William McAdams and Annie Eliza Curtis. One of the his first occupations was picking up Native American relics along the lower Illinois River for his father's museum collections. When he was nine, his family moved to nearby Alton, Illinois, where he attended public school. He began his newspaper career as a two-dollar-a-week printer's devil for the *Alton Democrat*, delivering papers and learning to set type. A part-time reporter while in high school, he quit Shurtleff College, Alton, after a year, in order to supplement the meager financial returns, which his father derived from scientific pursuits. In 1898, he received a place on the *Post-Dispatch*, thereafter his newspaper home except for a brief interval when he returned to Alton to edit the *Alton Republican*.

On the *Post-Dispatch*, McAdams was successively a reporter, feature writer, interviewer, drama critic, columnist, editorial writer, editor of the editorial page, and contributing editor. His "Just A Minute" column of prose and light verse became a widely quoted feature of the *Post-Dispatch* editorial page. Other famous verses were: "In Uganda," which satirized the African hunt of Theodore Roosevelt in 1909, and "Now I lay me down to sleep," a mock-serious "Senate debate" on the child's prayer in 1919.

McAdams worked to protect the trumpeter swan, to repeal prohibition, to save Sacco and Vanzetti and to bring out the full facts of the national political scandals of the 1920s. Succeeding George S. Johns as editorial page editor in 1929, he was sharply critical of the Hoover administration's handling of the economic crisis and enthusiastically welcomed the election of Franklin D. Roosevelt.

McAdams was relieved in July 1934 of the direction of the editorial page and was given the post of contributing editor due to differences over policy with the publisher. He continued to write trenchant editorials until his death the next year. Several of his editorials were printed as pamphlets by the *Post-Dispatch* and were widely distributed. He also taught journalism at Washington University in St. Louis, Missouri, from 1925 to 1927, and in 1931 he was invited to be editor of the *Nation*.

McAdams held many interests outside of the newspaper. He was president of the St. Louis Artists' Guild from 1912 to his death, chief founder and president of the Little Theatre of St. Louis, and a sponsor of many art competitions. The only journalistic organization with which he had much to do was the National Press Humorists Association, but he was for many years a director of the Missouri Fish and Game League and was editor of *Wild Life*, its official bulletin, from 1917 to 1920. In 1916 he was appointed by the secretary of agriculture as a member of the Federal Advisory Commission on Migratory Birds. He also carried on his father's archeological interests; in 1902, he was a member of the scientific expedition, which investigated the Mesa Verde cliff dwellings, and he published *The Archaeology of Illinois*. His hobby in his last years was motion-picture photography of wild flowers.

After an illness of several months caused by abdominal cancer, he died on November 29, 1935, at his home at age sixty-two. His body was cremated, and the ashes were placed in the mausoleum at Valhalla Cemetery, St. Louis, Missouri. His wife, Laura Swanwick Baker, was a native of Alton, whom he married on July 12, 1904.

McARTHUR, JOHN

(1826-1906) — Manufacturer and soldier, was born in Erkine, Scotland, to John and Isabella (Neilson) McArthur. His parents expected him to enter the Presbyterian ministry. He preferred his father's smithy, however, and one year after his marriage in 1848 to his neighbor, Christina Cuthhertson, he immigrated to America, joining his brother-in-law, Carlile Mason, in Chicago, Illinois. He eventually gained enough capital to become Mason's partner (1854-1858) in the ownership of the successful Excelsior Iron Works. From 1858 to 1861, McArthur conducted the business alone.

During these years, he rose from third lieutenant to captain of the Chicago Highland Guards, and in May 1861, he was at Cairo, as colonel of the Twelfth Illinois Infantry. Drilling, Kentucky reconnaissance, and railway patrol filled the rest of the year, and by its close he commanded the First Brigade of the Second Division. From Fort Henry (February 1862) until the Civil War ended, his troops were frequently on special duty. "Meritorious service" at Donelson made him a brigadier general (March 21, 1862), and at Shiloh, although wounded, he commanded his division after General W.H.L. Wallace was killed. He effectively led the Sixth Division, Army of the Tennessee, through the hard fighting around Corinth and Iuka. In the Vicksburg campaign, under

John McArthur

General McPherson, his men were often detached for emergency service to McClernand's, F.P. Blair's, or General William Sherman's command.

From the early autumn of 1863 to August 1, 1864, he was post commander of Vicksburg. For two months thereafter, he protected Sherman's line of communication about Marietta, Georgia, and was then ordered to Missouri to oppose Confederate General Stirling Price. In December, he was rushed to Nashville. On December 16, 1864, with only the silent sanction of his superior, Major General A.J. Smith, he charged the opposing heights, crushed John Bell Hood's left wing, and turned the battle of Nashville into a Confederate rout. McArthur was brevetted major general. Thereafter, until he was mustered out on August 24, 1865, he served under Major General E.R.S. Canly in the Alabama campaign and was stationed at Selma during the summer.

For twenty years after the war, McArthur suffered a series of reverses. Efforts to revive his foundry business failed. The Chicago Fire darkened his term as commissioner of public works (1866-1872), and while he was postmaster of Chicago (1873-1877), $73,000 of post-office funds disappeared in a bank crash. Bowing to a court decision, he used most of his fortune to make good this loss. Another of his ventures, the Chicago and Vert-Island (Lake Superior) Stone Company, succumbed to two successive ship disasters in the early 1880s. About 1885, he retired from business, but continued to take an active interest in the Presbyterian Church, the St. Andrew's Society, the Grand Army of the Republic, and the Loyal Legion.

He died of paralysis on May 15, 1906, and was buried in Rose Hill Cemetery, Chicago, Illinois. He was the father of seven children.

McCLURE, ROBERT ALEXIS

(1897-1957) — Army officer and first chief of psychological warfare, was born March 4, 1897, at Mattoon, Illinois, the son of George Hurlbert

McClure and Harriet Julia Rudy. His father died when McClure was young, and after his mother remarried, the family moved to Madison, Indiana. He attended public school there, and in 1912, he entered the Kentucky Military Institute in Lyndon, Kentucky, from which he graduated in 1915. The next year, he left home and enlisted in the Philippine Constabulary, and was commissioned a second lieutenant in the U.S. Army. On November 11, 1918, he married Marjory Leitch; they had two sons.

In addition to his tour of duty in the Philippines, McClure also served in China and Japan. In 1923, he returned to the United States for further military training at the Army Infantry School (1923-1924) and the Army Cavalry School (1925-1926). He served as an instructor at the Infantry School for four years (1926-1930). His next assignment was at the Command and General Staff School (1930-1932), and later, he studied at the Army War College (1935), where he remained as an instructor until 1940.

Soon after the outbreak of World War II in Europe, McClure was assigned to the American embassy in London as military attaché (1941-1942). In 1942, he was advanced to chief of intelligence for the American forces in the European theater of operations. As the G-2 (intelligence) officer on the staff of Lieutenant General Dwight D. Eisenhower, McClure was responsible for the security of the plans for the invasion of North Africa. In Africa, McClure was in charge of military information for the press for Eisenhower and served as censor.

McClure took charge of psychological warfare when it was established as a constituent responsibility of the Supreme Headquarters Allied Expeditionary Force (SHAEF) early in 1944. At first, McClure, then a brigadier general, was chief of a G-6 section that handled both public relations and psychological warfare. These responsibilities were separated in April 1944, with McClure at the head of the Psychological Warfare Division. He supervised activities such as radio reports on the course of the war beamed to enemy troops and civilians, as well as the printing and circulation of counterfeit ration stamps inside Germany. Combat psychological warfare teams accompanied field troops for broadcasting and leaflet distribution.

After the war ended, McClure was made director of the Information Control Division in Germany. This placed him in charge of developing print media, theater, film, music, and other information and cultural facilities organizations. His Information Control Service commands encompassed Bavaria, Wurttemberg-Baden, and Hesse.

McClure assembled a team of specialists that included linguists, lawyers, journalists, publishers, radio technicians and administrators, musicians, theatrical producers, psychologists, and academicians. McClure was known to allow women to advance to degrees not common to other SHAEF staffs.

In 1950, McClure began a three-year tour of duty as chief of the Psychological Warfare Division in the Pentagon. After Eisenhower's election as president, McClure was sent in 1953 to Teheran as head of the American military mission. In 1955, while on this assignment, he was awarded the rank of major general. The following year, he retired. He died on January 1, 1957, at Fort Huachuca, Arizona. At his instruction he was buried not in a military cemetery but in the family plot at Madison, Indiana.

McCONNEL, JOHN LUDLUM

(1826-1862) — Author, was born on November 11, 1826, in what was then Morgan but is now Scott County, Illinois, the son of Murray and Mary Mapes McConnell His father was a self-made pioneer lawyer who served in both branches of the state legislature and in the Black Hawk War, and was appointed by President Pierce one of the auditors of the U.S. Treasury, a post which he held for about five years. The eldest son John studied law under his father and at the Transylvania law school, from which he graduated in 1843 in a class of twenty-nine. He enlisted for service in the war with Mexico and before leaving the rendezvous of his company at Alton, Illinois, he was made first lieutenant. After the battle of Buena Vista, where he was wounded, he became captain in the 1st Illinois Volunteers. Returning to Jacksonville, he took over his father's practice, but he was as much interested in creative writing as in his professed deity, the law. His first works were melodramatic novels. *Grahame: or Youth and Manhood* (1850) is an improbable tale, which left the modern reader quite out of sympathy with any of the characters or situations. *Talbot and Vernon* (1850), a tale of love intrigue and the war in Mexico, with some excellent descriptions of that region and of court scenes in the West, and *The Glenns: A Family History* (1851), interesting for the author's pictures of the Southwest and the turbulent society of frontier Texas, throw valuable light on the social history of the period. *Western Characters: or Types of Border Life in the Western States* (1853) is a valuable descriptive volume, which portrays the picturesque figures of the frontier.

At the time of his premature death on January 17, 1862 he was engaged in a study to be entitled "History of Early Exploration in America," treating especially the work of the early Roman Catholic missionaries.

Shortly after his return from Mexico in 1847, McConnel was married to Eliza Deniston of Pittsburgh. She, with two children, survived him.

McCORMICK, CYRUS HALL
(1809-1884) — Inventor, manufacturer, and philanthropist, was born in Rockbridge County, Virginia, on February 15, 1809, the son of Robert and Mary Ann (Hall) McCormick. He was reared on his father's farm, and received his education from his parents and the rural school.

In 1831, he designed a hillside plow on which he obtained a patent. He also studied the problem of a reaping machine, then invented and built a better reaper. After an initial test and subsequent

Cyrus Hall McCormick

modifications, he gave the reaper a successful public trial during that year's harvest. In 1833, he invented and patented another hillside plow known as a self-sharpening horizontal plow.

Due to an account of the invention by Obed Hussey of a reaper apparently similar in some respects to his own machine, he took out a patent on his reaper in June 1834. He continued to work on his reaper, but did not attempt to place it on the market until after a failed investment in extracting crude iron left him and his father heavy in debt. In 1839, he held a public trial of his reaper on the farm of Joseph Smith of Augusta County, Virginia, and sold two reapers for the next harvest.

In 1841, having added further improvements, McCormick was able to guarantee his machine, and sold seven reapers for the harvest of 1842. He increased this number to twenty-nine in 1843, and to fifty in 1844, all manufactured in the farm blacksmith shop at Walnut Grove. In 1844, several machines were sent west by way of Richmond, Virginia; New Orleans, Louisiana; and Cincinnati, Ohio. McCormick followed, after the Virginia harvest of the same year, in order to see to proper assembling of his machine and correct instruction in its use.

As a result of this trip, he arranged for the manufacture of his machines in Brockport, New York, and Cincinnati, Ohio. After several years' experience under this arrangement, uncertain workmanship was endangering the reputation and general adoption of his machine. Accordingly, in 1847, with former mayor William B. Ogden, McCormick established his reaper factory, McCormick, Ogden & Company, in Chicago, Illinois, and discontinued production in other places. At the time of the expiration of McCormick's patent in 1848, Capitalists and other inventors successfully fought to prevent renewal of his patent. McCormick appealed his case to Congress but without success.

Despite the growing number of reaper manufacturers, McCormick retained his place not only as the inventor of the reaper but also as its foremost manufacturer. His opponents soon attempted to secure his later and unexpired patents, granted in 1845 and 1847, using expert patent lawyers. Failing in these efforts, they frequently infringed the patents. McCormick was continuously engaged in litigation from 1850 until the close of his career.

By 1850, McCormick had taken out a patent for his machine in England and was devising ways and means to extend his business abroad. He sent a reaper to the World's Exhibition in London in 1851, with the initial reception disappointing. However, a field trial of the machine astonished the English people, and the McCormick reaper was awarded the exhibition's Council Medal. In all of the seven world expositions held between that date and McCormick's death, his machines won gold medals and highest awards. In 1868, he was made a member of the Legion of Honor by the French government, and in 1878, he became an officer in that order. That same year, he was elected a member of the French Academy for his contributions to agriculture.

The McCormick reaper business in Chicago was conducted from 1847 until 1879, under various partnerships, all of which were headed by McCormick. The business was incorporated on September 11, 1879, as The McCormick Harvesting Machine Company, with McCormick as president, which office he held until his death

For a number of years, McCormick also served as a director of the Union Pacific Railway. In 1860, he bought the *Chicago Times*, a daily newspaper and published it for a year as a Democratic organ, advocating in it the friendly settlement of the differences between North and South. Between 1864 and 1884, he was at various times either a candidate or a nominee of the Democratic Party for governor of Illinois, congressman and senator from Illinois, and vice-president of the United States. He was chairman of the Democratic State Central Committee of Illinois, and for years, was a member of the Democratic National Committee. In 1859, he made a large contribution to the Theological Seminary of the Northwest in New Albany, Indiana, which moved to Chicago and later became the McCormick Theological Seminary (now the Presbyterian Theological Seminary). He endowed the chair of natural philosophy at Washington and Lee University and the chair of Oriental literature and biblical interpretation at the Union Theological Seminary, Hampden Sidney, Virginia. In 1872, he purchased the *Interior*, a religious periodical, which he published for many years, making it one of the leading Presbyterian journals in the country.

McCormick was married on January 26, 1858, to Nancy Maria (or Nettie) Fowler. The couple had seven children. On May 13, 1884, he died, his eldest son, Cyrus H. McCormick, Jr., succeeding him in the family business.

McCORMICK, JOSEPH MEDILL

(1877-1925) (husband of Ruth Hanna McCormick) Representative and Senator from Illinois; Senate Years of Service: 1919-1925; born in Chicago, Ill., May 16, 1877; attended preparatory school at Groton, Mass.; graduated from Yale University in 1900; engaged in newspaper work as reporter, publisher, and owner of the Chicago Daily Tribune, and later purchased an interest in the Cleveland Leader and Cleveland News; war correspondent in the Philippine Islands in 1901; vice chairman of the national campaign committee of the Progressive Republican movement 1912-1914; elected to the State house of representatives in 1912 and 1914; elected as a Republican to the Sixty-fifth Congress (March 4, 1917-March 3, 1919); elected to the United States Senate in 1918 and served from March 4, 1919, until his death; unsuccessful candidate for

Joseph Medill McCormick

477

renomination in 1924; chairman, Committee on Expenditures in the Department of Labor (Sixty-sixth Congress), Committee on Expenditures in Executive Departments (Sixty-seventh and Sixty-eighth Congresses); committed suicide in Washington, D.C., on February 25, 1925; interment in Middlecreek Cemetery, near Byron, Ogle County, Ill.

McCORMICK, ROBERT RUTHERFORD

(1880-1955) — Newspaper publisher, was born on July 30, 1880, in Chicago, Illinois, the son of Robert Sanderson and Katharine Van Etta Medill McCormick. His father was appointed secretary to the American legation in London, England, in 1889, and later became, successively, ambassador to Austria-Hungary, Russia, and France. When the family moved to England, McCormick's parents placed him in Ludgrove, a preparatory school. Returning to the United States around 1895, McCormick entered Groton, the exclusive Massachusetts preparatory school, from which he graduated in 1899. He then attended Yale, graduating in 1903.

McCormick entered the law school at Northwestern University in 1904, and although he did not complete the course of study, he was admitted to the bar in 1908. Meanwhile, in 1904, he was elected to the city council from a ward on the near North Side. In 1905, McCormick was elected president of the Chicago Sanitary District, where he promptly employed trained engineers to expand the sewage-drainage system for the city and to construct a generating plant at Lockport. His short-lived political career ended when he was not reelected to the sanitary board in 1910.

Before his death in 1899, Joseph Medill, McCormick's maternal grandfather, had devised a trust that controlled most of the shares of the *Chicago Tribune*, naming his sons-in-law, Robert Sanderson McCormick and Robert W. Patterson, as two of the three trustees. McCormick continued his diplomatic career, but Patterson became the editor of the *Tribune*. In 1910, Patterson died, and the stockholders contemplated selling the paper to Victor Lawson, owner of the successful *Chicago Daily News* and the less successful *Record-Herald*. Robert Rutherford McCormick and his cousin Joseph Medill Patterson (son of Robert Patterson) persuaded the stockholders not to sell, and in 1911, McCormick became president of the Tribune Company. In 1914, the two cousins established active control of the paper.

From 1914 to 1919, McCormick and his cousin ran the *Tribune* together. McCormick acquired cutting rights on a large tract of timberland in eastern Canada and constructed paper mills, therefore giving the *Tribune* a source of cheap newsprint. A fleet of *Tribune*-owned lake steamers transported the paper to Chicago. McCormick was also directly responsible for improvements in color presses.

After World War I broke out in 1914, *Tribune* editorials opposed American involvement. In 1915, McCormick journeyed first to England and the western front. After his marriage in the same year to Amy Irwin Adams, he traveled to Russia, where, because of his father's ambassadorship at Petrograd, he was welcomed by the czarist regime. After touring the Russian front, McCormick wrote a book, *With the Russian Army*.

Serving on the western front for the rest of the war, McCormick rose from major to colonel and took part in the battle of Cantigny, for which he later named his estate near Wheaton, Illinois. Just before McCormick returned from France, he and Patterson agreed to establish the *New York Daily News*, a tabloid, as an experiment under the aegis of the Medill trust. Under Patterson's editorship, the experiment proved a spectacular success; the *News* came to have the largest circulation in the United States. Therefore, in 1925, the two men separated, McCormick thereafter having sole charge of the *Chicago Tribune*, which achieved the largest circulation of a standard-size newspaper in the country.

McCormick took a proprietary interest in "Chicagoland"—the city and the surrounding five-state region served by the *Tribune*. His benefactions, totaling millions, included gifts to Passavant Memorial Hospital, Northwestern University's medical school, and the Medill School of Journalism. The publisher and his newspaper strove constantly to make Chicago a center of civic and cultural activity by fostering a music festival, the civic opera, and such sports events as the Golden Gloves, the Silver Skates, and all-star football and baseball games.

McCormick was vigorous in his defense of freedom of the press. Henry Ford, the auto manufacturer, sued the *Tribune* for $1 million, charging that an editorial criticizing Ford's stand against preparedness in 1915 constituted libel. Ford eventually won the case, but the jury awarded him only six cents. When Mayor Thompson sued for $10 million, charging that the *Tribune's* campaign against him was a libel upon the city of Chicago, the court sustained the paper's position on the ground that "the people have the right to discuss their government without fear of being called into account...." On a third occasion, the *Tribune* spent $350,000 supporting a small Minnesota paper's challenge of a state "gag" law prohibiting the press from freely criticizing public

479

officials; in 1931, the U.S. Supreme Court declared this law invalid. McCormick insisted that a guarantee of freedom of the press be written into the 1933 National Recovery Administration newspaper code.

McCormick had no children. His first wife died in 1939; in 1944, he married Maryland Mathison Hooper. On his death, April 1, 1955, in Wheaton, Illinois, most of his holdings went to the Robert R. McCormick Charitable Trust.

McCOY, JOSEPH GEATING

(1837-1915) — Pioneer cattleman, was born December 21, 1837, in Sangamon County, Illinois, the son of David McCoy and Mary (Kirkpatrick) McCoy. He went to the district school, and from 1857 to 1858, to the academic department of Knox College. On October 22, 1861, he married Sarah Epler, and the same year entered the cattle business.

In 1867, he left the prosperous farm in Illinois, and went west with the hope of getting beef from the southwest to the northern and eastern markets where there was a great scarcity. He found in Texas vast herds of cattle, which had been increasing for many years. Cut off from the markets, they were of so little value as to be neglected and permitted to roam the plains at will. Notwithstanding the failures of others, he moved swiftly toward success. He favored the plan of driving the cattle to some shipping point, but the railroads would take no part in his seemingly impracticable scheme. He was ridiculed, and some persons even thought him crazy. He chose for his shipping-point Abilene, Kansas, on the Kansas Pacific Railway and bought the whole town site with about 480 acres for $2,400. There, he built a three-story hotel and constructed his own stockyards. He hired surveyors, laid out and marked a trail across the prairies from Abilene to Corpus Christi, Texas, and arranged facilities for pasture and water.

He eventually persuaded ranchers to drive their herds to Abilene. The first drive passed over this trail in September 1867, and by the end of the year 35,000 cattle reached Abilene and were shipped east. Following that year a very great movement of livestock took place. Ten millions of cattle are said to have reached the market over this trail. The Kansas Pacific Railway agreed to give him one-eighth of the freight on each car of cattle shipped. After the second year, the sum of $200,000 was due him on this account. The company repudiated the contract on the ground that it was improvidently made, since such large shipments had not been anticipated. He surrendered his contract on a promise of another one, but the company never kept its promise. He sued for the amount due him, which he collected several years later, but the failure to receive the new contract cost him dearly. He served as mayor of Abilene and received many commissions from the federal government. His report on the livestock industry, as director of that branch of the 11th U. S. Census, attracted large capital to meet production in the grazing regions.

Rival interests finally diverted the trade from Abilene, but he followed the industry. He established the cattle drives to Cottonwood Falls, to Wichita, and helped open the famous Chisholm Trail. He went to Wichita in May 1872. In 1881, operating from Wichita, he served as agent for the Cherokee Nation in collecting their land revenues. He lived for a time in Oklahoma, where he took part in political conventions. A stanch Democrat, he was nominated for Congress in 1890, but was unsuccessful. He was the author of *Historic Sketches of the Cattle Trade* (1874) and was the original for the character thinly disguised as Joe McCoyne in Emerson Hough's *North of 36* (1923). He died on October 19, 1915, in Kansas. One son and two daughters survived him.

McCUMBER, PORTER JAMES

(1858-1933) — Lawyer and politician, was born on February 3, 1858, in Crete, Will County, Illinois, the son of Orlin McCumber and Anne Fuller McCumber. The family moved from Illinois to a farm seven miles southwest of Rochestor, Minnesota, the same year that he was born, and he attended the common schools of the county. He then attended the high school at Rochester, taught school for a few years, and graduated from the law department of the University of Michigan in 1880. He was admitted to the bar and began practice at Wahpeton, in what is now North Dakota, in 1881. Early in the following year, he formed a partnership with B.L. Bogart.

In 1884, he was elected to the Lower House of the territorial legislature, and in 1886, he was elected to the Upper House. For one term, 1889-1891, he was state's

Porter James McCumber

attorney for Richland County. The North Dakota Legislature elected him to the U.S. Senate in 1899. He was reelected in 1905, 1911, and 1916, and served continuously from March 4, 1899, to March 3, 1923.

In the Senate, his chief interests were pure-food legislation, pensions, Indian affairs, and the tariff. He wrote articles, made speeches, and eventually secured the passage of the national Food and Drugs Act. As chairman of the Senate Committee on Pensions, he effected legislation favorable to veterans of the Civil War. By 1922, he had become one of the leaders of the Senate and was by seniority the chairman of one of the most powerful committees, that of finance. Consequently he became a sponsor of the Fordney-McCumber Tariff Act. Defeated for the renomination in the North Dakota primary in 1922, he resumed the practice of law in Washington, D.C. In 1925, he was appointed by President Calvin Coolidge a member of the International Joint Commission, and served in that capacity until his death on May 18, 1933.

McCumber was married on May 29, 1889, to Jennie Schorning. They had a daughter, Helen, and a son, Donald.

McDOUGALL, JAMES ALEXANDER

(1817-1867) — Attorney general of Illinois and politician, was born in Bethlehem, New York, and attended the Albany, New York, public schools. After studying law, he was admitted to the bar and commenced practice in Cook County, Illinois, in 1837. As attorney general of Illinois (1842-1846), he made explorations of the southwestern part of the United States and finally settled in San Francisco, California.

He was attorney general of California from October 7, 1850, until he resigned on December 30, 1851. Elected as a Democrat to the Thirty-third Congress (March 4, 1853-March 3, 1855), he was not a candidate for renomination in 1854. Elected to the U.S. Senate, he served from March 4, 1861, to March 3, 1867, but was not a candidate for reelection.

A delegate to the Democratic National Convention at Chicago, Illinois, in 1864 and to the Union National Convention at Philadelphia, Pennsylvania, in 1866, he died in Albany, New York.

McKINLEY, WILLIAM BROWN

(1856-1926) Representative and Senator from Illinois; Senate Years of Service: 1921-1926; born in Petersburg, Menard County, Ill., September 5, 1856; attended the common schools and the University of Illinois at

Urbana; employed as a drug clerk in Springfield, Ill.; engaged in banking in Champaign, Ill., and also in the building and operation of public utilities and bridges; elected a trustee of the University of Illinois 1902-1905; philanthropist; elected as a Republican to the Fifty-ninth and to the three succeeding Congresses (March 4, 1905-Marh 3, 1913); was an unsuccessful candidate for reelection in 1912 to the Sixty-third Congress; chairman, Committee on Coinage, Weights and Measures (Sixtieth and Sixty-first Congresses); again elected to the Sixty-fourth,

William Brown McKinley

Sixty-fifth, and Sixty-sixth Congresses (March 4, 1915-March 3, 1921); was not a candidate for reelection, having become a candidate for Senator; elected as a Republican to the United States Senate in 1920 and served from March 4, 1921, until his death; unsuccessful candidate for renomination in 1926; chairman, Committee on Manufactures (Sixty-ninth Congress); died in Martinsville, Morgan County, Ind., on December 7, 1926; interment in Mount Hope Cemetery, Champaign, Ill.

McLAUGHLIN, ANDREW CUNNINGHAM

(1861-1947) — Historian, was born in Beardstown, Illinois, the son of David McLaughlin and Isabella (Campbell) McLaughlin. When he was a baby, the family moved to Muskegon, Michigan, where his father kept a store and doubled as superintendent of schools. In 1878, McLaughlin entered the University of Michigan at Ann Arbor. Graduating in 1882, McLaughlin returned to Muskegon as principal of the local high school; the following year, he went back to Ann Arbor for his law degree. There he came under the influence of Judge Thomas Cooley, author of the already classic *Constitutional Limitations*; when in 1887 Cooley went to Washington to be chairman of the new Interstate Commerce Commission, McLaughlin, who had been teaching Latin, shifted to the history department, taking over his mentor's classes in constitutional history.

Though teaching constitutional history, McLaughlin's early books explored the history of the Old Northwest: a biography of Lewis

Cass for the American Statesman series (1899) and volumes on government and on education in Michigan. In 1893-1894, McLaughlin spent a year studying in Germany. In 1901, he became managing editor of the *American Historical Review*, a post that he held for five years, and in 1903, he moved to Washington to head up the new Bureau of Historical Research of the Carnegie Institution. While there, he wrote for the American Nation series *The Confederation and the Constitution* (1905), a revisionist view of the Critical Period of American History. The book won immediate academic acclaim. President William Rainey Harper of Chicago University offered McLaughlin the chair of the history department, and he was instrumental in making it one of the most distinguished in the nation. Long a member of the Council of the American Historical Association, McLaughlin became president of that organization in 1914. In 1929, he retired formally from his professorship, but he continued for another decade to hold seminars and guide doctoral candidates in his chosen field.

McLaughlin kept up his research and writing during his teaching years. Several of his books, including *Courts, Constitution, and Parties* (1912) and *America and Britain* (1919), were made up of previously published articles. *Foundations of American Constitutionalism* (1932) was comprised of the Anson Phelps lectures that he gave at New York University. Three years later, he published the *Constitutional History of the United States*, which was awarded a Pulitzer Prize. His last major work was the *Constitutional History*.

On June 16, 1890, he married Lois Thompson Angell; together they had six children, James Angell, Rowland Hazard, David Blair, Constance Winsor, Esther Lois, and Isabella Campbell. He died on September 24, 1947, at his home in Chicago of pneumonia. He was buried in the family plot at Forest Hills Cemetery, Ann Arbor, Michigan.

McLEAN, JOHN

(1791-1830) (brother of Finis Ewing McLean and uncle of James David Walker) Representative and Senator from Illinois; Senate Years of Service: 1824-1825; 1829-1830; born near Guilford Court House (now Greensboro), Guilford County, N.C., February 4, 1791; moved with his parents to Logan County, Ky., in 1795; pursued an academic course; moved to Illinois Territory in 1815; studied law; admitted to the bar and commenced practice in Shawneetown, Gallatin County, Ill.; upon the admission of Illinois as a State into the Union was elected to the Fifteenth Congress and served from December 3, 1818, to March 3,

1819; unsuccessful candidate for reelection in 1818 to the Sixteenth Congress and for election in 1820 and 1822 to the Seventeenth and Eighteenth Congresses, respectively; member, State house of representatives 1820, 1826, 1828, and served as speaker; elected to the United States Senate to fill the vacancy caused by the resignation of Ninian Edwards and served from November 23, 1824, to March 3, 1825; was not a candidate for reelection; resumed the practice of law; again elected to the United States Senate and served from March 4, 1829, until his death in Shawneetown, Ill., October 14, 1830; interment in Westwood Cemetery, near Shawneetown, Ill.

John McLean

McROBERTS, SAMUEL
(1799-1843) Senator from Illinois; Senate Years of Service: 1841-1843; born near Maystown, Monroe County, Ill. (then a portion of the Northwest Territory), April 12, 1799; educated by private tutors; graduated from the law department of Transylvania University, Lexington, Ky.; admitted to the bar in 1821 and commenced practice in Monroe County, Ill.; clerk of the circuit court of Monroe County 1819-1821; State circuit judge 1824-1827; member, State senate 1828-1830; appointed United States district attorney by President Andrew Jackson in 1830 and served until 1832, when he resigned;

Samuel McRoberts

appointed by President Martin Van Buren receiver of the land office at Danville in 1832; appointed Solicitor of the General Land Office at Washington in 1839 and served in that capacity until his resignation in 1841; elected as a Democrat to the United States Senate and served from March 4, 1841, until his death; chairman, Committee on Engrossed Bills (Twenty-seventh Congress); died in Cincinnati, Ohio, March 27, 1843; interment in the Moore Cemetery, Waterloo, Monroe County, Ill.

Joseph Medill

MEDILL, JOSEPH

(1823-1899) — Editor and publisher; credited for building the *Chicago Tribune* into a powerful newspaper; former mayor of Chicago. Medill was born April 6, 1823, near Saint John, New Brunswick. He left Canada to publish papers in Ohio, including one in Coshocton from 1849 to 1951, and another in Cleveland from 1851 to 1855. In 1854 Medill helped found the Republican Party and gave the group its name.

In 1847, he joined the partnership that acquired the *Chicago Tribune* and was given the power to determine the paper's editorial policy. Medill focused on the slavery issue, demanding that slaves be freed and pushing for the nomination of Abraham Lincoln as a presidential candidate in the Republican Party. He continued to support Lincoln and his administration throughout the Civil War, and favored the Radical Republicans' program for reconstruction of the South.

One month after the 1871 Great Chicago Fire, Medill was elected mayor of Chicago. He used emergency powers to reorganize the municipal government and straighten out its finances. He also helped establish the Chicago Public Library. In 1871, Medill resigned as mayor and purchased controlling interest in the *Tribune*. He was named editor-in-chief, a position through which he advocated a free hand in business and fought liberal reformers.

Medill's love for journalism seemed to continue for generations, as three of his grandchildren became important newspaper publishers:

Robert McCormick of the *Chicago Tribune*, Joseph M. Patterson of the *New York Daily News*, and Eleanor M. Patterson of the *Washington Time Herald.*

Medill died March 16, 1899, in San Antonio, Texas. His family endowed the Medill School of Journalism at Northwestern University in Evanston, Illinois.

MEINZER, OSCAR EDWARD

(1876-1948) — Geologist, was born on November 28, 1876, near Davis, Stephenson County, Illinois, the son of William Meinzer and Mary Julia (Meinzer) Meinzer. After attending local schools and nearby Beloit Academy in Wisconsin (1896-1897), he entered Beloit College, from which he received a B.A. *magna cum laude* in 1901. He spent the next two years as a school principal in Frankfort, South Dakota, and in 1903, became a teacher of physical science at Lenox College in Hopkinton, Iowa. While teaching at Lenox College, he began graduate study in geology at the University of Chicago, Illinois.

In July 1907, Meinzer joined the U.S. Geological Survey as a junior geologist assigned to the investigation of groundwater. In Utah, New Mexico, and Arizona, he located water resources that made possible the irrigation and settlement of previously arid valleys. He became chief of the Division of Ground Water in 1913, a post he was to hold until his retirement in 1946.

Meinzer realized that, as water became an increasingly important natural resource, it would be necessary not only to discover underground reservoirs but also to find ways of measuring their storage capacities and their rates of discharge and renewal, and therefore arrive at a safe annual yield. His research in this area led to two publications that became standard references, *Outline of Ground-Water Hydrology, with Definitions* (1923), and *The Occurrence of Ground Water in the United States, with a Discussion of Principles* (1923). The latter was accepted as a dissertation by the University of Chicago, which awarded Meinzer the Ph.D. *magna cum laude* in 1922.

Meinzer also established a hydrologic laboratory, where, along with other experiments, he was able to prove that as long as the flow of water through granular material is laminar, the velocity is directly proportional to the hydraulic gradient, that is, the flow conforms to Darcy's law. For field investigations, he proposed and encouraged the development of geophysical techniques and such instruments as automatic water-stage recorders on wells. He was in the vanguard in urging pumping and other analytical tests on wells to obtain quantitative information on the properties of aquifers (water bearing strata of permeable rocks). Meinzer also directed studies of the chemical quality and geochemistry of water.

The droughts of the early 1930s and the onset of World War II greatly increased the demand for groundwater investigations. Meinzer and his assistants trained and supervised dozens of geologists and engineers, many of whom helped develop the more sophisticated tools, methodology, and techniques of modern groundwater hydrology. Meinzer was the recognized father of the science of ground water hydrology.

Meinzer was an active member of many scientific societies, and was president of the Society of Economic Geologists (1945) and the American Geophysical Union (1947-1948), whose Bowie Medal he received in 1943. For many years he taught boys' classes at Sherwood Presbyterian Church in Washington, D.C., and he was an active leader in the Boy Scouts.

He married Alice Breckenridge Crawford on October 3, 1906. They had two children, Robert William (adopted in 1913) and Roy Crawford. He died on June 14, 1948.

MICHEAUX, OSCAR

(1884-1951) — Film producer and author, was born near Metropolis, Illinois, the son of Calvin Michaux and Belle Willingham Michaux (as the family name was originally spelled). His background and life are obscure, but according to his thinly disguised autobiographical novel, *The Conquest: The Story of a Negro Pioneer, by the Pioneer* (1913), he was one of thirteen children, and the grandson of a slave. Shortly after Micheaux's birth, the family moved to Metropolis in order to further the children's education. Micheaux attended the local "colored" school for a few years, but returned with his family to the farm, where he worked as a vegetable vendor.

Micheaux left town when he was seventeen, and worked briefly in a railroad-car factory and in a coalmine in southern Illinois before going to live with an older brother in Chicago, Illinois, where he worked at the Union Stock Yards and held other irregular jobs. While working as a Pullman car porter, Micheaux learned from passengers of the opportunities for homesteading land in South Dakota. In 1904, he staked a claim in Megory County on what had been the Little Crow Reservation. He was the only African American in the area, but he prospered. If his novel *The Conquest* is accurate, Micheaux fell in love with a white woman, the daughter of a neighbor, but married an African American woman from Chicago, a minister's daughter who subsequently returned to her father.

Around 1908, Micheaux began his career in writing. After publication of *The Conquest* in 1913 he started traveling, particularly in the South, advertising his book and his ideas. Out of this promotional experience in the South came Micheaux's *The Forged Note: A Romance of the Darker Races* (1915). After his third book, *The Homesteader* (1917), Micheaux turned to a new medium, film. Approached for the motion picture rights to *The Homesteader*, he agreed to sell with the stipulation that he be allowed to direct the film. When his terms were refused, Micheaux decided to produce the movie himself. He raised the necessary money by the unusual method of soliciting advances against the rental of the film from owners or operators of movie houses, black and white. *The Homesteader* (1919) is considered by cinema historians to be the first all-black, full-length American film. Over the next three decades Micheaux produced thirty-three more movies.

Micheaux's low-budget productions were filmed on location at his New York City headquarters in four to six weeks. He used black players from established stage companies in the East. On March 20, 1926, Micheaux married Alice B. Russell, an actress who had appeared in his movies.

Micheaux made his first talking picture, *The Exile*, in 1931. He explored variations in genre in his films, although real or fancied miscegenation often served as the basis of plots. *Daughter of the Congo* (1930) had an African background; *Underworld* (1936) was a gangster film. In his last movie, *The Betrayal* (1948), he returned to the theme of the African American homesteader in South Dakota in love with a white woman.

During his years making movies, Micheaux also continued to write novels, including: *The Case of Mrs. Wingate* (1945), which utilized a war setting, a black German spy, and a Black detective; and *The Masquerade, an Historical Novel* (1947), a thinly disguised version of C.W. Chesnutt's *The House Behind the Cedars*. Micheaux died on March 26, 1951, in Charlotte, North Carolina, during a promotional tour of the South.

MIES VAN DER ROHE, LUDWIG

(1886-1969), was born in Aachen, Germany. He worked in the family stone-carving business before he joined the office of architect and furniture designer Bruno Paul in Berlin in 1905. He left Paul in 1907 and went to work for pioneering industrial architect, Peter Behrens, until leaving Behrens to open his own office in Berlin (1912).

During World War I, Mies served as an enlisted man, building bridges and roads in the Balkans. When he returned to Berlin in 1918, the fall of the German Monarchy and the birth of the Weimar Republic had helped inspire a burst of new creativity among modern artists and architects. The avant-garde school of the arts, The Bauhaus, was established. Mies joined the modernist movement, building several models of skyscrapers which experimented with steel frames and glass walls. Mies designed the German Pavilion for the 1929 Barcelona International Exhibition, and the Tugendhat House (1930) in Brno, (in what is now the Czech Republic). These buildings were long, low glass-sheathed structures, the interiors being a series of free-flowing spaces with minimal walls, typically of rare marbles and woods. For the Barcelona Exhibition, Mies designed the chrome and leather Barcelona chair, a recognized masterpiece in modernist furniture.

Mies was appointed director of the Bauhaus in 1930. Between Nazi attacks from the outside and left-wing student revolts from within, the school was in a state of perpetual turmoil. When the Nazis closed the school in 1933, Mies tried for a few months to revive it, but announced the end of The Bauhaus in late 1933. Four years later, Mies moved to the United States.

After settling in Chicago, Illinois, Mies (who added Van der Rohe, his mother's maiden name, to his name after establishing himself as an architect), was appointed director of the School of Architecture at Armour Institute (1938), where he would serve for the next twenty years. He trained a new generation of American architects and produced many buildings in the U.S, including skyscrapers, museums, schools, and residences. His 37-story bronze and glass Seagram Building in New York City, built in 1958 in collaboration with American architect Philip C. Johnson, is considered the most subtle development of the glass-walled skyscraper, while his Farnsworth House, built in 1950 in Fox River, Illinois, is the culmination of his residential architecture. Mies buildings exemplify his famous principle that "less is more," and demonstrate, despite their austere and forthright use of the most modern materials, his exceptional sense of proportion and concern for detail.

490

Ludwig Mies Van der Rohe lived out the remainder of his life in a spacious building near Lake Michigan in Chicago until his death in 1969. Along with French architect Le Corbusier and American architect Frank Lloyd Wright, Mies is one of the most influential architects of the Twentieth Century. Many of the skyscraper designs of the 1960s and 1970s were copied or adapted from his original designs.

MILLER, PERRY GILBERT EDDY

(1905-1963) — Teacher and scholar, was born on February 25, 1905 in Chicago, Illinois, the son of Eben Perry Sturgis Miller and Gertrude Eddy. Miller attended the Tilton School and Austin High School in Chicago, and in 1922, enrolled at the University of Chicago. He left the university the following year to try his hand at other things. He first went to Colorado, next to New York City and then abroad. The theater drew his attention in New York, and for a time he played bit parts in Paterson, New Jersey. He also performed around New York City with Edward H. Sothern and Julia Marlowe's Shakespeare Company. The stage did not hold Miller for long, and he next took to the sea. His travels, apparently for a time as a seaman, took him to Tampico, Mexico, the Mediterranean, and then to Africa, where he left his ship to work for an oil company in the Belgian Congo. On returning to the United States in 1926, he resumed his studies at the University of Chicago, where he received the bachelor's degree in 1928 and the doctorate in 1931; he spent the academic year 1930-1931 at Harvard. On September 12, 1930, Miller married Elizabeth Williams; they had no children.

Orthodoxy in Massachusetts, Miller's doctoral dissertation, was published in 1933. He had begun teaching two years earlier, as a tutor at Harvard's Leverett House. In 1933, with F. O. Matthiessen and Ellery Sedgwick, he began a survey course in American literature, one of the early courses in the field at an American university. Other innovative courses followed, including one on American romanticism that made Miller's reputation as one of Harvard's great teachers.

During the years before World War II, Miller completed the research for *The New England Mind: The Seventeenth Century* (1939). The war interrupted his studies, and he joined the U.S. Army in 1942, serving first as a captain and then in the Office of Strategic Services (OSS) as a major until his discharge in 1945. Harvard promoted him to full professor in 1946.

His writings included: a work edited with Thomas H. Johnson, *The Puritans* (2 vols., 1938), which proved valuable both to advanced scholars and to beginning students; an intellectual biography of Jonathan Edwards (1949); *Roger Williams: His Contribution to the American Tradition* (1953); and *The New England Mind: From Colony to Province* (1953), perhaps his finest work. He did not live to complete *The Life of the Mind in America*, though one volume of this work, *From the Revolution to the Civil War*, was published posthumously in 1965.

Miller died on December 9, 1963 in Cambridge, Massachusetts.

MILLIKAN, ROBERT ANDREWS

(1868-1953) — Physicist and educator, was born on March 22, 1868, in Morrison, Illinois, the son of Silas Franklin Millikan, a Congregational minister, and Mary Jane Andrews Millikan, who had been dean of Olivet College. When he was five years old, the family moved to McGregor, Iowa. In 1886, he entered Oberlin College, where he studied mathematics and Greek. The following year, however, his Greek professor asked him to teach a course in physics in the preparatory department. After Millikan graduated from Oberlin in 1891, he remained as a tutor in physics and served as acting director of the gymnasium. He earned his master's degree from Oberlin in 1893, then attended Columbia University, from which he received the Ph.D. in physics in 1895. His professor, the physicist and inventor Michael I. Pupin, advised him to study in Europe, and he spent most of 1896 at the University of Berlin in Germany.

In the fall of 1896, Millikan accepted an assistantship in physics at the new University of Chicago. In 1910, he became a full professor. While at Chicago, Millikan began his lifelong personal and scientific friendship with A.A. Michelson, the first American to win the Nobel Prize in physics. In 1902, Millikan married Greta Irvin Blanchard, a recent graduate of the University of Chicago, where she had majored in Greek; they had three sons.

Millikan spent many years obtaining an accurate measurement of the charge on the electron; the results of his experimentations were published in 1913. Millikan next tested the quantum theory of

Robert Andrews Millikan

radiation that had been suggested by Max Planck in 1900 and boldly extended by Albert Einstein in 1905. Millikan built an elaborate apparatus, housed in a high-vacuum chamber, with which he carried out an extensive series of highly precise measurements from 1912 to 1916. He confirmed Einstein's equation and determined Planck's constant, h. On the basis of this and the previous experiment, he was awarded the Nobel Prize in physics in 1923.

In 1917, George Ellery Hale, then director of the Mount Wilson Observatory in Pasadena, California, asked Millikan to join him in Washington, D.C. World War I was reaching a critical stage for the Allies, and the United States was about to become involved. Hale had been appointed chairman of the newly organized National Research Council, the operating arm of the National Academy of Sciences, and he appointed Millikan executive officer and director of research. He also worked in the area of antisubmarine warfare, and was instrumental in helping to eliminate enemy sinkings of Allied submarines.

As the war was coming to an end, Millikan and Hale supervised the conversion of the National Research Council into a permanent organization. Millikan declined the invitation to remain in Washington as its full-time chairman, but before leaving, he persuaded the Rockefeller Foundation to finance a program of National Research Council postdoctoral fellowships.

In November 1918, Millikan returned to the University of Chicago. For a year, however, he continued to spend a good deal of time in Washington fulfilling his duties as a member of the National Research Council and the National Academy of Sciences. His stay at Chicago was short-lived, however. As early as 1917, Millikan had been persuaded by Hale to spend some time in Pasadena at Throop College of Technology. In 1920, the trustees changed the name of the college to California Institute of Technology, and in 1921, they offered Millikan a new research laboratory and a $90,000-a-year research fund if he would come to Pasadena to head Cal Tech and direct its physics laboratory

For the next thirty-four years Millikan was the key figure in the development of Cal Tech, keeping the school small and select. He initiated high-voltage engineering research that made it possible to construct power lines that would bring electricity from the Sierras and Hoover Dam, and established a pioneering laboratory to study earthquakes. He also built a strong division of humanities to ensure that all students received a liberal education.

Millikan still pursued his own research in physics and guided the research of scores of graduate students and research fellows. He studied the ionization of air at high altitudes, as well as the far-ultraviolet spectra of atoms. Through these and many other research projects, the Norman Bridge Laboratory of Physics at Caltech became regarded as a center of science and engineering second in quality to none in the nation.

His scientific publications, many of outstanding importance, spanned fifty-four years (1895-1949). His college and high school textbooks in physics were the most widely used in America between 1902 and 1930; and one of them, first published in 1902, was, in a revised edition, still in use at the time of his death. He died in San Marino, California, on December 19, 1953. In 1966, one of Millikan's close friends, Seeley G. Mudd, donated funds to Cal Tech for construction of a towering library building, the Robert Andrews Millikan Memorial, in the center of the campus.

John Mitchell

MITCHELL, JOHN

(1870-1919) — Labor leader, was born in Braidwood, Illinois, the son of Robert Mitchell, a Civil War veteran and a coal miner, and Martha (Halley) Mitchell, who died when he was two and a half years old. His father was killed when John was six, and his stepmother, a devout Presbyterian, brought him up. He went to school a few weeks a season at the district school, then entered the mines at the age of twelve despite the state law that put the limit at thirteen. Faced by the industrial depression of 1886-87, he set out on two tramping trips to Colorado and Wyoming mines, but returned to Illinois as penniless as he left.

In 1885, he joined the Knights of Labor. Later, in 1890, when the Knights and the trade union joined to form the United Mine Workers of America, Mitchell joined the local branch. On June 1, 1891, he was married to Katherine O'Rourke. He joined in the many discussions with fellow workers on the remedies for unemployment and low wages, reading law for a year and studying social and economic problems.

In 1894, Mitchell was one of 125,000 men who participated in the strike of the United Mine Workers of America and was discharged at its end. Obtaining work in a near-by camp, he was found by an old acquaintance that picked the youthful miner to be secretary-treasurer of the union's sub-district. In 1897, he became a member of the State Executive Board. That year, he had an active part in the first victorious national strike called by the union. Elected a delegate to the national convention of the union, he was elected vice-president, and in September 1898, he stepped into the vacant presidency. In the anthracite coalfields of Pennsylvania in 1902, he brought together fifteen thousand mine workers, who by a five months' strike won an advance of wages, a reduction of hours, and an arbitration agreement.

At the age of thirty-two, he became the leader of the first successful organization of immigrant labor from eastern and southern Europe. He sought out the possible leaders of the many nationalities, trained them in the principles of united action, and won the support of public opinion, businessmen, and especially of Catholic priests. He himself in time accepted the Catholic faith. The depression in the bituminous coal fields, after 1904, and the failure of several strikes against a falling market, led to his defeat by the bituminous mine workers in 1907. At the conference called by President Theodore Roosevelt, Mitchell was bitterly assailed by the employers who had refused to confer until national pressure was brought to bear. In 1902, when he had organized and conducted the anthracite strike, he became a national figure.

Mitchell's presidency of the union ended in 1908, after which he lectured on trade unionism. He then became head of the trade-agreement department of the National Civic Federation, from which he resigned in 1911 on account of a resolution of the United Mine Workers calling for his resignation either from the union or from the Civic Federation. In 1915, he was appointed chairman of the New York state industrial commission, a position that he held until his death in New York City in September 1919.

He published *Organized Labor* in 1903. In 1913, he published *The Wage Earner and His Problems*, which gave in familiar terms the purposes of unions and the human needs they meet.

MOMOHOKO

(1800-?) — Native American Indian and descendent of the ruling clan called the Sturgeon of the Sauk tribe, who gave his support to Black Hawk during the great rivalry for tribal leadership. When the U.S. government ordered the Sauk to vacate their tribal homeland in Illinois and settle west of the Mississippi in Iowa, Black Hawk took over leadership of the resistance, while Keokuk spoke for those Sauk who agreed to submit to the government's demands. Mokohoko, a bitter enemy of Keokuk and the policy of appeasement, supported Black Hawk's ill-fated and short-lived war to maintain the Sauk land on Rock River.

MONROE, HARRIET

(1860-1936) — Poet and editor, was born on December 23, 1860, in Chicago, Illinois, to Henry Stanton and Martha (Mitchell) Monroe. She studied at Dearborn Seminary in her hometown, and at Visitation Academy in Georgetown, D.C. until 1879. At an early age, she became interested in literature, both to read and write it. In 1899, she wrote the lyrics to a cantata that celebrated the opening of the Chicago auditorium and in 1891, wrote a poem for the World's Columbian exposition, which was read and sung before a large audience in 1892. She also contributed art reviews to the Chicago *Tribune* and *Herald* as well as several magazines, including *Atlantic Monthly*, *Century* and *Scribner's*. She also published volumes of her poems, such as *Valeria and other poems* (1892), *John Wilborn Root- A Memoir* (1896), *Five Modern Plays in Verse* (1903), and others.

Her most well known achievement, however, was the establishment of *Poetry* magazine in 1912. As editor of the publication, she attracted the best of both British and American poets, and brought many unknown artists to fame, including Carl Sandburg: Ezra Pound, Willa Cather, Robert Frost, T.S. Eliot and Joyce Kilmer. In 1917, she edited *The New Poetry: An Anthology of Twentieth Century Verse*, which marked the upsurge of a new poetic movement. Her belief in poetry led her to help other poets achieve the notoriety she believed they deserved, although she didn't believe she had great talent herself. After publishing several more books of her own verse as well as more editions of the *Anthology*, she died on September 26, 1936, in Arequipa, Peru, while on tour.

MOONEY, THOMAS JOSEPH

(1882-1942) — Labor radical, was born on December 8, 1882, in Chicago, Illinois, the son of Bryan and Mary (Hefferon or Heffernan)

Mooney. After his father died in 1892, the family moved to his mother's hometown of Holyoke, Massachusetts. Mooney attended a Catholic parochial school for a short time, then transferred to public school. At the age of fourteen, he went to work in a local factory, and the following year, was apprenticed as an iron molder. He soon joined the molder's union, but found work in his trade only sporadically. On a trip to Europe in 1907, he converted to socialism. Back in the United States, he distributed Socialist literature from the campaign train of Eugene Debs during the 1908 presidential race. Two years later, he attended the International Socialist Congress at Copenhagen.

On July 3, 1911, in Stockton, California, Mooney married Rena Ellen (Brink) Hermann; they had no children. Settling in San Francisco, California, he affiliated with various radical and labor groups, including the Industrial Workers of the World and the left-wing faction of the San Francisco Socialists, whose newspaper, *Revolt*, he helped publish. In 1910, he ran as the Socialist candidate for Superior Court judge, and in 1911, for sheriff. He organized molders for William Z. Foster's Syndicalist League of North America and joined the International Workers Defense League, an organization formed to provide legal aid to radicals.

In 1913, Mooney and Warren Billings joined a prolonged, violent strike of electrical workers against the Pacific Gas & Electric Company. During the turmoil, Billings was arrested by a company detective, Martin Swanson, for carrying dynamite and was later imprisoned. Fearing that Swanson would try to implicate him as well, Mooney went into hiding, but was arrested near Richmond, California, and charged with illegal possession of high explosives. After two trials resulting in hung juries, he was acquitted in 1914.

During the San Francisco Preparedness Day parade (July 22, 1916), one of the many held throughout the United States to demonstrate for military readiness, a bomb exploded on Steuart Street, killing ten persons and wounding forty. Beyond a few fragments of shrapnel, little physical evidence was discovered; however, District Attorney Charles M. Fickert theorized that a time bomb had been carried to the scene in a suitcase. Acting on information supplied by Swanson, Fickert arrested Mooney, Mooney's wife, Warren Billings, and several others, charging them with the crime.

Billings was tried in September 1916 and sentenced to life imprisonment. Mooney, defended by Maxwell McNutt and Bourke Cockran, was tried in January 1917 before Judge Franklin A. Griffin.

Prosecution witness Frank C. Oxman claimed to have seen Mooney and Billings in the Steuart Street area carrying a suitcase, and Mooney was convicted of first-degree murder and sentenced to hang. Later, after a motion for a retrial was denied, it was revealed that Oxman had perjured himself in his affidavit to the district attorney, and that he had probably not even arrived in San Francisco until four hours after the crime. Despite this evidence, Fickert opposed a retrial. Rena Mooney was tried without Oxman's testimony in the summer of 1917 and was acquitted.

After Mooney's conviction, a number of groups, including the San Francisco Labor Council, joined in seeking a commutation of his sentence. In the protracted legal battle that ensued, Mooney was aided by Roger Baldwin of the American Civil Liberties Union; Frank P. Walsh, his chief defense attorney from 1923 to 1939; Fremont Older, editor of the *San Francisco Bulletin*; and Samuel Gompers of the A.F. of L. His case soon became an international *cause celebre*. When mobs protesting his conviction marched on the American embassy in Petrograd in 1917, President Woodrow Wilson urged California's governor to order Mooney to be retried. That summer Colonel Edward M. House persuaded a Federal Mediation Commission, appointed to investigate Industrial Workers of the World strikes against the copper and lumber industries, to look into the case; its report questioned the justice of the verdict. In November 1918, Governor William D. Stephens commuted Mooney's sentence to life imprisonment.

For two decades, his supporters continued their efforts to win his freedom, either through executive clemency or through legal action. An appeal to the U.S. Supreme Court on the ground that due process had been violated when Mooney was imprisoned as a result of perjured testimony brought a decision (*Moorzey vs. Holohan*, 1935) expanding the federal role in habeas corpus proceedings, but did not change Mooney's status. Governor Culbert L. Olson finally pardoned Mooney on January 7, 1939. Billings, whose cause had never received the same attention, was freed by commutation of sentence that October; he was officially pardoned in 1961.

After his release, Mooney went on tour under labor auspices. The years in prison having left him in poor health, he spent most of his last two years at St. Luke's Hospital in San Francisco. He died on March 6, 1942.

MORGAN, HELEN RIGGINS

(1900-1941) — Singer and actress, was born on August 2, 1900, in

Danville, Illinois, the only child of Frank Riggins of Danville and Lulu (Lang) Riggins. While she was still a small child, her mother divorced Riggins and married Thomas Morgan. They separated a few years later, and Lulu Morgan eventually moved to Chicago, Illinois. There, Helen Morgan attended Crane Technical High School, then left around 1918 to take a job packing crackers and then as a manicurist. Investing her wages in singing and dancing lessons, she began performing in Chicago speak-easies and was recruited by a talent scout

Helen Riggins Morgan

for the chorus of a Broadway musical, *Sally* (1920), produced by Florenz Ziegfeld. She then returned for another stint in small Chicago nightclubs.

Making her way again to New York, she secured a small singing part in *George White's Scandals* of 1925. She also sang that year at Billy Rose's Backstage Club, in a room so small and crowded she had to sit on the piano, a perch that became her trademark. She triumphed as the mulatto Julie LaVerne in Jerome Kern's *Show Boat* (1927-1928), where her greatest number, "Bill" (lyrics by P.G. Wodehouse), was a theme song for the "emancipated" but lonely city girl who desperately needed a man. She immortalized the Gershwins' "The Man I Love" ("Someday he'll come along"). Her hit songs in the Kern-Hammerstein musical of 1929, *Sweet Adeline*, in which she starred, "Don't Ever Leave Me" and "Why Was I Born?," reiterated her theme of alienation and isolation. So did the Victor Young-Ned Washington "Give Me a Heart to Sing To" from her 1935 film *Frankie and Johnny*.

She followed her 1929 film debut in *Applause* with half a dozen other movies, including the film version of *Show Boat* (1936), and also appeared on Broadway with the *Ziegfeld Follies* (1931) and *George White's Scandals* (1936) and on radio. Until moving to Hollywood, California, in 1935, she continued to work in Manhattan nightclubs she partly owned. In 1957 a film, *The Helen Morgan Story*, dramatized her life.

She was married twice. Her first marriage, on May 15, 1933, to Maurice Maschke, floundered during her constant engagements in New

York, London, England, and Paris, France. Her second marriage, on July 27, 1941, was to Lloyd Johnson. She died from cirrhosis of the liver and hepatitis on October 9, 1941, at the age of forty-one, in Chicago, Illinois.

MORRIS, NELSON

(1838-1907) — Stockbreeder and meatpacker, was born in Hechingen, province of Hohenzollern, Germany. He came to America as a boy and reached Chicago, Illinois, in the 1850s, looking for work. He was first employed at the Myrick Stock Yards, one of a number of small stockyards, which preceded the building of the Union Stock Yards. Later, John B. Sherman, the founder of the Union Stock Yards, gave him work. As Sherman's protégé, he evolved into a head-hog renderer, and after several years, left Sherman's employ to become a cattle trader on a small scale. Within a few years, he acquired a leading position in the live-cattle trade, not only from Chicago to the Atlantic seaboard, but also in transatlantic shipments.

Morris was a pioneer in transporting dressed beef from Chicago to the Atlantic seaboard. He early secured contracts to supply the French and other European governments with beef and he was also largely instrumental in supplying the commissariat department of the Union troops with livestock during the Civil War. By 1873, his company was earning more than $11 million a year. In 1874, he entered into partnership with Isaac Waixel, and for a while, the firm was known as Morris & Waixel. Eventually it became Nelson Morris & Company and later simply Morris & Company. The Morris plant was one of the first packinghouses to be opened in Chicago at the Union Stock Yards. Outside of Chicago, Morris established packing plants at East St. Louis, Illinois; St. Joseph, Missouri; and Kansas City, Kansas. He also owned large cattle ranches in the Dakotas and in Texas, and was one of the first to import Polled-Angus and Galloway cattle.

Morris became a director in various corporations. He was interested in a number of banks and other financial institutions, among which was the First National Bank of Chicago, in which he had always been a heavy stockholder and had taken a prominent part as a member of its board of directors. He also invested heavily in Chicago real estate. He established the Nelson Morris Institute of Pathological Research, for the purpose of study and original research in connection with diseases of all kinds, and contributed generously to public institutions, notably to the Michael Reese Hospital.

He married in 1863 to Sarah Vogel of Chicago. Of his five

children, Edward Morris succeeded him as president of Morris & Company. Morris died on August 27, 1907 in Chicago, Illinois.

MOSELEY BRAUN, CAROL

Carol Moseley Braun

(1947-) Senator from Illinois; Senate Years of Service: 1993-1999; born in Chicago, Ill., August 16, 1947; educated in Chicago public schools; graduated, University of Illinois 1969; graduated, University of Chicago School of Law 1972; admitted to the Illinois bar in Chicago 1973; prosecutor, office of the United States Attorney, Chicago 1973-1977; member and assistant majority leader, Illinois house of representatives 1978-1988; recorder of deeds, Cook County, Ill., 1988-1992; elected as a Democrat to the United States Senate in 1992, and served from January 3, 1993, to January 3, 1999; unsuccessful candidate for reelection in 1998; ambassador to New Zealand and Samoa, December 15, 1999-2001; candidate for the Democratic nomination for president in 2004; entrepreneur; is a resident of Chicago, Ill., Atlanta, Ga., and Union Springs, Ala.

MOTLEY, WILLARD FRANCIS

(1909-1965) — African American novelist, was born July 14, 1909, in Chicago, Illinois, the son of Florence Motley. He sometimes gave his year of birth as 1912. The Motleys were one of the few African American families in their neighborhood.

From December 1922 through January 1924, as the first "Bud Billiken," Motley edited and wrote a children's column in the *Chicago Defender*. In 1930, the year after his graduation from Englewood High School, he sought fame and adventure by riding a bicycle from Chicago to New York. The following years were spent largely in odd jobs and unsuccessful efforts to have his stories printed. In 1936 and 1938, he traveled by automobile to the West Coast. These two trips provided material for "Adventures and Misadventures of a Fool," several chapters

501

of which appeared as articles in *Commonweal* and various travel magazines.

In 1939, Motley moved to the Chicago slums. With Alexander Saxton, Motley founded and edited *Hull-House Magazine* (1939-1940), to which he contributed sketches of slum neighborhoods. From 1940 through 1942, he was employed by the Works Progress Administration Writers' Project, for which he conducted housing surveys in Chicago's Little Sicily and wrote civil defense material with novelist Jack Conroy. Motley's experiences in the slums resulted in his first novel, *Knock on Any Door*. At about six hundred thousand words, it was submitted to, and rejected by Harper's in 1943. It was accepted by Macmillan after extensive cutting and revision (to a little over tow hundred thousand words), but was then rejected as still too long and too sexually explicit. It was finally accepted by Appleton-Century and published in 1947. The novel remained on the *New York Times* bestseller list for ten months. In 1949, Columbia Pictures released a motion picture version starring Humphrey Bogart.

Motley's second novel, *We Fished All Night* (1951), was written with the support of Newberry and Rosenwald fellowships. This was followed by *Let No Man Write My Epitaph* (1958), which continued *Knock*'s plot and consisted of part of material previously cut from *Knock*. It sold fairly well and was made into a movie by Columbia Pictures (1960).

In September 1951, Motley left the United States for a proposed two-month trip to Mexico. He stayed there, except for occasional trips back to the United States, for the rest of his life. He lived on the outskirts of Mexico City until 1961, and then bought a house near Cuenavaca. An account of his life in Mexico entitled "My House Is Your House," and a novel-length work entitled *Remember Me to Mama*, were both rejected by publishers, although several sections of "My House" appeared in *Rogue*. Motley, who never married, adopted Sergio Lopez, a Mexican boy, as his son. He died in Mexico City in 1965. In 1966, G.P. Putnam's Sons published Motley's last novel, *Let Noon Be Fair*.

MOWRER, PAUL SCOTT

(1887-1971) — War correspondent, Pulitzer Prize winner and poet who was born in Bloomington, Illinois, and traveled all over the world, was born July 14, 1887, to Rufus and Nellie (Scott) Mowrer. He started reporting for the *Chicago Daily News* in 1905. He attended the University of Michigan from 1906 to 1908, but he did not complete his education.

Between 1907 and 1910, he took the opportunity to become a Paris correspondent, and in the meantime also married Winifred Adams, on May 8, 1909. He wrote for the allied armies during the first Balkan War, and then was assigned to the French General Headquarters in 1914, organizing and directing the *Chicago Daily News* war service. He stayed until the end of the war, and then was part of the *Chicago Daily News* Peace Conference Bureau. In April 1918, Mowrer was awarded the Legion of Honor at the French General Headquarters. He stayed in Europe covering the Moroccan campaigns in the Riff, and working as a general correspondent, political analyst, and head of the European Service.

In 1928, he won a Pulitzer Prize for his work as a correspondent, and won the Sigma Delta Chi foreign correspondent's award in 1932. In 1933, just before he returned to the states, Mowrer was promoted to officer of the French General Headquarters. Upon his return he was named associate editor of the *Chicago Daily News*, then was quickly promoted to editor-in-chief, were he stayed for nine years. Just before retiring from newspapers in 1945, he worked for one year as European editor for the *New York Post*. In 1941, he was given an honorary LL.D. from the University of Michigan.

While working as a correspondent, Mowrer was inspired to write poetry. Published collections included *Hours of France*, (1918), *The Good Comrade*, (1923), and after returning to the U.S. he wrote *Poems Between Wars*, (1941). After leaving the newspaper business he wrote numerous other works, including *On Going to Live in New Hampshire* (1953), *And Let the Glory Go* (1955), *Fifi* (1956), *Twenty-One and Sixty-Five* (1958), *The Mothering Land* (1960), *High Mountain Pond* (1962), *School for Diplomats* (1964), *This Teeming Earth* (1965), *Island Ireland* (1966), and finally, *The Poems of Paul Scott Mowrer* (1918-1966). He was editor of the *Golden Quill Anthology*, along with Clarence E. Farrar from 1966 to 1970. He was also a contributor to the *Atlantic, L'Illustration,* and *Writer's Digest,* among other publications. In 1961 and 1962, he was awarded the Lyric Poetry Award for traditional poetry.

Mowrer wrote books other than poetry as well, including *Balkanized Europe* (1921), *Our Foreign Affairs* (1924), his autobiography, *The House of Europe* (1945), *Six Plays*, (1968), and he edited *A Choice of French Poems* (1969). Mowrer died in Beaufort, South Carolina, April 4, 1971. He and his wife had three children.

MULFORD, CLARENCE EDWARD

(1883-1956) — Writer, creator of the western character, "Hopalong Cassidy," was born in Streator, Illinois, on February 3, 1883, the son of Clarence C. Mulford and Minnie Grace Kline. He was educated at the public schools of Streator and at Utica, New York, following the family's move there. After graduating from high school, Mulford began working on the *Municipal Journal and Engineer* in New York City. Then in 1899, he became a clerk in the marriage license bureau at Borough Hall in Brooklyn, New York. At the age of eighteen, Mulford sold his first story, "John Barrett," to *Metropolitan* magazine.

Mulford then published a series of connected stories about a ranch, the Bar 20, in Caspar Whitney's *Outing Magazine*; in 1907, the stories were collected into *Bar 20*. They centered on a rancher named William Cassidy. After Cassidy was wounded in the leg in a gunfight, he acquired the nickname "Hopalong." The book proved so popular that the character was continued in many others: *The Orphan* (1908), *Hopalong Cassidy* (1910), *Bar 20 Days* (1911), *The Coming of Cassidy* (1913), *The Man From Bar 20* (1918), *The Bar 20 Three* (1921), *Hopalong Cassidy Returns* (1924), *The Bar 20 Rides Again* (1926), *Hopalong Cassidy Takes Cards* (1937), and many more. The Cassidy series numbered twenty-eight books. His hardcover books sold more than 1.5 million copies, and were translated into German, Spanish, and Polish.

In 1934, Paramount Pictures decided to make a series of films with Cassidy as a hero. William Boyd was to be the villain, but he persuaded the producers to cast him as the hero instead. Sixty-six Hopalong Cassidy films were made. Mulford was appalled when he saw the result, calling the Cassidy in the movie "an absolutely ludicrous character." Mulford saw only six of the movies. Later, he sold the rights to the character to William Boyd. Mulford, in 1926, moved to Fryeburg, Maine, with his wife, Eva E. Wilkinson, whom he had married on January 5, 1920.

After World War II, Hopalong Cassidy became a great favorite not only in movies but also in the new medium of television, thereby earning Mulford hundreds of thousands of dollars in royalties. He used the money to establish the Clarence E. Mulford Trust Fund, a charitable and educational foundation intended to benefit worthy persons in the area around Fryeburg. In 1954, he gave his manuscripts, books, and card files to the Library of Congress. The Institute Litteraire et Artistique de France awarded him a laurette certificate, with gold medal, for his book *The Round-Up* (1933).

Mulford died on May 10, 1956, in Portland, Maine.

MULLIGAN, CHARLES J., "CHARLEY"

(1866-1916) — Sculptor, was born on September 28, 1866, in Riverdale, County Tyrone, Ireland, and came to this country at the age of seventeen. He found employment as a stonecutter in Pullman, near Chicago, Illinois. Here sculptor Lorado Taft, who was trying to forward artistic craftsmanship by means of a small vocational school in Pullman, discovered him. Soon Taft received him as pupil-assistant in his own studio in Chicago and called upon the apprentice to help in the carving of a marble bust. He also attended evening classes of the Art Institute of Chicago three evenings a week.

In addition to his Art Institute training, he had a brief period of study in Paris, France, under Alexandre Falguiere. In 1891, he was chosen by Taft to be the foreman of his exposition workshop. At the 1901 Buffalo Exposition, his statue *The Digger* attracted attention by its lively sincerity, while his four architectural figures of workingmen for the Illinois building stood forth as unusually good examples in this field. Later, he crafted *Miner and Child* or *Home*, now in Humboldt Park, Chicago. Garfield Park, of the same city, has his statues of *Lincoln as Railsplitter* and of John F. Finerty; his *President McKinley* is in McKinley Park.

He was instrumental in forming the nucleus of the artist colony, "Eagle's Nest," later established in Oregon, Illinois. He was one of the founders of the Palette and Chisel Club, a member of the Society of Western Artists, Society of Chicago Artists, Beaux Arts Club, the Cliff Dwellers, and the Irish Fellowship Club.

After Taft's resignation as head of the department of sculpture at the Art Institute, Mulligan was chosen to this position, in which he remained until his death. Among his many works in the West and South are *Justice and Power*, with *Law and Knowledge*, a pair of entrance groups for the Statehouse in Springfield, Illinois; an impressive statue of General George Rogers Clark in Quincy, Illinois; the soldiers' monument at Decatur, Indiana; and the Illinois monument, depicting Lincoln, the president; Grant, the warrior; and Yates, the governor, at Vicksburg, Mississippi.

In 1889 Mulligan married Margaret Ely, of Chicago; they had three sons. He died on March 25, 1916, in St. Luke's Hospital, Chicago, Illinois.

N

NEF, JOHN ULRIC

(1862-1915) — Chemist, the eldest son of Johann Ulric Nef and Katherine (Mock) Nef, was born in Herisau, Switzerland. In 1864, his father came to the United States and was employed as superintendent of a textile factory in Housatonic, Massachusetts. Four years later, the family joined him, and they settled on a farm near Housatonic. John Nef attended school at Great Barrington, four miles from his home. He had one year in a high school in New York City, and in 1880, he entered Harvard with the intention of studying medicine. He soon became fascinated with chemistry, and in 1884, was awarded the Kirkland Traveling Fellowship. After his graduation, he went to Munich, Germany, and began studying under Adolph von Baeyer, receiving the degree of doctor of philosophy in 1886. His thesis, entitled *Ueber Benzochinoncarbonsauren*, treated of the compounds related to succinosuccinic-ethyl-ester.

In 1887, he returned to the United States as professor of chemistry at Purdue University. Two years later, he went to Clark University as assistant professor of chemistry and was made acting head of the department shortly afterward. He remained until 1892, when he responded to the invitation of President Harper to organize and head the department of chemistry at the University of Chicago. He would hold this position until his death.

It was in Chicago, Illinois, that he met Louise Bates Comstock, who became one of his students and his wife on May 17, 1898; they had one son. She died March on 20, 1909. Nef died of heart disease at Carmel California (1915), while traveling with his son.

Nef's pioneer work on bivalent carbon, on the fulminates, on the sugars, on the mechanism of organic reactions, and on many other subjects contributed greatly to the advance of chemical knowledge. His work on the structure of quinone forms a very important part of the chemistry of dyes and is universally accepted. As a result of his research in organic chemistry, he published thirty-seven independent articles, most of which were written in German. Thirty-six others represent work carried on under him, twenty-eight of which were the theses of those taking the doctorate of philosophy with him. He may be said to have stood for an individual school of thought in organic chemistry, a fact recognized by its separate treatment in advanced texts in this field, but he never assembled his theories of organic chemistry in a single volume, nor wrote a textbook.

His scientific papers may be found scattered through *Justus Liebig's Annalen der Chemie* from volume CCLXX (April 27, 1892) to volume CCCCIII (September 28, 1913) and *Berichte der Deutschen Chemischen Gesellschaft*. His students Hedenburg and Glattfeld assembled after his death the remaining unpublished results of his researches, and published them in the *Journal of the American Chemical Society* (August 1917). Articles prepared in collaboration with his students appeared in the *American Chemical Journal* and the *Journal of the American Chemical Society* during the period of his active work.

NEIHARDT, JOHN GNEISENAU

(1881-1973) — Author and poet, was born on January 8, 1881, in Sharpsburg, Illinois, to Nicholas Nathan and Alice May (Culler) Neihardt. As a child, Neihardt and his family also lived in Kansas City, Missouri, northwestern Kansas, and in Wayne, Nebraska, where he attended Nebraska Normal College and graduated in 1897. After graduating from college, Neihardt worked at odd jobs. Having begun to write verse at the age of twelve, he published his first book, *The Divine Enchantment* in 1900.

In 1901, he went to live among the Omaha Native American tribe of Nebraska and studied their language, customs, religion, and philosophy for six years. He later studied the Oglala Sioux in the same manner. He began writing more, and from 1907 to 1916 he wrote *The Lonesome Trail, A Bundle of Myrrh, Man Song, The River and I, The Dawn-Builder, The Stranger at the Gate, Death of Agrippina, Life's Lure, The Song of Hugh Glass,* and *The Quest.* Other books he wrote include *The Song of Three Friends, The Splendid Wayfaring, Two Mothers, The Song of the Indian Wars, Poetic Values: Their Reality and Our Need of Them, Collected Poems, Indian Tales and Others, Black Elk Speaks, The Song of the Messiah,* and his autobiography, *All Is But a Beginning* (1972).

The Song of Three Friends won a prize from the Poetry Society of America, and in 1921 Neihardt was named poet laureate of Nebraska by special act of the State Legislature. From 1912 to 1923, he was the literary critic for the *Minneapolis Journal*. In 1923, he became professor of poetry at the University of Nebraska and was literary editor of the *St. Louis Post-Dispatch* from 1926 to 1938. From 1944 to 1948, he worked for the Office of Indian Affairs and in 1948, became poet in residence and lecturer in English at the University of Missouri. In 1935, he was honored as the foremost poet of the nation by the National Poetry Center. Other awards received include the Governor's Centennial Award as the Nebraska Poet of the Century in 1967; the Thomas Jefferson Award from the University of Missouri in 1968; the Prairie Poet Laureate of America by the United Poets Laureate International, 1968; the Golden Laurel Wreath from the president of the Republic of the Philippines, 1968; and an annual statewide Neihardt Day was proclaimed by the governor of Nebraska.

John Gneisenau Neihardt married Mona Martinsen, a sculptor, on November 29, 1980. The couple had four children: Enid Neihardt Fink, Sigurd Volsung, Hilda Neihardt Petri, and Alice Neihardt Thompson.

Mona Neihardt died in 1958. In 1961, a bronze bust of Neihardt, which his wife had done before her death, was placed in the rotunda of the Nebraska Capitol by an Act of the State Legislature. Neihardt died in Columbia, Missouri, on November 3, 1973.

NESTOR, AGNES

(1880-1948) — United States labor leader and reformer; she was born in Grand Rapids, Michigan, on June 24, 1880, the daughter of Thomas Nestor and Anna McEwen, second daughter of four children. Her father owned a grocery store at the time of her birth, but later constructed a successful career in local politics as alderman, marshal and treasurer. Her mother was a native of New York State and had worked in the cotton mills before moving. During Agnes' early childhood, the family lived comfortably until her father was defeated in an election for sheriff in the mid-1890s. With difficulty finding work outside of politics in the depressed economy, he moved alone at first, to Chicago in 1896; he became ill and could only find temporary employment. Young Agnes had to leave school and become employed. She would write later in her autobiography, "childhood was over." The rest of the family went to Chicago in 1897.

Agnes began working in the Eisendrath Glove Company factory, where the sixty-hour work week was exhausting; glove operators were made to buy their own needles and machine oil, and pay "rent" on the machines they used. She learned how a resourceful boss could expedite the production of piecework, that is, speed up the quantities being made without increasing the weekly pay. She suffered all the petty, discriminate, and arbitrary tyranny she could handle until she could no longer take it. She had discussed labor problems with her father in the past, but now she was ready for action.

In the spring of 1898 the women, encouraged by their unionized male co-workers, went on strike. Nestor was articulate and outspoken despite a frail appearance and she became spokesperson for the group. Within ten days of the beginning of picketing, all demands were met including an end to "machine rent," which operators had been forced to pay back to the company from the tiny wages, and the establishment of a union shop. In 1902, Nestor helped organize a female glove workers' local and as its president, she represented the local at the founding convention of the International Glove Workers Union (IGWU) later that year, and the following year she was elected as IGWU vice president. She served until 1906 when she was elected to a paid fulltime position as IGWU secretary-treasurer shortly after leaving factory work because of her chronic respiratory problems. Her new position, she later said, "changed the whole course of my life." She served there three years, and was elected president, becoming the first woman to head an international union. She was in that office until 1915.

Nestor realized that working women in all fields needed support despite her commitment to the glove workers' union, and that legal protection was as necessary as well as labor organization. In 1904, she found an institution that had the same concerns, the new National Women's Trade Union League. In 1907, Nestor became its national league board member and in 1913 she became the first working woman to serve as the president of the Chicago League; she held both posts simultaneously for the rest of her life. She worked to organize women in a wide variety of occupations on behalf of the league. She worked with a broad range of fields, from garment workers to milliners to stockyard workers. She helped lead numerous strikes, including the historic garment workers' strike of 1909 and 1910-11; she directed work in the field for the league's Training School for Women Organizers, and lectured often to middle-class audiences.

Nestor cultivated friendships with leading Chicago reformers through the league, such as Jane Addams, Mary McDowell, and Margaret Dreier Robins. With their support, she joined the fight for state laws to protect working women. She was courageous and a relentless lobbyist despite her small of stature physique and low-profile style. She was also very business-like, deeply committed, to many situations needing change, such as the eight-hour workday for women. When she finally realized that goal was not attainable politically, she played a leading role in persuading the state legislators to pass the Ten Hour-Day Law covering female factory workers in 1909. In 1911, a second related law extended the coverage to women in retail positions and clerical jobs. She also waged battles for child-labor laws, minimum wages for women, federal health programs for mothers and their babies, and creation of a public employment service and Women's Bureau in the U.S. Department of Labor.

She was on the National Commission on Vocational Education in 1914, and during World War I she served on a labor mission to England and France, the Woman's Committee of the U.S. Council of National Defense, and the Illinois Survey Commission. In 1928, she ran for the state legislature of Illinois against the incumbent for the Democratic nomination. Her opponent soundly defeated her, however, as neither Nestor's appeal for welfare legislation nor her status as a temperance-minded feminist proved appealing to the broader electorate, although labor and women's groups were supportive.

During the depression, Nestor served on numerous state and municipal boards having to do with labor issues. She played a pivotal role in finally winning the eight-hour workday for women in 1937. That year, her lifelong commitment to the IGWU faced a test, when many members began leaving for a rival union affiliated with the Congress of Industrial Organizations. Nestor remained loyal to the IGWU and worked with the American Federation of Labor (AFL) to restore the union to its former strength. She became the director of research and education for the union in 1938 and served the remainder of her life. During World War II, Nestor lobbied just as she did during World War I for rigid standards of worker safety and well being despite the pressures of wartime production. She wrote a Brief History of the International Glove Workers Union of America (1942) and served on an AFL postwar planning committee.

During her lifetime, Nestor had suffered from recurring serious colds, sinus infections, and bronchial asthma. On a number of occasions, overcome by complete physical and nervous exhaustion, she had to withdraw to sanatoriums for rest. She became weakened by what was diagnosed as rheumatic fever in 1946, and in 1948 she underwent surgery. On December 28, just a few months after being appointed to the Illinois Displaced Persons Commission, she died in Chicago, Illinois. Her contributions to working women can be measured in the institutions she formed and molded, including her own local, the IGWU, the National Women's Trade Union League and dozens of public and private boards.

It can also be measured in the lives she transformed, and the shining example of her own life. In her home state of Illinois, she is best remembered as a lobbyist for protective legislation for women and child workers.

NEWELL, PETER SHEAF MERSEY

(1862-1924) — Cartoonist and illustrator, son of George Frederick and Louisa N. Newell, was born near Bushnell, MacDonough County, Illinois. In spite of an early predilection for sketching and caricaturing, at the age of sixteen he attempted to work in a cigar factory. This experiment lasted three months and was followed by an apprenticeship to a maker of crayon portraits in Jacksonville, Illinois. He made enlargements, thereby gaining his first knowledge of drawing, and though he later studied in an art school he may be said to have been largely self-taught, for his work was free from the prevailing influences in illustration and he evolved a definitely original technique. At about this time he sent a humorous drawing to *Harper's Bazaar* with a note asking the editor whether it showed talent. The reply came back: "No talent indicated," but a check was enclosed. Successful contributions to the *New York Graphic* and various periodicals took him to New York in 1882, where he studied at the Art Students' League. He tolerated academic training only three months, believing that the value of his work would be sacrificed by adapting it to accepted methods. In 1893, using African American subjects in his new flat-tone technique, he achieved success with *Harper's Magazine* (August 1893) and sudden popularity by an amusing bit of nanete: "Wild Flowers."

He contributed full-page illustrations to holiday numbers of *Harper's Weekly* and *Harper's Bazaar*, continued to do comics with captions of his own invention, and then turned this knack to making children's books, starting with *Topsys and Turvys* (1893). This reversible little volume resulted from the distressing occasion upon which he discovered one of his children scrutinizing a picture book upside down. He determined to produce a book that could be looked at from any angle. Thereafter he illustrated contemporary fiction, notably John Kendrick Bangs's *A House-Boat on the Styx* (1896) and *The Pursuit of the Houseboat* (1897), and in 1901 tried his hand at *Alice in Wonderland*. The appearance of substitutes for Sir John Tenniel's inimitable illustrations was attended by considerable controversy. Newell defended the new edition in an article in *Harper's Monthly Magazine* (October 1901), in which he asserted that any distinctly personal reaction to character justifies a new version of interpretation.

Considered by his contemporaries to be an illustrator of ability and conspicuous originality, Newell survived by reason of his good humor rather than on grounds of artistic merit. Whenever his work lacked the animation of wit its execution appears unimpressive. The flat decorative use of wash does not conceal an inadequacy of drawing and composition. His strength lay in whimsical interpretation of nonsense set forth in simple and direct terms. He was inventive rather than imaginative, giving a certain zest to his own cartoons, which is not felt in his illustrations of the ideas of others.

Newell was married on February 5, 1884, to Leona Dow Ashcraft; they had two daughters. He died in 1924 at age sixty-two at Little Neck, Long Island, New York.

NICHOLSON, SETH BARNES

(1891-1963) — Astronomer, was born on November 12, 1891, in Springfield, Illinois, the son of William Franklin Nicholson and Martha Ames. He entered Drake University in Des Moines, Iowa, in 1908, and studied astronomy with D.W. Morehouse, best known for his 1908 discovery of the exceptionally bright comet that bears his name. As an undergraduate, Nicholson devoted his research time to comets and minor planets. In 1911, he and a fellow astronomy student, Alma Stotts, published a report of the computed orbit of the minor planet, Ekard, discovered in 1909. Nicholson also taught physics during his senor year. Nicholson graduated from Drake in 1912, then was appointed a fellow in the graduate program in astronomy at the University of California at Berkeley. Alma Stotts entered the program at the same time, and they were married on May 29, 1913. They had three children.

Beginning in the fall of 1913, Nicholson was instructor in astronomy at Berkeley for two years. He received the Ph.D. in 1915. In 1914, while serving as an assistant at the Lick Observatory, Nicholson was directed to observe the recently discovered eighth satellite of Jupiter. He took an unusually long exposure of Jupiter VIII to insure a superior photographic plate, and discovered yet another Jovian satellite at approximately the same distance from the planet. Calculating the orbital characteristics of Jupiter IX provided Nicholson with his doctoral dissertation. In 1938, he again observed Jupiter (this time with the 100-inch Mt. Wilson telescope) in an attempt to reconfirm the discoveries of the nine known moons. Upon developing his large collection of plates, he discovered two new satellites, raising the total to eleven. In 1951, while observing Jupiter X, he discovered a twelfth moon, therefore becoming, with Galileo one of the two astronomers to have discovered four Jovian satellites.

After completing his doctorate Nicholson joined the staff of the Mt. Wilson Observatory. Because this facility was devoted primarily to solar research during its early years, much of his work focused on the sun. Working with George Ellery Hale and other solar astronomers, he conducted long-term studies of solar spectra and surface features, providing an excellent record of sunspots and other solar phenomena. Later, with Harlow Shapley, Nicholson investigated the spectral patterns of Cepheid variables and collaborated with Walter Baade and Edwin Hubble in similar studies of several spiral galaxies.

During the 1920s and 1930s, Nicholson labored with Edison Pettit to adapt the vacuum thermocouple to measure temperatures of astronomical bodies. They used their new technique to establish the lower temperature of sunspots (compared with the solar surface), the low density of the Martian atmosphere, and the high surface temperature of Mercury. They also made extensive measurements of the rapid changes in the moon's surface temperatures during lunar eclipses, providing significant information about its surface and subsurface structure.

Between 1911 and 1963, he published 267 articles in scientific periodicals. He often lectured at the University of California during the summer, and after his retirement in 1957, served as western coordinator for the visiting professors program of the National Science Foundation and American Astronomical Association.

Nicholson served two terms as president of the Astronomical Society of the Pacific (1935, 1960), and edited its publications from 1940 to 1955. He was chairman of the astronomy section of the American Association for the Advancement of Science in 1944 and a member of the International Astronomical Union. In 1937, he was elected to the National Academy of Sciences. In June 1963, the Astronomical Society of the Pacific awarded Nicholson the Catherine Bruce Gold Medal for his many achievements. He died on July 2, 1963.

NICOLAY, JOHN GEORGE

(1832-1901) — Private secretary and biographer of Lincoln, was a German emigrant born on February 26, 1832, in the village of Essingen, near Landau, in the Rhenish Palatinate, Bavaria, the son of John Jacob and Helena Nicolay. The family, with its five children, sailed from Havre to New Orleans, Louisiana, in 1838, lived for a time in Cincinnati, Ohio;

moved to Indiana; shifted to Missouri; and later settled in Pike County, Illinois, where the father and brothers operated a flour mill for which John George acted as scribe and business interpreter. Upon the death of his parents, Nicolay clerked for a year in a store at White Hall, Illinois, then worked for the *Free Press*, published in the Pittsfield.

John George Nicolay

From printer's devil and typesetter, he became editor-proprietor of the paper in 1854. In 1856, he sold the *Free Press*, and became a clerk for the secretary of state in Springfield. Now an ardent Republican, he became acquainted with Abraham Lincoln, whose private secretary he became upon Lincoln's nomination for the U.S. presidency.

Nicolay fully enjoyed Lincoln's confidence. Sometimes his duties were more than secretarial, as when he attended the Republican convention at Baltimore, Maryland, in June 1864 to "watch proceedings" (that is, to promote Lincoln's interests). Nicolay served as consul at Paris, France, 1865-1869; in 1872, he became marshal of the U.S. Supreme Court, serving until 1887. For fifteen arduous years, 1875-1890, he collaborated with John Hay on the ten-volume biography entitled *Abraham Lincoln: A History* (1890). Nicolay spent six years collecting and arranging the elaborate mass of Lincoln papers loaned by Robert Lincoln. Besides the Lincoln collection, his other writings include *The Outbreak of Rebellion* (1881), which was the initial volume of a series published by Scribner's, entitled *Campaigns of the Civil War*; the article on Lincoln in the ninth edition of the *Encylopaedia Britannica* (1882); *A Short Life of Abraham Lincoln* (1902); the Civil War chapters in the *Cambridge Modern History* (1903); and numerous magazine articles.

On June 15, 1865, Nicolay was married to Therena Bates of Pittsfield, Illinois; she died in November 1885. His later years were spent in Washington, D.C., where he died on September 26, 1901, survived by his daughter. A son had died in infancy.

NORRIS, CHARLES GILMAN SMITH

(1881-1945) — Novelist, was born on April 23, 1881, in Chicago, Illinois, to Benjamin Franklin Norris and Gertrude Glorvina (Doggett) Norris. The family moved to Oakland, California, in 1884, and the following year to San Francisco. In 1887, they spent a year in London and Paris, where Norris wrote his first story, a historical romance about Louis XIV composed at age ten. Back in California, the boys' father abandoned his family in 1892, to be divorced by his wife five years later. Norris completed his education in California, graduating from the University of California with the Ph.B. in 1903.

He then went to New York City to serve as an assistant editor of the magazine *Country Life in America*. He returned to San Francisco in 1905 to become the circulation manager of *Sunset* magazine, then issued by the Southern Pacific Railroad. It was in *Sunset* that his first published fiction appeared: a sentimental story reminiscent of Bret Harte ("An Audience of One," December 1906); and it was during this period that he met a young San Francisco newspaper-woman, Kathleen Thompson, who became his wife on April 30, 1909. They were married in New York City, where Norris had moved the year before to become art editor of the *American Magazine*. They had three children: a son, Frank, who became a physician, and twin daughters who died in infancy. Some years later, in 1918, they adopted another son, William Rice Norris.

Charles Norris remained on the reform-conscious *American* staff until 1913, serving briefly also as assistant editor of the *Christian Herald* in 1912. He then resigned all regular employment, for the rapidly increasing income from his wife's fiction made it possible for both to become full-time writers.

Norris's first novel, *The Amateur* (1916), was followed by *Salt, or The Education of Griffith Adams*, (1918). Enlisting that year in the R.O.T.C., Norris served until the Armistice as an infantry officer. In 1919, he and his wife lived in Rio de Janeiro, where Norris wrote his third novel, *Brass* (1921), but the death of his mother brought them back to California, where they finally settled on a ranch in Saratoga.

His many works also include: *Bread* (1923), *Zelda Marsh* (1927), *Zest* (1933), *Hands* (1935), and *Bricks without Straw* (1938), *Pig Iron* (1925), *Seed* (1930), and *Flint* (1944). Norris's novels were generally well received. *Seed* sold more than 70,000 copies in its first edition and *Brass*, another bestseller, was made into a motion picture (1923). Aside from his novels, Norris wrote a few short stories and some poetic dramas for the Bohemian Club of San Francisco. He edited the manuscript of Frank Norris's (his brother) *Vandover and the Brute*, published in 1914 after Frank Norris's death.

He died on July 25, 1945, in Palo Alto of a heart ailment and was buried there at Alta Mesa Cemetery.

NORRIS, FRANKLIN, "FRANK"

(1870-1902) — Author, was born on March 5, 1870, in Chicago, Illinois, to Benjamin Franklin and Gertrude G. Norris. In 1884, Norris went with his family to San Francisco. He attended a boy's school at Belmont, California, and then studied art at the Julian Academy in Paris for two years. He enrolled in the University of California in 1890.

His first book, *Yvernelle*, a three-canto poem of medieval France, was published in 1891. He studied at Harvard University in 1890 and 1895, before he was sent to Johannesburg, South Africa, by the San Francisco *Chronicle*, Chicago *Inter-Ocean*, and *Harper's Weekly*. During the Jameson raid, he rode as a courier for John Hays Hammond and his allies. When the raid failed, he was ordered out of Transvaal by the Boer government. Returning to San Francisco, he contributed to the San Francisco *Wave* in 1896 and 1897. In 1898, Doubleday publishers sent Norris to Cuba as a war correspondent. During that same year, his first novel, *Moran of the Lady Letty*, was published. This was followed by *McTeague* (1899), *Blix* (1899), and *A Man's Woman* (1900). *The Octopus*, the first book in a trilogy, was published in 1901.

Unfortunately, Norris died before he could complete the trilogy. The second book, *The Pit*, was published posthumously. The third book was never written. Among the collected works, which were published after his death, were *A Deal in White*, *The Responsibility of the Novelist*, and *The Third Cafe*. Another novel, *Vandover and the Brute*, appeared in 1914.

Norris married Jeanette Williamson Black in 1899. He died on October 25, 1902, in San Francisco, California.

Franklin "Frank" Norris

517

NOVY, FREDERICK GEORGE

(1864-1957) — Microbiologist, was born in Chicago, Illinois, on December 9, 1864. He graduated with a B.S. from the University of Michigan in 1886. His first work after graduation, in the Department of Organic Chemistry at the University of Michigan, was on cocaine and its derivatives. In 1887, Victor C. Vaughan, professor of hygiene and physiological chemistry at the university, persuaded him to accept a position as instructor in that department.

Novy's first publication in bacteriological chemistry (1888), jointly with Vaughan, was on ptomaines and leucomaines. In the summer of 1888, he and Vaughan traveled to the Hygiene Institute in Berlin to study under Robert Koch, then the leading authority in bacteriology. On his return, Novy taught the first course on bacteriology to be offered at an American university. At the same time, he undertook research of the development of techniques for the cultivation of pathogenic bacteria. Novy received a Sc.D. in 1890 and an M.D. in 1891 from the University of Michigan. The latter year, he married; from this marriage there were five children. In 1894, he published his first text on bacteriology, *Directions for Laboratory Work in Bacteriology*. In the same year, he studied at the Pathological Institute in Prague. In 1897, he worked at the Pasteur Institute in Paris.

At Michigan, Novy made his first major discovery: the isolation of *Clostridium novyii*, an anaerobic bacillus capable of causing Latal septicemia in animals (1894). By 1900, he was an authority on bacteriology and communicable diseases. In 1901, he served on a federal commission investigating a possible bubonic plague outbreak in San Francisco. Novy also had been active on the Michigan Board of Health (1897-1899). He was involved in the founding of a number of societies and journals specializing in bacteriology, including the Society of American Bacteriologists, of which he became president in 1904. By then, he had become professor and head of the Department of Bacteriology at the University of Michigan.

Shortly after 1900, Novy began his work on trypanosomes and spirochetes. Once more, he concentrated first on the development of methods for laboratory cultivation. His work on spirochetes, the etiological agents of relapsing fevers, led to the identification of a particular organism, now called *Spirocheta novyi*. Novy's work on trypanosomes led to a lengthy period of investigation of the artificial stimulation of resistance to trypanosome infections. This work culminated in the publication, with P. H. de Kruif and others, of nine papers on anaphylactic shock (1917).

The last major research field in which Novy worked was the study of the metabolism of microorganisms, particularly the tubercle bacillus. In collaboration with Malcolm H. Soule, he published an account of the respiration of this organism and its dependence on the magnitude of the chemical potential of the oxygen in the host animal (1925).

Novy's later years were increasingly devoted to administrative matters. He was chairman of the Executive Committee of the University of Michigan Medical School from 1930 to 1933 and dean from then until 1935. Many honors were conferred on him, including election to the National Academy of Sciences in 1934.

His colleagues and former students at the University of Michigan continued Novy's work after his retirement. In fact, in 1953, eighteen years after his retirement, some tubes of dried rat blood, missing since 1920, were found and shown to contain a still-viable filterable agent that Novy had been investigating when the tubes were lost. Using Novy's carefully kept records from that era, workers were able to identify this filterable agent as a virus. This work was published in the *Journal of Infectious Diseases*, with Novy as one of the authors. He died on August 8, 1957, at Ann Arbor.

O

OBAMA, BARACK HUSSEIN

(1961-) — United States Senator, author, born on August 4, 1961, in Honolulu, Hawaii, the son of Barack Obama, Sr., and Ann Dunham. The senior Obama, born in Kenya, had grown up herding goats with his own father, but excelled in academics, which allowed him to study beyond Kenya's borders, and he earned a scholarship that took him to the University of Hawaii at Manoa, on the island of Oahu.

Obama's mother, born and raised in Kansas, had moved to Honolulu with her parents, and attended the University at Manoa's East-West Center, where she met the senior Barack Obama. The couple married in 1960.

When young Obama was just two years old, Barack senior and Ann separated, later divorcing. Obama senior went to Harvard University, in Boston, where he earned a Ph.D. in economics, and later returned to Kenya. Young Barack only saw his father once more, at age ten; and the senior Obama died in an automobile accident, in Kenya, in 1982.

Ann married an Indonesia army officer who was studying at the East-West center in Manoa, and in 1967, six year old Barack, whose name means "blessed," accompanied his mother and step-father to Jakarta, Indonesia, where Barack spent four years in school, learning the Indonesian language in just six months. Seeking to give her son a Western education, Ann sent Obama back to Hawaii, in 1971, where he lived with his grandparents, and attended the prestigious Punahou Academy, in Honolulu.

Barack Obama

He attended Occidental College, in Los Angeles, for two years, and then transferred to Columbia University, in New York, where he received his bachelor's degree in 1983, majoring in political science. After graduation, Obama

521

moved to Chicago, and worked as a community organizer, primarily among the residents of a housing project on the south side.

Continuing his formal education, Obama entered the Harvard School of Law in 1988. In 1990, he was selected as president of the school's *Harvard Law Review*, a respected legal journal. He received his J.D., in 1991, graduating *magna cum laude*.

Returning to Chicago after graduation, Obama worked as a civil-rights lawyer, and lectured on constitutional law at the University of Chicago Law School. Obama was active in politics as an organizer, and in 1992, worked on voter registration for future president Bill Clinton's campaign. In 1996, he ran for office as an Illinois State Senator, representing Hyde Park on the South Side, on the Democratic ticket.

In 2000, Obama lost an election for the 1st Congressional district in Illinois, to Rep. Bobby Rush, the incumbent. In 2004, he won decisively in an election for a U.S. Senate seat representing Illinois. Only the third African American to serve in the Senate since the days of Reconstruction, Obama gained national recognition when he delivered a stirring keynote address at the Democratic National Convention, in Boston, Massachusetts.

Obama is the author of two popular non-fiction books: *Dreams from my Father*, a 1995 autobiographical work, and *The Audacity of Hope*, a 2004 book of politics, patriotism, and values, that amplifies themes from his memorable keynote speech at the 2004 Democratic Convention.

In early 2008, the Senator is widely considered to be the top contender for nomination as the Democratic Party's Presidential Candidate for the fall, 2008 election. Married in 1992, to Michelle Robinson, the Obamas have two daughters. The family lives in Chicago, Illinois.

OCKERSON, JOHN AUGUSTUS

(1848-1924) — Engineer, was born in the province of Skane, Sweden, the son of Jans and Rose (Datler) Akerson. When he was two years old, the family immigrated to Chicago, Illinois. On the trip overland from New York, both parents and the eldest son died of cholera. He then lived with relatives who settled near Elmwood, Illinois, and received his early training in the Elmwood public schools. After coming to America, the family Anglicized the spelling of their name to Ockerson. In the spring of 1864, when only sixteen, he enlisted in the 132nd Illinois Infantry, but was mustered out after less than six months' service. In January 1865, he again enlisted, this time in the First Minnesota Heavy Artillery, with which he served until the end of the Civil War.

In 1869, he entered the civil engineering course at the University of Illinois, graduating in 1873. Upon leaving the University, he became principal assistant engineer in the federal Great Lakes Survey, and for five years was engaged in hydrographic, topographic, and triangulation surveys, including the survey for the famous jetties at the mouth of the Mississippi constructed by James Buchanan Eads. When an act of Congress established the Mississippi River Commission in 1879, Ockerson was appointed its principal assistant engineer in charge of surveys and physical examinations from the source of the river to the Gulf. Nine years later, when the work of the commission temporarily slackened because appropriations were reduced, he left the service for a short period to engage in a mining venture in Colorado. He returned to his old position in 1890, however, and occupied it until 1898, when he was appointed to a membership on the commission, which he held until his death.

In his later years, Ockerson was internationally recognized as a leading authority on river and harbor improvement, navigation, and related problems, and developed a large consulting practice at home and abroad. One of his greatest individual achievements, undertaken in 1910, was the construction of levees to control the floodwaters of the Colorado River, which threatened to overflow into the Salton Sea. For the successful completion of this work, Ockerson received personal commendation from President William H. Taft. He was the U.S. delegate to four International Congresses on Navigation (1900, 1905, 1908, 1912) and received many honors and decorations from foreign governments. In 1912 he was elected to the presidency of the American Society of Civil Engineers. His numerous contributions to technical literature were mostly in the form of official reports issued in connection with his work for the Mississippi River Commission. An especially elaborate report, on the opening and maintaining of navigation channels in rivers by hydraulic dredging, based as it was on original observation and experiment, will stand as one of the greatest contributions to this important field: "Dredges and Dredging of the Mississippi River."

Ockerson was twice married: on November 3, 1875, to Helen M. Chapin, who died in March 1886; and on June 4, 1890, to Clara W. Shackelford who survived him. He died on March 22, 1924, at his home in St. Louis, Illinois, after an apoplectic stroke.

OGDEN, WILLIAM BUTLER

(1805-1877) — Railroad president and manufacturer, was born in Walton, New York, and entered into a business career at an early age. In 1834 he also was member of the New York Legislature. The next year, he went to Chicago to investigate a land investment his brother-in-law had made there. To his dismay, he found it only marshland, knee-deep in water and smelling of wild onion.

He perceived the land to be worthless, and was astonished when he put it up for sale and made a huge profit. He then went into real estate for himself in the new city, seeing the land's value there triple in a few months. In 1837, Chicago was incorporated and Ogden become its first mayor, and was instrumental in aiding the city's industrialization and growth. By 1847, the area was a major trading center for farmer's grain and hundreds of wagons rode through the streets and ships docked in the swampy harbor to buy and sell goods. Ogden decided then that the city needed a railroad, and he became president of the new Chicago & Galena Railroad Company. In 1848, a train first pulled into Chicago with a carload of wheat. In the following years, Ogden also supported expanded ship canals through the Great Lakes, including one across the Michigan Peninsula. In 1855, he was president of the Chicago, St. Paul & Fond du Lac Railroad and merged it with his original company in 1864, calling the conglomerate the Chicago & Northwestern Railroad. He was also the first president of the Union Pacific Railroad, supporting efforts for passage to the Pacific. He also took a half-interest in the McCormick, Ogden & Company, which produced Cyrus McCormick's famous harvesters. He died in New York a millionaire in 1877.

William Butler Ogden

OGILVIE, RICHARD B.

(1923-1988) — Thirty-seventh governor of Illinois (1969-1973), was born in Kansas City, Missouri, to Edna May Buell and Kenneth S. Ogilvie. He studied at Yale University after attending schools in his hometown, and in 1942, enlisted in the U. S. Army, where he served for three years. He suffered face and jaw wounds in action as a tank commander in France.

After his discharge, Ogilvie returned to Yale and graduated in 1947, afterward attending law school at Chicago-Kent College. Upon passing the bar, he began practicing law in Chicago, from 1950 to 1958. He also held a job as Assistant U S. Attorney in 1954-1955, and his political involvement became deeper when he became Special Assistant to the U. S. Attorney General between 1951 and 1961.

Ogilvie was a leader in the movement against Chicago mobsters, heading a special Midwest office on organized crime. The reputation he gained in this position led to his election as the Republican candidate for Cook County Sheriff in 1962, and in 1966, he was elected president of the county's Board of Commissioners. Two years later, he was voted into the governor's seat, defeating Democratic incumbent Shapiro.

Richard B. Ogilvie

While in office, Ogilvie kept up the modernist reform movement that had swept the state in the mid-1960s. He hired young "whiz kids" to streamline and improve the quality of executive agencies and bring the state budget under control. A new income tax law doubled the state's income during his term, allowing more funding for local schools and police departments. Direct revenue sharing for local governments was also begun in these years. Ogilvie helped begin a massive road-building plan for the state, as well as the fast-growing higher education complex.

Ogilvie lost in the next gubernatorial election, and accepted an appointment as chairman of the Young Republicans of Cook County. He died in March 1988.

OGLESBY, RICHARD JAMES

(1824-1899) — Fourteenth, sixteenth, and twentieth governor of Illinois (1865-1869, 1873, and 1885-1889), was born in Kentucky to Isabel Walton and Jacob Oglesby. Orphaned at the age of eight, Oglesby was sent to Decatur, Illinois, to live with an uncle. After attending local schools and later the law school of Silas W. Robbins in Springfield, he began a law practice in Sullivan, Illinois.

When the Mexican War broke out, Oglesby was commissioned as a first lieutenant in Company C of the Fourth Illinois Infantry. In this capacity, he took part in battles at Vera Cruz and Cerro Gordo. The next year, he returned to Illinois to practice law at Decatur, and later graduated from the school of law in Louisville, Kentucky. For a time, Oglesby traveled around California mining for gold, but soon returned to practice law and enter political life.

He was an unsuccessful candidate in the race for U.S. House of Representatives in 1858, but was elected to the state senate in 1860.

Richard James Oglesby

After only one session, however, he responded to the call to arms and became colonel to a volunteer infantry in the Civil War. After a show of courage at Fort Henry, Oglesby was made a brigadier general. In a subsequent battle, however, he was so severely wounded that he was forced to return home.

After an eight-month recuperation, he addressed the state legislature in 1864. His speech denounced certain Democratic members of the senate and House for "treason" because of their efforts to nullify Governor Richard Yates' war measures. Many were impressed by Oglesby's speech, and a few months later, he resigned his appointment as Major General of the state's volunteers to accept an election as state governor.

His first term in office set the tone for the state's growth. During that time, a state board of equalization was formed, two amendments to the constitution were ratified, a penitentiary was built, and other institutions and asylums were constructed. He returned to private practice in 1869, but was reelected under the Republican Party ticket several years later.

Oglesby's second term only lasted a few months, however, since he was elected to the U.S. Senate. His third term, which began more than ten years later, was characterized by changes in the state's election processes. For example, the Citizen's Election Bill was passed, limiting the number of persons able to vote in a district to 450.

Oglesby was often referred to fondly as "Uncle Dick." After his third term in office, he retired to private life in Elkhart, Illinois, where he died in 1899.

P

PAINE, RALPH DELAHAYE

(1871-1925) — Journalist and author, was born on August 28, 1871, in Lemont, Illinois, the son of Reverend Samuel Delahaye Paine and Elizabeth Brown (Philbrook) Paine. The family moved to Jacksonville, Florida, where his father held a small parish. Paine saved enough from his salary as a twelve-dollar-a-week reporter to enter Yale College in the fall of 1890. He then began to cover the athletic news for a syndicate of over twenty newspapers and thereby pay for the whole of his own education and a part of his sister's schooling. Immediately after graduation in 1894, he joined the staff of the *Philadelphia Press*, and two years later he was sent to England to cover the Yale-Oxford crew race, serving again in 1904 in a similar capacity for *Collier's Weekly* at the track meet between the Yale-Harvard and Oxford-Cambridge teams.

Paine served as a war correspondent during the Cuban revolution and the Spanish-American War, combining newsgathering with filibustering under the doughty captain "Dynamite Johnny O'Brien." In 1900, Paine was sent to China to cover the Boxer Uprising, and in 1902, the *New York Herald* placed him in charge of its campaign against the beef trust, a campaign that brought him notice because of its notable success. After a brief connection with the *New York Telegraph* as managing editor, Paine gave up journalism and began his career as fiction writer and historian.

His researches as a historian led him to Salem, Massachusetts, where he delved into the history of Yankee shipping and published his results in *The Ships and Sailors of Old Salem* (1909), *The Old Merchant Marine* (1919), and *The Fight for a Free Sea* (1920). He wrote a number of boys' stories, such as *The Stroke Oar* (1908), *College Years* (1909), *Sandy Sawyer, Sophomore* (1911), and *First Down, Kentucky!* (1921), as well as a number of stories focused on the call of the sea, including *The Praying Skipper and Other Stories* (1906), *The Wrecking Master* (1911), *The Adventures of Captain O'Shea* (1913), *The Call of the Off-Shore Wind* (1918). In 1917, Paine was appointed special observer with the Allied fleets.

On April 5, 1903, Paine married Mrs. Katharine Lansing Morse of Watertown, New York, and in 1908 they moved to Durham, New Hampshire. Paine represented Durham in the State Legislature (1919) and served on the state board of education from 1919 to 1921. He was presented a medal by the citizens of Dunkirk, France, in gratitude for his kindness to the citizens of that city during the war.

He died on April 29, 1925, in Concord, New Hampshire. He was survived by his widow, and by five children, two of whom were stepchildren.

PALEY, WILLIAM SAMUEL

(1901-1990) — Owner and president of the Columbia Broadcasting System (CBS), was born on September 28, 1901, in Chicago, Illinois, to Goldie (Drell) Paley and Samuel Paley. He attended Western Military Academy at Alton, Illinois, and studied at the University of Chicago. He then went to school at the University of Pennsylvania where he graduated in 1922. After college, he worked for his father's cigar business and was soon vice-president in charge of advertising and production.

While Paley was overseas in the summer of 1927, his father and uncle negotiated an advertising contract with Independent Broadcasters network for thirteen weeks of radio broadcasting. When he came back from his trip, he discovered that sales were up because of the advertising and became extremely interested in radio. Paley bought the still fairly new but floundering network for a half a million dollars. At the time of Paley's purchase, the network, whose name he changed to Columbia Broadcasting System, had nineteen stations in the northeastern part of the United States. By 1940, Columbia had 121 stations in the United States, Canada and Puerto Rico.

Paley was the first ever to hire stars from other areas of the entertainment industry, such as Will Rogers and Paul Whiteman, to make appearances on radio. He also aired educational, religious and cultural programming as well as news. In the early years, Columbia covered such events as the abdication of King Edward VIII, the Austrian "Anchluss," and the Czech crisis.

Paley went overseas in 1943 to work for the Office of War Information as a civilian. He reorganized Allied radio activities in North Africa and restored radio service in Italy after the Germans were forced to leave. He received a commission to colonel in the U.S. Army in 1945, and became deputy chief of the Psychological Warfare Division. In 1945, he was discharged from active duty and returned to New York, where he began a reorganization of CBS.

Paley also purchased Hytron Radio and Electronics Corporation in order to manufacture television sets in the early 1950s. The venture supposedly cost CBS $50 million by the time it was abandoned. In 1953, the Federal Communications Commission (FCC) rejected the rotating disc system for color television developed by CBS because it was not compatible with existing black and white sets. The purchase of the New York Yankees baseball team in the late 1960s proved unsuccessful as well as the Electronic Video Recording (EVR) system.

Paley stepped down from the position of chief executive officer of CBS in 1977, but remained the chairman of the corporation until 1983, when he became executive committee chairman of the board of CBS. He also became a partner of the Whitcom Investment Company in that same year.

Paley wrote of his life and the history of CBS in his autobiography, *As It Happened: A Memoir*, which was published in 1979. He was also the recipient of many awards and honors including the Medallion of Honor of the City of New York, 1965; the Gold Achievement medal from the Poor Richard Club; the Keynote Award from the National Association of Broadcasters; a special award from the Broadcast Pioneers; the Concert Artist Guild Award; the Sknowhegan Gertrude Vanderbilt Whitney Award; and a gold medal from the National Planning Association.

William Paley married Dorothy Hart Hearst in 1932. The couple had a son, Jeffrey and a daughter, Hilary. Paley died on October 26, 1990, in Manhattan, New York.

PALMER, JOHN MCAULEY

(1817-1900) — Fifteenth governor of Illinois (1869-1873), was born at Eagle Creek, Kentucky, the son of Ann Hansford Tun and Louis D. Palmer. His family moved to Illinois because of strong anti-slavery principles in 1831. They settled near Alton, and three years later, John entered Shurtleff College at Upper Alton. He taught school while studying law and was admitted to the bar in 1839

After starting a practice at Carlinville, Palmer was appointed Probate Judge of Macoupin County in 1845, and in 1847, he helped

John McAuley Palmer

reframe the state constitution. Under the new constitution, he was elected County Judge in 1848, and gained enough support to be elected to the state senate in 1852. Two years later he resigned, however, because of political differences among his colleagues.

For a few years, he became involved in Republican Party activities, presiding over the first party convention in the state in 1856, and serving as a delegate to the national convention in 1859. He was also an elector to the ticket in 1860. After serving as a delegate to the Peace Convention in Washington in 1861, Palmer was commissioned a colonel in the Fourteenth Regiment of the state volunteer army. He was honorably mustered out after five years of service, which included his command of the first brigade of the First Division Army of the Mississippi and other major roles for which he was well honored.

Palmer returned to his Carlinville law practice, but soon became engaged in state politics again in Springfield. He was elected on the Republican ticket for governor in 1869. In 1871, he was successful in giving relief for victims of the Chicago fire.

During his governorship, Palmer also switched party loyalties, becoming a Democratic in order to support Horace Greeley for President. After 1873, Palmer once again returned to his law practice, this time in Springfield. He served as a delegate to the Democratic National Convention in 1884, and was elected as the liberal, pro-labor candidate for the U.S. Senate in 1891. He did not run for reelection in 1897, and in 1896, he was unsuccessful in a candidacy for President.

After returning once again to his law practice, Palmer died at his Springfield home in 1900. His family published his memoirs, *Personal Recollections of John M. Palmer-The Story of an Earnest Life,* in 1891.

PALMER, POTTER

(1826-1902) — Merchant, was born on May 20, 1826, in Albany County, New York, to farmers. After attending local schools, he left home to become a merchant. His first job, at seventeen, was at a dry-goods store in Durham, New York, and in two years he was made manager of the establishment. His father helped him open his own store in Oneida, New York, and soon he opened a larger store in Lockport, Illinois; however, he grew tired of small towns and in 1852, the year the railroads opened the way between the East Coast and the Midwest, he traveled to Chicago, Illinois, to open up a dry-goods store on Lake Street. The business quickly gained notoriety for its pioneering displays and advertising as well as Palmer's insistence on politeness in the store's clerks.

Geared toward "giving the Chicago lady what she wants," Palmer's store was the first to allow refunds on as much as it delighted the customers, but after ten years of business, Palmer was ready to retire as a wealthy man, the owner of the largest mercantile business in the city. In 1867, he decided to sell the business in the city to Levi Leiter and Marshall Field. He rested for a time at his physician's advice, but made investments which allowed him to buy a solid mile of land along the east side of State Street. Even after the fire of 1871, he made the

Potter Palmer

street into the business center it is today, first by building the enormous Palmer House and other buildings there, and also by widening the street by twenty feet. The street took on a characteristic look of Victorian opulence, and Palmer's mansion on the north side of the city set the trend for elite living. He also worked toward changing the swamps and sand dunes of the city into the now elegant Lake Shore Drive district. He died on May 4, 1902, in Chicago, Illinois.

PARRINGTON, VERNON LOUIS

(1871-1929) — Teacher, philologist, and historian, was born on August 3, 1871, in Aurora, Illinois, the son of John William and Louise (McClellan) Parrington. He attended the College of Emporia, a Presbyterian institution, for several years, was admitted as a junior to the class of 1893 at Harvard College, and after graduating, returned home to teach. He was instructor in English and French at the College of Emporia, 1893-1897; instructor in English and modern languages, 1897-1898, and professor of English, 1898-1908, at the University of Oklahoma; and assistant professor of English, 1908-1912, and professor of English from 1912 until his death at the University of Washington.

On July 31, 1901, he married Julia Rochester Williams; they had two daughters and a son. He taught in the summer sessions of the University of California in 1922, of Columbia University in 1923, and of the University of Michigan in 1927. At the University of Washington, he developed a notable series of courses in the history of American literature and thought. Outside the university he was little known until the first two volumes of his *Main Currents in American Thought* were published in the spring of 1927. The work was recognized at once as the most scholarly and original study of American literature.

Parrington's publications were "The Puritan Divines, 1620-1720," published in The Cambridge History of American Literature (1917); The Connecticut Wits (1926); Sinclair Lewis: Our Own Diogenes (1927); Main Currents in American Thought: An Interpretation of American Literature from the Beginning to 1920 (three volumes, 1927), the volumes bearing the subtitles of The Colonial Mind (1927), The Romantic Revolution in America (1927), and The Beginnings of Critical Realism in America (1930), which was published as he left it, incomplete and some of it not in its final form; articles entitled, "American Literature to the End of the Nineteenth Century" and "Nathaniel Hawthorne" in the Encyclopaedia Britannica (1929); the article on Brook Farm in the Encyclopaedia of the Social Sciences; the chapter, "The Development of Realism," in The Reinterpretation of American Literature (1928), edited by Norman Foerster; the introduction to James Allen Smith's The Growth and Decadence of Constitutional Government (1930); and a number of book reviews in the Nation, the Saturday Review of Literature, Books, and other periodicals. He died in 1929.

PARSONS, ALBERT RICHARD

(1848-1887) — Radical labor organizer, born on June 24, 1848, in Montgomery, Alabama, to Samuel and Elizabeth (Tompkins) Parsons. His parents died when he was five, and Parsons went to Texas to live with his older brother William. Parsons attended public schools until age thirteen, when he was apprenticed to a printer for the Galveston *Daily News*.

The Civil War broke out in April 1861, and Parsons joined the Confederate's military forces. He served in a number of different positions and eventually was in a company led by his brother. After the war, Parsons bought a farm in Waco and hired freedmen to help him work the land. The money generated from the farm allowed Parsons to briefly attend Waco University, where he learned typesetting.

Although he had fought for the Confederacy, Parsons joined the Radical Republicans and worked toward securing rights for African Americans. He helped freedmen register to vote throughout the state, an act that did not make him popular with most of the local white population. Parsons began publishing the Republican paper *The Spectator* in 1868. His newspaper, expressing his views in favor of the Reconstruction policies, did not make much money, and he had to stop its publication.

In the early 1870s, Parsons was selected by the Radical Republicans in Congress to fill a few government positions. He met his wife Lucy Eldine Gonzalez, who was believed to be of Mexican, Native American, and African American ancestry, while traveling through Texas in 1871. Even though Texas law prohibited people of different races to marry, Parsons claimed to have married her in 1872.

Albert Richard Parsons

His marriage, Republican affiliations, and his work in registering African Americans to vote made him extremely disliked. He was threatened numerous times, shot in the leg, and beaten for his activities. At the end of Reconstruction in 1873, he and his wife left Texas. They settled in Chicago, Illinois, where Parsons took a job as a typesetter at the *Times* and joined the Typographical Union.

The Parsons family lived in a poor immigrant neighborhood, where they saw the hardships workers faced. Parsons was outraged by the injustices these laborers faced, and he became a member of the Social Democratic Party of North America, and the Knights of Labor. He became an advocate for social change in Chicago. He helped rally the workers during the railroad strikes of July 1877. He was fired from his job at the *Times* and was blacklisted. His wife supported the family as a seamstress while Parsons continued to fight for rights for workers.

Parsons unsuccessfully ran for a number of political positions. After his lack of success in the political arena, he joined more radical trade unionists, many of which were anarchists. One of his allies was the anarchist August Spies. Parsons began editing the English language version of Spies' *Arbeiter-Zeitung*, *The Alarm*, which was a publication that called upon workers to rise up against their oppressors.

Labor leaders organized a mass demonstration in support of the eight-hour-day on May 4, 1886, at Haymarket Square. At the last minute, Spies, who was one of the organizers, asked Parsons to speak at the demonstration. Parsons spoke for an hour to a peaceful crowd and then went home. After he left, an unknown person threw a bomb into the crowd that killed a police officer. The police began shooting into the crowd. By the time the situation was under control, approximately fourteen people were dead (exact number unknown because many were afraid to visit hospitals), and many more were injured.

Several anarchists were arrested soon after the riot. Parsons left town, but returned and turned himself in to authorities. He was arrested and brought to trial. He used his trial to give a speech arguing for an eight-hour-day. Parsons was convicted, along with seven others, for causing the bombing in Haymarket Square. Parsons was sentenced to death. Although two of his convicted comrades sought clemency from the governor, Parsons refused, and was hanged on November 11, 1887, along side August Spies, Adolph Fisher, Louis Lingg, and George Engel. Parsons was survived by his wife and two children.

Lucy Parsons

PARSONS, LUCY

(1853-1942) — Writer and labor organizer, born Lucy Eldine Gonzalez, in Buffalo Creek, Texas. Nothing is known for certain about her parents. She is believed to be from African American, Native American, and Mexican ancestry. She reportedly used a few different maiden names before settling on Gonzalez. It is speculated that she may have been a slave on the Gathings' plantation in Texas.

She met her husband, Albert Parsons, in 1871, and married him the following year. They lived briefly in Waco, Texas, but moved to Chicago, Illinois, after her husband received numerous threats, and was shot in the leg for his work in registering freedmen to vote. They settled into a poor neighborhood inhabited by German immigrants. Surrounding them were sweatshops where Parsons witnessed the atrocities committed against workers.

Parson's husband joined the Social Democratic Party of North America, and through its members, Parsons came into contact with Marxist ideas, and came to believe that economics were the cause of oppression. Like her husband, she became a champion of the rights of workers, and became a radical activist. Parsons helped organize the Working Women's Union, and began advocating for socialist reforms through writing articles in such publications as the *Socialist*.

In 1877, a railroad workers strike swept the country. Beginning on the east coast, it spread to Chicago. Parsons' husband gave a speech to the railroad men, calling for a revolution. He was consequently fired from his job and blacklisted. Parsons had to support her family, which now had two more mouths to feed. She worked as a seamstress and opened her own dress shop. During this time, she continued to write and became more political. She joined the Socialist Revolutionary Club, and 1883, she helped August Spies found the International Working People's Association. In 1884, she published her most famous article, "To Tramps: The Unemployed, the Disinherited, and Miserable" in the *Alarm*, which her husband was editing.

Her views leaned more toward anarchism, and she was a supporter the Propaganda of the Deed philosophy, which was the belief that one violent act can inspire individuals to take action. She told workers to learn how to use explosives. She led demonstrations of the unemployed throughout the streets of Chicago. The city was charged with the working class' increasing discontent, and more and more people joined in the fight for a revolution.

On May 4, 1886, anarchist labor leaders organized a mass demonstration in support of the eight-hour-day at Haymarket Square. Parsons' husband was one of the speakers at the demonstration. He spoke for an hour to a peaceful crowd, and then they went home. After Parsons and her husband left, an unknown person threw a bomb into the crowd that killed a police officer. The police began shooting into the crowd. By the time the situation was under control, fourteen people were dead.

Anarchists were arrested after the incident, and a warrant was issued for the arrest of Parson's husband. She and her husband fled, but returned when the trial for their comrades was beginning. Her husband turned himself in to authorities, was tried with seven other radical labor leaders, and found guilty of inciting the bombing. She spent the next year and half trying to get her husband's death sentence commuted, but to no avail. He was hanged in November 1887. His death pushed Parsons to undertake her causes with more vigor. She went on a lecture tour as an advocate of the radical left, which lasted for fifty years. In March 1887, she was arrested in Ohio before one of her lectures. Her arrest turned her into a martyr for the working class.

In 1891, Parsons began to edit *Freedom, A Revolutionary Anarchist-Communist Monthly*. She used this publication to fight against racism in the South. Parsons joined the International Labor Defense to help fight for the release of African Americans who were unjustly imprisoned.

She continued to fight for labor reform, and helped found the Industrial Workers of the World (IWW) in the early 1900s. She worked alongside Mother Jones in the labor struggle. Parsons led hungers strikes, for which she was consequently arrested.

Toward the end of her life, Parsons became involved with the Communist Party. She died in 1942, in her home in Chicago, during an accidental fire. She was survived by her children, Lulu and Alfred. Prior to her death, many of her personal affects, including her writings, were seized by police.

PATTEN, JAMES A.

(1852-1928) — Grain merchant, capitalist, and philanthropist, was born on a farm at Freeland Corners, DeKalb County, Illinois, the son of Alexander Robertson Patten and Agnes (Beveridge) Patten. He had no middle name but used the initial "A" for purpose of euphony. Abandoning farming, Alexander Patten took charge of a general store at Sandwich, Illinois, which he ran successfully until his death in 1863. His widow, left to care for a family of five boys of whom Patten was the eldest, moved to her father's farm. Here Patten lived until he was seventeen. During the next two years, he attended the preparatory department of Northwestern University at Evanston.

Returning to Sandwich, he worked for a time as clerk in the country store, which had been his father's, and then spent a year on the farm of an uncle, John L. Beveridge, at that time governor of Illinois. In 1874, he received an appointment as clerk in the state grain inspection department at Chicago. He remained until 1878, when he went to work for G. P. Comstock & Company, Chicago grain brokers. Within two years the firm failed. Patten then went into the cash grain business for himself, taking as partners his brother George Patten and Hiram J. Coon. Soon, however, he joined with his brother in establishing the firm of Patten Brothers. The association of the two in the grain commission business remained unbroken until George Patten's death in 1910. In

1903, both brothers became members of the grain brokerage firm of Bartlett, Frazier & Carrington, later Bartlett, Patten & Company.

Patten joined Chicago board of trade in 1882, was elected a director in 1897, president in 1918, and remained a member until his death. He became successful as a speculator in the grain futures market. On several occasions, notably in 1908 and 1909, he succeeded in anticipating crop conditions in corn oats, and wheat so surely that he held virtual "corners" in all three grains successively. Later he was successful in cornering the cotton market. In connection with this venture he and three others were indicted in 1912 by the federal government for conspiracy. Patten elected to pay a fine of $4,000, but the other three fought the case and were acquitted. In addition to his other responsibilities, he was a director of the Continental and Commercial National Bank, the Chicago Title & Trust Company, Chicago, Rock Island & Pacific Railway, Peoples Gas, and Commonwealth Edison companies.

Patten gave $500,000 to promote the work of the Tuberculosis Institute and founded the Chicago Fresh Air Hospital. He made numerous gifts to small colleges in the Middle West, was a generous benefactor of Northwestern University at Evanston, where he made his home, and provided that half of his estate should go to charitable institutions upon the death of his widow. From 1901 to 1903, he was mayor of Evanston.

On April 9, 1885, he married Amanda Buchanan of Chicago; they had three children. He died in 1928.

PATTEN, SIMON NELSON

(1852-1922) — Economist, the son of William and Elizabeth Nelson (Pratt) Patten, was born in what is now Sandwich Township, DeKalb County, Illinois. When four years old, he came down with typhoid fever; his mother contracted the disease and died. Soon afterwards his father married Jane Somes. He passed through the district school, and at seventeen, as preliminary preparation for the law, he entered the nearby Jennings Seminary at Aurora, Illinois. He graduated in the spring of 1874. In the autumn of 1875, he entered Northwestern University as a freshman, but within a few months left to study in Germany at the University of Halle. He received a Ph.D. at Halle in 1878 and came home by way of England. He made another try at studying law, and in the fall of 1879, went to Chicago for study. After a few weeks, however, he developed eye trouble, which compelled his withdrawal. He received successful treatment by an eye specialist in Philadelphia, then undertook to teach the same little district school where he had learned his own letters; the next year he received a better position at Homewood, Illinois, and in 1888 was superintendent of schools at Rhodes, Iowa. During these years he had been working on the manuscript that was published as *The Premises of Political Economy* (1885).

The book secured Patten's appointment as professor of political economy in the University of Pennsylvania in 1888, and published a considerable amount in the aggregate. He introduced the concept of " solid economics, where the problems of a changing man can be treated in connection with changes in the physical world in which the man lives and through which he is conditioned." Patten's writing in the field of political economy as such may be said to have closed in 1899 with *The Development of English Thought*. Thereafter his interests expanded, and his speculations showed infusions of sociology, psychology, anthropology, and biology. Of his works in this later period, *The New Basis of Civilization* (1907) has had widest reading. After his death a number of his papers were collected and published under the title *Essays in Economic Theory* (1924), edited by R.G. Tugwell.

On September 2, 1903, at the age of fifty-one, he married Charlotte Kimball, much younger than himself; six years later they were divorced. In 1917, precisely at the entrance of the United States into World War I, the University of Pennsylvania notified Patten that he would be retired on account of having reached the age limit. He died five years later in 1922 at Brown's-Mills-in-the-Pines, New Jersey, after two paralytic strokes.

PATTERSON, ELEANOR MEDILL, "CISSY"

(1881-1948) — Newspaper editor and publisher, was born on November 7, 1881, in Chicago, Illinois, the daughter of Robert Wilson Patterson, Jr., and Elinor (Medill) Patterson. Her mother was a daughter of Joseph Medill, editor of the *Chicago Tribune*, the city's leading newspaper; her father succeeded Medill as editor. She was brought up by governesses, and received her education at Miss Hersey's School in Boston, Massachusetts, then at Miss Porter's in Farmington, Connecticut. At a ball in Vienna with her uncle, Robert S. McCormick, ambassador to Austria-Hungary, she met Count Josef Gizycki of Poland, whom she married him at the family's new mansion on Dupont Circle in Washington on April 14, 1904. She left him soon after the birth of their daughter, Felicia, in Poland. There ensued a headlined struggle for custody of the child, which she finally won, and eight years of divorce litigation was settled in June 1917.

Patterson bought a ranch near Jackson Hole, Wyoming. He first novel *Glass Houses* was published in French (in 1923), and was a satire on Washington society. *Fall Flight* (1928), a thinly disguised account of her harrowing marriage to Gizycki, was written after her second marriage, on April 11, 1925, to Elmer Schlesinger, a New York attorney. He died in February 1929.

In 1930, William Randolph Hearst took Patterson on as editor-publisher of his ailing *Washington Herald*. She covered some stories herself, walking in on Al Capone for an interview. She hired and fired editors often on impulse, and she launched campaigns for home rule in the District of Columbia, for hot lunches for schoolchildren, and for a cleaner Potomac. In the early New Deal years, the *Herald*, sympathetic within Hearst-imposed limits, brimmed with news and gossip. In August 1937, she leased from Hearst the *Herald* and his evening *Times*, and in January 1939, she exercised options to purchase them. She combined them into a single all-day paper with six editions, the *Washington Times-Herald*.

The paper backed Franklin Roosevelt in the 1940 election, but his lend-lease program soon roused isolationist feelings that led Patterson to join her brother and her cousin, Colonel Robert R. McCormick of the *Chicago Tribune*, in strident opposition. Foes termed the trio "the McCormick-Patterson axis," their antagonism to Roosevelt's policies continuing for the rest of his days.

She died on July 24, 1948, at her estate near Marlboro, Maryland, and was buried in the Medill plot at Graceland Cemetery, Chicago, Illinois. Short of capital, the *Times-Herald* executives to whom she left the paper sold it the following year to Colonel McCormick, who in turn sold it in 1954 to the *Washington Post*, with which it was merged.

PATTERSON, JOSEPH MEDILL

(1879-1946) — Newspaper publisher, was born on January 6, 1879, in Chicago, Illinois, the son of Elinor (Medill) Patterson and Robert Wilson Patterson, Jr. His maternal grandfather was Joseph Medill, editor and publisher of the *Chicago Tribune*. His father was managing editor of the *Tribune* and later Medill's successor at the paper. His sister, Eleanor ("Cissy") Patterson, later became owner and editor of the *Washington Times-Herald*. Patterson attended private schools in Chicago and France, and Groton School in Massachusetts (1890-1896). After a year spent on a

541

ranch in New Mexico, he entered Yale University in 1897, and received a B.A. in 1901. In the summer of 1900, he went to China to report on the Boxer Rebellion for the *Tribune*, and after graduating from college, he joined the paper's staff as a city reporter, subsequently rising to assistant editor.

In 1903, running as an opponent of boss rule, Patterson was elected to the Illinois House of Representatives, resigning from the *Tribune*. Two years later, Patterson supported the successful Chicago mayoral campaign of reformer Edward F. Dunne, and was rewarded by being named commissioner of public works. Believing that reform of the capitalist system was impossible and that socialism must replace it, he resigned his commissionership in 1906 and joined the Socialist Party. Patterson was named a member of the Socialist Party's executive council in 1906, but spent most of the next four years on a farm he purchased near Libertyville, Illinois, devoting himself to writing. Among the works he produced were the plays *Dope* and *The Fourth Estate*, and the novel, *A Little Brother of the Rich* (1908).

By 1910, when his father died, Patterson had become disillusioned with socialism. Returning to Chicago, he joined his cousin, Robert McCormick, as coeditor of the *Tribune*, taking over the editorial side of the business. More interested in reporting than editing, Patterson personally covered the border conflict with Mexico in 1914 and the beginning of World War I in Europe. In 1916, he joined the Illinois Field Artillery, and after the United States entered the war, he served in France in five major engagements, rising to the rank of captain. Before returning to the United States in 1919, Patterson stopped in London, England, where he was impressed by the success of the tabloid *Daily Mirror*. He was convinced that such a paper, based on photographs and mass appeal, could succeed in New York. Consequently, on June 26, 1919, he brought out the first issue of the *Illustrated Daily News* (which soon became the *Daily News*). Having run the *News* initially from his office in Chicago, in 1925, he gave McCormick complete control of the *Tribune* and moved to New York. In 1921, Patterson added a Sunday edition, and by 1925, the *News* had a circulation of over one million. It grew steadily until by the late 1930s it had the largest daily circulation in the United States and the largest Sunday circulation in the world.

The *Daily News* became somewhat more "respectable" in the 1930s, devoting more space to national and international affairs. The paper was an early supporter of Franklin D. Roosevelt's domestic policies, and Patterson became a frequent guest at the White House. His series of editorials in 1940 defending Roosevelt's bid for a third term helped him win a Pulitzer Prize. He broke with Roosevelt immediately after this election, when the president introduced the lend-lease bill. He attacked the administration bitterly in the editorial columns of the *News*, and although he unsuccessfully sought to reenlist in the army after Pearl Harbor, he continued throughout the war to question the wisdom of American involvement in Europe. He vigorously opposed the reelection of Roosevelt in 1944.

On November 19, 1902, he married Alice Higinbotham of Chicago, daughter of a partner of Marshall Field. They had three daughters: Elinor Medill, Alicia, and Josephine Medill, and adopted a son, James. In 1938 Patterson divorced his wife, from whom he had been separated for many years, and on July 7 of that year, married Mary King, women's editor of the *News*. Patterson died on May 25, 1946.

PAYTON, WALTER (JERRY)

(1954-1999) — Hall of Fame professional football player for the Chicago Bears, was born on July 25, 1954, in Columbia, Mississippi. He began playing football while a junior in high school, and wanted by several college recruiters, eventually settled on Jackson State University. He set his first record there when he accumulated 464 points, the highest number recorded in the history of the National Collegiate Athletic Association. He graduated with a B.A. in special education for the deaf.

In 1975, the Chicago Bears picked Payton in the first-round draft choice; he spent his off-season at Jackson State, working on his master's degree. In 1977, Payton helped lead the Bears to their first winning season since 1967. That year, Payton was first in yards rushing in the National Football League, with 1,852, and also broke O. J. Simpson's single-game record for most yards, with 275.

In 1977, Payton was chosen as Most Valuable Player in that year's Pro Bowl, as well as MVP for the league. By 1980, he became the only player to secure a fifth consecutive National Football Conference rushing title, with a total of 1,460 yards.

The Bears had a disappointing year in 1981, partly due to Payton's physical ailments, which included cracked ribs. The team revived itself in 1983, with Payton attaining over 2,000 yards in combined plays. That same year, Payton signed a history-making contract that guaranteed him $240,000 a year for life. Despite having undergone arthroscopic surgery on both knees, in 1984, Payton broke the nineteen-year, 12,312 rushing record set by Jim Brown.

In 1985, Payton helped lead the Bears to their National Football League Championship. He finished his career with ten NFL records and twenty-eight Chicago Bears records. His 16,726 rushing yards were an all-time NFL record. Payton retired from the Chicago Bears in 1988, and On July 31, 1993, he was inducted in the professional football league's Hall of Fame in Canton, Ohio. That same year, he took up racecar driving.

Along with his football activities, Payton established Walter Payton Enterprises, which invested in several different interests including real estate, timberland, and restaurants. He was also heavily involved in various charities, many of which help deaf and retarded children. He also became a successful businessman in real estate, banking, construction, and restaurants.

In February of 1999, Payton announced to the public that he had a rare disease of the liver, primary schlerosing cholangitis. That May, he also learned that he had a tumor in his liver, known as bile duct cancer. He spent his remaining months as a crusader for organ donorship and transplants.

Payton married Connie Norwood in 1976; the couple had two children, Jarret and Brittney. He died on November 1, 1999. The Walter Payton Cancer Fund was established to improve the quality of life for cancer patients as well as fund cancer research.

PEARSON, THOMAS GILBERT

(1873-1943) — Ornithologist and wildlife conservationist, was born on November 10, 1873, in Tuscola, Illinois, the son of Thomas Barnard Pearson and Mary (Eliot") Pearson. The family moved to Indiana, and in 1882 to Archer, Florida. There, he learned to shoot birds and collect eggs, activities that produced his first published work (in the *Oologist* January 1888) and paid for his first two years of board and tuition at Guilford College in North Carolina (given in exchange for his collection of eggs and mounted birds). Entering in 1891, Pearson studied for six years at Guilford, where he continued his work in natural history. In 1896, upon graduation, he received a job in the office of the North Carolina state geologist, and a salary that permitted enrollment at the University of North Carolina (B.S., 1899). For the next two years, he taught biology at Guilford, and from 1901 to 1904, he taught biology and geology at the State Normal and Industrial College for Women, Greensboro, North Carolina.

After Pearson's first book, *Stories of Bird Life* (1901), William

Dutcher, first president of the National Association of Audubon Societies, asked Pearson to organize the North Carolina Audubon Society, which was formed in 1902. In January 1905, he helped incorporate the National Association of Audubon Societies, acting first as secretary, receiving executive responsibility following Dutcher's paralytic seizure in 1910, and serving as president from the latter's death in 1920 until retirement in 1934. After 1911, he made his home in New York City.

Pearson continued both his field study and his professional writing while serving the Audubon societies. Bird protection had effectively begun late in the nineteenth century, but great obstacles remained. Many states had no laws protecting songbirds; others enforced such laws poorly. Game-bird laws were lacking or inadequate, permitting widespread market hunting and unchecked international trade. Commerce in millinery plumes and bird skins persisted, often without effective opposition, state or national. There were few wildlife sanctuaries, and many natural refuges were threatened by exploitation or by serious environmental changes. Pearson worked for protective measures and game-warden systems elsewhere in the South, addressing the legislatures of Tennessee and Arkansas and lecturing and lobbying in other states.

In New York, then the citadel of the millinery plume trade, Pearson for the first time registered as an avowed lobbyist, supporting the Audubon Plumage Bill. This notable measure was passed, and in other states various protective laws were obtained. Domestic laws varied widely, and they were also partly nullified by uncontrolled trade from abroad. The Federal Migratory Bird Law of 1913, passed with much Audubon help, largely remedied the first problem, but meanwhile Pearson had begun his campaign for international control by visiting President Diaz of Mexico in 1909, with only brief success. Later negotiations with Canada, in which Pearson joined, resulted in the important Migratory Bird Treaty of 1916. In 1922, Pearson visited Europe and at a London meeting founded the International Committee for Bird Preservation, serving as president until 1938 and as chairman of the U.S. section (and later the Pan-American section) until his death. The effort to establish refuges and maintain a favorable environment for birds and other wildlife in the United States was another aspect of Pearson's forty years of work with the Audubon movement.

On June 17, 1902, he married Elsie Weatherly of Greensboro,

by whom he had three children: Elizabeth, Thomas Gilbert, and William Gillespie. Pearson died on September 3, 1943, in New York, New York.

PEATTIE, DONALD CULROSS

(1898-1964) — Naturalist and historian, was born on June 21, 1898, in Chicago, Illinois, the son of Robert Burns Peattie and Elia Amanda Wilkinson. He grew up in Windsor Park, a Chicago suburb on the south shore. Encouraged by his family, Peattie began to write. He set type for his first work, *Blown Leaves* (1916), at University High School. He subsequently attended the University of Chicago (1916-1918), majoring in French. After his freshman year, Peattie tried reporting, but quit after two weeks on the *Tribune*. When his parents moved to New York City in 1918, Peattie joined them and became a reader for the publisher George H. Doran. After a visit to the Bronx Botanical Garden, Peattie quit his job and start training to be a scientific botanist. He spent the summer of 1919 on the southern Appalachian Trail, and entered Harvard that fall. His first scientific work was *Flora of the Tryon Region* (1928-1931).

Peattie received his B.A. in 1922 and won that year's Witter Bynner Poetry Prize. He then worked for two years under David Fairchild in the Bureau of Foreign Seed and Plant Introduction in Washington, D.C. On May 22, 1923, he married Louise Heegaard Redfield; they had four children. After his *Cargoes and Harvest* (1926), an economic botany, the Peatties collaborated on three books. In 1924, Peattie left the routines of plant identification and distribution to become a freelance writer. He had a column on the seasons in the *Washington Star* from 1925 to 1934, which was briefly revived in the *Chicago Daily News*. He wrote the biographies of many naturalists for the *Dictionary of American Biography*, and numerous magazine articles. In 1928, his wife's mother provided the couple with the money to travel to Paris, France. Their daughter died soon after they reached Paris.

The Peatties resided on the Riviera, first at Vence, then at Nice, and finally at Menton. Here they both wrote fiction, his wife more successfully, which included *Sons of the Martian* (1932), *Port of Call* (1932), and *A Wife to Caliban* (1934). By the time their money ran out, late in 1933, Peattie had written his *History of Vence* (1930), which was republished in America as *Immortal Village* (1945). The American edition borrowed from the Peatties' summary of their European years, *The Happy Kingdom* (1935).

After returning from France, Peattie lived in Illinois. He worked for the Field Museum, which had published his scientific study of the

Indiana dunes, *Flora of the Indiana Dunes* (1930). In the spring of 1934, he started what became the *Almanac for Moderns* (1935). Next came *Green Laurels* (1936), a collection of lives of naturalists; *A Book of Hours* (1937); and *A Prairie Grove* (1938), an "ecological novel." Peattie received Guggenheim fellowships from 1936 to 1938 to do a study of Robert Owen's community at New Harmony, Indiana. The results appeared in the *Reader's Digest* (November 1942) and in a chapter of *Journey into America* (1943).

In 1937, the Peatties moved to Santa Barbara, California. Already a frequent contributor to the *Reader's Digest*, Peattie became its roving editor in 1943. Only two of his projected four volumes on the trees of *North America* appeared (1948, 1950), and no major works were published after *The Rainbow Book of Nature* (1957), written for children. He died on November 16, 1964.

PECK, JOHN MASON

(1789-1858) — Educator, journalist and Baptist missionary of influence to Illinois territory; was born near Litchfield, Connecticut on October 31, 1789, to Asa Peck and Hannah Farnum, farmers; with hard work required on their farm, young John had little consideration given to schooling. He would overcome that problem by hard private study on his own. By 1807, he was teaching school. The same year, he was converted at a revival meeting in the Litchfield Congregational Church, where he also met Sally Paine, the New York lady he would marry two years later on May 8, 1809. In 1811, the Pecks moved to Greene County, New York, near Sally's home. Both were baptized in the New Durham Church that October. Peck was convinced that God was calling him to preach. He was license to preach the same year, and was ordained in Catskill, New York, in 1813. He worked as both a minister and teacher in various small towns such as Catskill and Armenia. In 1815, he met evangelist Luther Rice while attending an outreach service and was encouraged by the idea of missionary outreach.

In 1817, the Baptist Triennial Convention met and appointed Peck, along with James E. Welch, to serve as missionaries to the Missouri territory. The group had established headquarter in St. Louis and was attempting to form Baptist Churches wherever possible, and also to preach to Native American tribes. Peck immersed himself into this work, traveling in Missouri and Illinois, organizing the United Society for the Spread of the Gospel to organize Sunday schools and build churches. Funding for his work from the convention dissipated by 1820 but Peck persevered for what he had chosen as his lifelong work. In 1822, he moved to Rock Spring, Illinois, where he obtained a farm that served as center of his activities the next thirty years. He also became an agent for the Massachusetts Baptist Missionary Society, which provided him a salary of $5 per week, if he could collect from local patrons. Peck had as his primary interest the organizational aspects of ministry rather than revival preaching. A conversion experience was necessary for salvation he believed, but for him it was just as important to channel testimony by means of churches, schools and newspapers. Therefore, he established Rock Spring Theological Seminary and High School in 1827 to prepare both teachers and preachers; initially, it struggled to attract students. It was perhaps the first institution of higher learning in the state of Illinois. The school then moved to Upper Alton in 1832, and then became Shurtleff College in 1835, so-named in honor of a Boston sponsor Peck had influenced to secure as a gift $10,000 on a fundraising tour.

Peck was covering areas throughout western Indiana, Illinois, and Missouri but remained a trustee of the college he established for the remainder of his life. He continued to organize other Bible societies and Sunday schools, making it policy to visit each group regularly through a circuit-riding system. Obviously, Peck did not stay at one activity during his life, but in everything he did his objective was Baptist expansion. In 1829 he became a religious journalist, founding and editing the *Pioneer* newspaper, printed at his own farm. Ten years later it merged with the *Baptist Banner*, of Louisville, Kentucky. In its pages, Peck continued to promote the cause of missions. As an author during the 1830s, Peck wrote the *Guide for Emigrants* and a traveler's dictionary for Illinois; *Life of Daniel Boone* appeared in 1847. Other works include editing a "New Map of Illinois," and a revision of James H. Perkins' *Annals of the West* (1850).

In other issues of American life, Peck achieved notoriety: He was an unsuccessful candidate for the Illinois Constitutional Convention (1847-48). Peck vigorously opposed the introduction of slavery into Illinois. His efforts assisted in excluding the system north of the Ohio River; he condemned the extremist measures by abolitionists, however. Peck favored enforcement of the Fugitive Slave Law and in 1851 gave a sermon to that effect at the Springfield statehouse. As a far-ranging traveler, he earned a reputation as expert on midwestern land and settlements. Of course, some of his publica6tions were on Mississippi Valley histories and pioneer exploration and development. During his late years, Peck was active in various religious publication societies and held additional pastorates. He continued his service as secretary to the American Baptist Publication Society (1843-46) and had stints as a pastor in Edwardsville, Illinois; St. Louis, Missouri; and Covington, Kentucky. By 1855, Peck slowed down and he spent the last few years of his life at his farm home in Rock Spring, where he died on March 14, 1858. His geographical-interest journals and historical notes formed a contribution to the history of early Illinois settlers.

PEEK, GEORGE NELSON

(1873-1943) — Businessman, farm leader, and first administrator of the Agricultural Adjustment Administration, was born on November 19, 1873, at Polo, Illinois, the son of Henry Clay Peek and Adeline (Chase) Peek. In 1885, the family moved to a farm near Oregon, Illinois. After graduating from the Oregon high school in 1891, Peek attended Northwestern University in Evanston for one school year (1891-1892).

In January 1893, he obtained a job in Minneapolis with Deere and Webber, a branch of the John Deere Plow Company. In 1901, he was named general manager of the John Deere Plow Company in Omaha, and a decade later, he moved to the company's home office in Moline, Illinois, as vice-president in charge of sales. Meanwhile, on December 22, 1903, he had married Georgia Lindsey; they had no children.

Peek first achieved national attention in 1917, when he was appointed industrial representative on the War Industries Board. He became the board's commissioner of finished products in March 1918, working closely with the new chairman, Bernard M. Baruch. In February 1919, after the War Industries Board had finished its work, Peek was appointed chairman of the Industrial Board in the Department of Commerce; he resigned from his position at John Deere upon acceptance onto the board. Without real power to influence the economy during the period of reconversion, he and his fellow board members resigned in April.

Shortly after leaving government service, Peek accepted the presidency of the Moline Plow Company. After the postwar depression hit agriculture and the sale of farm machinery dropped sharply, Peek and Hugh S. Johnson, in 1922, came up with a plan of "Equality for Agriculture," which called for federal help in removing price-depressing surpluses from the domestic market. Resigning his business post in 1924, Peek thereafter devoted all his time and effort to organizing support for his farm relief plan.

549

Peek's ideas were incorporated in the successive McNary-Haugen bills, which were before Congress almost constantly between 1924 and 1928. Twice, in 1927 and 1928, a McNary-Haugen Bill passed both houses, only to be negated by presidential veto.

During the 1932 presidential campaign, Peek acted as an adviser on farm problems to Franklin D. Roosevelt. When Congress created the Agricultural Adjustment Administration in May 1933, Peek was named as its head to ensure the support of farmers and businessmen. Almost immediately, however, he found himself in sharp disagreement with Secretary of Agriculture Henry A. Wallace. His differences with Wallace became so severe that, in December 1933, President Roosevelt shifted Peek to a post as special adviser on foreign trade. But on November 26, 1935, he angrily resigned that position following a conflict with the administration over its reciprocal trade policies.

Peek then became a bitter and vocal critic of the New Deal. In 1936, he campaigned for the Republican presidential candidate, Alfred M. Landon, and in 1940, he worked vigorously for the America First Committee. Peek died on December 17, 1943, at his home near San Diego, California, where he had lived since 1937, and was buried in the family plot in the Moline Cemetery, Illinois.

PENDLETON, CLARENCE McLANE, Jr.

(1930-1988) — Business executive and political activist, was born in Louisville, Kentucky, on November 10, 1930, the son of Clarence and Edna Marie (Ramsaur) Pendleton. Pendleton grew up in Washington, D.C., and graduated from Dunbar High School. Pendleton then graduated from Howard University, earning a B.S. in 1954, and worked for a short time for the District of Columbia recreation department before joining the U.S. Army. He served with a medical unit at Fort Monmouth, New Jersey, and was released from active duty in 1957, having achieved the rank of specialist third class. He returned to Howard University as a physical education instructor, and during this time studied for a master's degree in education, which he received in 1961. Taking over Dr. Thomas F. Johnson's duties as swimming coach, his team won ten championships in eleven years and gained berths in national competitions. Pendleton also served as head baseball coach, head rowing coach and assistant football coach.

Pendleton left the field of education in 1968 to take a position as recreation coordinator with the Model Cities Program in Baltimore. He returned to Washington in 1970 to become the director of the urban affairs department of the National Recreation and Parks Association. He devoted his efforts to increasing community involvement in the establishment of recreation programs and persuaded the federal government of the need for year-round planning.

San Diego Mayor Pete Wilson recruited Pendleton in 1972 to head the Model Cities Program. After three-and-half years with the Model Cities Program, Pendleton succeeded John Jacob as executive director of the San Diego Urban League. In addition to pursuing an agenda in behalf of civil and social rights, Pendleton shepherded the organization into such innovative enterprises as packaging loans for small business and upgrading and managing small apartment units.

In 1981, President Ronald Reagan named Pendleton to replace the chairman of the U.S. Commission on Civil Rights, Arthur S. Flemming. The first African American chairman of the commission, Pendleton was an outspoken proponent of the administration's "color-blind" philosophy on civil rights. He adopted several stands that most observers would not have expected from an African American on the civil rights commission. For example, he opposed desegregation through busing because he felt such action violated the principle of neighborhood schools. Pendleton considered Affirmative Action a "bankrupt policy" that detracted from the legitimate achievements of those who would have succeeded in any case.

Pendleton continued to reside on the West Coast during his chairmanship, commuting to Washington, D.C., when necessary. Although he resigned his position with the Urban League in 1982, he remained active in San Diego business and public affairs. During this time, he was chair of San Diego Transit; president of Pendleton & Associates, a business development and investment firm; and chairman and president of the San Diego Local Development Corporation. In addition, he was a trustee of the Scripps Clinic and Research Foundation and served on the board of the Greater American Federal Savings and Loan Association and of the San Diego Coalition for Economic and Environmental Balance.

Pendleton married Margaret Krause in 1970; the couple had one daughter, Paula. Pendleton also had two children, George and Susan, by a previous marriage. Pendleton died on June 5, 1988.

PENTECOST, GEORGE FREDERICK

(1842-1920) — Clergyman and author, was born on September 23, 1842, in Albion, Illinois, the son of Hugh L. and Emma (Flower) Pentecost. In

1856, he went to Kansas Territory, where he became secretary to the governor and clerk of the U.S. District Court. He was a student at Georgetown College in Kentucky from 1860 to 1862, and enlisted in the army to serve for two years as chaplain of the 8th Kentucky Cavalry, U.S. Volunteers.

He entered the Baptist ministry in 1864, and served congregations at Greencastle and at Evansville, Indiana, for three years. He was then called to Covington, Kentucky, where he preached for another year. On leaving Covington, he entered upon the first of the two important Baptist pastorates of his career, Hanson Place church, Brooklyn, 1869-1872, and Warren Avenue church, Boston, 1872-1878. His abilities attracted the attention of Dwight Lyman Moody, with whom he occasionally joined in evangelistic work during the following two years. He returned to Brooklyn to become pastor of Tompkins Avenue Congregational church in 1880, and remained in this charge until 1887. He published *The Angel in the Marble* (1875); *In the Volume of the Book* (1879); *Out of Egypt* (1884); and *Bible Studies* (1880-89), twelve volumes.

Pentecost conducted evangelistic campaigns in several of the large cities of Scotland in 1887 and 1888; he traveled in India from 1888 to 1891, delivering special lectures to English-speaking Brahmans; and for six years, beginning in 1891, he was minister of Marylebone church, London. He published *The Birth and Boyhood of Christ and Forgiveness of Sins* (1897). He was pastor of First Presbyterian church in Yonkers, New York, during the next five years and published *Systematic Beneficence and Precious Truths* (1898).

In 1902, he visited Japan, China, and the Philippine Islands, as a special commissioner of the Presbyterian and Congregational Boards of Foreign Missions, to study Christian work in the Orient. For eleven years after his return from Asia, he lived in retirement, but in 1914, he was persuaded by his lifelong friend, John Wanamaker, to become the stated supply of Bethany Presbyterian church of Philadelphia. Two years later, he was formally installed as pastor.

He remained actively at work until his sudden death in 1920. He was survived by two children and his wife, Ada (Webber) Pentecost, whom he had married in Hopkinsville, Kentucky, on October 6, 1863.

PERCY, CHARLES HARTING

(1919-) (father-in-law of John D. Jay Rockefeller IV) Senator from Illinois; Senate Years of Service: 1967-1985; born in Pensacola,

Escambia County, Fla., September 27, 1919; attended public schools in Chicago and Winnetka, Ill.; graduated from the University of Chicago in 1941; joined the company of Bell & Howell; during the Second World War enlisted in the United States Navy in 1943 as an apprentice seaman and was honorably discharged in 1945 with the rank of lieutenant; after the war, rejoined the company of Bell & Howell, eventually becoming president, chief executive officer, and chairman of the board; appointed as President Dwight

Charles Harting Percy

Eisenhower's personal representative to presidential inaugurations in Peru and Bolivia with rank of special ambassador 1956; unsuccessful candidate for governor of Illinois in 1964; elected as a Republican to the United States Senate in 1966; reelected in 1972 and 1978 and served from January 3, 1967, until January 3, 1985; unsuccessful candidate for reelection in 1984; chairman, Committee on Foreign Relations (Ninety-seventh and Ninety-eighth Congresses); president, Charles Percy and Associates, Inc.; serves on the boards of several foundations and committees; is a resident of Washington, D.C.

PERKINS, GEORGE WALBRIDGE

(1862-1920) — Banker, was born on January 31, 1862 in Chicago, Illinois, the son of George Walbridge and Sarah Louise (Mills) Perkins. He did not attend the Chicago public schools until he was ten years old. At fifteen, he left school and became an office boy for the New York Life Insurance Company.

Rapidly advanced, he became first vice-president by the time he was forty-one. Among other reforms, he revolutionized the company's agency system. The practice had been to farm out territory to middlemen or general agents, who appointed those that did the actual soliciting for policies. These solicitors were often underpaid and improvident, frequently made misrepresentations in order to get initial premiums, and transferred their allegiance as the general agent did his. To end this shifting of personnel Perkins, in 1892, began to dispense with the general

George Walbridge Perkins

agents as fast as their contracts expired. He made the local agents and solicitors a loyal and permanently attached force by employing them directly and by introducing on January 1, 1896, the so-called "Nylic" system of benefits based on length of service and amount of policies written. He also made various trips abroad and obtained permission for his company to do business in Russia and other leading European countries. When he, after repeated solicitations, joined the banking house of J. P. Morgan & Company on January 1, 1901, he relinquished most of his duties with the New York Life but remained connected with it until 1905. He took a leading part in the formation of the International Harvester Corporation, International Mercantile Marine Company, and Northern Securities Company. He also further devised a working organization for the U.S. Steel Corporation and the scheme in force since 1903, of annual offerings of preferred stock to employees on advantageous terms.

At the close of 1910, he withdrew from Morgan & Company to devote himself public works. He believed that competition should be replaced by cooperation in the business world; that great corporations properly supervised were more efficient than small competing units, and that workers should receive retirement pensions and share in corporate profits. He made numerous addresses, many of which were later published. Of these perhaps the most important were "The Modern Corporation" in *The Currency Problem.... Addresses Delivered at Columbia University* (1908), *National Action and Industrial Growth* (1914); *The Sherman Law* (1915), and *Profit Sharing* (1919). He served as chairman from 1900 of the Palisades Interstate Park Commission, which he developed the park from a few hundred acres to fifty square miles of playground. In 1912, he joined the Progressive party, and became chairman of its national executive committee.

During the World War, Perkins was chairman of a joint state and municipal food supply commission for which he drew up an admirable report on marketing conditions in New York City. As chairman of a finance committee of the Young Men's Christian Association, he raised two hundred million dollars for welfare work among American soldiers abroad.

He died on June 18, 1920, at Stamford, Connecticut. He was survived by his wife Evelyn (Ball) Perkins, who he was married in 1889, and by their two children.

PINKERTON, ALLAN

(1819-1884) — Detective, was born on August 25, 1819, in Glasgow, Scotland, the son of William Pinkerton, a sergeant of the police force. When Allan was ten years old his father, on duty during Chartist riots, was so severely injured that he never walked again. Four years later he died. Forced to help maintain the family, the boy was apprenticed at the age of twelve to a cooper; at nineteen, he became an independent craftsman. His part in the Chartist demonstrations of 1842 led him to fear arrest, and he decided to go to America.

Alan Pinkerton

On the day before sailing, he married Joan Carfrae. They reached Chicago, Illinois, where Pinkerton found temporary employment in a brewery. The next year, they moved to the Scotch settlement of Dundee on the Fox River, where he established a cooper's shop of his own. One day, he chanced upon a rendezvous for counterfeiters, and led a party that captured the entire gang. Similar success followed in several local detective commissions, and in 1846, he was made deputy sheriff of Kane County, Illinois. An ardent abolitionist, he was also a "foreman" of the Underground Railroad and his shop was a station. He was invited to become deputy sheriff of Cook County, and he sold his business to move to Chicago, Illinois.

In 1850, he became a part of Chicago's newly organized police force as its first and at that time only detective. The same year, he established, in partnership with lawyer E.G. Rucker, a private detective agency, one of the first of its kind in the country. Rucker withdrew within a year, and Pinkerton resigned his city connections to work full time in his agency.

The solution of several Adams Express robberies gave the agency a national reputation. In January 1861, Pinkerton was employed by the Philadelphia, Wilmington & Baltimore Railroad to investigate threats by southern sympathizers against its property. While his operatives were working on the case in Baltimore, Maryland, they learned of an intended attempt on Abraham Lincoln's life to be made as he passed through the city on the way to his inauguration. With several of Lincoln's advisers, Pinkerton worked out plans for the president's unexpected night trip (February 22 1861) ahead of schedule to the capital. In April 1861, Lincoln invited Pinkerton to a conference on the subject of a secret-service department, but no action was taken. A few weeks later, at the invitation of General George B. McClellan, Pinkerton agreed to organize and conduct a secret service for the Ohio Department that McClellan commanded. Agents were immediately sent into Kentucky and West Virginia, and Pinkerton himself, in disguise, toured Tennessee, Georgia, and Mississippi. When in July McClellan was made commander-in-chief, Pinkerton accompanied him to Washington, D.C., and established headquarters at the capital and an office in the field. He now also directed important counter-espionage activities in Washington. During the war, Pinkerton enlisted under the name of Major E.J. Allen. He resigned upon McClellan's removal in November 1862, and thereafter served as an investigator of numerous claims against the government.

At the close of the war, he resumed the personal direction of his agency and established branches in Philadelphia, Pennsylvania, and New York, New York. Pinkerton also devoted much time to writing reminiscent detective narratives to the extent of eighteen volumes, based for the most part upon the agency's experiences.

From an autobiographical viewpoint the most valuable were *Criminal Reminiscences and Detective Sketches* (1879); *The Spy of the Rebellion* (1883); and *Thirty Years a Detective* (1884). After his death in 1884, his two sons took over the direction of the agency.

PONTIAC

(1720-1769) — Ottawa chief, joined with several tribes at the conclusion of the French and Indian War to launch simultaneous raids against British forts in the Great Lakes region, and nearly succeeded in wiping out the British presence in western Pennsylvania. Throughout the long imperial rivalry between the French and British, the Ottawa remained firmly allied with the king of France; most likely, it was Pontiac who led warriors from both the Ottawa and the Chippewa tribes in defeating the British column under General Braddock in 1755. Nonetheless, the French were defeated. The British did not treat the Native Americans as well as the French had. As ill-will intensified, Pontiac rose to a position of leadership by playing upon the tribes' hatred and fear of the British.

Meanwhile, the French traders and inhabitants in the region led Pontiac and other Indian leaders to believe that resistance to British

Pontiac

authority would elicit the aid of French troops. As the harshness of the British policy became clear, and the stream of white settlers penetrated the Indian lands of western Pennsylvania and Ohio, Pontiac made his decision to try and drive the Europeans out. By the end of April 1763, Pontiac had aligned the Ottawa, Huron, Potawatomi, Chippewa, and other tribes in a vast resistance to the British. His plan called for the simultaneous attack upon all twelve of the British outposts on Indian Territory, with the attack on Fort Detroit to be under his own supervision.

On the pretext of performing an Indian dance for the soldiers' amusement, Pontiac and about fifty of his followers gained admittance to the fort. Once inside, they noted the arrangement of sentries and guns, and then they promised to return in a few days for a good will council. On May 7, 1763, Pontiac returned to Fort Detroit, only to find that the British commander had learned of the plot and had prepared his forces to meet the attack. The Ottawa chief withdrew, but tried once again on May 9, but his plans were again thwarted. He decided that instead of attacking, he would lay siege to the British fort.

During the siege, Pontiac sent out other war parties to attack the other British outposts. By June 21, 1763, less than two months following Pontiac's initial foray against the British, every Ohio Valley and Great Lakes post had fallen except Fort Detroit and Fort Pitt. At Detroit, meanwhile, Pontiac held the confederation together and scored a smashing victory at the Battle of Bloody Run against a British reinforcement.

557

Yet, as time passed and the British failed to surrender, Pontiac's authority began to diminish. First, he lost the support of the French inhabitants, who now were convinced that French troops would never appear to aid the Native American. Then, his confederation faltered; throughout September and October 1763, several tribes made their peace with the British and went back home. By the end of October, a French officer brought confirmation that no French assistance would be forthcoming.

Pontiac attempted to revive the war against the British among tribes further west, but the French refused to supply him with ammunition. Throughout 1764, Pontiac refused to abandon his goal, traveling from village to village trying to forge another inter-tribal alliance. The British were more successful, however, convincing the tribes that resistance was futile and that there was more to be gained through peaceful commerce of furs for manufactured goods. British Indian policy was modified, and the tribes came to believe that the British presence was too powerful to be overthrown. By April 1765, Pontiac himself formally capitulated.

Pontiac performed a remarkable about-face and took the side of his former enemies when disputes arose between the Indians and the British. As a result, he lost nearly all of his prestige and power. He was scorned by nearly all of his former allies and was murdered in 1769 near present-day Cahokia, Illinois, by a Peoria.

POOLE, ERNEST COOK

(1880-1950) — Novelist and journalist, was born on January 23, 1880, in Chicago, Illinois, the son of Mary Nevin (Howe) Poole and Abram Poole. He attended the University School for Boys in Chicago, and in 1898, he followed his older brother, Ralph Poole, to Princeton University. He graduated with an A.B. *cum laude* in 1902, with honors in history, jurisprudence, and politics. He studied and imitated Alex Tolstoy, Ivan Turgenev, Guy de Maupassant, and Robert Louis Stevenson and found in Jacob Riis' *How the Other Half Lives* an impetus to make New York slum dwellers his initial subject matter.

Two years as a social worker with the University Settlement on New York's lower east side revealed to him the astonishing diversity and vigor of human existence in the frantic metropolis, which later became a part of his novels. He investigated firsthand the poverty, disease, and exploitation that awaited immigrants and sold his first piece to *McClure's* in 1903.

Commissioned to report on labor racketeering in Chicago, Poole returned to his hometown in 1904, and soon turned into a publicist for striking stockyard workers. The 1905 St. Petersburg, Russia, massacre impelled him to seek a wider perspective on mass social movements. Secretly carrying money and messages for the revolutionaries, he made the first of numerous trips abroad as a magazine correspondent for the *Outlook*. Poole then wrote and published a novel, *The Voice of the Street* (1906), inexpertly handling the grim, but fascinating, New York material that he continued to place successfully in the *Saturday Evening Post* and elsewhere.

On February 12, 1907, he married Margaret Winterbotham. They settled in Greenwich Village and grew more active in reform movements. Poole finally joined the Socialist Party, frequently contributing to its paper, the *New York Call*. A serious attempt at playwriting produced twelve scripts, usually with social messages. Most of them were torn up by Poole, but three had modestly successful productions.

The Harbor, Poole's semi-autobiographical second novel and his only book usually noted in literary histories, appeared in 1915. Further critical success came almost immediately with *His Family* (1917), a study of three sisters exemplifying roles available to modern women: reckless high society, dull domesticity, and frenetic social service. It won the first Pulitzer Prize offered in fiction.

In 1914, he reported World War I from the front lines. Then, breaking with the pacifism of his Socialist friends, Poole switched from journalist to propagandist, joining the Committee on Public Information headed by George Creel. A 1917 visit to Russia during the Kerensky government resulted in articles assembled into short books: *The Dark People* (1918), *The Village* (1919), and *The Little Dark Man* (1925).

Poole next wrote novels depicting American families caught in the threatening "winds," "storms," and "avalanches" of the "age of experiments" that had begun with a war to make the world safe. Later, in, Poole's title metaphor would represent his generation's life span. In 1936, his publisher, for the first time in twenty-five years, rejected a novel he submitted. When World War II broke out, his offer to serve again as government propagandist was refused.

His many works include: *Jazz Age, Blind* (1920), *Danger* (1923), *The Destroyer* (1931), *The Avalanche* (1924), *With Eastern Eyes* (1926), *Silent Storms* (1927), *Great Winds* (1933), *One of Us* (1934), *Giants Gone* (1943), *The Great White Hills of New Hampshire* (1946),

The Nancy Flyer (1949), and his autobiography, *The Bridge* (1940). He died on January 10, 1950, in New York, New York. He had three children: William Morris, Nicholas, and Elizabeth Ann.

PORTER, ELIZA EMILY CHAPPELL

(1807-1888) — Educator, welfare relief worker, and missionary especially remembered for numerous schools she helped establish throughout the United States; she was born on November 5, 1807 in Geneseo, New York, the fourth daughter and eighth of nine children to Robert Chappell and Elizabeth Kneeland, farmers. In 1811, her father died causing her added emotional attachment to her religious mother. Affluent relatives offered to raise the bright child and she agreed to live with them in Franklin, New York. After several homesick years, she returned to Geneseo at the age of twelve. She joined the Presbyterian Church that her mother belonged to when Eliza was fourteen but she never experienced a need for salvation until six years later during a grave illness. In 1829, lying on what many thought to be Eliza's deathbed, she had a powerful conversion experience and later resolved to devote her life to Christ. When she recovered, she moved with her mother to Rochester, New York, where she participated as a children's worker in the revivals of the Reverend Charles G. Finney. Eliza had begun teaching school at age sixteen and she established a small school in Rochester to instruct children in religion.

In 1831, Eliza's mother died; she traveled to the frontier settlement of Mackinac Island in Michigan territory at the request of Robert Stuart, an American Fur Company executive, as a private tutor for his children. Within a short time, she was teaching Stuart's associates' children, local poor children, and half-breed Native American children. She believed religious orientation was the key to personal development and moral progress, and opened a school to all who wished education; she was convinced the new school movement was "designed by God to open the way for the missionary of the cross." She was forced to leave Mackinac in September 1832 for health purposes; she had recurring stomach hemorrhages, and spent the winter recovering and securing support for the founding of more schools in the Northwest. She visited schools in New York and others, enlisting teachers to take over the school she started and to solicit funds to establish other schools.

In 1833, she returned to the Northwest long enough to open another school in the French and Native American settlement of St. Ignace, near Mackinac in Michigan, and then moved on to the tiny settlement of Chicago where she began a school in a log cabin that earned public support the next year: by December, it won praise from the *Chicago Democrat*, and later received an appropriation for public funding. She moved her school location in January 1834 to the newly constructed Presbyterian Church of the Reverend Jeremiah Porter, a missionary from Hadley, Massachusetts, who she knew in Mackinac. Miss Chappell began enrolling older girls from the outlying communities also, with the hope of training them to become teachers. Exhausted by her labors she again became seriously ill by the year's end. In 1835, she and Reverend Porter were married on June 15 in Rochester, New York; they had nine children, but only six survived infancy. After brief periods in Peoria and Farmington, Illinois, the Porter family settled in Green Bay, Wisconsin, in 1840, where they remained for eighteen years. Mrs. Porter cheerfully presided over a complex and large household that included nine children, invalid relatives, servants (who she inevitably taught to read), and missionary visitors. Porter perfected her managerial style that exemplified unselfishness, tact and kindness in training others to be self-sufficient. She was so busy, she did not read but instead had her husband read to her.

In 1857, Porter decided to upgrade the local schools and found rooms in the courthouse, and she recruited teachers locally and from New England and enrolled one hundred students, establishing a New England-style academy from which the grade schools in Green Bay later developed. In 1858, the Porters returned to Chicago where Reverend Porter assumed leadership of the Edwards Congregational Chapel, a city mission in a poor neighborhood. Soon after, the Civil War broke out and in 1861, Eliza Porter became an office manager of the Chicago (now Northwestern) Sanitary Commission to provide hospital supplies and relief for soldiers in the field. Her husband soon left to become chaplain of the First Illinois Light Artillery. Mrs. Porter at first supervised solicitation of food contributions, medical dressing and other medical supplies for use in military hospitals and at the front. By spring, however, she was convinced she could be more useful in the field. She escorted a group of Chicago women volunteers at the Battle of Shiloh in Cairo, Illinois, for hospital duty. She at once went to nearby Mound City, where along with a young Cairo volunteer named Mary Jane Safford, they met incoming hospital ships and helped transfer the wounded to local hospitals. After viewing battle firsthand, she returned to Chicago to recruit more nurses. These volunteers she escorted to Savannah, Tennessee, where a number of army field hospitals had been established.

She proceeded to Memphis in 1862 where her husband had been assigned as chaplain at the Fort Pickering Convalescent camp. She established a special diet kitchen for invalids and others, an innovation later introduced on a wider scale by Annie Wittenmyer. She made several trips through the farm country asking for eggs, butter, and other foodstuffs. She was also instrumental in Memphis in establishing a school and organized relief for African Americans. With her understanding of the public's hesitance to contribute to impersonal national organizations, Porter wrote letters from the battlefronts, personalizing relief and describing in graphic details the suffering of war, the usefulness of items contributed, and the gratitude the soldiers felt. She refused a salary for her works until April 1863 and shamed those who misappropriated commission supplies. She returned to Chicago in July 1863 where she again took charge of the Sanitary Commission offices during the temporary absence of regular directors. On January 1, 1864, in the middle of a freezing winter rainstorm, Porter arrived at the field hospital near Chattanooga where the undaunted Mary Ann Bickerdyke was already working to care for the wounded. The two caregivers had worked together before. Resourceful and relentless, the two did all types of work in the field hospitals, from cooking and laundering to emergencies and distributing relief supplies.

After a final summer of hospital work with Mrs. Bickerdyke, Porter traveled to Texas in October 1865 with her husband where they distributed Sanitary Commission supplies to Union troops stationed along the Mexican border and they visited military hospitals in Brownsville and Brazos. They moved to Brownsville in 1868, reopening a coeducational Rio Grande seminary she had founded earlier. In 1870, Reverend Porter was appointed a regular army chaplain and they traveled and lived for years, conducting religious services, teaching and conducting schools, passing out food and refreshments to needy people in army forts, and frontier territories in Texas, Oklahoma and Wyoming. She suffered intermittently from malaria and traveled sometimes to visit eastern friends. Following her husband's retirement in 1882, the couple spent their summers with their married children in Beloit, Wisconsin, and Detroit, Michigan; and wintered with friends in Florida, Texas or California. On New Year's Day, 1888, Eliza Emily Chappell Porter's boundless energy waned; she died on pneumonia in Santa Barbara, California. Following services there, and in the New England Congregational Church in Chicago, she was buried in Chicago's Rosehill

Cemetery. Her husband survived her by five years. Two of their children became ministers, and two others went as missionaries to China.

POWELL, ALMA WEBSTER

(1874-1930) — Singer and voice teacher, was born in Elgin, Illinois, the daughter of William Henry and Alma (Webster) Hall. She studied at the Girls' High School of Chicago, Illinois, and with private tutors in that city, and while she was still a young girl she went to New York to develop her vocal gifts, which were considerable. She secured a position as soprano in a leading church choir and in time came to the notice of A. Judson Powell, an organist and piano manufacturer, who devoted himself to the development of her voice and ultimately married her (April 16, 1891). In 1894 she went to Europe where, after studying with various masters, she made her debut in opera at Frankfurt-am-Main in the difficult coloratura role of Queen of the Night, in Mozart's *Magic Flute* on May 16, 1895.

She sang abroad until 1897, when she was engaged by the Damrosch-Ellis Opera Company. In that year she made a successful American debut in the Mozart role in Philadelphia, Pennsylvania, and in 1898 she joined the Savage Opera Company, scoring successes in *Martha*. Forced by a nervous breakdown to abandon singing for a time, she took a course in law at New York University and was granted an LL.B. in 1900. She then reentered the operatic field in Germany, singing at the Breslau *Stadt-Theater*, the royal opera houses of Berlin, in Munich, Dresden, and Prague, and at the Vienna Hofoper, appearing in *Martha*, *Lakme*, *Faust*, *Don Giovanni*, *Traviata*, and *Lucia* with notable success.

In Prague, on April 6, 1902, she created the role of Renata in Eugenio Pirani's *Das Hexenlied*. After three years of singing in concert and opera throughout Europe, she returned to the United States in 1904 and sang at the Metropolitan Opera House in New York. She then toured the United States and Canada with success, established the Powell Musical Institute (1905) in Brooklyn, New York, and founded the Webster-Powell Opera Company, which gave opera until 1912. In 1910 she had secured her Mus.B. at Columbia University, to which she added an M.A. in 1911 and a Ph.D. in political science in 1914. In 1913 she became codirector with Eugenio Pirani of the Powell & Pirani Musical Institute in Brooklyn, and in 1920, assumed the directorship of the Powell Vocal Academy in Brooklyn. She was the author of *Advanced School of Vocal Art* (1901), a textbook for singers and students; *Black Blood*, the libretto of a manuscript opera by Pirani, and *Music as a*

Human Need (1914), her doctoral thesis. During the war she served in the motor corps of the National League for Women's Service. She died of a heart attack following a fracture of the hip on March 11, 1930, in Mahwah, New Jersey.

PRYOR, RICHARD

(1940-2005) — Actor, comedian, was born in Peoria, Illinois on December 1, 1940, the son Leroy and Gertrude (Thomas) Pryor. He graduated from high school, and served in the United States Army from 1958 until 1960.

Pryor's comedic career began in the 1960s when he appeared on the television shows of "Ed Sullivan," "Merv Griffin" and "Johnny Carson." In 1977 he was the star of the "Richard Pryor Show" on NBC-TV.

He also pursued a motion picture career in movies such as *The Green Berets* (1968), *Silver Streak* (1976), *The Wiz* (1978), *Stir Crazy* (1980), *Brewster's Millions* (1985), *Harlem Nights* (1989) and *Lost Highway* (1996).

Pryor's writing successes are extensive. He was a scriptwriter for Flip Wilson's television series in the 1970s. He co-wrote television specials for Lily Tomlin, for which he won an Emmy in 1973 and an American Academy of Humor Award in 1974. For his script, *Blazing Saddles*, in 1973 he received the American Writer's Guild, American Academy of Humor Award. He was the writer, producer and director for the autobiographical, *JoJo Dancer Your Life Is Calling*, in 1986.

He won a Grammy Award for the comedy albums *That Nigger's Crazy* in 1974 and *Bicentennial Nigger* in 1976. In 1984 he was nominated for a Razzie Award as Worst Supporting Actor in Superman III. He was nominated for an Emmy in 1996 for his role as "Joe Springer" on "Chicago Hope" in the 1994 episode "Stand." He also received an Image Award nomination for that role.

The owner of Richard Pryor Enterprises in Los Angeles since 1975, Pryor suffered from Multiple Sclerosis (which he announced in 1986). Pryor continued to perform, although less frequently because of his declining health. He died from a heart attack on December 10, 2005; surviving him were his wife, Debbie; four children: Elizabeth Ann, Richard, Rain and Renee.

PULLMAN, GEORGE MORTIMER

(1831-1897) — Railroad entrepreneur, was born on March 3, 1831, in Brocton, New York, and at the age of fourteen he left home and school to learn cabinetmaking in Albion, New York. While there, he also worked as a contractor, moving many brick homes so that the Erie Canal could be built. In 1855, he moved to Chicago and continued construction work of buildings until he decided the railroad industry was more inviting. Inventors in the past had patented sleeping cars to tide over weary travelers and Pullman decided he wanted to build one. He remodeled two ordinary railway coaches into sleeping berths for the Alton Railroad in 1858, and they made their first run between Bloomington and Chicago that year. The sleepers were popular, but not so much as Pullman had hoped, and so he took off in the mine rush the next year and worked in a store in Colorado until 1863.

He returned to Chicago and spent $20,000 building a plush sleeping coach he named the Pioneer. This proved successful, and in the following years he built more trains, including a combination sleeping-dining car, which he called the "Pullman Hotel" car. In 1870, one of his cars carried people from Boston to San Francisco, the first such trip in the nation. In 1887, he founded and became president of the Pullman Palace Car Company, which expanded production of his patented cars and leased them to various railway companies. Employees of the new company were invited to live in his model community on the outskirts of Chicago, called Pullman City, which was hailed at first as the city of the future. However, other businessmen and members of the community soon found Pullman rents too high, services too costly, and employee wages too low.

Pullman City was now referred to as a "company-dominated serfdom operated for company profit." Pullman indeed fancied himself a medieval lord who resided over feudal-style landholdings. His "serfs" grew disillusioned, however, and in 1894, employees staged a strike in protest of wage cuts. After a great deal of violence among the strikers and federal troops, the strike

George Mortimer Pullman

broke. However, when Pullman died three years later on October 19, 1897, his once-glorious reputation had been seriously marred.

R

RAINEY, HENRY THOMAS

(1860-1934) — Speaker of the United States House of Representatives; he was born on August 20, 1860, in Carrollton, Illinois, the oldest of two children to John Rainey, a farmer and city councilman, and Catherine Thomas. He attended the public schools there, including Carrollton High School and then went to Knox College in Galesburg, Illinois for two years; he graduated with a bachelor's degree in 1883 from Amherst College in Massachusetts, where he excelled in athletics and public speaking. He then studied law at Union College of Law (now Northwestern University

Henry Thomas Rainey

Law School) in Chicago, receiving his law degree in 1885. Amherst bestowed upon him a Master of Arts degree in 1886, a customary practice for graduates who have completed two years of training. After being admitted to the Illinois bar in 1885, he began practicing in Carrollton, his hometown.

Rainey represented railroad interests as an attorney and also was a champion for civic development, especially for libraries and public education. Rainey's political interests in progressive and populist views were bolstered by his acquaintance with William Jennings Bryan. In 1888, Rainey married Ellenora "Ella" McBride; they had no children. She was an 1880 graduate of Knox College and active in several social welfare organizations. From 1903 until 1934, Ella served her husband as chief legislative aide. Rainey later explained his own theory of public service late in his career. He noted that the politician "established his self-respect only as his ambitions and efforts are for the good of others."

Rainey lived in the heavily based Democratic Twentieth Congressional District, and there was unsuccessful in his first three Democratic primary nominations until 1902, when he won the party primary in the first nominating primary in Illinois to use the secret ballot.

His victory was overwhelmingly by a 2-to-1 margin in the general election and he would be reelected every Congress until his death, with the lone exception of the Sixty-seventh (1921-23). At this time, the district included ten counties. Rainey was one of the original legislatures advocating the deepening of the Illinois River waterway. To the present day, the deepening has allowed continued use of the river for barge traffic, especially grains. Rainey diligently represented the interests of his agrarian district that borders the Mississippi River on the southwest, extending northeast along both banks of the Illinois River. He consistently was in favor of low tariffs for revenue only and the deeper waterway from the Great Lakes to the Gulf Coast. Unlike other advocates who only saw its regional economic advantages, Rainey supported the comprehensive resource management program to promote water and soil conservation also. In recognition of the part he played in flood control and water conservation, the Civilian Conservation Corps facility near Carrollton was renamed the Henry T. Rainey Camp in 1934. Rainey was sincerely concerned with the welfare of the urban working class, which led him to support liberal prolabor legislation.

In 1911, Rainey was first appointed to the Ways and Means Committee, and became an advocate of the progressive concept of a "scientific" tariff through an independent bipartisan tariff commission. He introduced a bill on February 1, 1916, to create a U.S. Tariff Commission and it passed as Section Seven of the Revenue Act of 1916. Rainey also served as acting chairman during much of the time between 1917 and 1919 due to the illness of Claude Kitchin. In that role, he was instrumental in the passage of war revenue bills, including the institution of income tax. In 1920, he was defeated in the election and it prevent Rainey from succeeding Kitchin to the position of ranking Democrat on the Ways and Means Committee, a position that went to John Nance Garner in the Republican-controlled Sixty-seventh Congress. By the time Rainey was returned to the committee in 1923, he had lost most of his seniority.

In 1931, Democrats regained control of Congress and elected Garner to the Speakership, while Rainey became the majority leader. The new Speaker had supported Rainey's election to the position, although the conservative Texan distrusted his Illinois colleague's intense liberalism. In the 1920s, Rainey had denounced Republican economic policies as reducing American farmers to the status of European peasants. Rainey saw that his new position would require him to act as a worker of compromise and "a healer of wounds." As majority leader, he initiated a plan for an international conference to reduce tariffs, but President Herbert Hoover vetoes the measure. He supported relief legislation but the measure he introduced was unsuccessful. He also supported the efforts to protect farmers from price fluctuations between domestic and international markets. He was hesitant but advocated a national sales tax measure, but its voted was defeated in 1932.

Rainey seemed to be likely successor to Garner as Speaker; Garner was elected vice president in 1932. However, the Democratic Party was divided along ideological and sectional lines. Southern conservatives opposed the election of a Midwestern liberal and chose to support Democratic Whip John McDuffie of Alabama. Rainey had pledged to pass President Franklin Roosevelt's legislative program and received the president's support, and also that of a majority of newly elected Democratic congressmen. Rainey received 166 votes to McDuffie's 112 in the part caucus in March 1933, and a few days later was confirmed as Speaker of the House.

As Speaker during the regular and special session of the Seventy-third Congress, Rainey assisted in promoting congressional support for the New Deal. He admired Roosevelt, who he once remarked "combined the idealism and the initiative of a (Woodrow) Wilson with the energy of a (Andrew) Jackson and the wide statesmanship of a (Thomas) Jefferson." Rainey nearly always supported the president's program and blocked any opposing legislation, and gave priority to the passage of relief measures such as the National Industrial Recovery Act. Only on the issue of remonetarization of silver did Rainey disagree with Roosevelt, and he led the House members in passing the Dies Bill, which required the administration to accept the compromise Silver Purchase Act of 1934. In 1933, Rainey was praised for leading the House with a firm but gentle touch, yet was criticized by the media in 1934 as "an easy-going person who is not much of a disciplinarian." Some observers felt the Illinois Democrat lacked the strength to manage the House, and were afraid that President Roosevelt might offer Rainey an appointment to the Supreme Court. Rainey remained loyal to the New Deal, however, and traveled around the United States during the summers of 1933 and 1934, rallying popular support. One day short of his seventy-fourth birthday, Rainey died unexpectedly on August 19, 1934, in St. Louis, Missouri. He was buried three days later in Carrollton following a funeral attended by President Roosevelt and twenty-five of the late Speaker's congressional colleagues. He was remembered best as an effective legislator for the New Deal. Some years later in the Rainey Memorial Park in Carrollton, a ten-foot bronze statue of Rainey was erected; during the ceremonial unveiling, many Illinois legislators and politicians were in attendance to pay tribute, along with his widow.

RANDALL, JAMES GARFIELD

(1881-1953) — Teacher and historian, was born in Indianapolis, Indiana, on June 24, 1881. Randall attended Butler College and then went to the University of Chicago, Illinois, where he received a doctor's degree in history, in 1911. He taught at numerous colleges including, Illinois College, the University of Michigan, Roanoke College, Harvard, and the University of California at Los Angeles. In 1920, he began teaching at the University of Illinois where he stayed for thirty-two years, until his retirement in 1949. Most of his books concerned President Abraham Lincoln and the Civil War, and he was regarded as an authority on the subject: *Constitutional Problems Under Lincoln, Civil War and Reconstruction, Lincoln and the South* and *Lincoln the Liberal Statesman.*

He attempted what was to be a definitive four-volume biography of Abraham Lincoln. His first was *Lincoln From Springfield to Bull Run* in 1945. Next came *Lincoln the President: From Bull Run to Gettysburg* also in 1945. In 1952, he published *Midstream: Lincoln the President.* He wrote the first eight chapters for the fourth volume, but died before he could complete it. Richard N. Current finished the book, entitled, *Last Full Measure*, using Randall's notes. It was published in 1955. J.G. Randall died of leukemia on February 20, 1953.

RAPP, WILHELM

(1828-1907) — Revolutionist and journalist, was born on July 14, 1828, in Leonberg, Wurttemberg, Germany, the son of a Protestant minister, Georg Rapp, and his wife, Augusta Rapp. While a student at the University of Tubingen, he became an ardent supporter of the revolutionary movement of 1848, and was sent by the "Demokratischer Verein" of Tubingen as their delegate to the convention at Reutlingen in May 1849. There, he advocated the union of the revolutionists of Wurttemberg and Baden in the cause of a politically free and united German nation. Joining the Tubingen volunteers, he took part in the Baden insurrection, and after the collapse sought refuge in Switzerland. At Ilanz in the Canton of Graubunden he taught in a private school, but while on a secret visit to his home in the Swabian highlands in January 1851, he was taken captive and transported to the prison of Hohenasperg, where he awaited trial for over a year.

He was acquitted of the charge of high treason at Ludwigsburg, but his refusal to recant deprived him of any chance of a career in his native land. He immigrated to the United States in 1852, and first attempted to support himself in Philadelphia, Pennsylvania. In the following year he received an offer from the Turners, convening at Cleveland, Ohio, to edit their journal. As editor of the *Turner-Zeitung*, in Cincinnati, Ohio, from 1855 to 1856, and at the same time as president of the Turnerbund, the organized union of German-American athletic clubs in the North and West. He traveled extensively in the West and East and became widely known as a political speaker.

In 1857, Rapp accepted the editorship of the German daily newspaper, *Der Wecker*, at that time the only newspaper in Baltimore, Maryland, supporting the Republican Party. In the turbulent month of April 1861, a Baltimore mob invaded the office of the *Wecker* and drove the editor out of that city. He returned to his newspaper before the occupation of Baltimore by General Butler, but soon accepted an invitation to join the editorial staff of the *Illinois Staats-Zeitung* in Chicago, Illinois, where he became one of the most effective supporters of the government and Union among the large German population of the Northwest. After the war, he returned to Baltimore as editor and part owner of the *Wecker* from 1866 to 1872.

He was married in that city in 1869 to Gesine Budelmann. He then again moved to Chicago, as editor and part owner of the *Illinois Staats-Zeitung*, on the invitation of the principal owner, A.C. Hesing, and editor-in-chief, Hermann Raster. When Raster died in 1891, Rapp assumed sole charge, and for seventeen years, led the German press of Chicago.

A number of his best speeches are contained in his *Erinnerungen eines Deutsch-Amerikaners*, which he published in 1890. He died in 1907.

REAGAN, RONALD WILSON

(1911-2004) — Fortieth president of the United States and thirty-third governor of California, was born in Tampico, Illinois, on February 6, 1911, the son of John Edmond and Nelle (Wilson) Reagan. Raised in nearby Dixon, Illinois, Reagan played high school football and worked as a lifeguard. As a student at Eureka College in Illinois, he helped lead a strike against budget cuts imposed by the college's president, and he was taken off a list of supporters for Helen Gahagan Douglas because his

Ronald Wilson Reagan

leanings were considered too liberal.

After college, he was a sports announcer in the Midwest for five years before moving in 1935 to California. After a Hollywood agent discovered him, Reagan joined Warner Brothers and made his film debut in *Love is On the Air* in 1937. Appearing in a total of fifty-two films, Reagan became a popular movie hero, his best roles considered those in *Brother Rat* (1938), *Dark Victory* (1939), and *Knute Rockne, All American.* In the 1942 film, *King's Row*, Reagan wakes up after his leg has been amputated and screams the line that later served as the title to his autobiography, *Where's the Rest of Me?* (1965). During World War II, he served in the Air Force, made training films, and was president of the Screen Actors' Guild.

After supporting Eisenhower and Nixon in 1962, Reagan changed his political party registration and became more active in politics. By 1964, he had emerged as a Goldwater Conservative. In 1966, Reagan ran against incumbent Governor Edmund G. "Pat" Brown, who was seeking a third term in office. In a surprise election, Reagan won by a two-to-one margin. He served as California's governor for two terms, 1967-1975, holding a conservative administration concerned with economy, particularly in the areas of higher education, social welfare, and medical aid.

In 1968 and 1976, Reagan ran unsuccessfully for the Republican presidential nomination. In 1980, however, he won the presidency over Democrat incumbent Jimmy Carter, with George Bush as his running mate. Although he claimed his "Reaganomics" would balance the budget and bring down taxes, thus spurring the economy, the federal deficit continued to climb at record rates. He had harsh critics among environmentalists, Blacks, and the unemployed, but he remained the darling of big businessmen. His inauguration marked a number of "firsts" for the presidential office: Reagan was the first divorcee, the first former union leader, the first Democrat-turned-Republican, and at sixty-nine years of age—the oldest.

In 1981, John Hinckley, Jr., made an assassination attempt on the president, shooting Reagan and three others, including Press Secretary James Brady. Reagan recovered quickly. Brady, shot in the head, was paralyzed.

In 1984, he was elected to a second term as president, defeating Democrat Walter Mondale and his female running mate Geraldine Ferraro. Reagan continued with his conservative agenda while attempting to stimulate economic growth, curb inflation, increase employment, and increase national defense. Meanwhile, his cabinet members developed a secret and illegal arms-for-hostages deal with Iran after Americans were taken hostage by pro-Iranian terrorists in Lebanon. When Reagan left office in January 1989, he passed the presidency to his vice-president and chosen Republican successor, George Bush.

The sale of arms to Iran came to light and a Senate investigation took place. Although Reagan has always denied knowledge of the secret deal with Iran, questions about his administrative dealings and leadership ability undermined his credibility and tarnished his image as the "Teflon President." In 1990, he published *An American Life: The Autobiography.*

Reagan married actress Jane Wyman on January 24, 1940. The couple had one daughter, Maureen, and adopted a son, Michael, before they divorced in 1948. Daughter Maureen died in 2001. Reagan was married a second time to actress Nancy Davis on March 4, 1952. They had two children: Patricia and Ronald. In November 1994 it is announced to the public that Reagan had Alzheimer's Disease.

Former President Ronald Reagan died on June 5, 2004, in Bel Air, California, due to complications of Alzheimer's Disease and pneumonia.

REDFIELD, ROBERT
(1897-1958) — Anthropologist and educator, was born on December 4, 1897, in Chicago, Illinois, the son of Robert Redfield and Bertha Alexandra Dreier. After tutoring at home, he entered the University of Chicago Laboratory School in 1910, and in 1915, went on to the University of Chicago. In the spring of 1917, Redfield enlisted for service in France as an ambulance driver in the American Field Service. His unit was disbanded that fall, and he was rejected by the draft because of a heart murmur. He then spent a brief period at Harvard studying biology. Next, he joined his family in Washington, D.C., where he served as Senate office boy and worked in the code room at Military Intelligence. After the war, Redfield decided to study law, and in 1920,

he received the Ph.B. *cum laude* from the University of Chicago. In 1921, he received the J.D., and in 1922, he was admitted to the Illinois bar.

On June 17, 1920, Redfield married Margaret Lucy Park. Dissatisfied with his job in his late father's law firm, Redfield went with his wife for a vacation in Mexico in the fall of 1923. While there, he met some *indigenista* intellectuals, including the anthropologist Manuel Gamio, who was then combining archaeological research with the study of contemporary Mexican communities. Converted to anthropology, in 1924, Redfield entered graduate study at Chicago.

After a year as instructor of sociology at the University of Colorado, Redfield won a Social Science Research Council fellowship to investigate the native cultural background of Mexican immigrants. In November 1926, he arrived with his family in Tepoztlan, a community near Mexico City that had long been a focus of *indigenista* interest. Although a flare-up of revolutionary violence forced the family's removal to Mexico City in February 1927, Redfield commuted to his fieldwork for four more months before returning to Chicago as instructor. He was promoted to assistant professor upon completion of his Ph.D. in August 1928. Save for summers teaching at Cornell (1928) and Stanford (1929), and later visiting professorships abroad, he remained at Chicago the rest of his life, ending his career as Robert M. Hutchins distinguished service professor (1953).

In 1930, Redfield undertook a long-term project in Yucatan for the Carnegie Institution. Converting geographical distribution into historical sequence, he organized investigations in four communities "along the scale of modernization." By 1941, Redfield, accompanied sometimes by his wife and children, had spent more than two years at field sites in Yucatan and Guatemala; to which the project was extended in 1935. Resulting publications included an ethnography of *Chan Kom* (1934), by Redfield and Alfonso Villa Roias, and Redfield's synthetic interpretation. *The Folk Culture of Yucatan* (1941). He later wrote *A Village That Chose Progress* (1950), *The Primitive World and Its Transformations* (1953), *The Little Community* (1955), and *Peasant Society and Culture* (1956). Redfield made two trips to "study of civilizations from the bottom up," to China in 1948 (constrained by the Communist revolution) and to India in 1955 (cut short by the onset of lymphatic leukemia).

For twelve years (1934-1940), Redfield served as dean of the Division of Social Sciences at Chicago. He was a frequent participant in the "Round Table" broadcasts, wrote numerous articles on civil liberties and educational policy, served as director of the American Council on Race Relations (1947-1950), and worked closely with the National Association for the Advancement of Colored People to end segregated education, most notably as expert witness in *Sweatt vs. Painter* (1950). A member of the social Science Research Council from 1935 to 1943, and of the board of directors of the American Council of Learned Societies from 1952 to 1955, he was also honored by election to the presidency of the American Anthropological Association in 1944, by an honorary degree from Fisk University in 1947, and by the Viking Fund (1955) and Huxley Memorial (1956) medals.

He was active until shortly before his death in Chicago, on October 16, 1958. His wife and three of their four children survived him.

REED, MYRTLE

(1874-1911) — Author, was born on September 27, 1874, in Norwood Park, Illinois, now part of Chicago, the daughter of Hiram and Elizabeth (Armstrong) Reed. Her father, at the time of her birth, edited a periodical called *The Millenarian* and lectured on religious topics. After graduating in 1893 from the West Division High School in Chicago, where she was editor of the school paper, she became a freelance journalist and magazine writer in her native city and in New York.

Her *Love Letters of a Musician* (1899), which she wrote with characteristic speed in the course of five hectic days, hit the popular taste, and was followed by *Later Love Letters of a Musician* (1900) and *The Spinster Book* (1901). Adding a thin strain of narrative to her meditations on romantic love, she produced a short novel, *Lavender and Old Lace* (1902), which belongs to publishing, if not to literary, history. It was an instantaneous success and went through forty printings during the nine years of her career. Her popularity, therefore established, suffered no diminution: her faculty for turning romantic day-dreams into deftly written novels of sentiment made her the most widely read and well remunerated authoress of her decade. Her subsequent volumes, issued by her publisher in a dainty format with lavender casing and profuse rubrication, were: *Pickaback Songs* (1903); *The Shadow of Victory: A Romance of Fort Dearborn* (1903); *The Master's Violin* (1904); *The Book of Clever Beasts* (1904); *At the Sign of the Jack o'Lantern* (1905); *A Spinner in the Sun* (1906); *Love Affairs of Literary Men* (1907); *Flower of the Dusk* (1908); *Old Rose and Silver* (1909); *Sonnets of a Lover* (1910); and *Master of the Vineyard* (1910). Under the pen name of Olive

Green, she published *What to Have for Breakfast* (1905), which was so successful that it became the first of ten cookbooks. Two volumes, *A Weaver of Dreams* (1911) and *The Myrtle Reed Year Book* (1911) were in the press when she died on August 17, 1911 and four others were issued afterward.

Myrtle Reed took a craftsman's pride in her writing and left several accounts of her habits of composition. When ready to write a novel, she would isolate herself from her friends and family, often going to a hotel in a distant city, and work at high nervous tension for four, five, or six weeks, completing her manuscript in that time. She had a rollicking sense of humor, was a loyal friend and daughter, and, though a free spender, managed her business affairs well. Her longing for affection was as apparent in her life as in her writings.

On October 22, 1906, she married James Sydney McCullough, an Irish-Canadian real-estate salesman then resident in Chicago. They were hopelessly incompatible, but she tried to conceal her misery from herself and her intimates until her mind collapsed under the strain and she ended her life with an overdose of a sleeping powder in 1911.

REEVES, JOSEPH MASON

(1872-1948) — Naval officer, was born on November 20, 1872, in Tampico, Illinois, the son of Joseph Cunningham Reeves and Frances (Brewer) Reeves. He attended the U.S. Naval Academy, where he became noted as an athlete, and graduated as cadet engineer in 1894. During the Spanish-American War, he distinguished himself aboard the battleship *Oregon*. Transferred to the line in 1899, he demonstrated remarkable ability in training gun crews. He was on duty at the Naval Academy from 1906 to 1908. His first command in 1913 was the experimental collier *Jupiter*, the navy's first ship with electric drive. Reeves commanded a second battleship, *Maine*, in World War I; was naval attaché to Italy; and from 1921 to 1923, commanded the battleship *North Dakota*. Then, for two years, he was a student and faculty member at the Naval War College, where his study of the principles of war as reflected in the battle of Jutland added a valuable document to naval literature.

In 1925, at the age of fifty-two, Reeves volunteered for duty as an aviation observer and took three months' intensive instruction in flying at Pensacola, Florida. In October, Reeves took command of Aircraft Squadrons, Battle Fleet, based at San Diego, California, which included the navy's first flight-deck carrier, *Langley*, (converted in 1921 from the former collier *Jupiter*). This force participated little in fleet operations, but devoted itself mostly to testing, breaking records, and stunt flying. In 1925, *Langley* had eight aircraft embarked; three years later, she was operating thirty-six with 200 landings a day. She also trained flight crews for the giant carriers *Saratoga* and *Lexington*, and when these joined the fleet in 1928, Reeves soon demonstrated that they were naval weapons of great power. In military exercises in 1928 and 1929, he conducted successful mock attacks on Hawaii and on the Panama Canal.

During the summer of 1927, Reeves was given temporary duty as adviser on aviation at the Geneva Disarmament Conference. Except for one year, Reeves remained in fleet aviation from 1925 to 1931, advancing in rank to rear admiral in 1927. In 1933, he became commander, Battle Fleet, and then for two years, was commander-in-chief, U.S. Fleet, the first aviation officer to hold this command. He retired in December 1936.

Reeves was recalled to active duty in 1940, and for the next six years, served on the lend-lease and munitions assignment boards. As a member of the Roberts Commission, which investigated the Pearl Harbor disaster, he was severe in his criticism of Admiral Husband E. Kimmel, commander of the Pacific Fleet at the time of the attack.

Reeves married Eleanor Merrken Watkins on July 1, 1896. They had three children: Ruth Drury, Joseph Mason, and William Cunningham. He died of a heart attack on March 25, 1948, in the Bethesda Naval Hospital, Maryland, and was buried at the Naval Academy.

REVELL, FLEMING HEWITT

(1849-1931) — Publisher, was born in Chicago, Illinois, the son of Fleming Hewitt Revell and Emma (Manning) Revell. The father, a descendant of French Huguenots who fled to the north of Ireland, was a shipbuilder in London, England, until, meeting with reverses, he brought his family to America, and in 1849 to Chicago, Illinois, where he built boats for the Lake Michigan traffic. Success did not attend him in Chicago either, and the only son had to leave school at nine years of age to help support his mother and three sisters. One of these sisters, Emma, married the evangelist, Dwight L. Moody, and it was under Moody's inspiration that Revell, not yet twenty, began in 1869 to publish *Everybody's Paper*, a little religious monthly. A pocket account book, in the possession of his son, shows that he traveled through the Middle

West securing subscriptions, five in one town and ten in the next. When the Chicago fire of 1871 burned his entire establishment, he started again. Doubtless the publishing of Moody's sermons, tracts, and other writings helped him to place his business on a firm basis, for these in cloth and paper bindings sold in time by the hundred thousands. To these were added the books of other evangelists suitable for the Moody audience, and by 1880 his list numbered about one hundred titles, besides booklets, gospel tracts, revival hymnals, and Sunday-school periodicals. A branch of the firm was opened in New York, New York in 1887, and ultimately branches in Toronto, Canada; London, England; and Edinburgh, Scotland were added.

By 1890 he was one of the largest publishers of religious books in America, having gradually widened his scope from strictly evangelical literature. He had a flourishing juvenile department, sold standard Sunday-school libraries of fifty volumes for $25.75, and distributed all the Sunday-school paraphernalia of the period, including picture cards and colored floral mottoes. He moved to New York about 1906 and some years afterward transferred the headquarters of his company to that city. His sixty years of religious publishing not only gave him a remarkable knowledge of the market possibilities of religious books of all kinds but permitted him to accumulate a comfortable fortune, which he invested wisely. Several years before his death he turned the presidency of his firm over to his son, Fleming Hewitt Revell, Jr., and became chairman of the board. He had married in 1872 Josephine Barbour of Romeo, Michigan, who died in 1924.

For years he was active in religious, educational, and financial affairs. Through his earlier association with Moody he developed a strong interest in the Northfield, Massachusetts, schools and contributed liberally to them. He was a trustee of the Northfield Seminary and of Wheaton College. He was long treasurer of the American Mission to Lepers and at different times a member of educational and mission boards of the Presbyterian Church. He was also a director of the New York Life Insurance Company. His extensive travels in Europe and the Near East during his yearly vacations gave him, in addition, a wide acquaintance with world problems. He died in 1931.

REVELL, NELLIE MacALENEY

(1872-1958) — Journalist, publicist, and radio personality, was born in Springfield, Illinois, the daughter of the editor and publisher of the *Springfield Republican*. She started her career on an opposition paper and was hired by her father after proving a worthy competitor for news. She married Joseph Revell; they had no children and were divorced. Revell left Springfield for Chicago, where she attracted attention as a writer for the *Chicago Journal*. Later in the decade, she reported for the *Denver Post*, the *Seattle Post Intelligencer*, the *San Francisco Chronicle*, and the *Chicago Times*. During this period, covered murder trials, then become a press agent for a circus.

New York was the center for American journalism at the turn of the century, and an offer from the *New York World* to become its first woman reporter lured Revell from the Midwest. She refused to have anything to do with the woman's page, and covered such pageantry as the coronation of Czar Nicholas II (1895) and Queen Victoria's funeral (1901).

She joined the *New York Evening Mail*, recently merged by Frank Munsey with the *New York Evening Telegram*, but quit when her column was moved to the woman's page. Shortly after this Revell became press agent for Al Jolson. Her interest in press agentry for circuses also continued, so that in the years following, she had as clients such Broadway stars as Lily Langtry, Norah Bayes, Lillian Russell, Elsie Janis, Eva Tanguay, and Will Rogers, as well as six circuses. Revell was head of publicity for the Keith-Orpheum motion-picture circuit and business manager of the Winter Garden.

In 1919, through an unfortunate investment, she lost her life's savings. Only weeks later, a severe spinal ailment developed that placed her in the hospital for years. While undergoing treatment, Revell published three books dealing with her battle for survival: *Right off the Chest* (1925), *Fighting Through* (1925), and *Funny Side Out* (1925). Funds to pay her hospital and medical expenses were also raised by a testimonial performance at the Cohan and Harris Theater.

By 1930, Revell had recovered despite all odds, and joined the National Broadcasting Company, where she became well known through her interviews with stage, screen, sports, and political figures. After her retirement in 1947, she continued to conduct a program called "Neighbor Nell."

Revell married Arthur J. Kellar; they had one daughter. Revell died on August 12, 1958, in New York City.

REYNOLDS, JOHN

(1788-1865) — Fourth governor of the state (1830-1834), was born in Pennsylvania to Irish immigrants Robert and Margaret (Moore)

John Reynolds

Reynolds. While he was still an infant, the family moved to Tennessee, but fear of the local Indians caused them to move again to Kaskaskia, Illinois, in 1800. Reynolds entered the College of Tennessee at Knoxville in 1809, and the next year began to study law. As a scout during the War of 1812, he was nicknamed "Old Ranger." Two years later, he passed the bar and began a law practice in Cahokia, Illinois, dealing mostly in litigation over land titles.

His political career began with his 1818 election as Justice of the Illinois Supreme Court. Although he was unsuccessful in his attempts for a U.S. Senate seat in 1823, Reynolds served in the state House of Representatives from 1826 to 1830. He aided in the attempt to revise the state constitution in favor of slavery in 1824. Six years later, he was elected governor by a small margin.

During his administration, the Black Hawk War (1831-1832) represented the culmination of conflicts between settlers and Indians concerning hunting and farming rights. Reynolds, acting as ex-official commander in chief of the militia, asked for volunteers to help fight the Indians. The governor's forces finally defeated the Indian tribes under Chief Black Hawk, forcing the Indians out of the state and across the Mississippi.

Reynolds resigned the governorship in 1834, after being elected to the U.S. House of Representatives. However, he was unsuccessful in his attempts for a state senate seat in 1848, and the state Superintendent of Schools post in 1858. He was elected an anti-Douglas delegate to the 1860 Democratic National Convention, but when he discovered Abraham Lincoln's popularity, he publicly stated his support for Douglas, and advised Southerners to take up arms against the North.

Reynolds died at Belleville, Illinois, in 1865.

RICHARDSON, WILLIAM ALEXANDER

(1811-1875) Representative and Senator from Illinois; Senate Years of Service: 1863-1865; born near Lexington, Fayette County, Ky., January 16, 1811; attended an academy at Walnut Hill, Ky., Centre College at Danville, Ky., and Transylvania University at Lexington, Ky.; taught school; studied law; admitted to the bar in 1831 and commenced practice in Shelbyville, Ill.; State's attorney 1834-1835; member, State house of representatives 1836-1838, 1844-1846, and served as speaker in 1844; member, State senate 1838-1842; presidential elector on the Democratic ticket in 1844; during the Mexican War enlisted as a captain and was promoted to the rank of major; moved to Quincy, Ill., in 1849; elected as a Democrat to the Thirtieth Congress to fill the vacancy caused by the resignation of Stephen A. Douglas; reelected to the Thirty-first and to the three succeeding Congresses and served from December 6, 1847, to August 25, 1856, when he resigned; chairman, Committee on Territories (Thirty-second and Thirty-third Congresses); elected to the Thirty-seventh Congress and served from March 4, 1861, until his resignation on January 29, 1863, having previously been elected Senator; elected as a Democrat to the United States Senate in 1863 to fill the vacancy caused by the death of Stephen A. Douglas and served from January 30, 1863, to March 3, 1865; was not a candidate for renomination in 1864; engaged in newspaper work; died in Quincy, Adams County, Ill., December 27, 1875; interment in Woodland Cemetery.

William Alexander Richardson

RICHBERG, DONALD RANDALL

(1881-1960) — Lawyer and writer, was born in Knoxville, Tennessee, on July 10, 1881, the son of John Carl Richberg, a lawyer and president of the Illinois Commission on Uniform State Laws, and Eloise Olivia (Randall) Richberg, who received her medical degree at the age of fifty and became a practicing physician as well as author. At the University of Chicago, Richberg lettered in track and was active in his fraternity. He graduated in 1901, and then earned his law degree from Harvard in 1904.

Richberg went into law practice with his father, and soon developed an interest in social issues.

He served for a number of years as the Chicago city treasurer and for the Cook County Board of Assessors. He became involved in the Bull Moose movement, led by Theodore Roosevelt, and from 1912 to 1916, was one of Roosevelt's closest advisors, helping to organize the Progressive Party. He served on the election committee of reform candidate C.E. Merriam for mayor of Chicago, and to the election campaign of Robert M. LaFollette in 1919. He was director of the National Legislative Reference Bureau of the Progressive Party in 1913 and 1914, then he ran for circuit judge himself as a Progressive Republican fusion nominee in 1915. From 1916 to 1919, he was master of chancery for the Circuit Court of Cook County.

As a crusading lawyer and special counsel to the city of Chicago, Richberg carried through twelve years of litigation with the Peoples Gas, Light & Coke Company resulting in the reduction of public utility rates. In 1922, he began representing the railway brotherhoods as chief counsel in a government injunction. He served as general counsel for the National Conference on Valuation of Railroads, and from 1926 to 1933, served as general counsel for the Railway Labor Executives Association. In 1926, he authored the Railway Labor Act, and defended it before the Supreme Court.

In 1932, Richberg went to work on the campaign of Franklin D. Roosevelt. After he was elected president, Roosevelt asked Richberg to assist in writing the labor and public works sections of the National Industrial Recovery Act, and after it was enacted, he was appointed general counsel to the National Recovery Administration. He took a leave of absence from this position to serve as executive secretary of the President's Executive Council, director of the Industrial Emergency Committee, and executive director of the National Emergency Council. Four months later, these three agencies were combined, and Richberg was appointed executive director of the new body.

In June 1935, the National Recovery Act was declared unconstitutional, and Richberg returned to private law practice, specializing in labor law. In 1945, he helped write the Ball-Burton-Hatch Bill, which was a labor relations bill that would establish a format for settling labor-management disputes. After two years it was defeated, but a similar bill, the Taft-Hartley Act, also co-written by Richberg, was passed.

In 1949, Richberg announced that he had accepted a teaching

position at the University of Virginia, where he stayed until retirement. As well as a crusading lawyer and teacher, Richberg was also an author of poetry and fiction. His poetry was published in a volume entitled *Old Faith and Fancies New*, and he wrote articles for the *New York Times Magazine*, the *New Republic*, and *Atlantic Monthly*. His fiction includes *The Shadow Men*, *In the Dark*, and *A Man of Purpose*. In addition, he wrote political studies, such as *Tents of the Mighty*, *Who Wins in November*, *The Rainbow*, and *Government and Business Tomorrow: A Public Relations Program*. His autobiography is entitled *My Hero*.

In 1924, he married Florence Weed, and they had one daughter. Richberg died on November 27, 1960, in Charlottesville, Virginia.

RIEGER, JOHANN GEORG JOSEPH ANTON
(1811-1909) — Pioneer Evangelical clergyman, was born on April 23, 1811 in Aurach, Bavaria, Germany. He was left an orphan before he reached the age of eleven, and for a time lived with an aunt in Epinal, France. From earliest childhood he had been destined for priesthood in the Catholic Church, but absorbed some Lutheran doctrine as a boy while helping a classmate with his catechism lessons. An open avowal of his Protestant leaning brought such strenuous opposition on the part of his aunt that he fled in 1832 to Basel, Switzerland, where he found refuge in the home of a Reformed minister and was brought in contact with the mission house of that place. Four years later when a group of American Christians applied to the Basel headquarters for German missionaries for the West, Rieger was chosen to go. He was among the first of the German missionaries who had the vision to introduce the use of English into the evangelical service.

His first mission field was at Alton, Illinois, where he arrived on November 28, 1836. During his ministry at this place, he lived at the home of Elijah Parish Lovejoy, and assisted in the latter's abolitionist activities, but his most strenuous efforts in the direction of a spiritual revival were so meagerly rewarded that he left in August of the following year for Beardstown, Illinois, where he stayed until the spring of 1839. In this year he returned to Germany where he made the acquaintance of Minette Schemel, who returned to the United States with him in 1840 as his bride. They settled first at Highland, Illinois, where their two children were born and died. In 1840, when the *Deutsche Evangelische Kirchen-Verein des Westen*, later called the *Evangelische Synode von Nord-Amerika*, was formed, Rieger was recognized as one of the dominating figures in the movement. In October 1843, two months after he had moved from Highland to Burlington, Iowa, his wife died. He made a second trip to Germany in 1844 and married Henrietta Wilkins at Bremen on April 15, 1845. For two years after his return to the United States he sold literature for the Bible and Tract Society of New York and then moved to Holstein, Missouri, where his two small daughters fell ill of cholera and died.

His principal work during these years was done in connection with the establishing of the Evangelical Seminary, at Marthasville, Missouri, in 1850, after it had been housed in his own home for two years. His ministry of thirteen years at Holstein ended when he moved to Jefferson City in 1860. He became one of the trustees of the Lincoln Institute, a college for African Americans, and did admirable work among the prisoners at the state penitentiary. He was universally beloved: southerners left their valuables in the safe-keeping of this abolitionist preacher when Federal soldiers approached; rich and poor, black and white, Catholic and Protestant sought out the humble clergyman for advice. When he died in 1909 the whole city went into mourning. His widow and seven children survived him.

ROBINSON, BENJAMIN LINCOLN

(1864-1935) — Botanist, was born on November 8, 1864, in Bloomington, Illinois, the son of James Harvey and Latricia Maria (Drake) Robinson. He received his early education at home and in local schools, then at Williams College and at Harvard University, where he graduated in 1887. Immediately thereafter, June 29, 1887, he married Margaret Louise Casson and went with her to Germany to continue his studies. Their only child, a daughter who died in early girlhood, was born there.

Robinson studied under Graf zu Solms-Laubach at Strassburg, and was awarded his doctorate in 1889. He had planned further study abroad, but was offered and accepted the position of assistant to Sereno Watson, curator of the Gray Herbarium at Harvard. Two years later, Watson died, and Robinson became curator. He took over the charge of a collection already distinguished and carrying the high repute of Asa Gray, but with very small resources. Eventually, with the anonymous aid of Mrs. Gray and a group of friends, the worst financial difficulties were overcome.

Naturally, Robinson succeeded to the unfinished work of Gray and Watson. With several collaborators, he edited and completed their manuscripts to bring out an additional volume of Gray's *Synoptical Flora of North America* (volume I, 1895-1897). Much of his predecessors' attention had been given to the study of pioneer collections of plants from the southwestern United States and Mexico; this work he carried on, largely from the especially discriminating and finely prepared collections of C.G. Pringle in Mexico. It resulted in numerous short taxonomic articles and monographs. Receipt of a large collection from the Galapagos was the occasion for his *Flora of the Galapagos Islands* (1902), one of the important documents relating to the natural history of that peculiar and much-discussed region. In collaboration with M.L. Fernald, he prepared the thoroughly rewritten seventh edition of Gray's *Manual of the Botany of the Northern United States* (1908). In his later years, he turned to monographic work, never finished as a whole but productive of a number of short papers, on a portion of the great family *Compositae*.

Robinson took part in the discussions that attended the launching of the American Code of Botanical Nomenclature in 1895, and during the thirty-five years when two codes were in use in the United States, he supported the conservative point of view and advocated action by international agreement rather than by American botanists independently. For more than thirty years he was the painstaking editor-in-chief of *Rhodora*, the journal of the New England Botanical Club.

He died on July 27, 1935.

ROBINSON, EDGAR MUNSON

(1867-1951) — Educator and youth group leader, YMCA official and one of scouting's "founding fathers," was born in St. Stephen, New Brunswick, Canada. He was the son of a local merchant and grew up working in the family store while getting his education at the local public schools. He eventually took over the family business. However, at the same time he cultivated an early interest in youth group service and over the next few years achieved some notoriety for his work at camp meetings and evangelical conferences. He married Serena Truman (date unknown); they had four children. In 18893, he formed a boys' camp, which he successfully operated himself. Robinson gave up his interest in the family store in 1894 after much indecision and migrated with his family to Springfield, Massachusetts where he met with Dr. Frank N. Seerley at the International Conference of the YMCA. He then began a lifetime association with that group. In 1898, he accepted a part time position of boys' work secretary for Massachusetts and Rhode Island. At the same time, he entered Springfield College as a student, where he was influenced by more liberal, progressive educational philosophies promoted by faculty members William G. Ballantine and college president Laurence L. Doggett. By graduation in 1901, Robinson had been transformed from an impatient, dogmatic evangelical to a more open-minded believer in Social Gospel. He was encouraged by YMCA superiors and colleagues to apply more liberal, flexible ways in working with boys.

Robinson became the first boys' work secretary for the International Committee of the YMCA in 1900, which included both Canada and the United States. For that position, he toured the continent encouraging the growth and development of the YMCA boys' work with emphasis on character building. Robinson came to value G. Stanley Hall's "recapitulation" theory, basically a child's life parallels human history and culminates in a civilized adulthood. He sought to apply this theory to regimented programs. As a pioneer camp director, he believed that summer camping experiences would lead adolescent boys into a "noble Christian life." In 1902, he initiated *Association Boys*, a magazine that became an effective publication of information for the progressive ideas of youth leaders. Nearly four hundred boys were workers under his (and his five associates) supervision by 1913.

Robinson was sympathetic and interested in other new youth movements, such as Ernest Thompson Seton's Woodcraft Indians and Dan Beard's Boy Pioneers. As early as 1909 he supported first efforts of YMCA units to organize Boy Scouts based on Lord Robert Baden-Powell's approach in England. However, after Robinson and others initiated the first National Boy Scout Committee in New York (1910), and after the first Boy Scouts of America (BSA) groups were formed he realized the YMCA and Boy Scouts were both independent and self-supporting. He remained a staunch BSA supporter and even served for a years as their first chief executive but resumed his work with the YMCA in 1911. Robinson also favored a less woodcraft mode of scouting and offered more democratic control by local leaders and members. In 1920, Robinson and Charles R. Scott were selected to go no a world tour on behalf of the YMCA. In 1922, Robinson was appointed boys' work secretary of the YMCA World Alliance. In this position he was instrumental in the planning of the 1923 Portschach conference, which considerably enhanced the World Alliance. Robinson was a member of numerous boards and committees; he held many honorary titles and received the Tarbell Medallion for citizenship, named after the journalist Ida Tarbell, and given in honor of his humanitarian achievements. He retired in 1927 at the age of sixty; he then became head of the Springfield College Faculty and head of its boys' work division. He maintained the college as his main interest throughout the remainder of his life and was critical in obtaining a pueblo for the college campus, which was named in his honor. Robinson published a historical recount of his YMCA youth work, The Early Years, in 1950. He died at his home in Springfield on April 9, 1951.

ROBINSON, JOHN MCCRACKEN

(1794-1843) Senator from Illinois; Senate Years of Service: 1830-1841; born near Georgetown, Scott County, Ky., April 10, 1794; attended the common schools and graduated from Transylvania University at Lexington, Ky.; studied law; admitted to the bar and began practice in Carmi, Ill., in 1818; judge of the State supreme court; served as general in the State militia; elected in 1830 as a Jacksonian (later Democrat) to the United States Senate to fill the vacancy caused by the death of John McLean; reelected in 1835 and served from December 11, 1830, to March 3, 1841; was not a candidate for reelection; chairman, Committee on Engrossed Bills (Twenty-second Congress), Committee on Militia (Twenty-second through Twenty-fourth Congresses), Committee on Post Office and Post Roads (Twenty-fourth through Twenty-sixth Congresses); elected an associate justice of the Illinois State supreme court in 1843 and served until his death two months later in Ottawa, Ill., April 25, 1843; interment in the Old Graveyard, Carmi, Ill.

John McCracken Robinson

ROSENWALD, JULIUS

(1862-1932) — Merchant and philanthropist, was born on August 12, 1862, in Springfield, Illinois, the son of Samuel and Augusta (Hammerslough) Rosenwald. He was educated in the public schools of Springfield, and in 1879, began his business career with Hammerslough Brothers, wholesale clothiers of New York City, remaining with that concern until 1885. He then became president of Rosenwald & Weil, a Chicago, Illinois, clothing firm, continuing in that capacity until 1906. From 1895 to 1910, he was also vice-president and treasurer of Sears, Roebuck & Company; from 1910 to 1925, president; and until his death, chairman of the board of directors.

Rosenwald regularly attended the religious services of Chicago Sinai Congregation, of which he was vice-president; and he freely confessed that he derived his social vision and social passion from that source. He was one of the leaders and pioneers who brought about the Federation of Jewish Charities in Chicago in 1923. As a member of the American Jewish Committee, he helped to protect the Jew against unjust discrimination. Feeling that the Jewish problem in Russia must be worked out in Russia itself, he contributed $6 million to further a plan for the colonization of Jews in that country. Through his far-sightedness, the Hebrew Union College of Cincinnati, and the Jewish Theological Seminary of America, in New York City, were put on a firm financial footing, though not endowed. He gave to the Hebrew University of Jerusalem and to other cultural agencies in Palestine, and aided in the relief of the unfortunate of that country. He also helped establish colleges in Assyria and Constantinople. Immediately after World War I, Rosenwald fed the hungry children of Germany; later, he established a dental clinic in Berlin. He contributed part of the total cost (about $3,850,000) of twenty-five Negro Young Men's Christian Association, and three Negro Young Women's Christian Association buildings in twenty-five cities with an approximately two million Negro population. He also contributed $3,660,000 toward the total cost of $23,200,000 for 4,500 Negro public schools in the South; 339 of these were built in 1929.

Civic minded, he was one of the founders of the Municipal Voters League. As a member of the Committee of Fifteen, he was fearlessly active in banishing the "red light district." During the race riots in Chicago, he served to restore peace and good will. He was an ardent champion of the Chicago Planning Commission, and president of the Jewish Charities of Chicago. He gave to the city, in 1929, an industrial museum, to be known as the Museum of Science and Industry founded by Julius Rosenwald. His gifts to the University of Chicago amounted to almost $5 million.

In 1916, President Wilson appointed Rosenwald a member of the Advisory Commission of the Council of National Defense and chairman of the committee on supplies. At the request of the secretary of war, he went on a special mission to France in 1918, and was a member of the Second National Industrial Conference in 1919.

His articles, "Principles of Public Giving" and "The Trend Away from Perpetuities," published in the *Atlantic Monthly* (May 1929 and December 1930, respectively) created history in the realm of philanthropy.

On April 8, 1890, he married Augusta Nusbaum of Chicago, who died May 23, 1929; they had five children. On January 8, 1930, he married Adelaide (Rau) Goodkind. He died on January 6, 1932, in Chicago, Illinois.

RUBIN, JERRY

(1938-1994) — Social activist and businessman, was born on July 14, 1938, to Jewish parents in Cincinnati, Ohio, but grew up in Avondale. His father was a bakery truck driver and union organizer. Rubin attended the local public schools and became interested in journalism. He worked for his high school's newspaper and also for *The Post*. He went to college at the University of Cincinnati, where he continued to work for *The Post*, and became its youth-page editor. While working for the paper, Rubin interviewed Adlai Stevenson, who was twice nominated for president by the Democratic Party. Stevenson's political beliefs greatly inspired Rubin.

In 1960 and 1961, Rubin's parents died, and he was left to care for his younger brother. He and his brother moved to Tel Aviv, Israel, where Rubin studied sociology. He returned to the United States in 1962, and settled in Berkeley, California, where he became involved in the Free Speech Movement. Later, he became one of the leaders in the youth, and anti-war movements. He organized the Vietnam Day Committee, and led many protests against the Vietnam War.

Rubin and fellow activist Abbie Hoffman joined together to in an effort to create awareness for their causes. They engaged in outrageous acts to attract the attention of the media. For example, in August 1967, Rubin, Hoffman, and others threw dollar bills down to the trading floor of the New York Stock Exchange, sending stockbrokers scurrying about the floor picking up the money.

In 1968, Rubin and Hoffman formed the Youth Party International. The members, referred to as "Yippies," engaged in outlandish public demonstrations. In August of that year, the Yippies gathered in Chicago to protest the Democratic National Convention's nomination of Hubert H. Humphrey for president. Before the protest, Hoffman made references to terrorizing Chicago by putting LSD into the city's water, among other things. The city's police regarded the demonstrators as a threat, and the Yippies peaceful protest quickly turned bloody as a riot broke out when the police began attacking the demonstrators. The media captured the violent clashes, but this time the public, while outraged over the police violence, were not sympathetic to the Yippies' disregard for social norms.

The Nixon administration brought charges of conspiracy to cross state lines with the intent to start a riot against Rubin and seven others. Bobby Seale, one of the defendants in the Chicago Conspiracy Trial, was separated from the group, and Rubin and the remaining defendants became known as the "Chicago Seven." Rubin and Hoffman made a spectacle out of the trial, engaging in attention-getting antics, such as dressing in judiciary robe instead of a suit. In all, over two hundred citations of contempt of court were given to the defendants. They were all found guilty of crossing state lines with the intent to start a riot, though the conspiracy charges were dropped. The convictions were appealed, and eventually overturned.

In the early 1970s, Rubin continued to be a social activist. He and Abbie Hoffman went to Miami to protest the Democratic Convention in 1972. Around this time, he realized that his popularity was fading. He went on a journey of self-exploration through the end of the decade. He became a Wall Street marketing analyst and started his own business, which proved to be very lucrative. His business activities generated criticism from social activists.

Rubin left New York and moved to southern California, settling near Los Angeles in the early 1990s. He worked as an independent marketer for a company that made nutritional drinks. In November 1994, Rubin was hit by a car while crossing the street. He died from his injuries on November 24. He was survived by his wife and daughter.

In 1970, Ruben published a book entitled *Do It! – Scenarios of A Revolution*. He also co-authored, with Abbie Hoffman and Ed Sanders, *Vote* (1972) about the presidential conventions in Miami.

RUBY, JACK L.

(1911-1967) — Night Club owner, assassin of Lee Harvey Oswald, was born Jacob Rubenstein on March 25, 1911, in Chicago, Illinois, the son of Joseph Rubenstein and Fannie Turek Rutkowski. He grew up in lower-class Jewish neighborhoods of Chicago, where Yiddish was the primary language in the home. In the spring of 1921, his parents separated. On June 6, 1922, the Jewish Social Service Bureau for truancy and incorrigibility referred Ruby to the Institute for Juvenile Research. The institute's psychiatric report stated that he was quick-tempered and disobedient. During the 1920s, he and several of his siblings lived in foster homes in the Chicago area.

Ruby dropped out of high school at the age of sixteen, and began working odd jobs. He became involved in commercial ventures on the streets of Chicago, scalping tickets to sporting events and selling novelty items and knick-knacks. During this time, he was arrested once after an altercation with a policeman concerning ticket scalping. In 1933, Ruby and a few of his friends went to Los Angeles, California, and later to San Francisco, California, where they supported themselves working off of the streets. In 1937, Ruby returned to the Chicago area, where he unsuccessfully attempted to organize the Scrap Iron & Junk Handlers' Union. He also helped organize the Spartan Novelty Company, which sold small novelty items.

In May 1943, Ruby joined the air force. Most of his service time was spent in the South. He attained the rank of private first class, and received the Good Conduct Medal before being honorably discharged in February 1946. He returned to Chicago and joined his three brothers in the Earl Products Company, a firm specializing in novelty items. In 1947, two of Ruby's brothers bought him out and Ruby moved to Dallas, Texas, where he helped his sister run the Singapore Supper Club, in which he was an investor. On December 30, 1947, he legally changed his name to Jack L. Ruby.

Ruby's main interest and source of income was the operation of nightclubs and dance halls in Dallas. He also engaged in speculative economic schemes, and in 1959, he became interested in a venture to sell jeeps to Cuba. By 1963, Ruby owned interest in two Dallas nightclubs, the Vegas Club and the Carousel Club. With his known violent temper, Ruby was frequently physically abusive to his employees and customers. Between 1949 and 1963, Ruby was arrested eight times on minor charges. By November 1963, Ruby also had serious difficulties with federal and state taxes that he owed.

Following the assassination of President John F. Kennedy in Dallas on November 22, 1963, the police arrested Lee Harvey Oswald for the murder of the president. Two days after the assassination, while the police were transporting the suspect, Ruby entered the Dallas Police Department basement through an auto ramp and shot Oswald in front of a TV audience of millions. Ruby claimed that he had shot Oswald to spare Jackie Kennedy the ordeal of returning to Dallas to testify in the trial of the president's alleged assassin. Two days later, he was indicted for murder. Ruby was convicted of murder on March 14, 1964, and was sentenced to death. During the trial, Ruby's lawyers offered a defense of insanity, and a psychiatrist testified that Ruby was a "psychotic depressive." Ruby avowed his sanity, a contention that was upheld in a Texas state court on June 13, 1966. The Texas Court of Appeals reversed the conviction on October 5, 1966, claiming that the trial judge had allowed illegal testimony. A second trial was ordered to take place with a change of venue to Wichita Falls, Texas.

While the trial was pending, Ruby was admitted to Parkland Memorial Hospital on December 9, 1966. Doctors diagnosed his illness as cancer; he died of a blood clot in his lungs in Dallas, Texas, on January 3, 1967. Ruby was buried in Chicago, Illinois.

After the murder of Oswald, various conspiracy theories attempted to link Ruby to a plot to kill President Kennedy. Some people made a big deal of Ruby's one or more visits to Cuba in 1959; others alleged that Ruby had been involved with organized crime through his dealings with the American Guild of Variety Artists. The Warren Commission Report of 1964 found no evidence that Ruby was part of any conspiracy. In 1975, the Rockefeller Commission, set up to investigate Central Intelligence Agency activities within the United States, concluded that neither Oswald nor Ruby had ties with the CIA, a charge made by several conspiracy theorists.

RYAN, GEORGE H.

(1934-) — Forty-first governor of Illinois (1999-2003), was born on February 24, 1934, to Thomas and Jeanette Ryan. Ryan attended local schools in Kankakee, Illinois, and attended Butler University in Indiana. From 1954 to 1956, he served in the U. S. Army in South Korea.

After returning from South Korea, Ryan attended and graduated from Ferris State College in Michigan with a degree in pharmacy. He then worked in the family pharmacy business, and in 1962, Ryan served as Senator Edward McBroom's campaign manager. From 1966 to 1972, he worked on the Kankakee County Board of Education. Ryan spent the following ten years in the Illinois legislature, and in 1982, was elected lieutenant governor under James R. Thompson, a position he held until 1991. He then served as secretary of state from 1991 to 1999, at which point he was elected and sworn in as governor of the state of Illinois.

Among the legislation that Ryan passed was the Illinois FIRST program, which provides twelve billion dollars to state road and transit system expansion and renovation, as well as for school renovation and environmental clean-up. He has also helped pass the CAP law, which aims to prevent child access to guns and a patient bill of rights for HMOs. In 2000, Ryan declared a moratorium on executions, and established a commission to review capital punishment, after thirteen people on death row were found to be wrongfully accused.

Due to mounting controversy over his service as secretary of state and the conviction of his former aides in that office, Ryan decided not to run for reelection in 2002. His last act as governor was to commute all the sentences of those on or waiting to be sent to death row because of his belief that the death penalty is inherently unfair. In December 2003, he was indicted of racketeering, fraud, and conspiracy; his trial began in September 2005.

Ryan married Lura Lynn Lowe in 1956; the couple has six children.

RYNNING, OLE

(1809-1838) — Immigrant leader and author, was born on April 4, 1809, at Ringsaker, Norway, the son of the Reverend Jens Rynning and Severine Cathrine Steen. He was tutored privately for matriculation at the national university in Christiania, where he studied from 1830 to 1833. He then opened a private school at Snaasen, and became interested in the economic conditions of Norwegian farmers and laborers. The Gordian knot of their difficulties could be cut, he believed, by emigration, and in 1837, he set out for America as the leader of a group of eighty-four emigrants who sailed from Bergen for New York on April 7, 1837, aboard the bark *AEgir*.

The *AEgir* reached New York on June 9, 1837, and a week later the immigrants started for Illinois. From Chicago, Rynning and three companions made their way to the Beaver Creek region in Iroquois County, where they selected a settlement site. The low land of the vicinity, dry in the late summer, was flooded the next spring; ultimately the colony was devastated by malaria, and it was abandoned in 1840. Meanwhile, Rynning wrote *A True Account of America for the Information and Help of Peasant and Commoner*, completed in February 1838. The next spring, Ansten Nattestad, a member of the colony, journeyed back to Norway by way of New Orleans, taking the manuscript with him. It was published at Christiania late in the year. A second edition appeared in 1839.

In September 1838, Rynning fell victim to the epidemic then

593

scourging the Beaver Creek colony and died.

S

SACHS, THEODORE BERNARD

(1868-1916) — Physician, the son of Bernard and Sophia Sachs, was born in Dinaberg, Russia. He received his education at the Kherson High School and the University of Odessa, from which he graduated in law in 1891. He then immigrated to America and settled in Chicago, Illinois. While attending the College of Physicians and Surgeons, he supported himself as a sewing-machine operator for a clothing manufacturer. He graduated in 1895, and after two years as intern and house physician at Michael Reese Hospital, established his office in the Jewish quarter of Chicago's west side.

In 1900, he established in the Jewish Aid Dispensary, the first clinic in Chicago devoted exclusively to patients suffering from pulmonary tuberculosis, denouncing the neglect of tuberculous patients at the county institutions at Dunning and Oak Forest. In 1905, he was attending physician to a camp for tuberculous patients at Glencoe, the first of its kind in the state. Later, a camp at Dunning was established, as well as the Edward Sanitarium at Naperville, where he was director and examining physician from its foundation to his death. He was in the forefront of the campaign successfully waged in 1909 for the establishment of the Chicago Municipal Tuberculosis Sanitarium, begun in 1911 and completed in 1915. As secretary of the first board of directors and later its head, he exercised much influence upon the plans of the buildings and upon the organization of its services.

After accusations of inefficiency and dishonesty against the board of directors by city officials, Sachs submitted his resignation on March 20, 1916, and two weeks later committed suicide by morphine poisoning at the Edward Sanitarium. He left a letter addressed to the people of Chicago that called for an inquiry into the affairs of the sanitarium and protested against its exploitation by politicians. A report of the finance committee of the Chicago city council later exonerated the sanitarium board of charges of any misuse of public funds.

In the midst of his municipal work Sachs was director and president of the Chicago Tuberculosis Institute, secretary of the United Hebrew Charities, and attending physician to several hospitals. In 1915-16, he was president of the National Association for the Study and Prevention of Tuberculosis. The most notable of his few articles are *Tuberculosis in the Jewish District of Chicago* (1904), *Children of*

595

Tuberculous Parents (1908), and *The Examination of Employees for Tuberculosis* (1912). He was greatly assisted in his investigations and writings by his wife, Lena Louise Wilson of Chicago, whom he married January 4, 1900.

Edith S. Sampson

SAMPSON, EDITH S.

(1901-1979) — Attorney, United Nations delegate, and Circuit Court judge, was born Edith Spurlock on October 13, 1901, in Pittsburgh, Pennsylvania, the daughter of Louis Spurlock and Elizabeth A. (McGruder) Spurlock. Sampson's family was poor, and during her childhood, public education was not compulsory, so she went to work full-time to help support her family. She did, however, manage to return to school, graduating from Pittsburgh's Peabody High School. Sampson's Sunday school teacher introduced her to Associated Charities, an organization that made it possible for her to attend the New York School of Social Work. During her schooling, after scoring the highest grade in a required course in criminology, Professor George W. Kirchwey told her that she should give up social work and become a lawyer.

Sampson continued her social work and moved to Chicago, Illinois, in the early 1920s, working for the Illinois Children's Home and Aid Society, where she again met Professor Kirchwey. This time she heeded his advice, and signed up for evening classes at the John Marshall Law School. During the day, she kept her jobs with the Young Women's Christian Association and the Illinois Children's Home and Aid Society. She received her bachelor of law degree in 1925, but failed the Illinois State bar exam. She then entered the Graduate Law School of Loyola University and received her degree in 1927, the first woman to receive an LL.M. That same year she was admitted to the Illinois State Bar.

Sampson began working for the Juvenile Court of Cook County in 1925, first serving as a probation officer and then as a referee. Two years later, she opened her own law firm on the south side of Chicago, specializing in criminal law and domestic relations. In 1934, Sampson was admitted to practice before the U.S. Supreme Court. As a leader in her community, Sampson became a member and chairwoman of the executive committee of the National Council of Negro Women. She gained international attention in 1949, when she was invited to participate in the *World Town Hall of the Air* lecture tour that toured the world debating political issues. She was elected president when the organization became permanent in 1950.

In August 1950, President Truman nominated her to serve as an alternate U.S. delegate to the fifth regular session of the United Nations General Assembly, becoming the first African American to be an official U.S. representative to the United Nations. She was assigned to Committee Three—the Social, Humanitarian, and Cultural Committee, and served with Eleanor Roosevelt. She was reelected in 1952.

By the early 1960s, Sampson was assistant corporation counsel of Chicago. In 1962, the local Democratic Party nominated her to fill an un-expired term as a Circuit Court judge. She won by a landslide, and in 1964, was elected to fill the seat for a six-year term, becoming the first African American woman ever to sit as a Circuit Court judge. Judge Sampson retired from the bench in 1978, just a year before her death.

She married Rufus Sampson; they divorced. She then married fellow lawyer Joseph E. Clayton on November 5, 1934. Sampson died on October 8, 1979, in Chicago, Illinois.

SANDBURG, CARL (AUGUST)
(1878-1967) — Author, poet, and biographer, was born on January 6, 1878, in Galesburg, Illinois, the son of Swedish emigrants. He received little schooling between jobs as a milk wagon driver, bricklayer, and barbership porter, but at the age of twenty he enlisted in the army for the Spanish-American War. He then entered Lombard College, working his way through until 1902, and began traveling around the country. He was a district organizer of the Wisconsin Socialist-Democrat Party for a year, and then secretary to the mayor of Milwaukee from 1910 to 1912. In 1913, he was made associate editor of *System* magazine and continued his journalism career as Stockholm correspondent for the Newspaper Enterprise Associates as well as editorial writer for the *Chicago Daily News*. He was involved with labor disputes in the city, and covered the Chicago race riots for the paper. He soon turned to his own writing, however, and began a tour around the country singing his own folk songs with a guitar. His greatest work, *Abraham Lincoln: The War Years* (1939), is regarded as a major historical biography in the nation and

Carl (August) Sandburg

garnered him the Pulitzer Prize in 1940. The book required of him thirteen years of research and took up four volumes.

His other great historical work, *The Prairie Years* (1926), also included biographical information about Lincoln. He wrote a Civil War book, *Storm over the Landrorn* in 1942, and a volume about World War II in *Home Front Memo* in 1943. Sandburg was also considered "poet laureate of industrial America," publishing books of verse which included *In Reckless Ecstasy* (1904): *Chicago Poems* (1915): *Corn Huskers* (1918); and other collections of both songs and children's stories. In 1929, he wrote a biography on his brother-in-law, Edward Steichen, the famous photographer. Sandburg was considered a "western Walt Whitman" in his time and he believed in a society where democracy, humanitarianism, and art were joined. His poetic language is simple and in the vernacular, often sympathizing with the urban working classes. He died in Flat Rock, North Carolina, on July 22, 1967.

SARGENT, FREDERICK

(1859-1919) — Engineer specializing in the design and construction of electrical generating stations, was born at Liskeard, Cornwall, England, the son of Daniel and Jane (Yates) Sargent. He became an apprentice in the famous engineering works of John Elder & Company on the Clyde, near Glasgow, and while serving his apprenticeship, attended night classes at Anderson's College, Glasgow.

In 1880, Sargent came to the United States and found employment designing marine steam engines in the shipbuilding yards on the Atlantic Coast. The following year, he worked as a designer for the Sioux City (Iowa) Engine Company, and in 1882, went to Milwaukee to join the engineering staff of E. P. Allis & Company. He soon became acquainted with the Western Edison Light Company of Chicago, and in 1884 went to work for them; on the organization of the Chicago Edison Company in 1887, he became its consulting engineer, holding this connection with the Edison Company and its successor, the

Commonwealth Edison Company, until his death.

To the duties of this post he added, in 1889, those of chief engineer of the Edison United Manufacturing Company, with headquarters in New York, and on the reorganization of this concern as the Edison General Electric Company, he became its assistant chief engineer. In August 1890, he returned to Chicago to establish himself as a consulting electrical and mechanical engineer, and in 1891, formed the firm of Sargent & Lundy. He was consulting engineer for the World's Columbian Exposition in 1891 and 1892. During the World War, he was consulting engineer for the government in connection with the Edgewood Arsenal and other projects.

While his early training had been in the design and construction of reciprocating engines, Sargent was among the first to recognize the great advantages of the steam turbine, and his purchase of the first large turbine for the Fisk Street Station, Chicago, began a new epoch in central station design. He saw the advantages in the use of high pressures and temperatures, took the lead in the introduction of pressures of 400 and 600 pounds, and had recommended the employment of 1200-pound pressures, which were introduced after his death. His mechanical mind indicated the economical and satisfactory solution of serious construction troubles in installations where large fluctuations in the condensing water levels existed.

Sargent was awarded a medal by the World's Columbian Exposition and was a member of the jury of awards for power engineering at the St. Louis exposition of 1904. He was a member of the American Society of Mechanical Engineers, the American Institute of Electrical Engineers, the Western Society of Engineers, and other organizations.

He married at Sioux City, Iowa, in 1885, Laura S. Sleep. His wife, with two sons and a daughter, survived him. He died in 1919 at his home in Glencoe, Illinois.

SAUGANASH

(?-1841) — Native American sub-chief, was born in Canada. His name is often spelled Sagaunash, and he is also known as "Englishman" or Billy Caldwell. His father was said to be William Caldwell, an Irish officer in the British service, and his mother was a Potawatomi. He was trained by Roman Catholic priests at Detroit, and, in addition to the several Indian dialects that he spoke, he acquired fluency in both French and English. From about 1807 he was closely associated with Tecumseh for some six years as an interpreter and perhaps as a secretary. He opposed the government of the United States and the frontier settlers, but there seems good authority for believing that he used his influence against the perpetration of atrocities.

He arrived at Fort Dearborn the day after the massacre of August 15, 1812, and it is certain that he was the means of saving several lives. He was probably at the Battle of the Thames on October 5, 1813, when Tecumseh was killed, and thereafter may have remained for some years in Canada. Under the British government he had the title of "captain of the Indian Department," which he is known to have used in signing documents as late as 1816. About 1820 he made his residence at the present Chicago and avowed his allegiance to the United States. In 1826 he was appointed a justice of the peace. With two other negotiators, he rendered valuable aid to the settlers and the government in 1827 by keeping the Winnebago chief, Big Foot, at peace. In 1828, at a point a few miles north of the mouth of the Chicago River, the government built for him a house, probably the first frame structure erected in the Chicago region. He again exerted his influence for peace in 1832 by dissuading Indians from joining Black Hawk's band. By successive treaties culminating in the one of 1833, at Chicago, the Potawatomi ceded virtually all of their lands east of the Mississippi, and in the summer of 1836 they began their long migration to western Iowa. Sauganash accompanied them. He died in the vicinity of the present Council Bluffs. Sauganash was more than six feet tall. By reason of his height, his powerful frame, and his erect bearing he was sometimes called the "Straight Tree." He was a man of exceptional intelligence and ability, and he was highly regarded by his white neighbors. Upon his tribesmen he urged the acceptance of the white man's mode of life and was especially interested in the education of Native American youth. He had but one wife, the sister of the Potawatomi chief, Yellow Hand, and but one child, a son who died before reaching manhood.

SCHLESINGER, BENJAMIN

(1876-1932) — Labor leader, was a native of Krakai, province of Kovno, Lithuania, and the son of Nechemiah and Judith Schlesinger. His father's family name is not known to his descendants, since at some time in his life Nechemiah adopted his wife's maiden name, Schlesinger, as his surname. Born into a rabbinical family, he enjoyed a superior intellectual environment and evidently inherited superior mental equipment. When transplanted from Krakai to Chicago in 1891, however, like most Jewish immigrant youths irrespective of their background, he was forced to resort to manual labor for a living. Accordingly, in common with large numbers of Russian Jews, he became a needle-trades worker, taking up the occupation of sewing-machine operator on cloaks and suits. Many of these superior immigrant youngsters pursued courses of study while plying their trade, thereby attaining a profession; but Schlesinger, from the outset, was caught in the vortex of official responsibilities connected with the labor movement, and his time and energy were absorbed in its service. From the age of seventeen, two years after he landed in America, he was a guiding spirit in the Jewish labor movement, either as a union official in the ladies' garment trades, or as manager of the *Jewish Daily Forward*, the outstanding Jewish Socialist and labor organ. Through these positions he played a dominant role in shaping the destinies of both the union and the publication in their rise from poverty to affluence and power.

His first office was that of secretary of the Chicago Cloak Makers' Union, and he had not held this a year when he was elected treasurer of the newly formed International Cloak Makers' Union of America. In 1903 he was made president of the International Ladies' Garment Workers' Union, which was founded in 1900, one of its chief objects being to eliminate sweatshops from the needlework trades. Because of factional differences he was defeated in 1904, but was selected as general manager of the New York Cloak Makers' Union. Three years later he became business manager of the *Jewish Daily Forward*, which was then experiencing a serious struggle for existence. In this capacity he served from 1907 to 1912. In the meantime, controversies within the Ladies' Garment Workers' Union created a critical situation and Schlesinger was again chosen, in 1914, to guide its fortunes, remaining its president until he resigned in 1923. Returning to the Forward as business manager of its Chicago affairs, he continued with the paper until 1931, when for the third time he was called to head the International Ladies' Garment Workers' Union.

He died in a sanitarium in Colorado Springs a few weeks after having been reelected, almost unanimously, at the 1932 convention. His wife, Rae (Schanhouse), two sons, and a daughter survived him.

SCHNEIDER, ALBERT

(1863-1928) — Bacteriologist, was born in Granville, Illinois, the son of John and Elizabeth Schneider. He married Marie Louise Harrington of Minneapolis, Minnesota, on June 28, 1892; they had one daughter. After taking an M.D. at the College of Physicians and Surgeons in Chicago, Illinois, in 1887, he became instructor in botany at the University of Minnesota; in 1897 he received a Ph.D. at Columbia University and returned to teaching. He was professor of pharmacology and bacteriology at Northwestern University, 1897-1903; of pharmacognosy and bacteriology at the University of California, 1903-1919; of pharmacology at the University of Nebraska, 1919-1922; and dean of pharmacy at North Pacific College of Oregon, Portland, 1922-1928. In addition, he was director of the experiment station of the Spreckels Sugar Company, 1906-1907; pharmacognosist, U.S. Department of Agriculture, 1909-1915; and editor of the *Pacific Pharmacist*, 1910-1915, through which he attempted to raise the standards of pharmacy as a profession and to secure pure foods and drugs. Apart from his strictly professional work, he was a man of some inventive genius. Apparatus and instruments of his design were to be seen in his laboratory, and he invented a ventilating system for Pullman cars. He was interested in the scientific detection of criminals, wrote several papers on the subject, re-introduced the "lie detector" in 1927, and lectured at the police schools in Berkeley, California, and Portland, Oregon, at various times.

His writings include books and articles on a wide range of subjects: bacteriology, botany, microscopy, food analysis, lichenology, toxicology, pharmacology, glandular therapy, and criminology. One of his early books was *The Limitations of Learning and Other Science Papers* (1900); later he wrote such technical books as *Pharmaceutical Bacteriology* (1912), *Bacteriological Methods in Food and Drugs Laboratories* (1915), *The Microbiology and Microanalysis of Foods* (1920), and *The Microanalysis of Powdered Vegetable Drugs* (1921). In 1896 he produced *A Compendium of General Botany*, translated from the German of Maximilian Westermaier. The papers he contributed with frequency to scientific journals exhibit great care in preparation. It was his habit to repeat experiments many times in a methodical way in order to satisfy himself that the results were worth publication; he strongly discouraged the type of research work that, as he expressed it, "clutters up" the journals. He was a member of the international jury of awards at the Panama Pacific International Exposition in 1915, one of a committee for the tenth revision of the United States Pharmacopoeia, a member of the American Pharmaceutical Association and of the American Association for the Advancement of Science. He died on October 27, 1928, in Portland, Oregon.

SCHNEIDER, GEORGE

(1823-1905) — Journalist and banker, was born on December 13, 1823, in Pirmasens, Rhenish Bavaria, the son of Ludwig and Josephine (Schlick) Schneider. He obtained his early education at the Latin school of his native town. Upon reaching his majority, he became engaged in journalism. Keenly interested in public affairs, he denounced the arbitrary government of his native state, and in 1848 joined an insurrection against it. Having eventually to leave the country because of his political views, he went first to France and then to the United States. He arrived in New York in July 1849, and was attracted by the stories of the new West. Within a few months, he had reached St. Louis and founded the *Neue Zeit*, a paper that soon became conspicuous for its opposition to the extension of slavery. In 1851, the home of the *Neue Zeit* was destroyed by fire, and in August of the same year, Schneider became managing editor of the *Illinois Staats-Zeitung*, a conservative weekly paper which he soon transformed into a thriving daily with a Sunday edition, the first in Chicago.

On January 29, 1854, Schneider convoked a public meeting, perhaps the first of its kind in the United States, to draft resolutions against the Nebraska Bill. On February 22, 1856, Schneider was one of a group of anti-Nebraska editors who assembled at Decatur, Illinois, and issued a call for the first Republican state convention in Illinois, to be held at Bloomington in the following May. At the Bloomington convention, with Abraham Lincoln's assistance, he managed to get a plank adopted that was a clear-cut pronouncement against Know-Nothing policies hostile to naturalized citizens, especially Germans. He was also chiefly responsible for the adoption of the tenth plank of the Philadelphia platform of 1856, which invited the "affiliation and cooperation of the men of all parties." He actively espoused Lincoln's candidacy for the presidency after his nomination in 1860, and the nation-wide circulation of the *Staats Zeitung* one of the most influential German papers in the Northwest, did much to consolidate the great foreign-born vote.

In 1861, he was appointed consul at Elsinore, Denmark, primarily to influence the public opinion of northern Europe in favor of the Union cause. Resigning from this office in 1862, he returned to the United States, and in 1863, became collector of internal revenue for the Chicago district, having in the meantime (1862) disposed of his interest in the *Staats-Zeitung*. After four years in the internal revenue service, he became chief executive of the State Savings Institution at Chicago, and in 1871, was chosen the first president of the newly organized National

Bank of Illinois, a position that he held until 1897.

Although he was now primarily interested in banking, he continued to be active in public life in Illinois. Declining to accept a diplomatic appointment to Switzerland in 1877, he became the treasurer of the Chicago South Park Board in the following year, serving in this capacity until 1882. He also served as a director of the Chicago Festival Association and the Illinois Humane Society, which through his efforts in 1879 established a separate department for helpless children.

On June 6, 1853, he married Matilda Schloetzer; they had seven children, all daughters. He died on September 16, 1905 in Colorado Springs, Colorado.

SCHUTTLER, PETER

(1812-1865) — Wagon maker, was born in the village of Wachenheim, Grand Duchy of Hesse Darmstadt, Germany. He came to the United States in 1834 and worked first in a wagon shop in Buffalo, New York, where he was paid seven dollars a month and his board, and then in Cleveland, Ohio. His inventive skill showed itself in a minor way in his use of a saw instead of an axe for cutting out wagon gearing. Having gathered together a little capital, he went into business for himself but he did not succeed, and after a year or two he moved to Sandusky, Ohio, where he worked at his own bench as a wagon maker for six years.

There he married Dorothy Gauch, a native of Prussia, by whom he had three children, a son and a daughter born during the sojourn in Sandusky and another son born in Chicago. Through careful saving he had accumulated from three to four hundred dollars, and with his mind bent on opening a wagon shop he left in 1843 by boat for Chicago. He found no less than thirteen wagon shops already established in the city. Nevertheless, he went to work and made by hand the frames of several wagons, which were ironed on shares by P. W. Gates. He built his own shop and lived in a board shanty behind it. A brief interlude in the brewery business with his father-in-law was marked by failure and left him firmly decided to continue with the wagon business.

With the settlement of the western states, the demand for wagons increased. He hired a blacksmith and helper and ironed his own wagons; later he installed an eight horse-power engine, all work having previously been done by hand in 1849, with the Gold Rush well under way, he built a new shop of brick, forty feet by seventy and four stories high, and began to manufacture buggies, carriages, and harness, as well as wagons. Though the shop burned to the ground in 1850, it was immediately rebuilt and he returned to the manufacture of wagons alone. The Schuttler wagon helped to displace the old prairie schooner, prevailingly in use until 1850; it had a capacity of thirty-five hundred pounds and was very strongly made, though it was of comparatively light weight and easy running, and commanded a premium of fifty dollars over other makes. The Mormons were among Schuttler's best customers. During the Civil War he refused to modify the design of his wagon in order to secure army contracts. By 1856 he had forty men at work and was turning out a hundred and thirty-five wagons a week. Up to this time, he himself worked in the plant, directed the work of his men, kept the books, and made the sales. In 1855 he traveled with his elder son, Peter, to Germany and returned to build the finest mansion in Chicago. He died a rich man, leaving the wagon business to Peter. His wife and the three children all survived him. The name of the company remained in the list of Chicago firms for many years; in 1934 it appeared in the Chicago telephone directory as "Peter Schuttler Company, Wagons," but no wagons were manufactured after 1925.

SCHWATKA, FREDERICK

(1849-1892) — Explorer, was born at Galena, Illinois, the son of Frederick Schwatka. At the age of ten his family took him to Salem, Oregon, where he worked as a printer and attended Willamette University. In 1867 he received an appointment to West Point, from which he graduated in June 1871. Commissioned as second lieutenant in the Third Cavalry, he served at various army posts throughout the United States and at the same time studied both medicine and law. He was admitted to the Nebraska bar in 1875 and the following year received a medical degree from the Bellevue Hospital Medical College in New York City. But it was neither as a lawyer nor as a doctor that he established his reputation. He became interested in exploration, and his adventurous imagination was seized by reports brought from the Arctic regions by Captain Thomas F. Barry concerning the fate of the famous expedition of Sir John Franklin.

For thirty years following the loss of this expedition, British and American explorers had sought the bodies or the papers of the Franklin party. Schwatka persuaded the American Geographical Society to organize a new search in the Arctic. This expedition, commanded by Schwatka and William Henry Gilder of the *New York Herald*, sailed from New York on June 19, 1878, in the *Eothen*. The explorers did not return for more than two years. During their search in King William Land in

1879-1880, they performed the longest sledge journey then on record, being absent from their base of supplies for eleven months and twenty days and traversing 2,819 geographical or 3,251 statute miles. Schwatka's search resolved the last doubts about the fate of the Franklin expedition. He discovered the wreckage of the one untraced ship, located many of the graves of members of the party, gave other mortal remains decent burial, brought back various relics, and established beyond doubt that Franklin's records were lost. "Schwatka's search," described by Gilder in articles in the *Herald*, became a popular phrase, and his discoveries were hailed as a triumph of Arctic exploration. In 1885 he resigned from the army and thereafter devoted himself to expeditions and to writing and lecturing. He explored the course of the Yukon River, described in his *Along Alaska's Great River* (1885) and *Nimrod in the North* (1885); he commanded the Alaskan expedition launched by the *New York Times* in 1886 and published his *The Children of the Cold* (1886); and he later visited northern Mexico and described the Tarahumari tribe of Chihuahua in a volume published posthumously, *In the Land of Cave and Cliff Dweller* (1893). His amazing and spectacular journeys, much as they appealed to the popular imagination, resulted in no great contributions to scientific knowledge; he did establish the fact, however, that White men could exist and carry on useful scientific work in the Arctic if they conformed to native habits. During the last years of his life he suffered intensely from a stomach complaint, which necessitated the use of laudanum. He died of an overdose of this drug on November 2, 1892, in Portland, Oregon.

SCOTT, HARVEY WHITEFIELD
(1838-1910) — Editor, was born on February 1, 1838, on a farm near Groveland, Tazewell County, Illinois, the son of Ann (Roelofson) and John Tucker Scott and brother of Abigail Jane Scott Duniway. He was a descendant of John Scott who settled in North Carolina shortly before the revolutionary war. In 1852 he went with his family overland to Oregon. After two years in the lower Willamette Valley he moved with his father to a farm near Shelton in the newly formed territory of Washington, but in September 1856 he returned to Oregon to work on a farm near Oregon City. In December he entered Tualatin Academy, but for lack of funds he was forced to leave school the next April and was unable to continue his education except irregularly until 1859, when he entered Pacific University in Forest Grove, Oregon. He graduated in 1863, supporting himself meanwhile by working as a teamster, a woodcutter, and a

teacher. After another year of school teaching he became librarian of the Portland library and studied law in a private office. Though he passed his bar examinations, he never actively practiced law. He married Elizabeth Nicklin of Salem, Oregon, on October 31, 1865, and after her death he married Margaret McChesney of Latrobe, Pennsylvania, on June 28, 1876.

In April 1865 he began to write editorials for the Portland *Morning Oregonian*, recognized as the chief spokesman in the state for the Republican Party, and a year later Henry Lewis Pittock, the owner of the paper, made him its editor. He also served as collector of the port of

Harvey Whitefield Scott

Portland from October 1870 to May 1876, when Senator John Hipple Mitchell of Oregon had him removed. According to Scott, this was because of his refusal to no longer contribute financial support to the *Portland Bulletin*, the newspaper organ of Mitchell and Ben Holladay. He had left the *Oregonian* in 1872, but in April 1877 he returned as editor and part owner, a connection that lasted until his death. He was never an avowed candidate for an elective office, although in 1903 he made overtures to Republican Party leaders for support in the legislative ballot for U.S. senator. He declined a diplomatic appointment to Belgium in 1905 and one to Mexico in 1909. He was president of the Oregon Historical Society, 1898-1901, of the Lewis and Clark Exposition, 1903-1904, and a director of the Associated Press 1900-1910. He died in Baltimore, Maryland, of heart failure following a surgical operation; his wife, three sons, and a daughter survived him.

SCRIPPS, EDWARD WYLLIS

(1854-1926) — Newspaper publisher, was born on June 18, 1854, on a farm near Rushville, Illinois, the son of James Mogg Scripps and his third wife, Julia (Osborn) Scripps. He attended a district school near his home and a private school conducted by his half-sister Ellen Browning Scripps. At eighteen, he began his newspaper work as an office boy on the *Detroit Tribune*, of which his half-brother James Edmund Scripps was manager. In 1873, when his brother started the *Detroit Evening News*, the first cheap, popular evening paper in the United States, Edward Scripps became first a member of the news staff and then city editor. In the fall of 1877, he gave up his position to accompany another half-brother, George H. Scripps, on a year's tour of Europe. During his travels he conceived the idea of establishing a paper of his own, and obtained financial backing from his two half-brothers and his cousin, John Scripps Sweeney, in support of a one-cent evening paper in Cleveland, Ohio. On November 2, 1878, he brought out the first issue of the Cleveland *Penny Press*.

In 1880, Edward and his brothers bought the two-cent *Evening Chronicle* of St. Louis, and a year or two later, bought a struggling paper in Cincinnati that they named the *Penny Post*, later the *Cincinnati Post*. These two papers with the Detroit *Evening News* and the Cleveland *Penny Press*, constituted the first chain of daily newspapers in the United States. Disagreements with James Scripps over the management of the papers led Edward Scripps to relinquish control of all the papers except the *Cincinnati Post*. He took Milton Alexander McRae into partnership in 1889, and formed the Scripps-McRae League of Newspapers with McRae and George H. Scripps in 1895. Following the decline of the old United Press in the nineties and the rise of the new Associated Press, organized in Chicago, Illinois in 1892, as the dominant news-disseminating agency in the United States, Scripps felt the need of an independent means of obtaining telegraph news, and in 1897, he organized the Scripps-McRae Press Association to cover the field west of Pittsburgh. In 1904, this organization purchased the Publishers' Press, a similar independent organization that covered the territory east of Pittsburgh. In 1907, the two agencies were combined into the United Press Associations generally known simply as the United Press, the first press association operated in connection with a chain of daily papers. The Newspaper Enterprise Association was organized in 1902 by Edward Scripps to supply his papers and others with cartoons, illustrations, and feature articles; this, known as the "NEA," became the first newspaper syndicate connected with a chain of daily papers.

In 1891, Scripps moved to San Diego, California. Two years later, he acquired an interest in the *San Diego Sun*, the first of the Scripps Coast League of newspapers, a chain that later included papers in Seattle, Tacoma, Spokane, Portland, Denver, San Francisco, Los Angeles; Fresno, and Sacramento. To serve these papers with telegraph news, he organized the Scripps Coast Press Association. In 1908, he and McRae retired in favor of Scripps' eldest son, James.

With his sister Ellen Browning Scripps, he endowed the Scripps Institution for Biological Research at La Jolla, California (later the Scripps Institution of Oceanography). In 1920, he established the Science Service, an organization designed to furnish the press with the results of research presented in popular form. He also provided for the Scripps Foundation for population research at Miami University, Oxford, Ohio.

Scripps married on October 5, 1885, Nackie Benson Holtsinger; they had six children. He died March 12, 1926.

SEMPLE, JAMES

(1798-1866) Senator from Illinois; Senate Years of Service: 1843-1847; born in Green County, Ky., January 5, 1798; moved with his parents to Clinton County; received private instruction and attended the common schools; enlisted in the Army in 1814; ensign in the Kentucky Militia in 1816; moved to Edwardsville, Ill., in 1818 and to Chariton, Mo., in 1819, where he engaged in business; elected as a commissioner of the loan office; studied law in Louisville, Ky.; admitted to the bar and commenced practice in Clinton County, Ky.; returned to

James Semple

Edwardsville, Ill., in 1827 and continued the practice of law; member, State house of representatives 1828-1833, serving as speaker four years; served as a private, adjutant, and judge advocate during the Black Hawk War; attorney general of Illinois in 1833; unsuccessful candidate for election in 1836 to the United States Senate; moved to Alton, Ill., in 1837; Charge d'Affaires to Colombia 1837-1842; judge of the State supreme court 1842-1843; appointed and subsequently elected as a Democrat to the United States Senate to fill the vacancy caused by the death of Samuel McRoberts and served from December 4, 1843, to March 3, 1847; was not a candidate for renomination in 1846; chairman, Committee on Revolutionary Claims (Twenty-ninth Congress); returned to Alton and engaged in the real estate business; moved to Jersey County,

Ill., in 1853 and founded the town of Elsah; continued in the real estate business; also engaged in literary pursuits; died in Elsah, Ill., December 20, 1866; interment in Bellefontaine Cemetery, St. Louis, Mo.

SENGSTACKE, JOHN HERMAN HENRY

(1912-1997) — Publishing company executive, was born in Savannah, Georgia, on November 25, 1912, the son of Reverend Herman Alexander Sengstacke and Rosa Mae (Davis) Sengstacke. His uncle was Robert Sengstacke Abbott, founder and publisher of the *Chicago Defender*, one of the largest and most influential African American publications in U.S. history. Sengstacke attended the Knox Institute in Athens, Georgia, and Brick Junior College in North Carolina. He graduated from junior college in 1929, and then attended the Hampton Institute in Virginia. He spent his summers working at the *Defender*. After graduating, he started working full-time as his uncle's assistant, and continued to take classes at the Mergenthaler Linotype School, the Chicago School of Printing, Northwestern University, and Ohio State University.

Under his uncle's guidance, Sengstacke advanced to vice-president and general manager of the Robert S. Abbott Publishing Company, his forceful editorials and comprehensive coverage growing the paper to a circulation of 230,000 nationwide. The company had two affiliated newspapers, the *Michigan Chronicle* and the *Louisville Defender*. In February of 1940, Sengstacke had just founded the Negro Newspaper Publisher's Association when his uncle died and he automatically became president of the company.

Soon after taking over, however, Sengstacke was asked to serve as chairman of the advisory committee on the African American press in the Office of War Information, and became chairman of the Chicago Rationing Board No. 2, the largest rationing board in the city. Sengstacke was also still active in the Negro Newspaper Publisher's Association, where he served as president for three terms, beginning in 1944. The Association made their correspondents part of the White House Press Corps, and they established a Washington news bureau for Association newspapers. Later, the Negro News Agency opened offices in New York and Chicago.

After the war, Sengstacke became director of the Urban League in Chicago, and of the Illinois Federal Savings and Loan Association. In addition, he served as vice-chairman of the South Side Planning Board, served on the Committee to Bring Olympics to Chicago, served on the Committee to Build a Greater Chicago, was a member of the Freedom

Train Committee, and was on the labor committee of the Mayor's Commission on Human Relations. He was named secretary of the President's Committee on Equality of Opportunity and Treatment in the Armed Services, plus he received certificates of merit from the Chicago Civil Liberties Committee, the Veterans of Foreign Wars, the National Urban League, and the American Legion.

Over the years, Robert S. Abbott Publishing Company grew as well. Affiliates included the *Tri-State Defender* in Memphis, Tennessee, the Michigan Chronicle Publishing Company in Detroit, Michigan, Florida Courier Publishing Company in Miami, Florida, Defender Publications in Chicago, and New Pittsburgh Courier Publishing Company in Pittsburgh, Pennsylvania. Sengstacke was chairman of the board of Sengstacke Newspapers, president of Amalgamated Publishers, Incorporated, and member of the Board of Directors of Virgin Island Corporation.

In the 1960s, Sengstacke became active in military issues again, serving as a member of John F. Kennedy's New Advisory Committee on Equal Opportunity in the Armed Forces, the U.S. Assay Commission, and the board of governors of the United Service Organizations (U.S.O.). He was appointed to the executive board of the National Alliance of Businessmen in 1968, and he had served as co-chairman of the United Negro College Fund Drive.

Sengstacke died in Chicago, Illinois, on May 28, 1997.

SENN, NICHOLAS

(1844-1908) — Surgeon, was born in Buchs, Canton of St. Gall, Switzerland, to John and Magdelena Senn, who immigrated to America about 1852 and settled in the village of Ashford, Wisconsin. After graduating from high school in Fond du Lac in 1864, he taught school and read medicine until 1866, when he entered the Chicago Medical College, from which he graduated two years later.

In 1869, he married Amelia S. Muehlhauser, who, with two sons, survived him. Following an internship of eighteen months in the Cook County Hospital, he settled for practice in Elmore, Wisconsin, but in 1874 he moved to Milwaukee, Wisconsin, where he was appointed attending physician to the Milwaukee Hospital. During 1877-1878, he studied at the University of Munich, Germany, which conferred upon him an M.D. Returning to practice in Milwaukee, he was in 1884 appointed professor of surgery at the College of Physicians and Surgeons in Chicago, Illinois; in 1890, he became professor of surgery and surgical pathology in Rush Medical College, and in the following year, he succeeded Charles Theodore Parkes as head of the department of surgery there. Later, he became professor of surgery at the Chicago Polyclinic, and lecturer on military surgery at the University of Chicago. For nine years, he traveled between Milwaukee and Chicago to fill his lecture and clinic engagements, until in 1893, he moved his residence to Chicago.

A pioneer in antiseptic surgery, with an unusual knowledge of surgical pathology, he quickly attracted the attention of the profession of the Middle West through his clinics. Senn was one of the first in this section to systematically pursue experimental surgery upon animals, and he devised one of the earliest mechanical aids for intestinal anastomosis. His experimental work upon abdominal surgery, including gunshot wounds of the intestines, gave him a local preeminence in this field. His practice was lucrative, and he was a liberal contributor toward the advancement of medical education. He gave a clinical building to Rush Medical College, and upon the death of Professor William Baum of the University of Gottingen, he purchased his library of old and rare medical books for the Newberry Library of Chicago.

Interested in military medicine, he served as surgeon general of Wisconsin for a time and later a brigadier general in the National Guard of Illinois. In 1891, he founded the Association of Military Surgeons of the United States and served as president for the first two years. During the Spanish-American War, he saw service in Cuba as chief surgeon of the VI Army Corps, with the grade of lieutenant colonel. In 1907, while in South America, he suffered an acute dilation of the heart, and was brought back to Chicago, Illinois, where he died in St. Joseph's Hospital.

Senn's many writings on surgical subjects, military medicine, and travel include: *Experimental Surgery* (1889), *Intestinal Surgery* (1889), *Surgical Bacteriology* (1889), *Principles of Surgery* (1890), *Pathology and Surgical Treatment of Tumors* (1895), *War Correspondence* (1899), and *Medico-Surgical Aspects of the Spanish-American War* (1900). From South America he sent a series of letters to the Journal of the American Medical Association, and in 1902 he published the well-illustrated *Around the World via Liberia*.

SHABBONA

(c.1775-1859) — Member of the Ottowa tribe, also known as Shabonee, Chambly, Chabonne, Shab-eh-nay or Sho-bon-ier, is remembered in Illinois as a prominent Ottawa chief in The Three Fires Confederacy. The confederacy consisted of the Potawatomi, Chippewa, and Ottawa, who resided north of Peoria on the Illinois River and throughout the northeastern part of the state. Several times, he represented his group at treaty councils with the white settlers. He grew to be a staunch friend of the latter. While it cannot be determined exactly when or where he was born, most believe it was around 1775 near the Maumee River in Ohio. Early in life, he joined the Three Fires group, and married at least one Potawatomi wife. During the War of 1812, he originally took up arms against the Americans, but switched his allegiance at the conclusion of this conflict.

Shabbona ruled as a village chief or peace chief of the Potawatomi, Ottawa, and Chippewa in Illinois. His name appears as a leader for the first time in a treaty negotiated at St. Louis on August 24, 1816. Nine years later, Thomas Forsyth (an agent at Peoria) declared that Shabbona acted as the principal chief of The Three Fires in his district. That same year, Shabbona participated in a treaty concluded at Prairie du Chien (August 19, 1825) as an Ottawa delegate. The following month, he drew rations and supplies at Fort Armstrong—on Rock Island—for his followers. At this time, his villages extended along the Spoon River, but in 1829, he complained to William Clark, superintendent of Indian affairs, that he had been threatened and driven from that location. His new settlement, called As-sim-in-eh-kon, lay in or near Paw Paw Grove, a wooded area now within Paw Paw Township of DeKalb County and Wyoming Township of Lee County, Illinois. Thus, the treaty of Prairie du Chien (July 29, 1829) reserved two sections of land at this site for his use.

When James M. Bucklin commenced surveying a route for the proposed Illinois-Michigan Canal in 1830, he engaged Shabbona as an expert guide. A year later, the chief still lived at Paw Paw Grove, although his reserve had not yet been surveyed and assigned to him.

With the coming of the Black Hawk War in 1832, Shabbona volunteered his expert services. Militia officers at Chicago, Illinois, however, refused his offer. Nevertheless, the chief led his warriors to the Rock River in June, and joined General Henry Atkinson's forces. In all, ninety-five men from The Three Fires (including twenty chiefs) were mustered into service on June 22, 1832. One month later, they all received discharges except Shabbona, Billy Caldwell, Waubonsee, and Perish LeClair, who served as guides, spies, and messengers.

On October 20, 1832, another treaty was signed with the Prairie and Kankakee bands of Potawatomi, and Shabbona's two sections of land were again mentioned as being reserved for him. By the treaty of

Chicago, September 26 and 27, 1833, The Three Fires gave up all their lands around Lake Michigan; Shabbona also witnessed this cession of land to the United States. One article stipulated that the faithful chief's two sections of land were now granted "in fee simple to him, his heirs and assigns forever." Because of his patriotic service in the Black Hawk War, he received in addition, a yearly pension of $200 for life.

From 1835 until 1838, many members of The Three Fires were officially escorted west of the Mississippi. Shabbona seems to have traveled with them, but later he returned to Paw Paw Grove. In 1838, he asked the government to survey his reserve. When Washington, D.C., officials appeared reluctant to permit an Indian to own land, Shabbona asked them in 1839 to buy back his grant, however, G.M. Butler laid out the reserve of 1,280 acres in December 1842. It included an area just north of Shabbona Grove in Shabbona Township of DeKalb County, but not Paw Paw Grove as the treaty had specified.

Since the old Chief often wandered about the country, squatters soon invaded his preserve, and the grant went up for sale on July 21, 1849. Before the buyers could obtain clear titles, however, the U.S. government was forced to appropriate $1,600 and purchase the tract from Shabbona in 1852.

He then resided west of the Mississippi for two or three years. He returned to Ottawa, Illinois, about 1855, where his friends purchased a parcel of land for him on June 27, 1857. It consisted of twenty acres.

Shabbona died on July 17, 1859. His wife, Pokanoka, drowned in the Mazon River on November 30, 1864, and was interred beside him. A grey boulder stands over their graves. This monument has been there since October 23, 1903. It bears the single word "Shabbona" and carries the dates 1775-1859.

SHAPIRO, SAMUEL H.

(1907-1987) — Thirty-sixth governor of Illinois (1968-1969), was born in Kankakee, Illinois, the son of Tillie Bloom and Joseph Shapiro. After attending St. Victor College, he received his law degree from the University of Illinois in 1929.

Shapiro practiced law in Kankakee for three years before being appointed City Attorney for his hometown in 1933. In 1936, he was appointed state's attorney for the county.

Shapiro ran successfully for lieutenant governor in 1960, and was reelected in 1964. When Governor Otto Kerner resigned, Shapiro took over his duties.

While Shapiro was in gubernatorial office, the controversial Democratic National convention was held in Chicago. He was unable to win the Republican nomination for governor in 1968, and after his short term as governor, Shapiro returned to his law practice. He died in March 3, 1987.

SHARP, KATHARINE LUCINDA

(1865-1914) — Librarian, library-school director, was born May 25, 1865, at Elgin, Illinois, the daughter of John William and Phebe (Thompson) Sharp. After preparing for college at Elgin Academy and the Oakland, California, High School, she entered Northwestern University, Evanston, Illinois, and graduated in 1885. Four years later, she was awarded the master's degree. She taught school at Elgin for a couple of years. In 1888, she accepted the proffered librarianship of the public library at Oak Park, a suburb of Chicago. She resigned her position after two years, and took a course at the New York State Library School. Just as she graduated in 1892, Chicago was busily engaged in assembling and arranging the various exhibits for the World's Columbian Exposition, and she was placed in charge of the exhibit of the American Library Association. She was then appointed director of the newly established department of library science, opened in the fall of 1893 at Armour Institute of Technology. When, four years later, the library school was transferred to the University of Illinois, she continued as director and became librarian of the University.

In 1894-96, Sharp was grand president of her college sorority, Kappa Kappa Gamma. She was director of the summer school of library science at the University of Wisconsin in 1895 and 1896, and lecturer on library economy at the University of Chicago in 1896. From 1895 to 1905, she was a member of the council of the American Library Association, and in 1898 and 1907, was vice-president; she was elected a fellow of the American Library Institute in 1906, and was president of the Illinois Library Association in 1903-04. She wrote frequently for library periodicals, and her 800-page monograph, *Illinois Libraries* (5 vols. 1906-08), remains the foundation work on that subject.

Sharp left the professional library field in 1907, because of impaired health, and became second vice-president and an executive in the Lake Placid Club in the Adirondacks, then rapidly developing under the presidency and leadership of Melvil Dewey. She served there for seven years before she died as the result of an automobile accident in

1914. In 1922, her former students presented a portrait tablet, executed in bronze in low relief by Lorado Taft, to the University of Illinois.

SHEEN, BISHOP FULTON JOHN

(1895-1979) — Roman Catholic priest, writer, and educator, was born on May 8, 1895, in El Paso, Illinois, to Newton Morris Sheen and Delia (Fulton) Sheen. He attended a parochial school in Peoria, Illinois, where the family moved while he was still young. He continued his education at Spaulding Institute, and later at St. Viator College in Bourbonnais, Illinois, where he received his B.A. in 1917, and his M.A. in 1919. He was ordained a priest in 1919. He attended seminary for a year in St. Paul Minnesota, and then went to the Catholic University of America, where he received S.T.B. and J.C.B. degrees together in 1920. Next, he went to Louvain University in Belgium and finished his Ph.D. in 1923. He became a D.D. of the University of Rome in 1924, and in 1925, Louvain University made him "Agrigi en Philosophie" and awarded him the Cardinal Mercier Prize.

When Sheen came back to America, he was assigned to a poor Peoria parish to serve as priest. In 1926, he joined the faculty of the Catholic University where he became a professor in the department of scholastic philosophy. He preached at summer conferences at Westminster Cathedral; lectured in the Catholic Summer School in Cambridge, England; preached Sunday evening services at the Church of the Paulist Fathers in New York; and was Lenten orator at St. Patrick's Cathedral also in New York. In 1934, Pope Pius XI Papal Chamberlain appointed him Right Reverend Monsignor, and the following year, Domestic Prelate. In 1936, he won the Cardinal Mazella Medal in philosophy.

Sheen was perhaps most well known to the public as the Sunday "Catholic Hour" preacher. He began speaking on the show in 1930. His television series, "Life Is Worth Living," won an Emmy Award in 1952.

In 1967, Sheen's disagreement with the church on its position regarding the American troops in Vietnam caused him to break with it for a while. Also, during his tenure as bishop of Rochester, New York, he rocked the boat considerably with such actions as naming a young priest who had been active among African Americans as his vicar for urban affairs, giving his priests permission to say mass in private homes, moving the favored age of confirmation to the late teens, proposing that the church give 5 percent of its revenues to the poor and voicing his opinion that no new church should cost more than one million dollars to build.

Sheen contributed articles to a number of Catholic magazines such as Commonweal, America, and New Scholasticism. He also authored several books including God and Intelligence in Modern Philosophy, Religion without God, The Life of All Living, The Divine Romance, Old Errors and New Labels, Moods and Truths, Way of the Cross, The Seven Last Words, Hymn of the Conquered, The Eternal Galilean, and many more including his autobiography, Treasure in Clay: The Autobiography of Fulton J. Sheen. He wrote the columns "God Loves You," for the Catholic Press and "Bishop Sheen Speaks," syndicated in secular publications. When the March of Time produced The Story of the Vatican, the first complete motion picture ever made inside Vatican City, Father Sheen was the narrator. He died on December 9, 1979, in New York, New York.

SHERMAN, LAWRENCE YATES

(1858-1939) Senator from Illinois; Senate Years of Service: 1913-1921; born near Piqua, Miami County, Ohio, November 8, 1858; moved with his parents to Illinois in 1859; attended the common schools, Lee's Academy in Coles County, and McKendree College, Lebanon, Ill.; studied law; admitted to the bar in 1882 and commenced practice in Macomb, Ill.; city attorney 1885-1887; judge in McDonough County 1886-1890; member, State house of representatives 1897-1905, and served as speaker 1899-1903; lieutenant governor and ex officio president of the State senate 1905-1909; president of the State board of administration of public charities 1909-1913; continued the practice of law in Springfield, Ill.; elected on March 26, 1913, as a Republican to the United States Senate to fill the vacancy caused by the unseating of William Lorimer; reelected in 1914 and served from March 26, 1913, to March 3, 1921; chairman, Committee on the District of Columbia (Sixty-sixth Congress); resumed the practice of law in

Lawrence Yates Sherman

617

Springfield, Ill.; moved to Daytona Beach, Fla., in 1924 and continued the practice of law; also engaged in the investment business; retired from active business pursuits in 1933; died in Daytona Beach, Fla., September 15, 1939; interment in Montrose Cemetery, Effingham County, Ill.

SHORT, WALTER CAMPBELL

(1880-1949) — U.S. Army officer, was born on October 30, 1880, in Fillmore, Illinois, the son of Hiram Spait Short and Sarah Minerva (Stokes) Short. After a preliminary education in public schools, he entered the University of Illinois, from which he received a B.A. in 1901. He then taught mathematics at Western Military Academy until 1902, when he accepted a commission in the U.S. Army. Short's army career began with the Twenty-fifth Infantry at Fort Reno, Oklahoma. Between tours into Alaska and into Mexico with the punitive expedition of 1916-1917, Short served as secretary of the School of Musketry at Fort Sill, Oklahoma. While there, he married Isabel Dean of Oklahoma City on November 4, 1914. They had one child: Walter Dean.

With America's entry into World War I, Short went to France with the First Division in June 1917. He held a series of increasingly responsible training positions while rising to the temporary rank of colonel. He won the Distinguished Service Medal for his service. Returning to the United States in 1919, Short taught at the General Service Schools at Fort Leavenworth, Kansas, where he wrote a textbook, *Employment of Machine Guns* (1922). He was later co-inventor of a low-slung machine-gun carrier.

Walter Campbell Short

Short graduated from the School of the Line in 1921, and from the Army War College four years later. Following various troop and staff assignments, and another tour at Leavenworth, he obtained his first regimental command, that of the Sixth Infantry, in 1934. He was promoted to the rank of brigadier general in 1936, during a brief assignment as assistant commandant of the infantry school at Fort Benning, Georgia. In 1939, he took command of a division.

As America mobilized in

1940, Short took command of provisional corps in maneuvers, and the First Corps later the same year. In February 1941, he took charge of the army's Hawaiian Department, with the rank of lieutenant general. Serious concern in early 1941 over a possible surprise attack on the Pacific fleet and its Pearl Harbor base gradually faded during the year. Both in Washington, D.C., and in Hawaii, it was generally assumed that the Japanese would not dare risk a strong carrier-based air attack on Oahu while the American fleet was based there. The real danger seemed to Short and others to lie in the half of Oahu's population that was of Japanese descent. However, the Japanese attacked on December 7, 1941, with Short receiving much of the blame.

After the attack, Short quickly instituted a tight military control of Hawaii and set in motion measures that greatly strengthened the army's defenses. The success of the surprise attack had stunned the nation. President Franklin D. Roosevelt, on December 15 and 16, 1941, appointed an investigating commission headed by Supreme Court Justice Owen J. Roberts, and on December 17, 1941, directed the relief from duty of both Short and the fleet commander, Admiral Husband E. Kimmel. The commission's report, in January 1942, accused the Hawaiian commanders of poor judgment and dereliction of duty. Short submitted a request for retirement, and at the president's order Short and Kimmel were retired on February 28, 1942, "without condonation of any offense or prejudice to any future disciplinary action," a phrase leaving open the way to court-martial. While awaiting his day in court, Short worked as traffic manager for the Ford Motor Company in Dallas, Texas, which remained his home thereafter.

Short finally received the opportunity to testify publicly before the congressional committee investigating Pearl Harbor in early 1946. He readily acknowledged, as he had in earlier secret testimony, that he had made the wrong decision about an alert before the attack; but he denied that his estimate of the situation was the result of any carelessness on his part or on the part of his military associates in Hawaii. He also believed that he had acted in accordance with his instructions, that Washington had withheld significant information from him that might have persuaded him to act differently, and that in effect the army had made him its scapegoat for the disaster. Heart trouble led to Short's complete retirement after the congressional inquiry, and he died in Dallas, Texas, on September 3, 1949. He was buried in Arlington National Cemetery.

SILLS, MILTON (GEORGE GUSTAVUS)

(1882-1930) — Actor, was born on January 12, 1882, in Chicago, Illinois, the son of William Henry and Josephine Antoinette (Troost) Sills. He graduated from the University of Chicago in 1903 with an A.B., and for a year and a half, remained there as a scholar and fellow in philosophy. In 1906, he made his professional debut as an actor at New Palestine, Ohio, in an old melodrama entitled *Dora Thorne*. A season of barnstorming through towns of the Middle West followed, and then he went to New York, where he was soon playing roles under the management of Frohman, Shubert, and Belasco. He also performed Shakespearean plays with Charles Coburn's repertory company, and for a time, was leading man with Blanche Bates in *The Fighting Hope*. His other works during this time included: *This Woman and This Man*, *Just Married*, *The Governor's Lady*, *The Law of the Land*, and *A Happy Marriage*.

In 1914, he deserted the stage for the screen, and in 1916, after preliminary experience in the studios of New York, went to Hollywood, California. His first appearance on the screen was in a motion picture version of Frank Norris's novel, *The Pit*, with Wilton Lackaye. Later, he played leading characters in *The Barker*, *Burning Daylight*, *The Sea-Hawk*, *Men of Steel* (of which he was part author), and *Paradise*. His marriage to Gladys Edith Wynne in London, England, on May 26, 1910, resulted in divorce in 1925, and on October 12, 1926, he married actress Doris Margaret Kenyon.

Sills delivered occasional lectures at colleges and universities on various subjects connected and unconnected with the stage; in 1927 he spoke at the Harvard School of Business Administration on conditions in the motion picture world. He was the coauthor with Ernest S. Holmes of a book, published after his death, entitled *Values: a Philosophy of Human Needs* (1932), and he was one of the organizers of the Academy of Motion Picture Arts and Sciences. He died suddenly while playing

Milton (George Gustavus) Sills

tennis with his wife at their home in Santa Monica, California, on September 15, 1930. With her survived a son and a daughter by the first marriage.

SIMMS, RUTH HANNA McCORMICK

(1880-1944) — U. S. Congresswoman and political leader, woman suffrage movement activist; she was born on March 27, 1880, in Cleveland, Ohio, to Marcus "Alonzo" Hanna, industrialist and political Republican National Chairman who managed William McKinley's presidential campaign, and to Charlotte August Rhodes. Her father was known as a "political king maker," running various political campaigns. She married Joseph Medill McCormick in 1903, of the *Chicago Tribune* newspaper family. It was a great political event attended by President Theodore Roosevelt, who was eager for Hanna's endorsement. They had three children. She was later remarry Albert Gallatin Simms.

She attended Hathaway Brown School in Cleveland, Dobbs Ferry School in New York, and Miss Porter's School in Farmington, Connecticut; as a teenager, Ruth worked for her father, Senator Hanna, as his private secretary in 1897 on Capitol Hill. In Chicago, Ruth and Medill McCormick were involved in progressive reform activities. They lived for a while behind the stockyards at the University of Chicago Settlement House. Ruth was active in the Consumers' League and the Women's Trade Union League, and worked for better management relations in the women's division of the National Civic Federation. By 1912, Medill had left the newspaper to enter politics, and both McCormicks endorsed and campaigned for Roosevelt's Progressive Party. Medill was elected to state legislature in 1912 and his wife joined him to lobby for a suffrage bill in Springfield, Illinois. The bill passed east of the Mississippi, allowing women the right to vote in presidential and municipal elections. Ruth McCormick was chosen to replace Alice Paul, head of the Congressional Committee of the National Woman Suffrage

Ruth Hanna McCormick Simms

Association, when Paul proved too controversial. Ruth McCormick worked at the state level to elect prosuffrage members to Congress. In 1918, the Republican Party appointed her to chair their new National Women's Executive Committee to attract female voters. She also became associate member of the national committee (1919-1924). Ruth and her friend Alice Roosevelt Longworth lobbied members of Congress in their salons, while the "Republican irreconcilable" Medill McCormick was elected the U.S. House of Representatives (1916) and the Senate (1918). He was called that because he was among those who blocked America's entry into the League of Nations.

In 1920, after passage of the Nineteenth Amendment, the Republicans reorganized themselves to include eight woman in its 21-member executive committee, with McCormick in charge of the central division. She believed women should join the major political parties, and argued that organizations like the League of Women Voters diluted women's political strength; for this reason, and to assist Medill in the reelection of 1924, she organized Republican's women's clubs all through the state of Illinois. By the end of the 1920s, it claimed more than 200,000 members. Medill McCormick was defeated in a close election in the primary by Charles S. Deneen, who was elected in November. Tragically, just before his Senate term expired in February 1925, Medill, who had been subject to depression, committed suicide.

Ruth McCormick had other interests, such as her dairy farm in Byron, intended to supply safe milk for city children, newspapers and a radio station in Rockford, and later a ranch in Colorado. However, she was fond of saying that her profession was politics. In 1928, she ran for one of two seats for congressperson at large from Illinois. She easily beat seven male opponents after waging a vigorous campaign. While many voters were opposed to the idea of a woman legislator, many hoped this difference would signal a departure from the factionalism of Illinois politics. Shortly after taking office, she began campaigning for the Senate in 1930. Though her statewide constituency was faith, more roadblocks existed for a woman senator. She utilized organized labor and the African-American community and denounced Deneen for his World Court advocacy, which was unpopular in Illinois. She thoroughly beat Deneen in the primary but lost in the Democratic landslide of 1930.

She married Simms of New Mexico, a former fellow congressman in 1932; they had no children. She moved to Albuquerque and although she campaigned for Alf Landon in 1936, she was more active in civic affairs rather than politics. She founded the Manzano and

Sandia schools for girls and the supporting arts. After the death of her son in 1938, McCormick reentered the political arena. In the fall of 1939, she became the principal management force behind Thomas Dewey's 1940 presidential campaign. Dewey was young and not yet well known outside New York and New England; McCormick was well experienced and connected politically. Both agreed on the need to keep the U.S. out of the war in Europe; as the international situation escalated, however, the convention turned to Wendell Willkie, and internationalist. Dewey removed himself from close alliance with McCormick but she continued to work for him.

On December 31, 1944, former Congresswoman Ruth Hanna McCormick Simms died in Chicago, Illinois. Interment was in Fairview Cemetery in Albuquerque, New Mexico. She attracted large numbers of women into partisan politics as a leader in the suffrage movement and the Republican Party, as well as successful campaigner. She had the background and determination to take on the issues of women in electoral politics in the first half of the twentieth century.

SIMON, PAUL MARTIN

(1928-2003) Representative and Senator from Illinois; Senate Years of Service: 1985-1997; born in Eugene, Lane County, Oreg., November 29, 1928; attended the public schools of Eugene and Concordia Academy High School, Portland, Oreg.; attended the University of Oregon, Eugene 1945-1946 and Dana College, Blair, Nebr., 1946-1948; pursued career as a newspaper editor and publisher in Troy, Ill., eventually building a chain of fourteen weeklies; served in

Paul Martin Simon

the United States Army 1951-1953; teacher at Sangamon State University, Springfield, Ill., 1972-1973, and Harvard University's John F. Kennedy School of Government 1973; served in the Illinois house of representatives 1955-1963 and in the Illinois State senate 1963-1968; lieutenant governor of Illinois 1969-1973; author; elected as a Democrat to the Ninety-fourth Congress in 1974 and reelected to the four succeeding Congresses (January 3, 1975-January 3, 1985); was not a candidate for reelection in 1984 to the House of Representatives, but was elected to the United States Senate; reelected in 1990 and served from January 3, 1985, to January 3, 1997; was not a candidate for reelection in 1996; unsuccessful candidate for the Democratic presidential nomination in 1988; director, Paul Simon Public Policy Institute, Southern Illinois University, 1997-2003; was a resident of Carbondale, Ill., until his death following heart surgery in Springfield, Ill., on December 9, 2003; interment in a family plot near Makanda, Ill.

SIMONS, HENRY CALVERT

(1899-1946) — Economist, was born on October 9, 1899, in Virden, Illinois, the son of Henry Calvert Simons, a lawyer, and Mollie Willis (Sims) Simons. He graduated from the Virden High School and the University of Michigan (B.A., 1920), where he specialized in economics. For the next seven years, he taught at the University of Iowa, initially as teaching assistant, then as instructor and assistant professor. During summers and the academic year 1925-1926, he pursued graduate study, first at Columbia (1922) and then at the University of Chicago. Simons moved to the University of Chicago faculty in 1927. There, Simons remained for the rest of his life, becoming associate professor in 1942 and professor in 1945.

The Great Depression, which destroyed so many careers, galvanized Simons. Aroused by the nation's calamity and by the threat to political liberty he saw in the New Deal's economic planning, he devised a highly personal program of economic reform. The initial, yet most comprehensive, formulation of this program was a powerfully written pamphlet, *A Positive Program for Laissez Faire: Some Proposals for a Liberal Economic Policy* (1934). Simons advocated a strong, decentralized economy, achieved by a vigorous antitrust policy and statutory limitations on corporate size and reinforced by free international trade. Where competition was unattainable, industries were socialized (preferably by local governments). He was as strongly egalitarian as most Socialists, and he proposed a radical reform of the tax system under which highly progressive personal income taxes would become the mainspring of the revenue system.

The details of Simons' tax proposals were spelled out in a work that has become a classic of public finance, *Personal Income Taxation* (1938), subsequently elaborated in *Federal Tax Reform* (1950). He had a comprehensive income concept (including in income capital gains, gifts, etc.), and he made an influential case for income averaging. This program was the intellectual source of the famous Carter Commission on Taxation in Canada, whose proposals led to a restructuring of that nation's federal taxation much along Simons' recommendations.

Simons also argued with great force for the guidance of monetary policy by fixed rules rather than by administrative discretion, with the goal of establishing a stable price level. He proposed that the federal government take primary responsibility for determining the money supply, reducing commercial banks to money warehouses through a hundred-percent reserve requirement. He also suggested reducing the variety of private forms of ownership and debt, as well as eliminating short-term governmental debt. He was an early interventionist during World War II, and he envisioned a postwar federation of nations bound together by a commitment to both peace and free trade.

Simons was a major contributor to the formation of the "Chicago School" of economists, whose members share a belief in the importance of free markets and the need for quasi-constitutional rules to achieve stable monetary policy. On May 30, 1941, he married Marjorie Kimball Powell; they had one child: Mary Powell. Simons died of an accidental overdose of sleeping pills on June 19, 1946, in Chicago, Illinois.

SIMPSON, CHARLES TORREY

(1846-1932) — Scientist, was born on June 3, 1846, in Tiskilwa, Illinois, the son of Jabez and Matilda (Cook) Simpson. He was educated in the public schools of the neighborhood, and at the age of seventeen, enlisted in the Fifty-seventh Illinois Infantry as carpenter's mate. During his extensive travels, he made a large collection of seashells, which led to his appointment on December 14, 1889, as aid in the division of mollusks in the U.S. National Museum. He held this position until 1902.

During his connection with the National Museum, he made a number of trips to various parts of the West Indies and the Bahamas in quest of mollusks, and later in search of plant life for "The Sentinel," his estate in Little River, Florida, which he developed into a veritable botanic paradise. The place soon attracted the attention not only of the lay public, but also of the scientific world, and secured for him on June 1, 1914, the appointment of collaborator in the Bureau of Plant Industry of the U.S. Department of Agriculture, which position he held until June 30, 1932. He was also awarded on April 2, 1923, the Frank N. Meyer medal of the American Genetic Association for distinguished service in plant introduction. The Simpson Memorial Park, a five-acre tract, part of the

Brickell hammock, Miami, Florida, is named for him.

Simpson was the author of about sixty scientific contributions to knowledge of mollusks, chief among which were "Distribution of the Land and Fresh-Water Mollusks of the West Indian Region, and Their Evidence with Regard to Past Changes of Land and Sea" in the *Proceedings of the United States National Museum* (1895); "The Mollusca of Porto Rico" in the *United States Fish Commission Bulletin for 1900* (1901), prepared in collaboration with William H. Dall; and *A Descriptive Catalogue of the Naiades or Pearly Fresh-Water Mussels* (1914). He was also the author of two works of a popular nature: *In Lower Florida Wilds: A Naturalist's Observations on the Life, Physical Geography, and Geology of the More Tropical Part of the State* (1920) and *Out of Doors in Florida: The Adventures of a Naturalist Together with Essays on the Wild Life and the Geology of the State* (1923). He published *Florida Wild Life: Observations on the Flora and Fauna of the State and the Influence of Climate on Their Development* (1932). His immense collection of mollusks he willed to Miami University, Miami, Florida.

He was twice married: first, on June 29, 1878, to Cornelia H. Couch, who died in 1898; second on September 17, 1902, to Mrs. Flora Gertrude Roper, who survived him. By his first marriage he had a son, Pliny Ferd. He died on December 17, 1932, in Miami, Florida, at the age of eighty-seven.

SINCLAIR, UPTON BEALL

(1878-1968) — Novelist and political figure, was born on September 20, 1878, in Baltimore, Maryland, to an old, formerly wealthy family. His father, a liquor salesman, moved the family to New York when Sinclair was a boy, and at fourteen, he entered the City of New York College, receiving his bachelor's degree in 1897. He also worked his way through graduate school at Columbia University by writing adventure stories for pulp magazines as well as jokes for comic periodicals. His earliest writings were romances: *Springtime in Harvest* (1901) and *The Journal of Arthur Stirling* (1903), as well as a Civil War novel, *Manassas* (1904). However, he lived in poverty with his wife in the country during those years, which may have brought him to his belief in socialism and his involvement in the Socialist Party. This belief inspired him in the rest of his writing, making him an internationally known controversial figure. His novel, *The Jungle*, written in 1906, was a result of his studies of the Chicago meatpacking industry for the party, was meant to attack all of capitalism. However, it had most of its effect on the meatpackers, who were under immense attack from the public and press for producing the spoiled and often poisonous food Sinclair described in the novel. President Theodore Roosevelt and Congress soon pushed through pure food laws, which required much more stringent packing standards. Only his novel written in 1927, *Oil*, approached *The Jungle*'s influence on the nation.

His later novels were not so concerned with muckraking as with stories about modern-day heroes, such as Lanny Budd in the *World End* series. These ten volumes covered American and European history through the life of Budd from 1913 to 1946, and the 1942 volume, *Dragon's Teeth*, won a Pulitzer Prize for its treatment of Nazism in Germany. He also wrote treatises on his political beliefs, including *The Industrial Republican*. He died in Bound Brook, New Jersey, on November 25, 1968.

SLADE, (JOSEPH ALFRED), "JACK"

(1824-1864) — Gunfighter, murderer of the American West, and reputed "bad man," also variously known as "Alf" and "Cap" Slade, was born at or near Carlyle, Clinton County, Illinois. The earliest available record concerning him is of May 22, 1847, when he enlisted in the army. After more than a year's uneventful service in New Mexico, he was mustered out at Alton, Illinois, in October 1848. He is next heard of, in the late 1850s, as a freighter and wagon train boss in the employ of Russell, Majors & Waddell. In the spring of 1860, after the firm had organized its overland stage service, he was made a division agent at Julesburg, in what is now Colorado, with instructions to rid the region of bandits preying upon the company's property. In an encounter with "Old Jules" Reni, Slade shot his antagonist to death, cut off his ears, and nailed them up to dry; later, it is said, wearing one of them as a watch-charm.

Transferred to a more westerly division, he continued to prove a scourge to evildoers. Mark Twain, who in August 1861 met him at a Wyoming station, says that he then bore the reputation of having killed twenty-six men. In 1862 the stages were withdrawn to a more southerly line, and Slade was transferred to a new station, Virginia Dale, a hundred miles north of Denver, Colorado. Unaccountably, he had by this time become a brawling drunkard, and in the fall of the year was discharged. With his companion, a dashing and attractive frontier woman whose given name was Maria Virginia and whose surname may have been Dale, he set out in the spring of 1863 at the head of a small freighting outfit for

627

the Montana gold diggings. Settling on a small ranch near Virginia City, he conducted a number of freighting expeditions and for a time was peaceful. Later, he again began drinking heavily and indulging in outbursts of drunken rowdyism. When arrested in March 1864, he defied the People's Court, and subsequently, revolver in hand, made threats against the judge. A joint meeting of the Vigilantes of Virginia City and the miners of the adjoining camp of Nevada decreed his execution, and though he begged pitifully for his life, he was promptly hanged on March 10, 1864, in Virginia City, Montana. The body was embalmed in alcohol and buried in Salt Lake City.

Slade was of sturdy build. When sober he was genial and friendly, but when drunk, he was a ferocious ruffian. Though the accounts of his numerous killings have been disputed by some writers, they were fully accepted by Frank A. Root, who entered the company's service in Colorado only a few months after Slade's departure and who had every opportunity to learn the facts.

SLATTERY, JAMES MICHAEL

(1878-1948) Senator from Illinois; Senate Years of Service: 1939-1940; born in Chicago, Ill., July 29, 1878; attended the parochial schools and St. Ignatius College, Chicago, Ill.; employed as a secretary with the building departments of the city of Chicago in 1905; graduated from Illinois College of Law at Chicago in 1908; admitted to the bar the same

James Michael Slattery

year and commenced practice in Chicago, Ill.; member of the faculty, Illinois College of Law 1909-1912; superintendent of public service, Cook County, Ill., 1910-1912; secretary of Webster College of Law, Chicago, Ill., 1912-1914; counsel for the Lincoln Park Commission 1933-1934 and for the Chicago Park District 1934-1936; chairman, Illinois Commerce Commission 1936-1939; appointed on April 14, 1939, as a Democrat to the United States Senate to fill the vacancy caused by the death of James Hamilton Lewis and served from April 14, 1939, to November

628

21, 1940, when a duly elected successor qualified; was an unsuccessful candidate for election to fill the vacancy; resumed the practice of law in Chicago, Ill.; died at his summer home at Lake Geneva, Wis., August 28, 1948; interment in Calvary Cemetery, Evanston, Ill.

SMALL, LENNINGTON

(1862-1936) — Twenty-eighth governor of Illinois (1921-1929), was born in Kankakee, Illinois, the son of Calista Currier and Dr. Abram Small. After attending local schools, and later, the Northern Indiana Normal School, he was a member of the state senate beginning in 1905.

In 1904, he was a member of the state treasury, a position he held until 1908. In 1912, he was assistant treasurer in charge of the U. S. Sub-treasury in Chicago, and in 1917, he won in the race for state treasurer. He registered as a Republican, and in 1920, was elected governor under that party.

When he took office, Small worked for improvements in the state's highway system. In his inaugural address, Small recognized the growing need for more roadways. During his eight years in gubernatorial office, the state's highways grew to be the longest in the United States as he replenished the funds available for building.

The economic boom of the early twenties aided Small's efforts for road building, and as the number of automobile purchases increased, so did the demand for roads. Small used this to his advantage politically by nominating local candidates for election, promising to build roads in the area if his protégés were elected, and then living up to that promise. Despite criticism of his "machine" methods of party politics, Small was reelected in 1924. By the time he left office, state roadways spanned 7,000 miles.

Small came under attack for charges of corruption early in his term in 1921, when he was tried on charges of conspiracy and embezzlement from his years as state treasurer. He was not found guilty, but was forced to pay 650,000 dollars to settle a civil suit in that case.

In 1932, Small ran for governor once again, and although he won the Republican nomination, he lost to Democratic candidate Henry Horner. He tried again in 1936, but was not nominated to his party for governor. Small continued to live on his farm in Kankakee during this time, and published the town's *Daily Republican* newspaper. He died at his farm in 1936.

SMITH, ALEXANDER

(1865-1922) — Chemist, educator, and author, was born on September 11, 1865, in Edinburgh, Scotland, the son of Alexander and Isabella (Carter) Smith. In preparation for the University of Edinburgh, he studied for seven years at the Edinburgh Collegiate School. While he received a B.S. in chemistry in 1886, he devoted a good part of his four years at the university to the study of astronomy and published four semi-popular articles on it before he graduated. Finding that there was little prospect of a successful career in that subject, however, he turned to the study of chemistry under Adolph Ritter von Baeyer at the University of Munich, specializing in organic chemistry. After securing a Ph.D. at Munich in 1889, he was assistant in analytical chemistry at Edinburgh for a year, and gave a course of lectures on organic syntheses. During a visit to the United States in the summer of 1890 he was appointed professor of chemistry and mineralogy at Wabash College, Crawfordsville, Indiana, a position he held for four years. He also continued his researches in organic chemistry. In 1891 he became a member of the Royal Society of Edinburgh.

In 1894, he was invited by John Ulric Nef to take charge of the work in elementary inorganic chemistry at the University of Chicago, Illinois. He was assistant professor, 1894-98; associate professor, 1898-1904; and professor, 1904-11. From 1900 to 1911, he was also dean of the junior colleges. Thoroughly trained in physics and mathematics, he soon became a distinguished name in physical chemistry, which was rapidly coming into vogue in America. His most important studies in the new field were on the forms of sulfur, for which the Royal Society of Edinburgh in 1912 awarded him the Keith prize and medal, and on vapor pressure measurements at comparatively high temperatures. In a series experimental researches, he threw a flood of light on the conditions for the formation and existence of the different solid and liquid forms of sulfur. He also devised new methods for the determination of vapor pressures and through them demonstrated that the vapor above solid calomel consists of a mixture of metallic mercury and mercuric chloride.

As a teacher, Smith made a very careful study of the best methods for presenting chemistry to beginners. His ideas were crystallized in a book on *The Teaching of Chemistry and Physics in the High School* (1902), written with Edwin H. Hall. His *Introduction to General Inorganic Chemistry*, (1906), was translated into German, Italian, Russian, and Portuguese.

On February 16, 1905, he married Sara (Bowles) Ludden; they

had a son and a daughter. Six years later, in 1911, he became head of the department of chemistry at Columbia University, a position he held until 1919, when he retired because of failing health. He became president of the American Chemical Society, 1911; a member of the Society of Physics and Chemistry of Madrid, 1911, and a member of the National Academy of Sciences, 1915. He died on September 8, 1922 in Edinburgh.

SMITH, GEORGE

(1806-1899) — Banker and financier, was born on February 10, 1806, in the parish of Old Deer, Aberdeenshire, Scotland. He arrived in Chicago around 1834, and invested what little money he had in lots and wild lands. Following the boom in land values in 1835 and 1836, he sold his holdings. In 1836, he became associated with the Chicago Marine and Fire Insurance Company. The following year, he went back to Scotland and organized the Scottish Illinois Land Investment Company.

On his return to America in 1839, he found that the legislature of Illinois had passed a law that suppressed the banking operations of his Chicago corporation. He therefore went to Wisconsin and chartered a similar organization. The Wisconsin Marine & Fire Insurance Company was chartered February 28, 1839.

Smith made Alexander Mitchell secretary of the company. Throughout the forties, the territorial legislature endeavored to repeal the company's charter. Mitchell's contention that the legislature could not determine the rights of a company while "acting in the three-fold capacity of a party interested, a jury, and a court" did not fall upon deaf ears, and the matter was never carried to the courts. After Wisconsin became a state, in 1848, the attorney general began *quo warranto* proceedings to test the legality of the charter, but on the promise of either Smith or Mitchell to incorporate as a state bank in the event that the Wisconsin free-banking law was adopted by a vote of the people, proceedings against the company were dropped. In 1853, the Wisconsin Marine & Fire Insurance Company became a state bank.

In 1854, Smith sold his stock to Alexander Mitchell, and proceeded to Georgia. Here, he obtained from the state a charter incorporating a bank of issue located at Atlanta. He had hoped to make his Chicago institution and Mitchell's bank at Milwaukee the fountainhead of his Atlanta bank, but following the adoption of free banking in Midwest states, it seemed implausible, and in 1856, he closed out his Atlanta bank.

631

Between that date and the outbreak of the Civil War, he made several trips to Scotland. On his last return to America in 1860, he invested his huge fortune in Chicago real estate and the securities of the Rock Island, Northwestern, and St. Paul railroads. During the troublesome days of wildcat money, the credit of George Smith & Company was as good as the government's and better than that of most states. The rapid economic expansion of Wisconsin and Illinois in the forties would not have been possible without the aid of "George Smith's money." From 1860 to his death, he divided his time between his castle in the Scottish Highlands and the Reform Club of London. He never married and had no close relatives. He died at the Reform Club in London in 1899.

SMITH, JOHN EUGENE

(1816-1897) — Soldier, was born on August 3, 1816, in the canton of Berne, Switzerland. His father, John Banler Smith, was an officer in one of the Swiss regiments that accompanied Napoleon from his ill-fated Moscow campaign to Waterloo. Before John Eugene was a year old, his parents immigrated to America and settled in Philadelphia, Pennsylvania. There he received an elementary education and learned the jeweler's trade. In 1836, after having followed his trade for a few years in St. Louis, Missouri, he moved to Galena, Illinois, and established a jewelry business. During the same year he was married to Aimee A. Massot of St. Louis. In 1860 he was elected treasurer of Jo Daviess County, Illinois. When the Civil War broke out, he at once offered his services to Governor Yates, and, after serving on the staff of the latter for a few months, he organized the Forty-fifth Illinois Infantry, known as the Washburne Leadmine Regiment, and became colonel on July 23, 1861. During 1862 he led his regiment with bravery and distinction in the operations against Forts Henry and Donelson, was in the thickest of the fight at Shiloh, and temporarily commanded a brigade at the siege of Corinth. He was appointed brigadier general of volunteers on November 29, 1862.

In the spring of 1863 he was given command of a division, under General Grant, which he led ably throughout the Vicksburg campaign, participating in the expedition to Yazoo Pass, the battles of Port Gibson, Raymond, Jackson Champion's Hill, Big Black River, and the final siege and capture of Vicksburg. Smith, with his division, was then transferred to the Army of the Tennessee, made a brilliant charge at Missionary Ridge, Tennessee, and accompanied General Sherman on his march to the sea. A prompt and effective deployment of his division at Savannah, Georgia, on December 20, 1864, was instrumental in causing the Confederates to evacuate the city. In June 1865 he was assigned to command the district of western Tennessee where he remained until he was mustered out of the service on April 30, 1866. The following July he was commissioned colonel of the Twenty-seventh Infantry in the regular army. He served at various frontier posts, and by his coolness and prompt action at Fort Laramie, Wyoming, helped to quell an outbreak of the Sioux Indians under Spotted Tail. Smith retired from active service in May 1881, and settled in Chicago, Illinois, where he died on January 29, 1897. His body was taken to his old home at Galena for interment. He had been three times honored with brevet rank: in 1865, as major general of volunteers for service and gallantry in action; in 1867 as brigadier general in the regular army for gallantry at the siege of Vicksburg; and again in the same year, as major general in the regular army for action at Savannah, Georgia. He died in 1897; three sons survived him.

SMITH, JOHN MERLIN POWIS
(1866-1932) — Biblical scholar, was born in London, England, the son of William Martin Smith and Anne (Powis) Smith. He attended private schools at Leominster, Hereford, and at Dawlish, Devon, and in 1881, he successfully passed the entrance examination for Cambridge, his primary interest being in Biblical study. He immigrated to Denison, Iowa, in 1883, and worked for a time on the farm of an uncle, but soon became teacher of the local school. In 1889, he found his way to Des Moines College, where he joined the Baptist Church. He graduated with an A.B. in 1893.

He became instructor in Greek in Cedar Valley Seminary, Osage, Iowa, but in the summer of 1894, enrolled as a graduate student in Semitics in the first summer session of the new University of Chicago. A year later, he gave up his teaching post and enrolled at Chicago as a candidate for a Ph.D. in Semitics. On July 1, 1899, he was awarded that degree *cum laude* and was appointed to the teaching staff of the department of Semitics as docent. His marriage to Catherine McKlveen of Chariton, Iowa, followed on September 19 of the same year. He attracted the attention of President William Rainey Harper, who made him his literary secretary. He became assistant professor in 1908, associate professor in 1912, and in 1915, was made professor and charged with the editorship of the *American Journal of Semitic Languages*, in succession to R. F. Harper. He fulfilled the duties of both

633

positions with distinction until the day of his death.

His contribution to the scientific literature of Biblical scholarship was notable. His more important works include commentaries on Micah, Zephaniah, Nahum, and Malachi in the International Critical Commentary Series; *The Prophet and His Problems* (1914); *William R. Harper's Elements of Hebrew* (1921) and *Harper's Hebrew Method and Manual* (1921); *The Religion of the Psalms* (1922); *The Moral Life of the Hebrews* (1923); *The Prophets and Their Times* (1925); *The Old Testament: An American Translation* (1927), of which he was general editor as well as translator of large sections of the text; and *The Origin and History of Hebrew Law* (1931). He also wrote more than seventy technical and popular articles.

His standing was recognized by the fraternity of Orientalists in his appointment in 1927 as annual professor in the American School of Oriental Research in Jerusalem, and by his election in 1931 as president of the Society of Biblical Literature and Exegesis and vice-president of the American Oriental Society. He died in 1932 as his ship was docking in New York harbor.

Joseph Smith

SMITH, JOSEPH

(1805-1844) — American religious leader, founder of the Church of Jesus Christ of the Latter-day Saints, commonly known as the Mormon Church, was born in Sharon, Vermont, the son of Joseph Smith, Sr., and Lucy Mack. In 1816, the family moved to Palmyra, New York, and finally settled just south of Palmyra in Farmington (later named Manchester) in 1818. Along with his father and neighbors, Smith spent much of his childhood and youth searching for buried treasure as a diviner, a practice combining quests for religious enlightenment with the exercise of magical powers. He was literate, but unschooled.

Smith claimed that he received his first vision at the age of fourteen. In this vision he saw two beings that introduced themselves as the Father and the Son. These beings forgave him of his sins and told him that none of the churches were right. Later visions led to the alleged receiving of golden plates containing the record of prophecy from ancient America. Smith translated these plates, written in what he claimed was a reformed Egyptian, with the aid of translation stones found with the plates. The translation was published as the *Book of Mormon* in 1830.

On April 6, 1830, Smith, now in Fayette, New York, organized his followers into the Church of Jesus Christ of the Latter-day Saints. Smith saw the formation of his church as a restoration to the Christian gospel as taught by Jesus and the first apostles, not as the formation of a new religion. He named himself as first elder of his church. His other titles within the church included that of seer, translator, and prophet.

Smith maintained that he led the church by direct revelation. He reportedly received multiple revelations that dealt with trivial administration details and guidelines for everyday living. He also reported many visions of the afterlife that awaited his followers. In 1835, Smith published a collection of his revelation called *Doctrine and Covenants*. Both the *Book of Mormon* and *Doctrine and Covenants* were seen as scriptural writings on par with the Bible. The Church of Jesus Christ of the Latter-day Saints continues to see these publications in the same way.

Smith, at the direction of his visions, led his church first to Kirkland, Ohio, in 1830, and then to Independence, Missouri, in Jackson County, where he hoped to build a new Zion. Smith himself stayed behind in Ohio in order to direct new converts to the future site of the new Zion. However, due to growing hostility, citizens of Jackson County, Missouri, eventually drove the congregation out of the county in the fall of 1833. Smith's efforts to reinstate his followers on their properties with the formation of his own militia named Zion's Camp proved unsuccessful.

In Kirkland, Ohio, Smith continued to plan for Zion. He sent missionaries throughout the United States and into England while seeing to the construction of a temple in Kirkland, dedicated in 1836. Smith formed a bank as part of a broad economic program, but the bank collapsed in 1837. Smith and the church were blamed for the damages that the collapse caused, and Smith and other church leaders fled Kirkland for Missouri in early 1838.

Smith and his fellow leaders met with their Missouri followers who had congregated in Far West, Missouri, after their forced removal from Jackson County. Here enmity towards Smith and his followers escalated into pitched battles between the citizens of Missouri and the

635

Church of Jesus Christ of the Latter-day Saints in the summer and fall of 1838. Lives were claimed on both sides and Smith was arrested on October 31, 1838, along with some of his leaders. The rest of his followers fled Missouri for Illinois. Smith escaped in April of 1839, and promptly joined his followers who were now residing in Quincy, Illinois.

Later that year, Smith went to Washington to seek redress from the federal government for the loss of property in Jackson County Missouri. President Martin Van Buren denied his request. Smith then asked the Illinois legislature to charter a new city, to be called Nauvoo, where the church could control all agencies of the government within the city. His request was granted and the Church of Jesus Christ of the Latter-day Saints renewed their missionary efforts with Nauvoo as their headquarters. It was here, in 1841, that Smith began to preach on the idea of eternal marriage and plural marriages.

With Smith's teachings deviating more and more from conventional Christian teachings, opposition to the Mormon Church continued to grow. A small but influential group broke away from the church and joined anti-Mormon forces. Smith's announced candidacy for the presidency in 1844. His use of church missionaries to campaign on his behalf, only confirmed the fears of his enemies and prompted them to publish a newspaper, the *Nauvoo Expositor,* aimed at exposing Smith's errors. Acting as Nauvoo mayor, Smith declared the paper a threat to the peace of the community and had it closed down. This ignited the opposition and Smith was charged with inciting a riot for destruction of the press on June 12, 1844. With new threats of violence escalating and Smith's use of the Nauvoo militia, Smith was also charged with treason and conspiracy. He finally submitted to arrest and was moved to nearby Carthage under the governor's protection. On June 27, 1844, a mob stormed the jail where Smith and his brother Hyrum were awaiting trial and killed them both. The bodies were returned to Nauvoo the next day.

Smith had married Emma Hale in 1827. Together they had nine children. With his death in 1844, the church became divided. The majority migrated to Salt Lake, Utah, under the leadership of Brigham Young. A smaller group rejected the Utah Church and settled in Independence, Missouri, under the leadership of Smith's eldest surviving son, Joseph Smith III, as the Reorganized church.

SMITH, RALPH TYLER
(1915-1972) Senator from Illinois; Senate Years of Service: 1969-1970; born in Granite City, Madison County, Ill., October 6, 1915; attended

public schools in Granite City; graduated from Illinois College at Jacksonville in 1937 and from Washington University Law School at St. Louis in 1940; admitted to the bar in 1940 and commenced practice in Granite City; enlisted in the United States Naval Reserve immediately after Pearl Harbor, ordered to active duty in July 1942, commissioned an ensign in October 1942 and served until January 1946; resumed the practice of law in Alton, Ill., in 1946; elected to the Illinois general assembly in 1954, and was reelected for seven succeeding

Ralph Tyler Smith

terms; majority whip in 1963; elected speaker in 1967 and reelected in 1969; appointed on September 17, 1969, as a Republican to fill the vacancy in the United States Senate created by the death of Everett M. Dirksen and served until November 3, 1970; unsuccessful candidate for election to fill the unexpired term in 1970; resumed the practice of law; died in Alton, Ill., August 13, 1972; interment in Sunset Hill Cemetery Mausoleum, Edwardsville, Ill.

SNYDER, JOHN FRANCIS

(1830-1921) — Physician, Confederate soldier, archaeologist, and author, was born on March 22, 1830, in Prairie du Pont, Saint Clair County, Illinois, the son of Adelaide (Perry) Snyder and Adam Wilson Snyder. He was first educated at Belleville, Illinois, at McKendree College, Lebanon, Illinois, and at the St. Louis University. During the winter of 1849-1850, he was a student at McDowell Medical College in St. Louis, Missouri, and the following summer, he crossed the plains to California. He visited the Sandwich Islands in 1852, returned home that year by way of the Isthmus of Panama, and arrived at Philadelphia, Pennsylvania, in time to enter Jefferson Medical College, where he graduated in 1853.

For a short period thereafter, he was in government medical service in western territories and went over the old Santa Fe trail to Taos and Albuquerque, New Mexico; then he resigned and began the practice of medicine at Bolivar, Missouri, where on September 27, 1854, he married Annie E. Sanders.

He was admitted to the Missouri bar in 1859, but he never practiced law. In June 1861, he joined the Confederates under General Sterling Price as a colonel, and served through the Civil War, taking active part in the battles of Wilson Creek, Lexington, Pea Ridge, Helena, Corinth, and Baldwin. Returning to Illinois after the war, he resumed the practice of medicine at Virginia. He was elected a member of the Thirty-first Illinois Legislature, where he gave a good account of himself, but declined further participation in party politics.

One of the founders of the Illinois State Historical Society in 1899, he became its president, 1903-1905, and contributed many important papers to it. He was also affiliated with the St. Louis Academy of Sciences, the Illinois Academy of Science, and other organizations. He took part in the survey and mapping of the Cahokia mounds (1880) and advocated their preservation. For many years, he was a research correspondent of the Smithsonian Institution, which published several of his shorter papers. His most important writings are *The Field for Archaeological Research in Illinois* (1900); *Captain John Baptiste Saucier at Fort Chartres in the Illinois 1751-1763* (1901), reprinted in *Transactions of the Illinois State Historical Society, 1919* (1920); *Adam W. Snyder and His Period in Illinois History, 1817-1842* (1903); "Prehistoric Illinois: Its Psychozoic Problems" (October 1911), "The Kaskaskia Indians" (July 1912), and "The Great Cahokia Mound" (July 1917) in the *Journal of the Illinois State Historical Society*. He was the first to indicate cultural differences between prehistoric tribes of southern and central Illinois, and explorations by the University of Illinois from 1922 to 1927 proved his hypothesis. He died in Virginia, Illinois, in 1921, at the age of ninety-one.

SPALDING, "A. G." ALBERT GOODWILL, "AL"

(1850-1915) — Sportsman and merchant, was born on a farm in Byron, Ogle County, Illinois, on September 2, 1850, the son of James Lawrence and Harriet Irene (Goodwill) Wright Spalding. He was educated in the public schools of Byron and Rockford, Illinois, and at the Rockford Commercial College. His first employment was as a grocer's clerk. At the age of seventeen, he became an outstanding player with the Forest City team of Rockford. After the establishment of professional baseball, Spalding joined the Boston team managed by Harry Wright in 1871. Spalding was pitcher and captain until 1875, and during that time, the team won the championships of the National Association of Professional

Base Ball Players from 1872 to 1875, inclusive.

In 1876, William A. Hulbert of Chicago, Illinois, with Spalding as aid and adviser, formed the National League of Professional Base Ball Clubs, and Spalding became pitcher, captain, and manager of the Chicago team. In March of the same year, he organized, with his brother James Spalding, a business firm to manufacture and sell baseball equipment and other sporting goods, under the name A.G. Spalding & Brother. Two years later his brother-in-law, William T. Brown, joined them and the firm name became A.G. Spalding & Brothers. Spalding maintained a connection with the Chicago Club for many years, however. Upon the death of William A. Hulbert in 1882, Spalding became its president and continued as such until 1891, when he felt it necessary to give all his time to his sporting-goods business.

"A. G." Albert Goodwill "Al" Spalding

As early as 1874 he made the arrangements for a tour of England and Ireland by two baseball teams, in an endeavor to impress the good points of the game on the followers of cricket and football. Again, in 1888-1889, he organized and took personal charge of a trip around the world made by his Chicago team and another group known as the All-American players. They gave exhibitions of baseball in Australia, Ceylon Egypt, Italy, France, and the British Isles. He was chosen as director of the section of sports for the United States at the Olympic games of 1900, held in connection with the World's Fair at Paris, France, that same year. For his work in this capacity, he later received from France the rosette of the Legion of Honor. From 1878 to 1880, he edited *Spalding's Official Baseball Guide*, and in 1911 published *America's National Game*, a comprehensive history of baseball.

He spent the last fifteen years of his life as a resident of Point Loma, California, and it was there that he died on September 9, 1915. His first wife, whom he married on November 18, 1875, was Sarah Josephine Keith; they had one son; she died in 1899, and in 1900 he married Mrs. Elizabeth Churchill Mayer, who survived him.

SPALDING, ALBERT

(1888-1953) — Violinist, was born on August 15, 1888, in Chicago, Illinois, the son of James Walter Spalding and Marie Boardman Spalding. At the age of seven, Spalding received his first violin, a half-size instrument, as a Christmas present. He practiced under the teaching of Ulpiano Chiti and Jean Buitrago, and at the age of fourteen, entered and passed with highest honors the examination for the diploma at the Bologna Conservatory of Music, although he had not studied there. He continued his studies privately in Paris, France, where he made his debut on June 6, 1905, performing Saint-Saens's *Concerto No. 3 in B Minor* and the *Chaconne* from Bach's unaccompanied *Partita No. 2*. Through his teacher Lefort, Spalding met Camille Saint-Saens. The respected composer, more than fifty years his senior, became his friend and mentor, and prevailed on the conductors Hans Richter and Walter Damrosch to invite Spalding to appear with their orchestras.

Spalding made his American debut in Carnegie Hall on November 8, 1908, with the New York Symphony Orchestra conducted by Damrosch. He subsequently performed widely in the United States and Europe until the outbreak of World War I, when he enlisted in the Air Service of the U.S. Signal Corps. Commissioned first lieutenant and sent to Italy, he served as assistant to Major Fiorello H. La Guardia on the Joint Army and Navy Aircraft Board, accompanying La Guardia on a secret mission to Spain to arrange the transport of raw materials to Italy.

Spalding returned to the concert stage in Paris, and on July 19, 1919, he married Mary Vanderhoef Pyle; they had no children. The following year, with composer-pianist John Powell, he toured Europe with the New York Symphony Orchestra. In 1923, he sat on jury examinations at the National Conservatory of Music in Paris, the first American so honored. Four years later, to the surprise of many Europeans, the German conductor Karl Muck invited "der Amerikaner" to be soloist in the Beethoven Violin Concerto at the Beethoven Centennial Festival in Hamburg. In addition to his concert tours, Spalding taught master classes at the Julliard School of Music in New York City from 1933 to 1944. From 1940 to 1942, Spalding was soloist and master of ceremonies in a popular series of weekly musical programs broadcast by a national radio network.

Commissioned colonel during World War II, Spalding directed psychological warfare operations in North Africa and Italy, and made radio broadcasts as "Major Sheridan" to rally Italian partisans. After the war, he was decorated by the French and Italian governments, and received the Medal of Freedom from the American government. He resumed his concert career in 1945, but decided to retire five years later, and made his farewell appearance at Lewisohn Stadium in New York City on June 20, 1950. After retiring, he taught at the Boston University College of Music and at the University of Florida at Tallahassee.

Spalding composed more than 100 works, including songs, chamber works, orchestral compositions, and cadenzas to violin concertos. He was also author of *A Fiddle, a Sword, and a Lady* (1953), a novel based on the life of the eighteenth-century violinist Giuseppe Tartini. He died on May 26, 1953, in New York, New York.

SPIES, AUGUST

(1855-1887) — Radical labor leader, born in Landeckerberg, Germany. He was tutored privately and then attended the Polytechnicum in Cassel. When he was seventeen, his father died and Spies quit school in order to save the money his father had left for the rest of his family. He immigrated to the United States in 1872. He arrived in New York, and then made his way to Chicago where he found a job doing upholstery.

August Spies

Appalled by the horrible conditions the working class faced and the high rate of unemployment, Spies began researching the working conditions, and attended a meeting of the Workingmen's Party of Illinois. It was at this meeting that Spies first came in contact with Socialism. He began reading more about it, and in 1877, he became a member of the Socialist Labor Party. He ran for political office a few times, but was unsuccessful, citing a conspiracy against the workingmen.

In 1876, Spies opened his own shop and began caring for his family, who came to Chicago the same year. He continued to advocate his Socialist ideals and champion the rights of the working class during this time.

Spies became the editor of the German-language magazine the *Arbeiter Zeitung*, an organ for the working class. His friend and fellow reformer, Albert Parsons, began editing the English-language edition.

Spies' political agitation quickly made enemies out of government officials. In 1881, he was a delegate to the congress of Revolutionary Socialists, and two years later, to the International Working People's Association (an anarchist organization that called for a revolution among the working class to end capitalism). Spies became one of the leaders of this organization, and helped form the campaign for the eight-hour day.

On May 1, 1886, Spies led eighty thousand workers in a parade, known as the National Strike of May 1, a day that has been associated with anarchy ever since Spies' demonstration. The goal of his demonstration was to secure an eight-hour workday by striking. Over the next couple days, over three hundred forty thousand workers went on strike. Spies published a leaflet *Revenge! Workingmen to Arms*, wherein he called upon the working class to rise up and "destroy the hideous monster that seeks to destroy you. To arms we call you, to arms." On May 4, labor leaders organized the Haymarket Square rally to advocate for an eight-hour workday. Spies was one of the first speakers at the rally and left before the violence erupted. Later that day, however, an unknown assailant threw a bomb into the crowd and the police began firing at the demonstrators. Approximately fourteen people were killed, and over two hundred were injured. Eight labor reformers, including Spies, were later arrested.

Spies and his co-defendants were found guilty of inciting the throwing of the bomb and Spies was given the death penalty. He was hanged on November 11, 1887. He was buried at the Haymarket funeral. His funeral was attended by a great number of the working class to whom he became a martyr. His final words were: "The day will come when our silence will be more powerful than the voices you are throttling today."

ST. CLAIR, ARTHUR

(1736-1818) — Revolutionary war soldier and governor of the Northwest Territory (1787-1802), was born on March 23, 1736, in Thurso, Caithness County, Scotland. He is often mistakenly said to have been the son of Margaret Balfour (Wedderburn) and James St. Clair, an officer in the French army, and the grandson of the Baron of Rosslyn. He was probably the son of William Sinclair, a merchant, and the great-grandson of James Sinclair, second Laird of Assery. His mother may have been Elizabeth (Balfour) Sinclair. He attended the University of Edinburgh for part of one term and had an unsuccessful apprenticeship under William Hunter, the celebrated anatomist of London. In 1757, he became an ensign in the British army and served with Amherst in Canada. On May

15, 1760, he married Phoebe Bayard of Boston, Massachusetts; they had seven children.

He resigned from the army in 1762, with the commission of lieutenant, and later, with a legacy of his own military service claims, he purchased a 4,000-acre estate in the Ligonier valley of western Pennsylvania. As the largest resident property owner in Pennsylvania west of the mountains, he was made the agent of colonial government in this frontier country in 1771. As justice of the county court of Westmoreland

Arthur St. Clair

County after its formation in 1773, he was obliged to extend the form but not the substance of government into the Pittsburgh area, at the same time that John Connolly, captain of the militia and after 1774 justice of the district of west Augusta County, Virginia, sought to extend the substance as well as the form of Virginia control over the same region. St. Clair was unsuccessful before the superior military force and greater popular appeal of the Virginians, who rebuilt and garrisoned the fort abandoned by the British in 1772 and prepared for the surveying and occupation of the Kentucky country. Supported by the fur traders, he refused to cooperate in these and other actions offensive to the Shawnee tribe and thus probably relieved Pennsylvania of the vengeance of that tribe in Dunmore's War of 1774. He favored rewarding the Delaware Native Americans for their neutrality in the face of frontier insults, but complied in the refusal the legislature to establish and garrison a satisfactory trading post in the Delaware town of Kittanning.

With the onset of the Revolutionary War, he was made a member of the Committee of Safety of Westmoreland County, but he was powerless to extend Pennsylvania control over the Pittsburgh area, as the Virginia committee sent John Neville to occupy the fort and as Virginia's commissioners undertook most of the financial burdens and diplomatic manipulation at the treaty of Pittsburgh in 1775, by which the outstanding issues of Dunmore's War were settled and a Loyalist-Native American uprising prevented. At this treaty, he occupied the minor position of secretary to the relatively insignificant commissioners of the Continental Congress. In the winter of 1776-1777, as brigadier general, he was with Washington in the campaign and the battles of Trenton and Princeton. In the spring of 1777, as major general, he was ordered to the defense of Fort Ticonderoga, which was popularly considered as indestructible. His evacuation of the post, probably as the result of factors beyond his control, filled the public mind with such dismay that Congress recalled him from service in the field. Although he was completely exonerated by a court martial in September 1778, he was not, for the rest of the war, placed in a position to render noticeable service.

Upon his return to civil life, he entered Pennsylvania politics as an anti-constitutionalist. As a member of the council of censors in 1783, he unsuccessfully opposed the constitution of 1776, and he wrote the majority report recommending a new constitutional convention in order to abolish the single legislative chamber and other radical features. Elected state delegate to the Continental Congress, he served from November 2, 1785 to November 28, 1787, and was president in 1787. With the creation of the Northwest Territory in 1787, he was appointed governor and served until 1802. As administrator of Indian affairs, he was obliged to defend the treaties made with the tribes in 1784 and 1785, which deprived them of much land north of Ohio, and which the Indians claimed had been forced upon them by fraud and military compulsion. They insisted upon a treaty to make the Ohio River the boundary and to be drawn up at a grand council in which all the tribes were fairly represented. At the treaty of Fort Harmar in 1789, however, he met only part of the Tribes concerned, permitted those present to weaken their strength by quarreling among themselves and finally manipulated the tribes into an apparent acceptance of the earlier and much hated treaties. The resulting dissatisfaction led into a war in which he, as major general and commander of the federal army, was overwhelmingly defeated on November 4, 1791, on a branch of the Wabash about a day's march from the site of Fort Wayne. A confederated Native American army administered the defeat with the Miami, Little Turtle, which was inferior in numbers to the American army.

St. Clair was under positive and unalterable orders to erect a chain of military posts from Fort Washington, near the mouth of the Miami, to the rapids of the Maumee in the heart of the country of the then powerful Miami confederacy; few military enterprises have been more poorly planned and executed. He was originally directed to set out from Fort Washington in July, but he did not do so until September. The result was that the frosts destroyed the grass, which was the only source of food for the horses and cattle. The delay was caused in part by the prolongation of the peace mission of Thomas Proctor, until the final and unsuccessful outcome of which St. Clair was obliged to postpone all offensive movement. Blundering in the quartermaster's department resulted in the failure to provide adequate supplies and arms. The morale of the army, two-thirds of which was militia and from which many had deserted, was also undermined by the fact that during their six months' service they received their monthly pay of three dollars but once, by short rations, and by the rigorous and non-military services required of them by St. Clair. He himself was not so experienced in frontier and Native American tribe warfare as was his second in command, General Richard Butler, though he seems to have been more able. He declined to accept Butler's opinions and advice on certain technical matters, and the resulting estrangement continued throughout the campaign. At no time during the expedition did St. Clair have sufficient knowledge of the numbers and location of the tribes opposing him. The disaster was most humiliating, and although he was exonerated from blame by Washington and by a committee of the House of Representatives, he resigned from the army and devoted himself to the duties as governor of the Northwest Territory. His ambitions for advancement in Federalist politics were, of course, checked.

In governing the Northwest Territory frontiersmen, he sought to enforce the spirit and the letter of the highly centralized and undemocratic Ordinance of 1787. With an overbearing manner and a paternal zeal too uncomplimentary to his frontier citizens, he objected to proposed legislation that was aimed to decentralize the functions and control of local institutions. He objected to statehood as premature and sought to divide the territory into smaller territories so as to postpone statehood indefinitely. The result was a movement by the local Jeffersonians in 1801 to remove him from office. They were successful in the latter but failed in the former, until St. Clair at the constitutional convention of 1802 denounced as a nullity the Ohio enabling act of Congress. Jefferson thereupon removed him from office. He retired to his home, the "Hermitage," near Ligonier, Pennsylvania, where he developed his estate and built an iron furnace to manufacture stoves and castings. Owing to generous lending of money, signing notes for friends, and the failure of the Republican Congress to reimburse him for moneys advanced for government use while he was the Federalist governor of the Northwest Territory, he lost the whole of his fortune. In 1812, he published in defense of himself, *A Narrative Of The Manner In Which The Campaign Against The Indians (1791) As Conducted Under The*

Command Of Major General St. Clair, Together With The Reports Of The Committees Appointed To Inquire Into The Causes Of The Failure Thereof.
His later years were spent in poverty and political oblivion. After being thrown from his wagon, and he died on August 31, 1818, in the log cabin that was his home on Chestnut Ridge.

STELLE, JOHN H.

(1891-1962) — Thirty-first governor of Illinois (1940-1941), was born in McLeansboro, Illinois, the son of Laura Blades and Thompson Beveny Stelle. His father, a county judge, sent him to Western Military Academy in Alton after an elementary education, and from 1914 to 1915, he studied law at Washington University in St. Louis.

Stelle practiced law in his hometown until 1917, when he enlisted in the state's National Guard. As an officer in the U. S. Army, he was sent to France in the 115th Machine Gun Battalion, and in 1919, was discharged as a captain after being wounded in battle. After recuperating and spending several years involved in business interests, Stelle served as assistant state auditor from 1933 to 1934, and as state treasurer from 1934 until 1936. That year, he was elected lieutenant governor under Governor Henry Horner. When Horner became ill in 1938, Stelle took over his duties. At Horner's death, Stelle officially took over the governorship until the end of his term, in January of the following year. While in office, Stelle fired Horner's appointees and appointed his friends to the state administration.

Stelle did not receive the Democratic nomination for the next term in 1940, and returned to his business interests. In 1941, he became president and owner of Arketex Ceramic Corporation; he was also president of the Evansville Coal Company and McLeansboro Shale Products Company. Stelle died in McLeansboro, his hometown, in 1962.

STETTINIUS, EDWARD REILLY

(1900-1949) — Corporate executive and U.S. secretary of state, was born on October 22, 1900, in Chicago, Illinois, the son of Edward Reilly (Riley, Rilley) and Judith (Carrington) Stettinius. He grew up in Chicago and in Staten Island, New York. After graduating from the Pomfret School in Connecticut, he entered the University of Virginia in 1919. He neglected his studies for YMCA work, Sunday school teaching, and missionary work among the poor in Albemarle County, Virginia, and left college without a degree in 1924. On May 15, 1926, he married Virginia

Gordon Wallace; they had three children: Edward Reilly and twins, Wallace and Joseph.

Stettinius, an Episcopalian, considered becoming a minister, but was persuaded by John Lee Pratt, vice-president of General Motors, to apply his humanitarian ideals to a business career. He began after college as a stockroom clerk at GM's Hyatt roller-bearing division and soon rose to employment manager. In 1926, as special assistant to Pratt, he instituted one of the automobile industry's first group insurance plans, improved working and sanitary conditions, and helped formulate advertising policy. He became assistant to President Alfred P. Sloan, Jr., in 1930 and, a year later, vice-president in charge of industrial and public relations. Stettinius moved in 1934 to the U.S. Steel Corporation as a vice-president, and was influential in the company's decision to recognize the steel workers' union in 1937. The following year, he became chairman of the board of U.S. Steel.

Stettinius supported the basic economic goals of the New Deal. In 1933, President Franklin D. Roosevelt appointed him to the Industrial Advisory Board to act as a liaison officer with the National Recovery Administration. Roosevelt called Stettinius into government service again in 1939, as chairman of the War Resources Board, and the following year, placed him on the new National Defense Advisory Commission, at which point Stettinius resigned from U.S. Steel to devote full time to government service. He became director of priorities of the Office of Production Management in January 1941, and nine months later, administrator of lend-lease.

In September 1943, Roosevelt appointed Stettinius under-secretary of state and charged him with the task of reorganizing the State Department, whose structure had failed to adapt to its expanded functions during World War II. Among other changes, Stettinius eliminated administrative duplication, created a set of offices to deal with daily problems, therefore giving the under-secretary and the assistant secretaries more time for broad policy questions, and established two top-level committees, one on policy and one on postwar programs. He also strengthened the department's relations with the White House, Congress, and the public. On December 1, 1944, after the resignation of the ailing Cordell Hull, Roosevelt named Stettinius secretary of state.

Stettinius' most notable contributions as secretary of state centered on his vigorous efforts to establish the United Nations. As under-secretary, he had headed the American delegation to the seminal Dumbarton Oaks Conference in 1944, at which the Allies accepted as a basis for negotiation the State Department's proposals for structure of the United Nations. In February 1945, he accompanied Roosevelt to the Yalta Conference with Winston Churchill and Joseph Stalin, at which it was decided to call a conference in San Francisco, California, at the end of April to form the new organization. Stettinius subsequently attended the Inter-American Conference in Mexico City to reassure the nations of Latin America that the creation of the United Nations would not prevent the development of a hemispheric security system. The resulting Act of Chapultetec laid the foundation for the Organization of American States in 1948.

After Roosevelt's death in April 1945, President Harry S. Truman asked Stettinius to continue in office and head the American delegation to the San Francisco Conference. Truman accepted Stettinius' resignation as secretary of state at the close of the San Francisco Conference, but appointed him chairman of the U.S. delegation to the United Nations Preparatory Commission, and in January 1946, chairman of the American delegation to the first session of the U.N. General Assembly, as well as American representative on the Security Council. He resigned in June of that year.

For three years after his return to private life, he served as rector of the University of Virginia. A longtime friend of William Tubman, the president of Liberia, he helped form (1947) and headed as board chairman the Liberia Company, a partnership between the Liberian government and American financiers to provide funds for the development of that African nation. He died of a coronary thrombosis on October 13, 1949, in Greenwich, Connecticut, and was buried in the family plot at Locust Valley, Long Island.

STEVENSON, ADLAI (EWING)
(1835-1914) — U.S. Representative from Illinois and vice-president of the United States, was born in Christian County, Kentucky, on October 23, 1835, the son of John T. and Ann Eliza (Ewing) Stevenson. He was brought up on his father's farm, and was educated in the public schools and at Center College, Danville, Kentucky. When he was sixteen years old, he moved with his family to Bloomington, Illinois, where he studied law under Judge Davis and Robert E. Williams, and was admitted to the bar. Stevenson opened a law office at Metamora, Illinois, in 1859, and practiced there for ten years, during which he was master of the Circuit Court for four years and district attorney for the same period.

In 1864, the Democratic Party nominated him for presidential elector. In the interest of George McClellan, the nominee of his party for the presidency, he canvassed the entire state, speaking in every county. At the end of his term as district attorney in 1869, he returned to Bloomington and formed a law partnership with Judge James S. Ewing, which continued for twenty-five years.

The Democrats of the Bloomington district nominated Stevenson for Congress in 1874. The district had been safely Republican, and his opponent, John McNulta, was one of the leading Republican

Adlai (Ewing) Stevenson

orators of the state. Stevenson, however, was successful. He was in Congress during the exciting scenes incident to the Tilden-Hayes contest in 1876. He was defeated for a second term in 1876, but in 1878, was again elected.

At the end of his second term, Stevenson resumed the practice of law in Bloomington. He was a delegate to the Democratic National Convention of 1884, in Chicago, Illinois, and after the election of Grover Cleveland as president of the United States, was appointed first assistant postmaster general, which position he held until 1889. In 1892, he was elected vice-president for Cleveland's second term, following the Democratic convention in Chicago, at which he was chairman of the Illinois delegation.

Rutherford B. Hayes appointed him a member of the board to inspect the military academy at West Point in 1877, and in 1897, he was a member of the commission that met in Belgium to try to secure international bimetallism. Stevenson was a nominee for vice-president on the ticket with William Jennings Bryan in 1900, and was a candidate for governor of Illinois in 1908, but was defeated by Charles S. Deneen.

He was the author of *Something of Men I have Known* (1909). He was well versed in the history of Illinois and Kentucky, and in 1903, delivered the annual address before the Illinois Historical Society, his subject being, "The Constitution and Constitutional Conventions of Illinois." He was an honorary member of the Chicago Historical Society.

He was married on December 20, 1866, to Letitia Green of

Danville, Kentucky, and had one son, Lewis Green, and three daughters: Mary (who died in 1892), Julia, wife of Martin D. Hardin of Chicago, Illinois, and Letitia Stevenson. Adlai E. Stevenson died at his home in Chicago, Illinois, on June 24, 1914.

STEVENSON, ADLAI E.

(1900-1965) — Thirty-third governor of Illinois (1949-1953), was born in Los Angeles, California, to Helen Louise Davis and Lewis Green Stevenson. His grandfather was vice president to President Grover Cleveland.

When he was eighteen years old, Stevenson left home to join the U. S. Naval Reserve as an apprentice seaman. He studied at Princeton University, graduating in 1922. From that time until 1926, he completed his study of law at Northwestern University in Evanston while working as assistant managing editor of the Bloomington *Daily Pantograph.* He also became a resident of Illinois.

In 1927, Stevenson set up a law practice with the firm of Cutting, Moore and Sidley, which led him to the position of special counsel for the Agricultural Adjustment Administration in 1933. His legal knowledge also helped him gain an appointment as Assistant Counsel for the Federal Alcohol Control Administration in 1934. During World War II, he was Special Assistant to the Secretary of the Navy, at which time he was appointed head of the Italian Section of the Foreign Economic Mission. He also served as senior advisor in the San Francisco conference of 1945, where the United Nations was formed; the next year he was a member of the United States delegation to that body.

His renown in both international and state services led Stevenson to be elected governor of Illinois in 1948, defeating the Republican incumbent by about six hundred thousand votes. His platform was for liberal reform in the state. His success triggered a reform movement within the Democratic Party, which at that time had grown almost indistinguishable from Republicans in its orientation and platforms.

While in office, Stevenson sponsored mining law revisions and effectively broke up syndicated gambling, prostitution, and loan shark rings in Rock Island, Peoria, Joliet, Decatur, Springfield and East St. Louis by putting state police on the merit system. Corrupt links between the underworld and politicians in these cities diminished markedly. He also increased the state gasoline tax to finance the state's highway system. However, in spite of his successes, Stevenson found it difficult to deal with local and legislative officials, and showed a preference for international affairs.

In 1952, he did not run for gubernatorial reelection and was instead nominated for the Democratic Presidential race. He was defeated by Dwight Eisenhower both that year and in 1956. He continued his law practice and was, from 1955 through 1960, in partnership with Rifkind and Wirtz. From 1961 until his death, he served as U. S. Ambassador to the United Nations. He was buried at Bloomington, Illinois in 1965.

STEVENSON, ADLAI EWING III

(1930-) (great-grandson of Vice President Adlai Ewing Stevenson) Senator from Illinois; Senate Years of Service: 1970-1981; born in Chicago, Cook County, Ill., October 10, 1930; attended grammar schools in Illinois and Milton Academy, Massachusetts; graduated from Harvard College in 1952, and from the law department of the same university in 1957; entered United States Marine Corps as a private in 1952, served as a tank platoon commander in Korea, discharged as a first lieutenant in 1954 and from the Reserves in 1961 with the rank of captain; law clerk to justice of Illinois Supreme Court 1957-1958; admitted to the bar in 1957 and commenced practice in Chicago, Ill.; member, Illinois house of representatives 1965-1967; treasurer, State of Illinois 1967-1970; elected in a special election on November 3, 1970, as a Democrat to the United States Senate to fill the unexpired term caused by the death of United States Senator Everett M. Dirksen; reelected in 1974, and served from November 17, 1970, to January 3, 1981; was not a candidate for reelection in 1980; chairman, Select Committee on the Senate Committee System (Ninety-fourth Congress), Select Committee on Ethics (Ninety-fifth and Ninety-sixth Congresses); resumed the practice of law; unsuccessful Democratic candidate for governor of Illinois in 1982 and 1986; discontinued practice of law in 1992; founded and served as chairman of investment banking firm of SCM Investment Management 1992-; is a resident of Hanover, Ill.

Adlai Ewing Stevenson, III

651

STOCK, FREDERICK AUGUST

(1872-1942) — Orchestra conductor, was born on November 11, 1872, in Jülich, near Cologne, Germany, the son of Friedrich Karl and Louise (Leiner) Stock. His father, a bandmaster in the Prussian army, gave him his first music lessons. At fourteen, he entered the Cologne Conservatory as a violin pupil of Georg Japha, studying theory and composition with Engelbert Humperdinck and Gustav Jensen. He joined the violin section of the Cologne Municipal Orchestra (also known as the Gurzenich Orchestra) in 1891. Theodore Thomas, the conductor of the Chicago Orchestra, heard him there and engaged him. When Stock arrived in Chicago, Illinois, in October 1895, however, there was no vacancy in the violin section, and he was assigned to the violas.

In 1899, Thomas, in his sixties and wishing, chose Stock as assistant conductor. Although he continued to play viola, Stock began to conduct occasional rehearsals and to direct accompaniments for soloists, especially on tour. Stock's growing gifts as a composer were recognized when Thomas conducted his *Symphonic Variations* in 1903. When Thomas died on January 4, 1905, three weeks after the opening of Orchestra Hall, the orchestra's first permanent home, Stock was asked to serve until a new permanent conductor could be found. Unsuccessful negotiations with several eminent Europeans followed, after which, in April 1905, the trustees elected Stock conductor. He was not yet thirty-three and relatively unknown outside Chicago.

Stock gave careful attention to the construction of his programs, introduced works by contemporary composers, encouraged young performers, and took the orchestra on tours throughout the Middle West and South. He also made significant innovations. Thomas had conducted occasional popular and children's concerts, but Stock expanded these into regular series: the popular concerts, for which low-priced tickets were distributed through civic organizations, in 1914, and the children's concerts in 1919.

The steady growth in influence of the Chicago Symphony Orchestra under Stock's direction was disrupted by anti-German prejudice during World War I. Although Stock had applied for U.S. citizenship on his first day in Chicago, he had neglected taking out his second papers within the allotted time. With the declaration of war in Europe, he announced to the orchestra that from this time rehearsals would be conducted in English rather than in German, as they had been since the orchestra's inception. Feeling against Germans increased with America's entry into the war, and on August 17, 1918, believing that his presence was damaging the orchestra, Stock resigned as conductor. The trustees regretfully acquiesced and appointed Eric DeLamarter, a local organist and composer, as assistant conductor to fill what they hoped would be a temporary interregnum. During the season of 1918-1919, Stock observed the orchestras in such cities as Boston, Massachusetts; New York, New York; and Philadelphia, Pennsylvania. On February 7, 1919, he filed his application for second papers; on February 19, 1919, the orchestra's trustees invited him to resume conducting; and on February 28, 1919, he appeared on the stage for the first time since the close of the preceding season, receiving an ovation. He became a citizen on May 22, 1919.

The dislocations of the war had made evident the shortcomings of the United States as a training ground for orchestral performers. In a farseeing plan, Stock suggested to the trustees of the Chicago Symphony the formation of a training orchestra designed to teach the orchestral repertoire and the necessary routine in ensemble work. The formation of the Civic Orchestra was announced on December 4, 1919, with Stock as director; he conducted its first concert on March 29, 1920. He also gave much attention to encouraging musical education in the public schools and sometimes conducted concerts by high school orchestras.

Besides his regular conducting in Chicago, Stock participated in numerous music festivals and served as guest conductor for the New York Philharmonic (1926, 1927) and Philadelphia orchestras. His own compositions included two symphonies, three overtures, a violin concerto *March and Hymn to Democracy* (1919), and other orchestral works, as well as numerous orchestral arrangements, chamber works, and songs.

Under Stock, the Chicago Symphony Orchestra dominated the musical life of the Middle West. He conducted a Mahler Festival in 1917, and performed works by other major composers, such as Stravinsky's *Rite of Spring*, years before they were heard in New York. When Howard Hanson in 1938 made a survey of American performances of works by American composers over the previous twenty years, he reported that the Chicago Symphony Orchestra headed the list, having played 272 compositions by eighty-five composers.

Stock received honorary degrees from several universities including Northwestern (1915), Michigan (1924), and Chicago (1925); he was made a chevalier of the Legion of Honor (France) in 1925. He married Elizabeth (Else) Muskulus in Milwaukee, Wisconsin, on May 25, 1896; they had one child, Vera Fredericka. Stock died of a coronary thrombosis at his Chicago home on October 20, 1942, shortly before his seventieth birthday. His ashes were placed in Rosehill Cemetery, Chicago.

STONE, MELVILLE ELIJAH

(1848-1929), — journalist, was born in Hudson, Illinois. At the age of twelve, he moved with his parents to Chicago, Illinois, where he graduated from the high school in 1867. In 1869, Stone purchased an interest in a foundry and machine-shop. He was successful in his business until his earnings were swept away in the great Chicago fire of 1871.

After the fire, Stone turned his interest to journalism. After four successful years as correspondent and editor, Stone established his own evening paper. On Christmas day, 1875, he published the first edition of *The Daily News*. On the editorial side, Stone assembled a splendid staff of writers, including George Ade, Bill Nye, and Eugene Field. Stone's own specialty was what he called "detective journalism." For Stone, this usually meant exposing official corruption and punishment of the "public offenders." Though it began rather crudely, the *Chicago Daily News* quickly caught on.

By the 1880s, *The Daily News* had passed Chicago's *Tribune* and *Times* to become the most popular newspaper in the city, with a circulation more than 100,000. Circulation hit 200,000 by 1895, making the *Daily News* the first medium of mass communication in Chicago. The *Chicago Daily News* was a penny paper, a small-format, four-page sheet. In appearance alone, it was strikingly different from other newspapers of the time. Everything was on a smaller scale, with smaller pages, fewer stories, and fewer departments; everything was tightly edited and drastically condensed. But, in a more subtle sense, its philosophy was as different as its look. The *Daily News* also reflected the social values of the dominant, Protestant, native-born elites of Chicago. Yet from the start, the paper promoted an urban culture much less dominated by rigid notions of private property and individualism. In both editorial philosophy and journalistic technique, the *Chicago Daily News* was an urban newspaper, an activist portrayer and promoter of public life and urban community.

Because of this belief in the interdependent nature of society, the *Daily* laid the blame for social problems upon the heads of individual people, as did most papers of the time. Stone argued that the poor were poor because of hard times; prostitutes were prostitutes because they could find no honest work; bad boys were bad because of poor nurture in

654

the schools and churches. Rarely did the *Daily News* blame individuals. With such a view of the power of environment and community over individual, it is not surprising that the *Daily News* was a strong advocate of charity. The paper urged the creation of all sorts of philanthropic organizations, including shelters for prostitutes and the homeless, public baths, soup kitchens, and unemployment relief agencies. Almost always, interdependence was the key idea.

The *Daily News* also urged formal public action through government. Stone was no socialist, in an ideological sense; and like other editors, he complained about high taxes and government corruption. But most of the time, the *Daily News* advocated increased government intervention in business and in urban life. The paper demanded sweeping government regulation of business, large-scale public works, and expanded human services. In a remarkable editorial during its first month of existence, the *Daily News* even called upon the city to provide a job to every person who needed one.

In 1893, Stone became the general manager of the modern Associated Press, a new organization designed to compete with the Associated Press of New York, which Midwestern publishers denounced as a selfish monopoly in collusion with the United Press and Western Union Telegraph. The new AP quickly became a formidable national force in newsgathering. During his 25 years as head of the Associated Press, Stone began and ran the organization's first steps into becoming the international newsgathering organization it is today. Under Stone's leadership, the Associated Press adopted the most advanced telegraph, cable, and wireless technologies. He also moved the headquarters from Chicago, the home of the old Western Associated Press, to New York.

Under the direction of Melville Stone, the Associated Press became the leading news agency. Offering honesty, impartiality, and public service, it became the quintessentially American doctrine of journalism in the Twentieth Century. Melville Elijah Stone died in New York City in 1969.

STONE, ORMOND
(1847-1933) — Astronomer, was born on January 11, 1847, in Pekin, Illinois, son of the Reverend Elijah and Sophia Louise (Creighton) Stone. He was able to secure a good preliminary education, and entered the University of Chicago in 1856, studying there until 1870. Meantime, he was instructor at Racine College, Wisconsin, in 1857-1868, and taught at Northwestern Female College, Evanston, Illinois, in 1869. His ability in

Ormond Stone

mathematics led to his appointment as assistant in the U.S. Naval Observatory in 1870, where he remained until 1875. In this latter year, he received an A.M. from the University of Chicago.

While he was at the Naval Observatory, his work was largely with the two transit circles and in the routine computing. Simon Newcomb was so impressed by his ability that Stone was strongly recommended for the directorship of the Cincinnati Observatory, which position he occupied from 1875 to 1882. He and his assistants used the eleven-inch refractor there in the discovery and measurement of southern double stars, though the measures were made under considerable difficulties from lack of a driving clock. Stone is credited with the discovery of forty-four pairs, which come under the modern definition of double stars.

Stone was appointed director of the University of Virginia observatory, to which Leander McCormick had given a new refractive lens, and began his new duties in 1882. In 1884, he founded the *Annals of Mathematics* and was one of its editors for many years. Besides what appears in the publications of the three observatories with which he was connected, he contributed over a hundred shorter articles to scientific journals. He retired on the Carnegie Foundation in 1912 and lived on his farm at Clifton Station, Virginia, until his death, taking an active part in the local affairs of his county.

On May 31, 1871, he married Catharine Flagler of Washington, D.C., who died on January 8, 1914, and, on June 9, 1915, he married Mary Florence Brennan of Lansing, Michigan, who died in 1932. He had no children. He was struck and instantly killed by an automobile, on January 17, 1933.

STRATTON, WILLIAM G.

(1914-2001) — Thirty-fourth governor of Illinois (1953-1961), was born in Ingleside, Illinois, the son of Zula Van Wormer and William Stratton. His mother taught school, and his father was prominent in the state's

Republican Party, having been the Director of Conservation and later the Secretary of State of Illinois.

Stratton attended local schools before attending the University of Arizona, from which he graduated in 1934. He majored in political science, and was a member of that state's National Guard while in college, but decided to return to Ingleside after graduation.

While working as a salesman, he was a delegate to several Republican State conventions over the next five years, and in 1940, was nominated by his party for the U. S. House of Representatives, where he served for one term. As the youngest member of the House, Stratton voted against arming merchant ships, extending military service to eighteen months, and the ship seizure bill, but favored registering teenagers for military service.

Stratton returned to Illinois in 1942, and served four years as state treasurer. In 1945, he joined the U. S. Navy with the rank of lieutenant. On the way home from his duty abroad, Stratton learned from a radio broadcast that he was once again nominated to represent the state in Congress. He served in Washington until 1950, with a record of overriding at least six significant Presidential vetoes. After this term, he again took the position of Illinois State Treasurer.

Two years later, Stratton was elected the Republican candidate for governor of the state. In 1953, he appointed the first woman ever to a governor's cabinet post, approved a bond issue to finance expressways, and began an open door policy toward his constituents. He held a weekly open house in Springfield, so that people could speak with him directly about state affairs. During his second term in office, Stratton approved an increase in state sales tax to raise money for schools, and pushed for reform in state hospitals for more beds.

Although he disapproved of presidents holding office for more than two terms, Stratton ran again for a third term as governor in 1960, but lost to Democrat Otto Kerner. After his term ended, he returned to his Black Angus cattle farm. He tried again for Governor in 1968, but finished third in the primary race.

He retired to Chicago, and died on March 2, 2001.

STRAWN, SILAS HARDY

(1866-1946) — Lawyer and businessman, was born on December 15, 1866, on a farm near Ottawa, Illinois, the son of Abner Strawn and Eliza (Hardy) Strawn. After graduating from Ottawa High School in 1885, Strawn supported himself as a teacher, and while reading law, as a clerk and court reporter. In 1889, he was admitted to the Illinois bar, practicing initially in the office of Bull and Strawn. Beginning in 1892, Strawn practiced in Chicago, Illinois, at the offices of Winston & Meagher, and in 1894, he was made a partner. On June 22, 1897, Strawn married Margaret Stewart; they had two daughters, Margaret and Katherine.

The firm of Winston, Strawn, Black, & Towner was one of the oldest and largest in Chicago that engaged in general practice. At one time or another, the firm represented the Chicago Great Western Railroad Company; the Union Stock Yards & Transit Company; the Michigan Central Railroad Company; the Chicago & Alton Railroad; the Chicago, Indianapolis & Louisville Railway Company; the Nickel Plate Railroad; the Mutual Life Insurance Company of New York; and Montgomery Ward. Strawn took a particular interest in Montgomery Ward, serving for twelve years on the executive board, and for a few months in 1920, as president of the corporation.

Strawn was a member of the New York bar, as well as a member, officer, and active participant in the appropriate local, state, and national bar associations. He served the Chicago Bar Association as president from 1913 to 1914, the Illinois State Bar Association from 1921 to 1922 as its president, and from 1927 to 1928, he presided over the fiftieth anniversary of the American Bar Association. He became a member of the executive council of the American Society of International Law, a trustee of the Carnegie Endowment for International Peace, and president of the Chicago Council on Foreign Relations. He attended the foreign conventions of the International Chamber of Commerce in 1923, 1927, 1931, and 1933 as an American committee delegate, and was elected to an honorary vice-presidency in the U.S. Chamber of Commerce in 1928. From 1930 to 1933, Strawn was chairman of the American committee, and during those same years, was also honored as president of the U.S. Chamber of Commerce, serving in that office from 1931 to 1932, and on that organization's senior council from 1932 to 1940.

In 1925, President Calvin Coolidge appointed Strawn as one of the two American commissioners to represent U.S. interests at the Chinese tariff conferences at Peking. Apparently at Strawn's own suggestion, Coolidge also appointed him sole commissioner of the United States on the international commission to investigate extraterritorial jurisdiction in China. Both commissions failed in the face of the Chinese revolution.

Strawn received honorary LL.D. degrees from the University of

Michigan (1928), Lake Forest College (1928), Knox College (1930), Northwestern University (1930), and Middlebury College (1935); and became Chicago's recognized elder statesman. He spent his later years speaking and writing against the New Deal and its alphabetical agencies, attacking them in the courts, and assailing their intrusions, real and imaginary, into business and private affairs.

Strawn died of a heart attack on February 4, 1946, and was buried first in Ottawa, then in Lake Forest, Illinois.

STRONG, JOSIAH

(1847-1916) — Clergyman, social reformer, and author, was born on January 19, 1847, in Naperville, Illinois, the son of Josiah and Elizabeth C. (Webster) Strong. In 1852, his parents moved to Hudson, Ohio, then the site of Western Reserve College. Strong graduated from this institution in 1869, and at once entered Lane Theological Seminary in Cincinnati, Ohio. He began his professional career in 1871 at Cheyenne, Wyoming, where he was ordained on September 8, 1871, and installed as pastor of a Congregational church; ten days before (August 29, 1871), at Chardon, Ohio, he had married Alice Bisbee, daughter of Charles and Cordelia (Packard) Bisbee.

After only two years in Cheyenne, Strong returned to Western Reserve College to serve as chaplain and instructor in theology. Three years, later he accepted a call to a pastorate in Sandusky, Ohio. In 1881, he became a secretary of the Congregational Home Missionary Society, for the work in Ohio, Kentucky, West Virginia, and western Pennsylvania. In 1884, he returned again to the parish ministry as head of the Central Congregational Church in Cincinnati.

He published his book, *Our Country*, in 1885. This work had its origin in a small manual of the same title, issued years before by the Congregational Home Missionary Society, which he had been asked to revise and bring up to date; but instead made the book his own with a collection of new material. The book was translated into foreign languages, and reissued in new and revised editions in America. His second book, *The New Era*, was published simultaneously in the United States and England in 1893, and had instant circulation of wide dimensions.

Strong was made president of the Evangelical Alliance, but that society proved to be too conservative in its ideas, too pietistic in its practices. In 1898, there fore, he resigned his office and founded his own organization, the League for Social Service, which was reorganized in

659

1902 as the American Institute for Social Service. He was also an active participant in the establishment of the Federal Council of the Churches of Christ in America. He went to England in 1904 to organize the British Institute of Social Service, and five years later (in 1909-1910), visited South American countries. His books written during this period include *The Twentieth Century City* (1898), *Religious Movements for Social Bettermernt* (1900), *Expansion under New World Conditions* (1900), *The Times and Young Men* (1901), *The Next Great Awakening* (1902), *Social Progress: A Yearbook* (1904-1906) *The Challenge of the City* (1907), My *Religion in Every-Day Life* (1910), *Our World: The New World Life* (1913) and *Our World: The New World Religion* (1915), the first two of four projected volumes. He also edited *The Gospel of the Kingdom*, a monthly begun in October 1908, and published numerous sermons, addresses, and pamphlets.

Strong died on April 28, 1916, at age seventy, after a prolonged and painful illness.

Louis Henri Sullivan

SULLIVAN, LOUIS HENRI
(1856-1924) — Architect, was born on September 3, 1856, in Boston, Massachusetts, to Patrick Sullivan, a music and dancing academy owner, and Adrienne (List) Sullivan. Louis attended public schools in Boston before taking courses at the Massachusetts's Institute of Technology (1872). He also spent two years at the Beaux Arts in Paris, studying under Joseph Auguste Emile Vaudremer. In 1875, he returned to the United States and joined his parents, who had moved to Chicago, Illinois. There, he worked in various offices and in 1879 he began as a probationary partner under the prestigious Dankmar Adler. In 1881, he was named as Adler's full partner. The two strove to design buildings in the city so that more light would shine within, at the same time making them taller. The early designs were a strange combination of Victorian Gothic, English "Eastlake," and French' Neo Grecian. In 1886, Adler and Sullivan won

the contract to build the Chicago Auditorium, since their ability to master the problem of acoustics was impressive. The building was completed in 1890, and gained for Sullivan international recognition. He also designed the Wainwright building in St. Louis, Missouri (1900), later described by Frank Lloyd Wright as "the master key to the skyscraper as architecture the world over." His designs became more and more original, and he introduced the new method of skeleton construction, which later produced the steel-constructed skyscrapers of the early twentieth century. After Adler's death in 1900, Sullivan worked on his own, and in 1924 he wrote the famous *Autobiography of an Idea*, setting forth the thesis that "form follows functions." His philosophy of ornament is displayed in twenty original drawings at the Art Institute in Chicago, and he wrote several articles for architectural periodicals throughout his career. He died in Chicago, Illinois, on April 14, 1924.

SWANSON, GLORIA MAY JOSEPHINE SVENSSON

(1899-1983) — Actress, was born in Chicago, Illinois on March 27, 1899. She went to public schools in Chicago, Key West, Florida, and San Juan, Puerto Rico.

Her film debut was in 1915 as an extra in The *Fable of Elvira* and *Farina and the Meal Ticket*. The next year she had leading roles in Keystone films, then spent a year working for Triangle films. In 1919, she received a contract from C.B. DeMille, which was a turning point in her career. Films include *Queen Kelly*, shot in 1928 and produced by Joseph Kennedy and directed by Eric von Stroheim. In 1934 she survived the switch to "talkies" when she learned how to sing for her role in *Music in the Air*.

In the 1940s, Swanson returned to the stage for roles in *Reflected Glory, Let Us Be Gay* and *A Goose for a Gander*.

She was also a clothes designer and artists, founder of Essence of Nature Cosmetics, and made television appearances throughout the 1960s and 70s.

Swanson received Best Actress nominations for Sadie Thompson in 1929, *The Trespasser* in 1931 and *Sunset Boulevard* in 1951. She won a Golden Globe Award for Best Actress in 1951 for *Sunset Boulevard*.

She was married seven times: to Wallace Berry in 1916; to Herbert K. Somborn in 1919; to William Somborn in 1919; to Marquis Henri de la Falaise in 1924; to Michael Farmer in 1931; to William

Davey in 1945; and to William Duffy in 1974. Gloria Swanson died on April 4, 1983.

SYMONS, (GEORGE) GARDNER

(1865-1930) — Landscape painter, was born in Chicago, Illinois, of Jewish descent. After studying at the Art Institute of Chicago, he was a student in Munich, Germany; London, England; and Paris, France. He returned to the United States in 1909 and took up his residence in Brooklyn, New York. He spent most of his life in New York but made frequent sketching trips to the Berkshire Hills, the valley of the Deerfield River; Gloucester, Massachusetts; Cornwall, England; various parts of Europe, whither he went almost every year to paint, and to southern California. In the latter part of his life he did much of his work at his country home in Colrain, Massachusetts. He specialized in winter landscapes. He won the Carnegie prize of the National Academy of Design in 1909 for his *Opalescent River* and in 1911 became an academician. In 1912 the National Arts Club conferred on him a gold medal and a prize of $1,000 for his painting of *The Sun's Glow and Rising Moon*. He was awarded a bronze medal at the International Exposition, Buenos Aires, 1910; the third W. A. Clarke prize and Corcoran bronze medal, Corcoran Gallery of Art, Washington, D.C., 1912; and the Saltus medal for merit, National Academy of Design, 1913. At the inaugural exhibition of the Toledo Museum of Art in 1912, he exhibited *Rock-ribbed Hills of New England* and *Snow-clad Fields in Morning Light*; at the Carnegie Institute in Pittsburgh, Pennsylvania, 1913, *Breaking of the Winter Ice* and *November, Dachau, Germany*; and at the sixth annual exhibition of the Concord Art Association in Concord, Massachusetts, *Morning Light*. He died in Hillside, New Jersey, at the home of a brother-in-law. He was a member of numerous clubs and societies of artists both in the United States and abroad.

His *Snow Clouds* is in the Corcoran Gallery of Art; *The Winter Sun* in the Art Institute of Chicago. There are other examples of his work in art museums in Los Angeles, California; St. Louis, Missouri; Toledo, Ohio; Brooklyn, New York; Pittsburgh, Pennsylvania; and in numerous other cities throughout the country. *Opalescent River*, a typical Symons painting in the Metropolitan Museum of Art, New York, shows bright sunlight shining on the snow and floating ice in the river, with groups of trees and farm buildings beyond, and hills in the distance. His pictures, which have been praised for their strength and originality, are characterized as well by great sincerity and truth, and by a warm sympathy of imagination. He died in 1930.

T

TAFT, LORADO ZADOC

(1860-1936) — Sculptor, was born on April 29, 1860, in Elmwood, Illinois, the son of Don Carlos and Mary (Foster) Taft. His father was appointed professor of geology at the new Illinois Industrial University (later the University of Illinois) at Urbana in 1871, and Taft received his early education at home from his parents. He helped patch together plaster casts in a collection purchased by the university in 1874, and entered the university in 1875. He graduated with honors in 1879, and received an M.A. in 1880. He then left for Paris, France, where he spent three years as a student at the École des Beaux Arts under Augustin A. Dumont, J.M.B. Bonnassieux, and Jules Thomas.

In 1886, Taft settled in Chicago, Illinois, and opened a studio. That same year, he began teaching at the Chicago Art Institute, where he pioneered in new methods of sculpture instruction, introducing marble carving and assigning group compositions in place of individual projects. In 1890, he married Carrie Bartlett of Boston, Massachusetts, only to lose her in childbirth the next year.

His first national recognition came in 1893, with his groups for the Horticulture Building at the Columbian Exposition. For the rest of the century, in addition to sculpting, he lectured at the University of Chicago, contributed regularly to periodicals, and took a prominent part in many art organizations. In February 1896, he married Ada Bartlett, a cousin of his first wife; they had three daughters: Mary, Emily, and Jessie Louise.

Taft's *Solitude of the Soul* (1901, Chicago Art Institute) and *The Blind* (1908, University of Illinois) were awarded important national prizes. His *History of American Sculpture* was published in 1903, and he began a long and successful career as a professional lecturer on sculpture. The "Clay Talk"—a lecture-demonstration of sculptural processes, was his most popular. His *Blackhawk* (1911), a huge concrete figure of a Native American chief, overlooks the Rock River at Oregon, Illinois. Other major works include: *Columbus Fountain* (1912, Washington, D.C.), *Fountain of the Great Lakes* (1913, Chicago), and *Thatcher Memorial Fountain* (1917, Denver, Colorado).

Taft moved to an old barn in the Chicago Midway, the nucleus of the famous Midway Studios, a collection of buildings housing an ever-changing group of independent artists and students. An ardent supporter of art education in public schools, he gave a brilliant series of talks in the high schools of Pittsburgh and Chicago, wrote and produced a renaissance art pageant for children, and devised his "Peep Shows"— little sculptural dioramas showing famous sculptors at work.

Taft still continued to produce as a sculptor. Following the monumental cast-concrete *Fountain of Time* (1922, Jackson Park, Chicago) came *Lincoln, The Young Lawyer* (1927, Urbana, Illinois), *The Pioneers* (1928, Elmwood, Illinois), the three-figure *Alma Mater* for the University of Illinois (1929), two colossal stone pylon groups for the Louisiana Capitol (1932), and, completed in his last year, the relief of the *Lincoln-Douglas Debate* (Quincy, Illinois). His honors included membership in the American Academy of Arts and Letters, medals from the Holland Society and from five world's fairs, and honorary degrees from Northwestern University, the University of Colorado, and the University of Illinois.

Taft died of a heart attack following a paralytic stroke on October 30, 1936, in Chicago, Illinois. His ashes were scattered over his parents' graves at Elmwood, Illinois, and a bronze reduction of his *Memory* was erected there.

TALBOT, ARTHUR NEWELL

(1857-1942) — Civil engineer and engineering educator, was born on October 21, 1857, in Cortland, Illinois, the son of Charles A. Talbot and Harriet (Newell) Talbot. After earlier education in Cortland and the high school in nearby Sycamore, Talbot taught country school for two years. He then entered Illinois Industrial University (later the University of Illinois) at Urbana, where he majored in civil engineering. After graduating with a B.S. in 1881, he worked in railroad location, construction, and maintenance in Colorado, New Mexico, Kansas, and Idaho. Four years later, he returned to the University of Illinois as assistant professor of engineering and mathematics. He was promoted in 1890 to professor of municipal and sanitary engineering, and held this position until his retirement in 1926.

Talbot developed formulas for computing the rates of maximum rainfall and the size of waterways for bridge and culvert design. In 1899, he published *The Railway Transition Spiral*, which went through numerous editions and became a basic treatise for laying out easement curves. His interest in practical municipal problems led to the establishment of a center for laboratory research and the consequent founding (1903) and administration of the Engineering Experiment Station at the University of Illinois.

Talbot was a member of the Joint Committee on Concrete and Reinforced Concrete of the American Society of Civil Engineers and the American Society for Testing Materials, to which he was appointed in 1904 (and whose subcommittee on design he headed until 1909). The committee's twelve-year investigation into the properties of reinforced concrete and its use in beams, slabs, columns, footings, pipes, frames, and buildings formed one of the major foundations of the modern construction industry.

He also made extensive studies of the construction, mode of action, and resistances of railroad rails, ties, ballast, and roadbed under different loads traveling at varying speeds. Begun in 1914 under the sponsorship of the American Society of Civil Engineers and the American Railway Engineering Association, these studies continued for nearly three decades. Talbot's report in the *American Railway Engineering Association Bulletin* (August 1933) helped modify the design of rolling stock and right-of-way construction and is considered one of the earliest reliable contributions to the scientific understanding of safe, high-speed transportation.

Talbot served in administrative capacities in many engineering societies, including as president (1890-1891) of the Illinois Society of Engineers (which he had helped found four years earlier), of the Society for the Promotion of Engineering Education (1910-1911), of the American Society for Testing Materials (1913-1914), and of the American Society of Civil Engineers (1918), and vice-president of the American Association for the Advancement of Science (1928).

Among his honors were: the George Henderson Medal of the Franklin Institute (1924), for his innovations in railway engineering; the Henry C. Turner Medal of the American Concrete Institute (1928), for his work on reinforced concrete; the Benjamin Garver Lamme Medal of the Society for the Promotion of Engineering Education (1932), for his achievements in engineering education; and the John Fritz Medal of the United Engineering Societies (1937). He also received honorary doctorates from the universities of Pennsylvania (1915), Michigan (1916), and Illinois (1931). In 1938, the University of Illinois named a laboratory building for him, the first time a living individual had been so honored.

On June 7, 1886, Talbot married Virginia Mann Hammet, who died in 1919. They had four children: Kenneth Hammet, Mildred Virginia, Rachel Harriet, and Dorothy Newell. He died on April 3, 1942.

TANNER, EDWARD EVERETT, III

(1921-1976) — Author, was born on May 18, 1921, in Chicago, Illinois. As a boy, he attended various private schools in Chicago and Evanston, Illinois, but was expelled by some of them. After leaving school, he went to work for the Stebbins Hardware Company and then for Columbia Educational Books, Inc. Tanner left Columbia Books to serve as an ambulance driver for the American Field Service in Arabia, North Africa; Italy; and France during World War II. He was attached to the armed forces of seven nations: Great Britain, Australia, Union of South Africa, New Zealand, Greece, Poland, and France. Twice he was wounded in service. In 1945, Tanner was discharged and went to live in New York City. He worked for a while with Franklin Spier, Inc., an advertising agency, and with Creative Age Press as an advertising manager. He then became promotion director of *Foreign Affairs* magazine and worked there until 1956. Tanner started his literary career by revising other people's works and doing ghost writing. He used the pseudonym of Patrick Tanner for his personal life, which he had started using as a boy in school. He ended up using several aliases throughout his life, even though it made things confusing at times. One of the names he wrote by was Virginia Rounds, under which he wrote *Oh, What a Wonderful Wedding* (1953). Under the same pseudonym, he published *House Party* a year later and then *The Loving Couple* and *Love and Mrs. Sargent*.

The first book Tanner wrote was *Auntie Mame; An Irreverent Escapade in Biography*, which took him years to develop the plot but only ninety days to write the story. It then took another three years to get the book published, which it finally was in 1955, and made the bestseller list for the next two years. It was later adapted for a Broadway production which ran from October 3, 1956, to June 28, 1958. A film version was later released on December 4, 1958. After *Auntie Mame* came *Guestward Ho!, As Indiscreetly Confided to Patrick Dennis, The Pink Hotel, Around the World With Auntie Mame, Little Me, Genius, First Lady: My Thirty Days Upstairs in the White House, The Joyous Season, Tony, How Firm a Foundation, Paradise, Three-D*. He contributed articles and short stories to national magazines and was drama critic for the *New Republic* starting in 1957. Tanner also set a record as the only author to ever have three novels on the *New York Times* bestsellers list at once.

Tanner married writer Louise Stickney on December 30, 1948, and had two children, Michael and Elizabeth. He died on November 6, 1976, in New York City.

TANNER, JOHN RILEY

(1844-1901) — Twenty-third governor of Illinois, (1897-1901), was born in Booneville, Indiana, to Eliza Downs and John Tanner. He lived on the family farm until 1861, when he enlisted in the army with all other male members of his family. Until 1865, he fought with the Ninety-eighth Illinois infantry, and afterwards returned north to purchase his own farm in Clay County, Illinois.

Five years later, he was elected sheriff of the county, and from 1872 to 1876, served as clerk of the Circuit Court. In 1880, he was nominated for state senator of his district and won. He continued his political career with an appointment as U. S. Marshall in 1883, and an election as state treasurer in 1886. Under Governor Fifer's administration, Tanner worked as Railroad Commissioner, but he resigned in 1891 to fill an appointment as U. S. Treasurer in Chicago. He was a gubernatorial candidate on the Republican ticket in 1896. His efforts to reorganize the party two years earlier, while he was still a state central committee chairman, helped him become the victor.

Although Tanner's accomplishments in party organization brought forth Republican representation in the legislature and in the governor's seat, his term in office was tumultuous from the beginning. Coal strikes in Virden, Pana, and Carterville broke into violence after he refused to send troops to protect strikebreakers. After some lost their lives, Tanner sent guards, but gave them strict orders not to allow strikebreakers into the mines.

Tanner became unpopular with voters when he approved the Allen Bill, allowing city councils to grant fifty-year franchises to street railway companies. Financial problems also caused the governor embarrassment. When he took office, there were deficits in almost every state agency, and no money was left in the treasury to pay the bills. He reached an agreement with some companies to buy products at wholesale prices and on credit. By the end of his term, the state debt had been paid. The governor was also involved in the war with Spain, sending 10,000 troops within two days of his call for volunteers.

Despite his successes, Tanner lost favor with the majority of the state and decided not to run for reelection. After his term ended, he was an unsuccessful candidate for the U. S. Senate. He died shortly thereafter at Springfield in 1901.

TEEPLE, JOHN EDGAR

(1874-1931) — Chemical consultant, was born on January 4, 1874, in Kempton, Illinois, the son of William Harvey and Abby (Hinckley) Teeple. He was left an orphan at an early age, and grew up in the family of a neighbor. His early education consisted of local schooling. From 1888 to 1894, he was able to attend Valparaiso University, Valparaiso, Indiana, for a total of about three years, being employed the remainder of the time. He received a B.S. there in 1893, and that of A.B. in 1894. He then became professor of chemistry and mathematics in the Nebraska Normal College, Fremont, Nebraska, serving in that capacity for four years. From 1898 to 1903, he was instructor in organic and physiological chemistry at Cornell University, where he received a B.S. in 1899 and that of Ph.D. in 1903. The following year, he went to New York City to become a consulting chemist and chemical engineer, and until 1908, was in charge of The Industrial Laboratories, a consulting and research organization owned by a corporation. He left in 1908 to establish his own office.

Much of his work was that of designing, organizing, and directing chemical plants. One of his notable achievements was his direction of the research and development that resulted in the remarkable industry at Searles Lake, California, where potash is prepared in its purest form from complex dry salts. The deposits there were owned by the California Trona Company, which in 1914 was succeeded by the American Trona Corporation, and this, later, by the American Potash and Chemical Corporation. Teeple became connected with the enterprise in 1919. He recorded his experiences in a monograph entitled *The Industrial Development of Searles Lake Brines* (1929). He is credited with building up the American potash industry almost single-handed after the First World War, when German supplies were again flooding the market. The Perkin medal was awarded him in 1927 for "significant scientific, technical, and administrative achievements, and particularly the economic development of an American potassium industry." He is also well known for his work in the utilization of waste wood and for his accomplishments in the perfection and manufacture of decolorized carbon.

He served the American Chemical Society as its treasurer for twelve years. He also found time to devote to the service of the Chemists' Club, New York City, of which he was president for two years. One of his hobbies was archeology, and in August 1930 the Carnegie Institution of Washington published a volume by him entitled

Maya Astronomy.

On August 17, 1897, in Fremont, Nebraska, he married Lina Pease, by whom he had three children, John Hazen, Charlotte Marion, and Granger Odell. He died on March 23, 1931, at the Presbyterian Hospital, New York.

THAYER, TIFFANY ELLSWORTH

(1902-1959) — Novelist, actor, and advertising scriptwriter, was born on March 1, 1902 in Freeport, Illinois, the son of Elmer Ellsworth Thayer and Sybil Farrar. His parents were actors, and were divorced when Thayer was five. He lived with his father in Rockford, Illinois, until 1916, when he ran away to join his mother in Chicago. After dropping out of high school in his third year, he worked for a commercial artist, and in 1917, as a copyboy on the *Chicago Record-Herald.*

Thayer joined a dramatic and operatic stock company in Oak Park, Illinois. From 1918 to 1922, he played in theaters in Illinois, Indiana, and elsewhere in the Midwest. He had roles in *Her Unborn Child* and *Up the Ladder*, and in 1918, appeared with Lillian Kingsbury in *The Coward.* He worked as a newspaper reporter between theatrical seasons, and for a time, he clerked in bookshops specializing in old and rare books in Chicago and managed bookshops in Cleveland and Detroit In 1926, Thayer moved to New York City. His savings ran out before he could find an acting role, and he took a job as an advertising copywriter.

Written during evenings and weekends in 1928 and 1929, Thayer's first novel, *Thirteen Men*, was published in May 1930. Soon afterward, he sailed for Europe. On his return to New York that fall, he found that he had produced a best seller. Thayer wrote more than twenty other novels, some of which were published under the pseudonyms Elmer Ellsworth, Jr., and John Doe, including: *Call Her Savage* (1931), *Thirteen Women* (1932), *An American Girl* (1933), *One Woman* (1933), *The Old Goat* (1937), and *Rabelais for Boys and Girls* (1939).

From 1930, Thayer was advertising manager of the Literary Guild, and in 1931, he founded the Fortean Society honoring Charles Fort, a critic of science and expounder of unconventional theories of scientific phenomena. Thayer was permanent secretary of the society and editor of its magazine, *Doubt.*

In the mid-1930s, Thayer spent time in Hollywood as a scenarist and part-time actor. He appeared in a stage revival of *Whistling in the Dark.* He then returned to New York, and from 1938 to 1948, worked as a radio-advertising writer for J. Walter Thompson Agency. After 1948, he wrote for the advertising firm of Sullivan, Stauffer, Caldwell, and Bayles for six months, and spent the other half of the year writing at Nantucket, Massachusetts. In 1939, Thayer began a story of the Renaissance in Italy with the aim of discovering the reasons for the Mona Lisa's enigmatic smile. The first three of twenty-one projected volumes were published in 1956 as *Mona Lisa: The Prince of Taranto.*

Thayer married three times; his widow was the former Kathleen McMahon. He died of a heart attack on August 23, 1959, at Nantucket, Massachusetts. He had no children.

Jesse Burgess Thomas

THOMAS, JESSE BURGESS
(1777-1853) Delegate from Indiana Territory and Senator from Illinois; Senate Years of Service: 1818-1829; born in Shepherdstown, Va. (now West Virginia) in 1777; studied law in Mason County, Ky., where he also served as county clerk until 1803; moved to Lawrenceburg, Indiana Territory in 1803 and practiced law; appointed deputy attorney general of Indiana Territory in 1805; member, Territorial house of representatives 1805-1808, and served as speaker 1805-1808; elected as a Delegate from Indiana Territory to the Tenth Congress to fill the vacancy caused by the resignation of Benjamin Parke and served from October 22, 1808, to March 3, 1809; moved to Kaskasia in 1809, then to Cahokia, and later to Edwardsville, Ill.; upon the organization of Illinois Territory was appointed judge of the United States court for the northwestern judicial district 1809-1818; delegate to the State constitutional convention in 1818 and served as president of that body; upon the admission of Illinois as a State into the Union in 1818 was elected as a Democratic Republican to the United States Senate; reelected as a Crawford Republican (later Adams Republican) in 1823, and served from December 3, 1818, to March 3, 1829; declined to be a candidate for reelection in 1829; chairman, Committee on Public Lands (Sixteenth and Seventeenth Congresses); moved to Mount Vernon, Ohio, in 1829; committed suicide at Mount Vernon, Ohio, May 2, 1853; interment in Mound View Cemetery.

THOMPSON, ("BIG JIM") JAMES ROBERT

(1936-) — Thirty-ninth governor of Illinois (1977-1991), was born in Chicago, Illinois, the son of Agnes Josephine Swanson and Dr. James Thompson, a pathologist. He grew up on the west side of Chicago, in Garfield Park, where he became interested in politics at an early age.

Thompson attended the University of Illinois from 1953 to 1955, and Washington University from 1955 to 1956. In 1959, he graduated from Northwestern University School of Law and was admitted to the bar that year. For the next few years, he served as an assistant on the prosecutorial staff of the Cook County State Attorney (1956-64).

After becoming an associate professor of law at Northwestern University for four years, from 1969 to 1970, Thompson was Assistant Attorney General of the state. He also lectured at the University of California, Davis, and at Michigan State University. His specialty is criminal law, and in 1967, he was a member of the president's task force on crime.

Thompson used his expertise in the Attorney General's office to become Chief of the Criminal Division and Chief of the Department of Law Enforcement and Public Protection. In 1970, he became first assistant to the United States Attorney for the Northern District of the state, and the next year was appointed U. S. Attorney for the district, where he served until 1976.

Thompson's efforts produced convictions and sentences for 90 percent of over three hundred indictments he handled, some of which included corrupt public employees. His prosecution of a Chicago police officer for brutality against a young African American ended in the first civil rights conviction against a policeman in the city's history. Other convictions included city aldermen and a former Cook County clerk. But Thompson's most significant success was in the case of former governor Otto Kerner for seventeen counts of tax evasion, bribery, fraud, perjury, and

("Big Jim") James Robert Thompson

673

conspiracy in connection with a racetrack scandal.

These successes led Thompson to vaulting fame, and in 1976, he was elected governor on the Republican ticket. Soon after he took office, he worked with Chicago officials to establish a mass transit and highways program, and pushed through a stringent anti-crime law, as well as a plan for a balanced state budget in spite of the Democratic controlled state legislature.

Although he originally planned to serve a two-year term in order to prevent Illinois gubernatorial elections from coinciding with presidential elections, he was reelected to a four-year term in November 1978, and was continually reelected until the 1990 election, when Republican Jim Edgar won the gubernatorial office.

In 1993, Thompson became chairman and CEO of Winston and Shaw LLP, a position he still holds today. From 2003 to 2004, he served on the 9/11 Commission, and has represented United Airlines against charges of negligence concerning the September 11th attacks. He is a director and head of the audit committee for Hollinger International.

THOMPSON, SEYMOUR DWIGHT

(1842-1904) — Jurist, was born on September 18, 1842, in Will County, Illinois, the son of Seymour and Betsy (McKee) Thompson. In 1855, the Thompsons moved to a farm in Fayette County, Iowa, where his father and brother died in a prairie fire in 1858. The survivors returned to relatives in Illinois. Without a permanent home, he managed to secure a fair education by attending Clark Seminary at Aurora, and Rock River Seminary at Mount Morris, working meanwhile as farm laborer, peddler, and grammar school teacher.

When the Civil War began, he went back to Iowa and enlisted on May 21, 1861, in the Third Regiment of that state. He was made a first sergeant on September 4, 1862, and in 1866, was mustered out of military service at Memphis, Tennessee, with the rank of captain. He took part in the Battle of Shiloh and the siege of Vicksburg, and witnessed the riotous burning by Union soldiers of Holly Springs, Mississippi. In 1864, he published *Recollections with the Third Iowa Regiment*, an unromantic presentation of actual warfare.

After the war, he remained in Memphis for five years, making his living as a policeman, as a balloonist, as a court clerk, and after he was admitted to the bar in 1869, as a self-educated lawyer. In 1872, he moved to St. Louis, Missouri, where he soon attracted the attention of John Forrest Dillon then U.S. circuit judge. Dillon appointed Thompson to a fairly lucrative position as master in chancery, and in 1874, founded the *Central Law Journal* with himself as editor and Thompson as associate editor. In 1875, Thompson became editor of the publication and served in that position until 1878. From 1883 until his death, he was principal editor of the *American Law Review*. From 1880 to 1892 he was a judge of the St. Louis Court of Appeals, and from 1892 to 1898 practiced law in St. Louis, although chiefly engaged in authorship. Thereafter until his death, he maintained a law office in New York City for consulting work.

Thompson's distinction rests mainly on his many read treaties, which contained vigorous and constructive criticism of law as announced by judges or established by statute. His more important works were *A Treatise on Homestead and Exemption Laws* (1878), *The Law of Negligence in Relations Not Resting in Contract* (two volumes, 1880), *A Treatise on the Laws of Trials* (two volumes, 1889), and *Commentaries on the Law of Private Corporations* (seven volumes, 1895-1899). This last work was the most extensive legal treatise on a single topic ever published in the English language up to the time of Thompson's death.

In January 1865 he married Lucy A. Jennison, who with three sons and two daughters survived him. He died on August 11, 1904 in East Orange, New Jersey.

THOMPSON, WILLIAM HALE, "BILL"

(1869-1944) — Chicago mayor, was born in Boston, Massachusetts, to William and Medora (Gale) Thompson. While still a boy, his family moved to Chicago, Illinois, where young William attended public schools. He worked as a ranch hand in Colorado, Montana, and Wyoming from the time he was fourteen until he was nineteen, and then he bought a ranch of his own in Nebraska. When his father died in 1891, he returned to Chicago to take over the family real estate business, and became a member of the city's Real Estate Board. In the next few years, he was also active in athletic clubs and events in the city, and in 1900 he was elected alderman in his ward of Chicago. Two years later he was elected Cook County commissioner. In those positions, he was active in acquiring the first municipal playgrounds for children. He ran for mayor in 1915, and won on the Republican ticket. In his first term, he faced two major strikes as well as corruption in the police department and city hall. From 1916 to 1920, Thompson served as his party's national committeeman for Illinois, but was unsuccessful in a campaign for U.S. senator in 1918. He won the race for the second term as mayor in 1919,

William Hale "Bill" Thompson

and stayed in the post for four years. He decided not to run for a third term in 1923, but in 1927, he was elected again. While in office, Thompson allied his interests with Governor Len Small in the effort to build more roads in the state, and soon he was referred to as "Big Bill the Builder" for his administration's improvements in Chicago. He pushed for widening streets as well as building the Michigan Avenue link bridge, which helped southwest travel within the city. "Big Bill" was also the subject of controversy because of his isolationist views during World War I, as well as his firing of Chicago's school superintendent for encouraging the use of anti-American and pro-British histories in the classroom. After two more attempts for the mayor's seat, Thompson retired to private life and died in 1944 in Chicago, Illinois.

THURSTONE, LOUIS LEON

(1887-1955) — Psychologist, was born on May 29, 1887, in Chicago, Illinois, the son of Conrad and Sophie Stroth Thurstone. The family lived in several communities, including Jamestown, New York, where Thurstone graduated from high school. He then attended Cornell University, receiving a degree in mechanical engineering in 1912. While at Cornell, he invented a flickerless motion-picture projector. He demonstrated it to Thomas A. Edison, who did not choose to produce it but offered him a position in his laboratory in East Orange, New Jersey. Thurstone worked there during the summer of 1912, and then took an instructorship in drafting and descriptive geometry at the University of Minnesota. He gradually became more interested in psychology, and enrolled as a graduate student in that subject at the University of Chicago in 1914. Three years later, he received his doctorate.

Meanwhile in 1915, Thurstone had accepted an assistantship in psychology at the Carnegie Institute of Technology in Pittsburgh, Pennsylvania. After 1917, he rose rapidly, eventually becoming full professor and the head of the department. His work during those years was primarily in designing tests, including oral trade-aptitude tests for the army during World War I and college entrance examinations for the American Council of Education. In 1924, he married Thelma Gwinn. She received the Ph.D. in psychology in 1926 and collaborated with her husband on many research projects and publications. They had three sons.

Also in 1924, Thurstone returned to the University of Chicago as associate professor of psychology, and three years later, he was promoted to full professor. There, he developed a psychometric laboratory. In 1932-1933, he was president of the American Psychological Association. A founder of the Psychometric Society and of its journal, *Psychometrika*, he served as its first president in 1936. In 1938, Thurstone was named Charles F. Grey distinguished service professor. He served as visiting professor at Frankfurt in 1948 and at Stockholm in 1954, and was made an honorary fellow of the British and Swedish psychological societies. He retired in 1952.

While at the University of Chicago, Thurstone began researching the basic theory behind psychological testing, and in several papers written during the 1920s, explored the theory of scaling tests, the significance of the dispersion of the scores of different groups as well as the means of their scores, the mental-age concept, and other aspects of test theory. In regards to the nature of intelligence, Thurstone, in 1934, analyzed the results of fifty-seven tests administered to 240 students and concluded that they demonstrated the existence of seven primary mental abilities: numerical ability, spatial visualization, perceptual speed, rote memory, verbal meaning, verbal fluency, and reasoning.

Using matrix algebra, Thurston developed the theory and procedures of multiple-factor analysis, widely used ever since in the study of mental characteristics in general. He and others have used it in studies of personality, creativity, temperament, and other broad human characteristics. *The Vectors of Mind* (1935) and *Multiple-Factor Analysis* (1947) are probably his most important works in this field.

Thurstone, who was interested in measuring such mental responses as social, moral, or aesthetic evaluations, envisioned the extension of psychophysics (the study of the relation between physical stimulus and mental response) to include mental responses to mental stimuli, and provided a basis for the quantitative study of social attitudes and other matters that had previously been handled only descriptively. His *Law of Comparative Judgment* (1927) provides a mathematical principle for testing internal consistency in studies of this nature.

Following Thurstone's retirement in 1952, he and his wife joined the faculty of the University of North Carolina and established a psychometric laboratory there. He died on September 29, 1955.

TODD, HENRY ALFRED

(1854-1925) — Romance philologist and editor, was born in Woodstock, Illinois, the son of a Reverend Richard Kimball Todd and Martha (Clover) Todd. His father directed his early education. In 1876, he graduated from the College of New Jersey (later Princeton University), where for the next four years he taught French. In 1880, he went abroad to continue his studies, first at Paris, France, then at Berlin, Germany, where he followed the courses of Adolph Tobler, at that time the chief German authority on Old French syntax. Going then to Rome, Italy, he worked for one semester under Ernesto Monaci, a leading Italian philologist, after which he passed to the Central University of Madrid in order to attend the courses of literary critic Marcelino Menendez Pelayo for one semester. Returning to Paris in 1882, he spent a year studying Romance philology and literature, as well as Sanskrit, under Gaston Paris, Paul Meyer, Arsene Darmesteter, and Abel Bergaigne. During this time, he was commissioned by the Societe des Anciens Textes Francais to edit for its series an Old French text, *Le Dit de la Panthered'Amours* (Paris, 1883), by Nicole de Margival.

From 1883 to 1891, he was instructor in romance languages at Johns Hopkins University in Baltimore, Maryland, where he was awarded a Ph.D. in 1885. During this time, he collaborated with A. Marshall Elliott in founding and editing *Modern Language Notes*, of which the first number appeared in January 1886, and in organizing the Modern Language Association of America (1883). He later served as treasurer of the Association (1886-1891), member of the editorial committee (1894-1895), member of the executive council (1893, 1908-1911), and president (1906).

On July 30, 1891, he married Miriam Gilman. The following autumn, he was called to Leland Stanford University as professor of romance languages and head of the department. Two years later (1893), he became professor of romance philology at Columbia University, a chair that he held until his death. He was one of the chief organizers of the celebration held in March 1894 to commemorate the centenary of the birth of Friedrich Christian Diez, the founder of romance philology; in collaboration with Adolphe Cohn, he founded and edited until his death the *Columbia University Studies in Romance Philology and Literature*; and in 1909, with three colleagues, he founded at Columbia the *Romantic Review*, a quarterly journal devoted to research in romance philology and literature, the first of its kind to be established in the United States. With Raymond Weeks, he continued joint editorship of the *Review* until his death. He was a life member of the Institut Francais aux Etats Unis; president of the committee on courses and lectures of the Institute; president of the French Union, university branch of the Institute from 1917; and vice-president of the council of administration of the Musee d'art Francais. In 1919 he was sent to France by the U.S. government as a member of the Mission de Rapprochement. He died in 1925 in New York City; survived by his wife, two daughters and a son.

He was author of nearly one hundred books, articles, and book reviews. His chief publications include the following editions of Old French manuscripts: "Guillaume de Dole" (1886), "La Naissance du Chevalier au Cygne" (1889), "La Vie de Sainte Catherine d'Alexandrie" (1900), "The Old French Versified Apocalypse of the Kerr Manuscript" (1903) all in *Publications of the Modern Language Association of America*; "An Unpublished Fourteenth-Century Invocation to Mary Magdalen" in *Studies in Honor of A. Marshall Elliott* (n.d.); a French poem of the twelfth century; and, in collaboration with F.C. Ostrander, *Li Romans dou Lis* (1915). After his death, his colleagues, friends, and pupils issued the *Todd Memorial Volumes: Philological Studies* (two volumes, 1930), edited by John D. Fitz-Gerald and Pauline Taylor.

TOMBAUGH, CLYDE WILLIAM

(1906-1997) — Astronomer who discovered Pluto, the ninth planet in the solar system, was born on February 4, 1906, in Streator, Illinois, the son of Muron D. Tombaugh and Adella Pearl (Chritton) Tombaugh. Clyde received an A.B. from Kansas University in 1936, and an M.A. in 1939. He later obtained an D.Sc. from Arizona State College in Flagstaff in 1960. Tombaugh was an assistant observer at the Lowell Observatory from 1929 until 1938. It was there that in 1930, while he was examining some photographic plates with a blink microscope, that he discovered the planet Pluto. Percival Lowell had predicted the general location of Pluto fifteen years earlier. Tombaugh became the astronomer at the observatory in 1938. He was also a science instructor at Arizona State College from 1943 until 1945, and a visiting assistant professor of

Clyde William Tombaugh

astronomy at the University of California at Los Angeles from 1945 until 1946. In 1946, Tombaugh became an astronomer at the Aberdeen Ballistics Labs Annex at the White Sands Proving Grounds in Las Cruces, New Mexico, where he engaged in ballistics research. His work was applied to ballistics rockets and missiles. Other discoveries were a globular star cluster in 1932, and later six galactic star clusters. Tombaugh's research also included the hypothetical geology of Mars and an interpretation of Martian features.

Tombaugh received numerous honors and awards including the Jackson-Gwilt Medal from the Royal Astronomy Society in 1931, and a Distinguished Service Citation from the University of Kansas in 1966. He married Patricia Irene Edson on June 7, 1934. The couple had two children. He died in Las Crues, New Mexico, January 17, 1997.

TOMLINS, WILLIAM LAWRENCE

(1844-1930) — Musician and teacher, was born on February 4, 1844, in London, England, the son of William and Sarah (Lawrence) Tomlins. He began his career as a choirboy in London, and during that period of service he was a pupil of George Alexander Macfarren and Eduard Silas. At the age of fifteen, he became organist and choirmaster of a London church and at seventeen began conducting oratorio. At eighteen he was made a government inspector and examiner of music teachers in the public schools of England, in the department of theory and harmony. In 1864 he was made one of the examiners of the Tonic Sol-Fa College in London. He married Mrs. Elizabeth (Stripp) Squire in 1868.

Tomlins came to America in 1870, settling in Brooklyn, New York. There he attracted the attention of the Mason & Hamlin Company for his remarkable mastery of the harmonium, and in 1875 that concern sent him to Chicago, Illinois to demonstrate their orchestral organ. Remaining in Chicago, he became during that same year conductor of the

Apollo Club, then a male chorus, which in 1876 was changed to a mixed chorus. Tomlins was its conductor for twenty-three years. He began in 1883 to organize classes of school children for choral singing and in this type of work specialized for many years, producing astonishing results. In 1893 he had charge of choral singing at the World's Columbian Exposition, Chicago, for which he trained a chorus of twelve hundred children. Five years later he resigned his position as conductor of the Apollo Club in order to devote his entire time to his work with children. In 1903 he established in Chicago the National Training School for School Music Teachers and in the same year was engaged by the Chicago board of education as instructor of music teachers in the grade schools. Returning to England in 1906, he carried on his work with children for two years, in four different centers, with notable success. He then came back to America and thereafter until nearly the end of his life spent most of his time lecturing and illustrating his ideas throughout the country.

In his teaching of children, Tomlins' original purpose was simply to establish in early life normal habits of musical expression so as to facilitate later musical studies. In time, however, he came to believe that the act of singing is capable of influencing the character of the singer by liberating the moral and spiritual faculties, and he then endeavored to stimulate the inner life through breathing, rhythm, the song voice, and "a vital, reverent attitude toward the Human Spirit, Nature, and God." Profoundly religious, though not in any orthodox sense, since he could not bring his philosophy within the limits of any creed, he made a definite effort, as part of his instruction, to awaken his pupils to spiritual values. His system became known as "The Tomlins Idea."

Tomlins was the author of *Children's Songs and How to Sing Them* (1884) and editor of *The Laurel Song Book* (1901). He died in his eighty-seventh year, September 26, 1930 at the home of a daughter in Delafield, Wisconsin.

TONTY, HENRI DE

(c.1650-1704) — Explorer and founder of the first settlements in the Mississippi Valley, and lieutenant to Rene-Robert Cavelier, Sieur de LaSalle, during his North American explorations, was born probably in Paris, France, the son of Lorenzo de Tonti, originator of the tontine form of life insurance, who had fled from Naples, Italy, after taking part in an insurrection. Tonty's mother was Isabelle de Liette (or Desliettes), and he was the eldest of three children, all of whom later came to New France.

Henri de Tonty

Henri entered the French army at the age of eighteen and, serving in Italian waters, lost his right hand in the explosion of a grenade. He replaced it with a metal hand, which he wore covered with a glove, and which he sometimes used with great effect upon rebellious Indians; from this he was known as "the man with the iron hand." Prince de Conti introduced Tonty to the explorer La Salle in 1678, when the latter was seeking assistance in France for his exploration projects in North America. Tonty immediately enlisted in La Salle's service, and gave him a loyalty and devotion that were La Salle's greatest aids in carrying out his plans. After their arrival in Canada they went at once to La Salle's seigniory at Fort Frontenac on Lake Ontario; Tonty was detailed to the Niagara River to superintend the building of La Salle's ship, the *Griffon*, the first sailing vessel on the upper Great Lakes. Tonty went in advance at the time of sailing and was taken on board at the Detroit River. He and La Salle sailed for Michilimackinac, where Tonty again left ship, coasting down the east shore of Lake Michigan to join LaSalle at the St. Joseph River. Together they advanced into Illinois and in the winter of 1679-1680 built Fort Creveccur on Lake Peoria. In the spring La Salle found it necessary to return to Fort Frontenac, and Tonty was left in command in the Illinois country. There his men soon deserted; he was unable to complete his fort and the summer was filled with difficulties of every sort. Yet he never despaired, and when in the autumn a war party of Iroquois entered the Valley breathing vengeance upon the Illinois, he fearlessly visited their camp to protest their raid upon French-allied Indians. He was seriously wounded, but escaped with his life. Then, finding he could not calm the storm, with five companions he retreated through the Wisconsin woods, living upon roots and gleanings from the deserted Native American villages. Toward the end of the year 1680 he finally reached Green Bay, Wisconsin, and safety. After recruiting his health and recovering from his wound, he left for Michilimackinac, which he reached in June 1681 just too late to meet his cousin Daniel Greysolon Duluth. La Salle, arriving the next day, was overjoyed at finding Tonty, who he feared had perished in Illinois. Together they returned once more and built Fort St. Louis in Illinois, and gathered there a settlement of French and Indians. In the spring of 1682 they explored the Mississippi, finding its mouth and there taking possession of the whole Valley for France. In the spring of 1683 La Salle left for France to prepare to colonize Louisiana. Tonty never saw his chief again. In France, La Salle secured a captaincy for his faithful lieutenant left in Illinois.

It was 1686 before Tonty could undertake a voyage to join La Salle; that year he went down the Mississippi without finding any trace of his leader, and returned unsuccessful. The next year he was called upon by Governor Denonville of New France to lead his forces against the Iroquois. At Fort des Sables he also met his cousin Duluth and returned west with him in the autumn of 1687. At his post in Illinois he found Jean Cavelier, brother of La Salle, and Henri Joutel; neither revealed to him the fact of La Salle's death. In March 1689 he was still unaware of it, but in September of that year one of his men, whom he had left to found a settlement in Arkansas, brought him news of his beloved leader's assassination. He started south in December to try to find the colonists La Salle had left, but returned unsuccessful. For a decade longer he remained in Illinois, bringing settlers, trade goods, and missionaries from Canada. He was respected and beloved by all, and was the true founder of Illinois. In 1700, hearing of the settlement made by Pierre le Moyne, Sieur de'Iberville, near the mouth of the Mississippi, he asked permission to join the new colony, and for four years gave his valuable services to Louisiana in exploration and in conciliation of the Indians. He died near Mobile, Alabama, probably from yellow fever. He never married, and left his property to his younger brother Alphonse.

Tonty's exploits have not been as much noticed as they deserve. He wrote two brief memoirs of his experiences, one covering the years 1678-1683, the other covering the years 1678-1691. A later memoir published under his name *Dernieres Decouvertes dans l'Amerique Septentrionale de Monsieur de la Salle par Chevalier de Tonti* (1697), he declared spurious. He was a modest person, not given to boasting of his undertakings. He has been regarded only as a faithful lieutenant of La Salle; in fact he was himself a great explorer and an able administrator who succeeded where La Salle failed. He secured the respect and confidence both of the Indians and of his men; he was popular with the missionaries of every group; and his courtesy and consideration enabled him to accomplish his ends.

TORME, MELVIN HOWARD

(1925-1996) — Singer, songwriter, film and television entertainer, was born on September 13, 1925 in Chicago, Illinois. He studied drums at the age of seven.

Torme began his career acting in radio soap operas. He also sand with Buddy Rogers and other name bands during his early career, including touring with the Chico Marx band in 1942-43.

Torme's motion picture debut was in Higher and Higher in 1943. Other motion picture appearances include: Pardon My Rhythm (1944), Words and Music (1948), Walk Like a Dragon (1960) and others.

The lead singer of the group the Mel-Tones in California, he also performed as a solo singer.

Some of the recordings by Torme are: Live at the Maisonette, Mel Torme and Friends, Recorded at Marty, Songs of New York, Round Midnight, Together Again, The London Sessions, (1992), Mel Torme in Hollywood (1992), Nothing Without You (1993), Christmas Songs (1993), Sixteen Most Requested Songs (1993), A Tribute to Bing Crosby; and many others.

He was also the author of two books: *The Other Side of the Rainbow* (1970) and his autobiography *It Wasn't All Velvet* (1988).

Torme was the recipient of a Grammy Award for Best Male Jazz Vocal Performance in 1983 and 1984. Torme married Janette Scott; they had two children. The marriage ended in divorce.

His 65-year singing career came to a close in August 1996; Torme died after suffering the lingering effects of a stroke.

Lyman Trumbull

TRUMBULL, LYMAN

(1813-1896) — Jurist, U.S. Senator, was born on October 12, 1896, in Colchester, Connecticut, the son of Benjamin Trumbull and Elizabeth (Masher) Trumbull. He attended Bacon Academy in his native town, and in 1833, went to Greenville, Georgia, where he taught school for three years. In the meantime, he read law and was admitted to the bar in

1836. The following year, he began practice in Belleville, Illinois, and soon entered politics. He was elected to the state legislature as a Democrat in 1840, but resigned in 1841 to accept appointment as secretary of state, in which capacity he served until 1843. He then practiced law and was a candidate for various offices until 1848, when he was elected justice of the state supreme court; in 1852, he was reelected for a term of nine years.

He had served two years of this term, however, when he took a seat in the Senate. The three terms that he served (1855-1873) were marked by the bitter struggle over slavery and Reconstruction, during which he was first a Democrat, next a leading Republican, and ultimately a supporter of the ill-fated Liberal Republican movement. During the war, he was at once President Abraham Lincoln's able helper and stanch opponent, his attitude being determined by that of the executive toward the Constitution. He opposed legalizing Lincoln's extraordinary acts performed, such as suspensions of the writ of habeas corpus, while Congress was in recess. In introducing his radical confiscation bill (December 1861), he declared that he wanted "no other authority for putting down even this gigantic rebellion than such as may be derived from the Constitution properly interpreted." He would suppress the "monstrous rebellion according to law, and in no other way."

In 1864, as chairman of the judiciary committee, he introduced the resolution that became the basis of the Thirteenth Amendment to the Constitution. Trumbull's powerful personal and committee influence aided the Radicals in the early stages of the fight with President Andrew Johnson. His bill to enlarge the powers of the Freedmen's Bureau failed to pass over the veto. The veto of his civil rights bill, designed to give effect to the Thirteenth Amendment, alienated him from the. He urged its repassage to offset the actions of the executive. These episodes mark an opposition that lasted until the impeachment measures against the president. Trumbull was one who was "willing to be radical lawfully" and his viewpoint drove him to oppose the impeachment proceedings, becoming one of the famous seven who saved Johnson from conviction. This, together with his reconstruction attitude, lost him Republican leadership. The excesses of the Ulysses S. Grant administration drove him into the Liberal Republican movement. He was among those suggested for the presidential nomination. After the movement collapsed, he finished his senatorial term and then retired to Chicago, where he practiced law.

Trumbull's appearance as counsel for Samuel Tilden's side in the disputed election of 1876 marked his return to the Democratic fold, and he was that party's unsuccessful candidate for the governorship of Illinois in 1880. His last political excursion found him skirting the edges of Populism; in 1894, he drafted a platform that Chicago Populists took to a national conference in St. Louis.

He was twice married: first, June 21, 1843, to Julia Maria Jayne, who died in August 1868; and second, November 3, 1877, to Mary Ingraham; he had three sons by his first wife who survived him. He died on June 25, 1896.

TURNER, AVERY

(1851-1933) — Railroad executive, was born on March 8, 1851, in Quincy, Illinois, the son of Edward and Lucretia (Newhall) Turner. He received his early education at Quincy Academy and at the age of eighteen entered Cornell University, where he specialized in engineering. When he left college, Turner went to Colorado as a surveyor on the Maxwell land grant, but he soon became associated with the Santa Fe Railroad. During his railroad career, Turner was to see the Santa Fe develop into a transcontinental system comprising 14,000 miles. After serving as trainmaster at La Junta, New Mexico, Turner became superintendent of the Newton, Kansas, division, in 1889. He served also as assistant general superintendent at Topeka, Kansas, and as superintendent of the Chicago division before he became vice-president and general manager of the Pecos Valley lines in 1902, when he was sent to Amarillo, Texas, to extend the Santa Fe system over the South Plains. He was especially active in sponsoring "Home Seekers" Excursions. He left his work at Amarillo only twice: to take charge of the importation of Mexican labor at El Paso, Texas, during World War I, and to serve for a few years as receiver for the St. Louis & San Francisco Railroad. Turner was married to Mary Honeyman Ten Eyck of New Jersey in 1886. He was a member of the Episcopal Church and the Masonic lodge. He died at his home in Amarillo, Texas, on April 15, 1933.

TURNER, GEORGE KIBBE

(1869-1952) — Journalist, editor, and author, was born on March 23, 1869, in Quincy, Illinois, the son of Rhodolphus K. and Sarah Ella Kibbe Turner. His father died when Turner was young; his mother subsequently married James Dayton of Quincy. Turner graduated from Williams College with an A.B. in 1890, and the following year became a reporter on the *Springfield Republican* in Massachusetts, then under the editorial leadership of Samuel Bowles. Turner began to write for magazines; and by 1899, he had placed stories in *McClure's*, which also published his first novel, *The Taskmaster* (1902). In 1906, editor S.S. McClure enlisted Turner as a staff member and writer, a connection that continued until 1916.

Turner became *McClure's* specialist on urban problems. His first major assignment was to report on the new commission form of municipal government set up in Galveston, Texas, after the devastating hurricane of September 1900. Turner's article, "Galveston: A Business Corporation," was published in October 1906. The response was immediate and dramatic. Leaders in many cities sought reprints; Seattle, Washington, called for 20,000 copies and Philadelphia, Pennsylvania, issued its own pamphlet. Some newspapers ran the article in full. The total circulation was estimated at twelve million. Many states amended their statutes to permit adoption of the commission form.

McClure's then sent Turner to Chicago, Illinois, where he prepared the preface for a collection of articles from Chicago newspapers recording day-to-day criminality and violence. Digging into hidden causes, Turner produced an analytical report so revealing and convincing that *McClure's* printed it as a long article, "The City of Chicago: A Study of the Great Immoralities," in the April 1907 issue. Turner's article brought the White slave traffic into the open for public discussion. Chicago's reformers demanded action; and in 1910, the mayor appointed a commission on vice composed of prominent educators, clergymen, industrialists, and civic leaders. Turner's disclosures were pursued in the commission's plainspoken report, "The Social Evil in Chicago." It was widely noted in other cities that set up their own investigations into commercialized vice.

Turning to New York City, in June 1909, he contended in "Tammany's Control of New York by Professional Criminals," also published in *McClure's*, that prostitution had been virtually legalized in the city. That November, in "The Daughters of the Poor," he said bluntly that New York City had become "the leader of the world" in the "recruiting and sale of young girls of the poorer classes by procurers" who operated a nationwide network as well as a trade in immigrants. This article, probably the most memorable of Turner's contributions to *McClure's*, was followed only one month later by the introduction in Congress of the bill that became the Mann Elkins Act of 1910, banning the White slave traffic from interstate commerce. Within two months, reform forces had established a New York grand jury headed by John D.

Rockefeller, Jr., to investigate Turner's charges. Turner backed up his writings with testimony before grand juries in New York and other cities.

In 1907, Turner went to Boise, Idaho, and obtained a jail-cell confession from Harry Orchard that he had assassinated the state's governor, Frank R. Steunenberg, in 1905 at the instigation of William Dudley ("Big Bill") Haywood. This sensational revelation was published as a McClure book, *The Confession and Autobiography of Harry Orchard* (1907).

After the decline of muckraking, Turner returned to fiction and wrote film scripts. His works included: *Red Friday* (1919), *Memories of a Doctor* (1913), *The Last Christian* (1914), *The Biography of a Million Dollars* (1918), *Hagar's Hoard* (1920), *White Shoulders* (1921), and *The Girl in the Glass Cage* (1927).

On October 19, 1892, he married Julia Hawks Parker of Bennington, Vermont; they had no children. He died on February 15, 1952, in Miami, Florida.

V

VAN DOREN, CARL CLINTON

(1884-1950) — Literary critic and biographer, was born on September 10, 1884, in Hope, Illinois, the son of Charles Lucius Van Doren and Dora Anne (Butz) Van Doren. In 1900, the family moved to Urbana, Illinois, where the father retired from medical practice, farmed, and speculated in various business enterprises, often unsuccessfully. Van Doren attended Thorburn High School, where he played football and was president of his class. He was at the University of Illinois in Urbana from 1903 to 1907, when he received his B.A.

In September 1908, Van Doren left home to attend Columbia University on a graduate scholarship. He took his Ph.D. in 1911, with a dissertation on Thomas Love Peacock; his biography of Peacock was already in type when he submitted it to his committee at Columbia. He taught at Columbia, on a part- or full-time basis from 1911 to 1930. On August 23, 1912, he married Irita Bradford, and had three daughters: Anne, Margaret, and Barbara. Irita Van Doren was to become a prominent literary figure in her own right as editor of the *New York Herald Tribune* book section. The Van Dorens were divorced in 1935. Van Doren's second marriage, to Jean Wright Gorman on February 27, 1939, ended in divorce in 1945.

Van Doren became literary editor (1919-1922) of the newly revitalized *Nation*, where he was a strong supporter of "new" or "modern" writers. Van Doren lent his authority as a literary scholar and Columbia professor to his many genial, hospitable pieces about the new novelists and poets. He kept a graduate course in American literature at Columbia even when he was briefly (1916-1918) headmaster of the Brearley School. He was managing editor of the *Cambridge History of American Literature* (1917-1920) and literary editor of the *Century* magazine (1922-1925). In 1921 he published *The American Novel*, which he described as "the first history of that literary form," and in 1922, *Contemporary American Novelists*, "the first systematic study of postwar American literature." He collected his literary reviews in *The Roving Critic* (1923) and *Many Minds* (1924), and did early studies of Cabell (1925) and Lewis (1933). His novel, *The Ninth Wave*, was written in 1926. His most successful narrative was his biography, *Benjamin Franklin* (1938), which won the Pulitzer Prize for biography. Other studies of the Revolutionary period included: *Secret History Of The*

689

American Revolution (1941); *Mutiny in January* (1943), about an incident in the Continental army in 1780-1781; *The Great Rehearsal* (1948), about the making and ratifying of the Constitution as a possible guide to the United Nations; and *Jane Mecom* (1950), a life of Franklin's sister.

Van Doren died of a heart attack complicated by pneumonia on July 18, 1950, in a hospital in Torrington, Connecticut. After cremation, his ashes were scattered over Wickwire, his home in Cornwall, Connecticut.

VAN HORNE, Sir WILLIAM CORNELIUS

(1843-1915) — Railroad executive, was born in Will County, Illinois, on February 3, 1843, the son of Cornelius Covenhoven Van Horne and Mary Minier (Richards) Van Horne. The family moved to Illinois in 1832, where his father farmed, milled, and practiced law. His mother had charge of his education until 1851, when the family moved to Joliet, Illinois. In Joliet, his father was elected the first mayor of the city, and Van Horne attended the public school.

Cornelius Van Horne died in 1854, and the family was left practically penniless. William Van Horne worked intermittently delivering telegraph messages and learned to send and receive in the Morse code. At the age of fourteen, he was given his first full-time job, as telegraph operator, with the Illinois Central Railroad. Later, the Michigan Central Railroad engaged him in similar capacity. When the Civil War began, he promptly enlisted, but his superintendent secured his release because his services as telegraph operator and general assistant were important to the railroad.

In 1862, Van Horne transferred his service to the Chicago & Alton Railroad as ticket agent and operator in Joliet; in 1864, he became train dispatcher for the same railroad in Bloomington, Illinois. Four years later, he was appointed superintendent of telegraph, and two years afterward, superintendent of

Sir William Cornelius Van Horne

transportation. In 1872, he became general superintendent of a subsidiary line, the St. Louis, Kansas City & Northern Railway. His success in that position led in 1874 to his appointment as general manager and subsequently as president of the Southern Minnesota Railroad, with offices in La Crosse, Wisconsin. In 1879, he returned to the Chicago & Alton as its general superintendent. After brief service with his old employers, however, he became general superintendent of the Chicago, Milwaukee & St. Paul.

James J. Hill recommended him to the directors of the Canadian Pacific Railway for the task of creating the proposed transcontinental line from Montreal to a terminus on the Pacific Ocean, and Van Horne took charge of the work of construction at Winnipeg on December 31, 1881. The project was carried to completion in 1886, and Van Horne, who had served from 1881 to 1884 as general manager, and from 1884 to 1888 as vice-president, was elected president of the railway in August 1888. The eleven years of his presidency were marked by further growth in mileage, earning power, and ramification of auxiliary services. Failing health led him to resign on June 12, 1899, and accept election as chairman of the board of directors and member of the executive committee. In 1910, he withdrew from all official connection with the Canadian Pacific.

While still with the Canadian Pacific Railway, Van Horne established a 350-mile railroad through the eastern provinces of the island of Cuba, originally under a revocable license in lieu of a charter. The charter was granted soon after the Republic was organized, and on December 1, 1902, the Cuba Railroad was opened for traffic. He also directed the construction of the last sixty-five miles of a railroad from Puerto Barrios to the city of Guatemala, the last spike being driven in January 1908.

Coinciding with his railroad activities, he was a director or officer in several large industrial enterprises, such as the Laurentide Pulp Company, Grand Mere, Quebec; a salt company at Windsor, Ontario; tramway systems in several Canadian cities, as well as in Mexico and Brazil; and the Dominion Coal Company and the Dominion Iron and Steel Company of Cape Breton. Van Horne was also a member of the board of the Equitable Life Assurance Society. In 1894, he accepted royal appointment as an honorary knight commander of the Order of St. Michael and St. George; prior to 1890, he had become naturalized under the Canadian laws.

In March 1867, he married Lucy Adaline Hurd. Three children were born to them, including a son who died in his fifth year. Van Horne died in Montreal, Canada, on September 11, 1915.

VASEY, GEORGE

(1822-1893) — Botanist, was born on February 28, 1822, near Scarborough, England, of English parents, who moved the year following to Central New York, settling at Oriskany. He was the fourth of ten children, and had to quit school at twelve to work in a village store. Already deeply interested in plants, he devoted his spare time to their analysis and made the acquaintance of Dr. P.D. Knieskern, John Torrey, Asa Gray, and other botanists. After graduation from the Oneida Institute, he began the study of medicine, attending the Berkshire Medical Institute in Pittsfield, Massachusetts.

Toward the end of 1846, he married a Miss Scott, of Oriskany, and began the practice of medicine at Dexter, New York. In 1848, he moved to northern Illinois, where, at Elgin and Ringwood, he spent eighteen years in professional practice. During this period, he continued his botanical studies, collected extensively the prairie flora of the region. He helped organize the Illinois Natural History Society and was its first president. Early in 1866, his wife's failing health led him to move to the southern part of the state, where she soon died. Late in 1867, he married Mrs. John W. Cameron.

In the latter half of 1868, Vasey accompanied his friend Major John Wesley Powell on an exploring expedition to Colorado as a botanist. Shortly after his return, he was made curator of the natural history museum of the State Normal University of Illinois, and in 1870, was associated with Professor Charles V. Riley in the editorship of the *American Entomologist and Botanist*. On April 1, 1872, he was appointed botanist of the U.S. Department of Agriculture, in Washington, D.C., and put in charge of the U.S. National Herbarium, which had been transferred from the Smithsonian Institution in 1868.

In preparation of an exhibit of the woods of American forest trees, accompanied by herbarium specimens, for the Centennial Exhibition in Philadelphia, he published a guide to the exhibit entitled *A Catalogue of the Forest Trees of the United States Which Usually Attain a Height of Sixteen Feet or More* (1876). His other publications include: *Agricultural Grasses of the United States* (1884); *A Descriptive Catalogue of the Grasses of the United States* (1885); *Grasses of the Southwest* (two volumes, 1890-1891) and *Grasses of the Pacific Slope* (two volumes, 1892-1893), published also under the title *Illustrations of North American Grasses* (two volumes, 1891-1893); and *Monograph of the Grasses of the United States and British America* (1892). Under his direction, also, experimental studies of grasses and other forage plants suited to arid regions of the West were initiated.

Vasey died in 1893 at his home in Washington, D.C., survived by his wife and six children.

W

WACKER, CHARLES HENRY

(1856-1929) — Brewer, executive and city planner, was the only child of Frederick Wacker, a German emigrant who settled in Chicago, Illinois, in 1854, and his wife Catharine Hummel. He was educated in the schools of Chicago and studied one year at Lake Forest Academy. He started in business as an office boy, 1872-1876, in the firm of Carl C. Moeller & Company, grain commissioners, and then toured Europe and Africa for three years, spending some time studying in Stuttgart and Geneva. Returning to his position in 1879, he remained there until the following year when his father took him into partnership in the malting business to form the firm of F. Wacker & Son, which in 1882 became Wacker & Birk Brewing and Malting Company. From 1884 until 1901 he was president of this firm, and, from 1895 to 1901 he was also president of the McAvoy Brewing Company, with which it was consolidated in 1889. In 1901 he turned his attention to real estate, and from 19O2 to 1928 he was president of the Chicago Heights Land Association.

His interest in civic affairs was given an impetus by his connection with the World's Columbian Exposition in Chicago in 1893 as a member of the board of directors and of various committees. He became an enthusiastic supporter and eventually the leader of a movement, started by the Merchants and Commercial Clubs, to beautify the city of Chicago. He was vice-chairman of the Merchants Club's Committee from 1907 to 1909, and its chairman for a short time in 1909. In 1909 Mayor Busse and the City Council created the Chicago Plan Commission to improve and beautify Chicago's "loop" and lakefront, and appointed Wacker chairman. He held this position until November 4, 1926, when he resigned because of illness. In appreciation of his remarkable work and untiring efforts in sponsoring and developing the Chicago Plan, the City Council renamed South Water Street, the double-decked drive along the river, which Wacker had been most influential in securing as a part of the Plan, Wacker Drive.

He was made secretary of the Chicago Zoning Commission in 1920, was president of the Chicago Relief and Aid Society, and, when it merged with the Chicago Bureau of Charities to form the United Charities of Chicago, became the first president of that body (1909-1912). He was a director of many important companies, and a member of a great many social clubs, German clubs, and singing societies. In 1921 he was awarded a medal of honor by the Societe des Architectes Francais. Some of his articles and addresses on the Chicago Plan were published; among them are *An S-O-S to the Public Spirited Citizens of Chicago* (1924), and articles in the *American City* (October 1909) and in *Art and Archarology* (September-October 1921).

He was twice married: first to Ottilie Marie Glade on May 10, 1887; and, after her death, to Ella G. Todtmann on March 19, 1919. By the first marriage there were two sons and a daughter, who, with his second wife, survived him.

WALGREEN, CHARLES RUDOLPH

(1873-1939) — Pharmacist and drugstore chain founder, was born on October 9, 1873, on a farm near Galesburg, Knox County, Illinois, the son of Charles Walgreen and his second wife, Ellen (Olson) Walgreen. In 1887, the family moved to Dixon, Illinois, where Charles Walgreen attended public schools and a local business college. After employment as a bookkeeper in a general store, he went to work in a Dixon shoe factory. However, an accident there cost him the first joint of a finger on his left hand, and the doctor who dressed his finger influenced him to take a job as a druggist's apprentice. In 1893, Walgreen went to Chicago, Illinois, where he worked in drug stores and began the serious study of pharmacy at night, becoming a registered pharmacist four years later. With the outbreak of the Spanish-American War, he enlisted in the First Illinois Volunteers, and while on duty in Cuba, he contracted malaria and yellow fever.

Following his discharge from the army, Walgreen secured work as a pharmacist with the druggist Isaac W. Blood in Chicago. In 1902, when Blood decided to retire, Walgreen bought him out. In 1909, when another of his former employers retired, Walgreen acquired his store and organized C.R. Walgreen & Company, the beginning of the later nationwide chain. In 1916, when the name was changed to Walgreen Company, there were seven stores. By 1927, the number had grown to 110, and at the time of Walgreen's death in 1939 to 493.

Walgreen has been called the father of the modern drug store. His company pioneered in the development of much of the modern equipment now in use and in clean, well-lit stores. Walgreen early began the manufacture of his own ice cream, candy, and certain drug items, and over the years his manufacturing facilities became unusual in their range and diversity. Walgreen remained as president of the company until his retirement in August 1939, when his son Charles Rudolph, Jr. succeeded him.

In 1935, Walgreen withdrew his wife's niece from the University of Chicago, publicly charging that she was being indoctrinated with un-American teachings. His action resulted in a full-scale investigation of the university by a committee of the Illinois legislature. Except for the pacifist leanings of one or two faculty members the committee found little to object to. After subsequent discussions with President Robert M. Hutchins, Walgreen gave the university $550,000 in 1937 for the establishment of the Charles R. Walgreen Foundation for the Study of American Institutions, with the object of spreading among the students a deeper understanding and a greater appreciation of the American way of life.

An aviation enthusiast, Walgreen donated the Dixon Municipal Airport to his hometown. He was an active Mason and a loyal Republican. On August 18, 1902, he married Myrtle R. Norton of Normal, Illinois. They had three children: Paul Olin, who died in infancy; Charles Rudolph; and Charlotte Ruth Walgreen, who died of cancer in Chicago and was buried in Dixon. He died on December 11, 1939, in Chicago, Illinois.

WALKER, DANIEL

(1922-) — Thirty-eighth governor of Illinois (1973-1977), was born in Washington, D. C., the son of Virginia Lynch and Lewis W. Walker. His father was a chief radioman for the U. S. Navy, and he was raised at the San Diego, California base.

Walker served as a seaman in the Navy from 1939 to 1942, and after graduating from the Naval Academy in 1945, he entered Northwestern Law School in 1947, where he was editor of the university's *Law Review.* He ranked second in his 1950 graduating class.

For a year afterward, Walker worked as a law clerk to Supreme Court Justice Fred M. Vinson. In 1951, he assisted Illinois Governor Adlai Stevenson. After practicing law with two successful law firms, he took a position as vice president and general counsel for Montgomery Ward Company in 1966. Two years later, he was vice president and general counsel for MARCOR, Incorporated.

He tried and failed in his first bid for public office, losing the Democratic nomination for state attorney general in 1960. However, Governor Otto Kerner appointed him to the Illinois Public Aid Commission to oversee the state's welfare programs. In other commissions, he fought for more open occupancy of middle income housing in the traditionally white suburbs of Chicago, and published two pamphlets disclosing local business interests of mobsters. These activities gave him the reputation of a liberal; in 1968, he was chosen by the National Commission on the Causes and Prevention of Violence to lead an investigation on the bloody confrontations between Chicago police and antiwar demonstrators at that year's Democratic National Convention. Walker blamed municipal government orders, particularly from Mayor Daley, for police disorderliness in the week-long riots earlier.

Although his accomplishment caused much local criticism for Walker, he also received supportive national recognition. After serving as campaign manager in Adlai Stevenson's successful bid for the U. S. Senate in 1970, Walker announced his intentions to run for governor in 1972 as a reform Democrat.

His alienation from the large Chicago Democratic "machine" did not defeat Walker. Instead, he won the primary and defeated incumbent Governor Richad Ogilvie in a close race. While in office, he trimmed the state payroll by 10 percent, and sought for austerity in his office by dismissing personal security guards and substituting his own Dodge for three official limousines. He also implemented energy-saving measures for state buildings, and approved a Regional Mass Transit Authority. In his attempt for second term, he was defeated at the Democratic primary by a Chicago "machine" candidate, Michael J. Howlitt.

After stepping down from office, Walter entered private business with a chain of oil-change franchises and two Savings and Loans. In 1987, he was convicted for improprieties in handling the Savings and Loans, and spent two years in prison. He then retired to California.

WALLACE, HENRY CANTWELL

(1866-1924) — Agricultural journalist and U.S. secretary of agriculture, was born in Rock Island, Illinois, the son of Nannie (Cantwell) and Henry Wallace. He attended the city schools and helped his father on the farm, at the same time learning the printer's trade in the newspaper offices in Winterset, Iowa. From 1885 to 1887, he attended the Iowa State Agricultural College, now the Iowa State College of Agriculture. He then rented one of his father's farms, and married Carrie May Broadhead on November 24, 1885. They had six children.

Returning to the Iowa State Agricultural College in 1891, he graduated in 1892, and obtained appointment as assistant professor of agriculture in dairying. In 1894, he became part owner and publisher with Charles F. Curtiss of the *Farm and Dairy*, published at Ames, Iowa. In a few months, he, his father, and his brother, John P. Wallace, became the owners and decided to move it to Des Moines, Iowa. The name was changed to *Wallace's Farm and Dairy* and later to *Wallace's Farmer*. Henry C. Wallace became associate editor, and on the death of his father, editor.

Henry Cantwell Wallace

Wallace was involved in various farm organizations, including the Cornbelt Meat Producers Association, of which he was the secretary for fourteen years. He labored for the equalization of railroad rates for farm products and became a recognized leader of national movements for the advancement of agricultural interests. During World War I, he bitterly opposed the food administration policy of Herbert Hoover.

When the Republicans returned to power in 1921 on a platform promising farm relief, President Warren Harding appointed him as secretary of agriculture, and reappointed by President Calvin Coolidge, he served in this capacity until his death. He opposed the transfer of all marketing functions to the Department of Commerce, and urged that the Department of Agriculture should not only assist the farmer in increasing the efficiency of production but that it should also develop improved systems of marketing. He fought for the retention of the forest service, which Secretary Fall attempted to have transferred to the Department of the Interior, had an important part in framing agricultural legislation, and supported the principles of the McNary-Haugen Bill. He reorganized the department into more unified and effectively correlated bureaus, established the bureau of agricultural economics and the bureau of home economics, and inaugurated the radio service for market reports. He was a zealous advocate of education, being concerned primarily with the improvement of the rural schools, the establishment of courses in agriculture in the high schools, and the advancement of the agricultural colleges along scientific and practical lines.

After Wallace's death in 1924, *Our Debt and Duty to the Farmer* (1925) was published with a last chapter written jointly by Nils A. Olsen and Henry A. Wallace, his son. His funeral services were held at the White House, and he was buried in Des Moines, Iowa.

WALLER, WILLARD WALTER

(1899-1945) — Sociologist, was born on July 30, 1899, in Murphysboro, Illinois, the son of Elbert and Margaret Dora (Clendenin) Waller. After completing high school at Albion, Illinois, in 1915, Waller entered McKendree College at Lebanon, Illinois. Two years later, he transferred to the University of Illinois, where he studied sociology under Edward C. Hayes. A tour of duty in the navy in 1918 delayed his graduation by one semester. He received the B.A. in 1920, and following a short stint as a reporter on the *Evansville* (Ind.) *Courier*, took a job near Chicago, Illinois, at the Morgan Park Military Academy, where for the next six years, he taught Latin and French. On January 3, 1922, he married Thelma A. Jones of Evansville.

In 1921, Waller began taking courses on a part-time basis at the University of Chicago, at first in education, then in law, and finally in sociology. He completed his M.A. in 1925. Having separated from his wife, he transferred to the University of Pennsylvania, where he was both instructor and graduate student. He received a Ph.D. in 1929 with a study of divorce, *The Old Love and the New* (1930), in which he analyzed the process by which married people become alienated from each other and provided original insights into the nature of marital dissolution and readjustment. On August 13, 1929, he married Josephine Wilkins of Philadelphia; their children were Peter, Bruce, and Suzanne.

In the fall of 1929, Waller went to the University of Nebraska as an assistant professor of sociology. Parents and fellow instructors complained about Waller's teaching procedures, which included encouraging students to do case studies on their own families, and when a university official discovered in February 1931 that his unmarried and pregnant daughter had been confidentially counseled by Waller, he was immediately dismissed. Paid the balance of his salary, Waller moved to Chicago, where he completed his second book, *The Sociology of Teaching* (1932), depicting schools in terms of symbolic social interaction.

Waller next (May 1931) joined the faculty of Pennsylvania State College (later University) as associate professor of sociology; he was promoted to professor in 1933. He published two important studies in the *American Sociological Review*, "Social Problems and the Mores" (December 1936) and "The Rating and Dating Complex" (October 1937). In the first he contended that social problems are actually perpetuated by so-called respectable social institutions. In the second he analyzed student dating patterns and ratings of self and others, material that appeared also in his textbook, *The Family* (1938), which drew on his parents marriage for illustration. Waller soon began giving advice to troubled married couples.

In 1937, he accepted the chairmanship of the sociology department at Wayne University in Detroit, but then negotiated his release to take an associate professorship at Barnard College, Columbia University. He utilized his location in New York City, and began publishing popular articles and giving radio speeches on social policy. At the outbreak of World War II, concerned about the long-term effects of the organization of American society into a war-making machine, he wrote *The Veteran Comes Back* (1944), a plea for a humane, planned demobilization of returning veterans, and toured the country to publicize the need for government programs to ease the adjustment of veterans. He died on July 26, 1945, of a heart attack in the subway station near Columbia.

WALSH, BENJAMIN DANN

(1808-1869) — Entomologist, was born in Clapton, London, England, the son of Benjamin Walsh. Intended for the church, he attended Trinity College, Cambridge, where he received a B.A. in 1831, became a fellow in 1833, and in 1834, was awarded an M.A. He resigned the fellowship, however, and declined to follow the study of divinity. For some years, he wrote for *Blackwood's Magazine*, and published *The Comedies of Aristophanes, Translated into Corresponding English Metres* (1837). About this time, he married Rebecca Finn, and at the age of thirty, immigrated to the United States, expecting to settle in Chicago. He finally made his home in Henry County, Illinois, near the town of Cambridge, where for thirteen years, he engaged in farming. He then moved to the town of Rock Island, where he carried on a successful lumber business for seven years.

Retiring from business about 1858, he devoted the rest of his life to entomology. He wrote many articles for the agricultural newspapers and published a number of admirable articles in the *Proceedings of the Boston Society of Natural History* and in the

Transactions of the American Entomological Society. He also became one of the editors of a journal started in Philadelphia known as the *Practical Entomologist*. In 1868, with Charles V. Riley, he founded and edited the *American Entomologist*.

Walsh's bibliography shows 385 titles of individual record and 478 in co-authorship with Riley, among which is "On Certain Entomological Speculations of the New England School of Naturalists." In 1867, he was appointed state entomologist of Illinois, and assumed the duties of that position, although his appointment was not confirmed until the next biennial session of the legislature. Walsh's sole report was published in the *Transactions of the Illinois State Horticultural Society* for 1867.

Walsh died in 1869, as the result of a railway accident near Rock Island. Walsh's collections and many of his notes were destroyed in the Chicago fire of 1871.

WARD, ARCH BURDETTE

(1896-1955) — Sportswriter and promoter, was born on December 27, 1896, in Irwin, Illinois, the son of Thomas Stephan and Nora Gertrude O'Conner Ward. His father, a brakeman for the Illinois Central Railroad, died in a railway accident when Ward was four years old. Shortly thereafter, he and his mother moved to Iowa to live with relatives. In 1914, Gertrude Ward arranged for the president of St. Joseph's College and Academy (later Loras College), in Dubuque to become Arch's legal guardian. Ward took odd jobs, including menial assignments with a Dubuque newspaper, in order to complete high school and two years of college at St. Joseph's. He then left school to write for the *Dubuque Telegraph-Herald*.

In 1919, Ward enrolled at the University of Notre Dame. He worked as campus correspondent for the *South Bend Tribune*, and filed stories with other newspapers, including the *Chicago Tribune*. At the behest of Knute Rockne, Notre Dame's football coach, Ward also acted as the university's first athletic publicity director. Ward left Notre Dame in 1921 to become sports editor of the *Rockford Morning Star*. Although he attended the university again for a brief period in 1931, he never earned a degree.

In 1921, Ward married Helen Carey of Chicago; they had two children. In 1925, he joined the *Chicago Tribune* as a copy editor, and within five years, had risen to sports editor. On June 14, 1937, he began to write "In the Wake of the News"; originated in 1905, it is the oldest continuous sports column in American journalism.

Ward often covered only the biggest events and permitted staff members to ghostwrite about one-third of his columns. Still, under Ward, the *Tribune* developed the largest sports staff of any American newspaper of the era.

As a promoter, Ward started or assisted the organization of the Silver Skates and Golden Gloves competition, as well as sundry golf, bowling, swimming, and horseracing events. Each promotion raised funds for charity. In 1933, he was asked to devise a sports event to coincide with the Chicago Century of Progress Exposition. Seizing upon the idea of an all-star baseball game, he overrode the objections of skeptical owners who doubted that the game would attract a sufficient crowd to pay expenses. The contest drew 47,000 spectators at Comiskey Park and became an annual event. The following year Ward conceived the idea of an all-star football game to be played for the benefit of charity. He arranged for the professional champion Chicago Bears to compete against a team of college all-stars. The game was held at Chicago's Soldier Field in August 1934, before nearly 80,000 fans, the largest crowd that had seen a professional football team play. It, too, became an annual event.

In the 1950,s Ward took on a local television program and a national radio broadcast in addition to his *Tribune* duties. He died on July 9, 1955, in Chicago, Illinois.

WARD, LESTER FRANK

(1841-1913) — Sociologist, was born on June 18, 1841, in Joliet, Illinois, the son of Justus Ward and Silence (Rolph) Ward. The family later moved to Buchanan County, Iowa. At the age of seventeen, he went to Pennsylvania, where, at Myersburg, his brother, Cyrenus Osborne Ward, later a labor leader, was then manufacturing wagon hubs. Beginning in 1861, he spent four terms at the Susquehanna Collegiate Institute at Towanda. In August 1862, he enlisted in the Union army, and served until November 1864, when he was discharged on account of wounds received at Chancellorsville. On August 13, 1862, just before his enlistment, he married Elizabeth Carolyn Vought, by whom he had a son who lived less than a year; his wife died in 1872, and on March 6, 1873, he married Rosamond Asenath Simons.

In 1865, he secured a position in the U.S. Treasury Department at Washington, D.C., with which he remained connected until 1881. Meanwhile, he studied at Columbian College (now George Washington

Lester Frank Ward

University), from which he received his A.B. in 1869, his LL.B. in 1871, and his A.M. in 1872. After leaving the Treasury Department, he became assistant geologist in the U.S. Geological Survey. He was appointed geologist in 1883, and paleontologist in 1892. His chief contributions to the natural sciences include "Types of the Laramie Flora" published in *Status of the Mesozoic Floras of the United States* (1905), a monograph of the survey, and various articles in its Annual Reports.

Valuable as are Ward's studies in the natural sciences, he is best known because of his leadership in the field of American sociology. He became the great pioneer of modern and evolutionary sociology in the United States, through the publication of *Dynamic Sociology* (1883). This was followed by *The Psychic Factors of Civilization* (1893); *Outlines of Sociology* (1898); *Pure Sociology* (1903); and *Applied Sociology* (1906). The *Textbook of Sociology* (1905), by J.Q. Dealey and Ward, is mainly a condensation of the *Pure Sociology*.

Ward sought and obtained a call to the chair of sociology in Brown University. This chair he held for the remainder of his life. In *Glimpses of the Cosmos*, he republished his minor writings in their biographical and historical background. It also contains a summary of what he considered to be his chief contribution to social philosophy.

He traveled widely over the United States and Europe and in 1903, as president of the Institute International de Sociologie, he presided over the deliberations of that learned body at the Sorbonne, Paris. He died on April 18, 1913, in Washington, D.C.

WARMAN, CY

(1855-1914) — Journalist and author, was born near Greenup, Illinois, the son of John and Nancy (Askew) Warman. He was educated in the common schools, and for a time, was a farmer and wheat broker at Pocahontas, Illinois. In 1880, he went to Colorado, where he worked in the railroad yards at Salida, and was successively locomotive fireman and engineer for the Denver & Rio Grande Railroad. Forced by poor health to give up railroading, he went to Denver to enter journalism, and in 1888, became editor of the semi-monthly paper *Western Railway.* In 1892, he started a paper called the *Chronicle* at the new silver mines of Creede, Colorado. Meanwhile, both as railway worker and as journalist, he began writing poetry. In 1891, one of his poems, "The Canyon of the Grand," won a prize, and in 1892 Warman published a slender volume entitled *Mountain Melodies.* On September 4 of that year, Charles A Dana, editor of the New York *Sun,* published a group of Warman's verses in his paper. Raymond Moore set one of these lyrics, "Sweet Marie," to music and a million copies were sold in six months.

The silver boom at Creede having collapsed, Warman went to New York City in 1893. About this time, he offered to ride a thousand miles in a locomotive cab and write his story for *McClure's Magazine.* The story was hugely successful, and Warman went on to produce a long series of short stories and novels depicting the romance and adventure of the frontier. These tales were collected in a series of volumes: *Tales of an Engineer with Rhymes of the Rail* (1895); *The Express Messenger and Other Tales of the Rail* (1897) *Frontier Stories* (1898); *The White Mail* (1899); *Snow on the Headlight; a Story of the Great Burlington Strike* (1899); *Short Rails* (1900); *The Last Spike and Other Railroad Stories* (1906); *Weiga of Temagami and Other Indian Tales* (1908). He also published a history of American railroad enterprise, *The Story of the Railroad* (1898), and another volume of verse, *Songs of Cy Warman* (1911).

Warman stayed only a few months in New York. For two years he traveled in Europe and the Orient, and for two more he lived in Washington, D. C. He then built a house at London, Ont., which was his home for the rest of his days. He was twice married first, 1879, to Ida Blanch Hays, of St. Jacobs, Illinois, who died in 1887; second, May 17, 1892, to Myrtle Marie Jones, the inspiration of the song "Sweet Marie," whom he met at Salida and married at Denver. Warman died in a Chicago hospital in 1914.

WASHINGTON, HAROLD

(1922-1987) — First African American mayor of Chicago, was born in Chicago, Illinois, on April 15, 1922, the son of Roy L. Washington and Bertha (Jones) Washington. He attended public schools, and starting at a young age, ran errands for the Democratic precinct on Chicago's south side where his father was a precinct captain. After a stint in the Army Air Force during World War II, Washington enrolled at Chicago's Roosevelt

Harold Washington

University and received a B.A. in 1949. He continued his education at Northwestern University Law School, earning a J.D. in 1952. In 1954, Washington took his father's place as precinct captain after the latter's death. That same year, he began serving as assistant city prosecutor, a post he held until 1958. Between 1960 and 1964, Washington worked for the Illinois Industrial Commission as that organization's arbitrator.

Next, Washington served six terms (1965 to 1976) in the Illinois House of Representatives, and then three years (1977 to 1980) in the Illinois Senate. Known for his progressive outlook, he was responsible for the passage of bills that provided better protection for crime witnesses, an upgrading of the Illinois Fair Employment Practices Commission, and the implementation of a state holiday on the birth date of the Reverend Martin Luther King, Jr. He pushed to obtain separate funds for minority contractors, and was instrumental in the creation of a Department of Human Rights. In addition, he co-created the Black Caucus within the Illinois Legislature.

After the death of Chicago's longtime mayor, Richard J. Daley, Washington ran in the special election that was held to fill the incumbent's post, but came in third, with Michael Bilandic winning the race. In 1980, Washington ran successfully as a Democrat for the U.S. Congress. Three years later, he ran again for Chicago's mayorship on the Democratic ticket against incumbent Jane Byrne and Richard A. Daley in February 1983. He geared his campaign toward the minority community, and promised that he would work on the huge unemployment rate pervasive in the Black community. He won "an upset primary victory" over Byrne and Daley, and was successful in the general election against Republican Bernard Epton.

Once Washington took office, he had to face a lack of support from twenty-nine out of fifty aldermen, who, with their leader, Alderman Edward Vrdolyak, were determined to fight him on every decision he made. He used his veto to put various council decisions on hold, and eventually, his opponents got tired of the fight. Washington nominated

Fred Rice to become the city's first African American police commissioner. He also came through on his promise to eliminate the city's patronage system, urged city employees to form a union, decreased the inherited budget deficit to a more reasonable amount, and filled top city jobs with minorities and women. Washington ran for and won a second mayoral term in April of 1987. Washington's second term was cut short by his death in Chicago, Illinois, on November 25, 1987. Washington was buried in Oakwood Cemetery.

WAYMACK, WILLIAM WESLEY

(1888-1960) — Journalist and government official, was born on October 18, 1888, in Savanna, Illinois, the son of William Edward Waymack and Emma Julia Oberheim. He began elementary school at Savanna, but before completing the eighth grade, went to Mt. Carroll, Illinois, to live with his mother's parents. After graduating from high school, he worked as a section hand and did other jobs in the Savanna area.

Beginning in 1908, Waymack worked his way through Morningside College in Sioux City, Iowa. During his senior year, he was the college correspondent for the *Sioux City Journal*. He graduated with a B.A. in 1911, and on June 27 of that year, married Elsie Jeannette Lord. They had one son. Waymack then went to work as a reporter on the *Journal*. In 1914, he was established as city editor and chief editorial writer. He held these positions until 1918, when he joined the Cowles newspaper organization in Des Moines to write editorials for the morning *Register* and the evening *Tribune*. Three years later, he was moved to the managing editor's desk, which he administered until 1929. After a period of ill health, he was chosen a director of the publishing company and placed in charge of the editorial sections in 1931. They remained his responsibilities until 1946.

Waymack became a spokesman for Iowa's farm belt. Showing that by 1936 some 40,000 Iowa farmers had become tenants or had been forced off the land altogether, Waymack calculated the costs in human as well as economic terms. He sought to hold down the annual "massive" March first migration of farmers (before the crop-planting season) by which, he said, everyone lost—tenant, landlord, and "the social soundness of Iowa." From 1930, he lived on a 275-acre farm at Adel, twenty miles west of Des Moines.

But Waymack's horizon extended beyond the rural Middle West to the sharecropping South, the industrial East, and on to the international scene. He campaigned for a wider, more effective role for the United

States in global affairs, supported freer world trade, and called for entrance of the United States into the League of Nations. He also advocated wage and price controls to combat inflation.

Second in the Pulitzer Prize competition for editorial writing in 1936, Waymack received the top award a year later for his commentaries on "man and the land." In 1938, he was given the first-place editorial award of Sigma Delta Chi, a professional journalistic society. In October 1946 Waymack gave up his newspaper responsibilities to accept appointment by President Harry S. Truman to the newly created Atomic Energy Commission. He served for two years before retiring because of ill health.

From 1941 to 1959, Waymack was a trustee of the Carnegie Endowment for International Peace, and he was a director of the Twentieth Century Fund from 1942 until his death. He was a director of the Federal Reserve Bank in Chicago, a member of the War Labor Board, a member of the National Council for NATO, an adviser to the State Department after the bombing at Pearl Harbor, and a national committeeman for the American Civil Liberties Union. He was a pioneer advocate of radio and television as potential instruments for education, and was among the first users of aviation, which he enthusiastically promoted. He married Elsie Jeannette Lord in 1911. He died on November 5, 1960, in Des Moines, Iowa.

WEBSTER, "H. T." HAROLD TUCKER

(1885-1952) — Cartoonist, was born in Parkersburg, West Virginia, on September 21, 1885, and grew up in Tomahawk, Wisconsin. He began drawing at the young age of seven. As he got older, he began studying composition, portraiture, cartooning, and lettering under Frank Holmes. After saving some money, he went to Chicago, Illinois, to study at Holmes' School of Illustration; however, less than a month later the school closed.

After failing to find work with various newspapers, Webster migrated to Denver, Colorado, where he eventually got a short-term job with the *Denver Post*. He then returned to Chicago, and after enduring unemployment for a time, both the *Chicago Daily News* and the *Chicago American* began accepting his cartoons. The *Daily News* eventually hired Webster, who worked there from 1903 to 1905. In the latter year, Webster went to work for the *Chicago Inter-Ocean*, where his political drawings were printed on the front page. He next accepted a job with the *Cincinnati Post*. While the bulk of his work was political, he also began branching out and drawing cartoons that were of the human-interest variety. He drew a whole series in that genre including *Little Tragedies of Childhood* and *Life's Darkest Moment.*

After taking a long trip around the world, Webster returned to the United States, settling in New York and eventually securing a job with Associated Newspapers. He continued to provide political cartoons, but soon his human-interest sketches were being published more often. From 1919 to 1923, He worked for the *New York Tribune*, then joined the staff of the *New York World.* As he set about to prepare enough cartoons for three and a half months in one month's time, he strained his right hand and it became paralyzed. Undeterred, Webster practiced drawing with his left hand until he became proficient at it.

Some of Webster's cartoon series included The Thrill that Comes Once in a Lifetime, They Don't Speak Our Language, The Boy Who Made Good, and Poker Portraits. He also published several compilation books of his works including Our Boyhood Thrills and Other Cartoons (1915), Boys and Folks (1917), Webster's Bridge (1924), Webster's Poker Book (1925), and Culbertson Webster Contract System (1932). Ring Lardner contributed the introduction to Webster's book, The Timid Soul, which was published in 1931. In 1933, Webster wrote an article that was published in Forum concerning one of his series entitled They Don't Speak Our Language. Two more of his collections were published in 1945: Webster Unabridged and To Hell With Fishing.

Webster married Ethel Worts in 1916, and the couple made their home in Connecticut. He died on September 22, 1952, in Stamford, Connecticut.

WEIDIG, ADOLF

(1867-1931) — Composer, teacher, and conductor, was born on November 28, 1867, in Hamburg, Germany, the son of Ferdinand and Hulda (Albrecht) Weidig. His father was a trombonist for thirty-eight years in the City Theatre orchestra at Hamburg. He received his general education in the schools of that city, and began to study violin at the age of twelve with Johannes Jagan, a member of the City Opera orchestra. From 1882 to 1887, he studied in the Hamburg Conservatory with K. L. Bargheer (violin), Hugo Riemann (theory and composition), and J. von Bernuth (piano). When he was sixteen, he became a member of the Hamburg Philharmonic Orchestra. He entered the Munich Conservatory in 1887, and became a pupil of Rheinberger (harmony, theory, and composition) and Abel (violin), graduating in 1891. In the meantime,

1888, he had composed a string quartet that won him the Frankfort "Mozart Prize," yielding an annual allowance of 1800 marks for four years. In June 1892, he came to America and settled in Chicago. He entered the Chicago Symphony Orchestra, and then the Thomas Orchestra, where he was a member of the first violin section from 1892 to 1896. In the latter year, he resigned to devote himself to teaching.

In 1893, he joined the American Conservatory of Music in Chicago, as teacher of violin and theory, and from 1907 until his death, he was an associate director of this school. His scholarly and comprehensive treatise, *Harmonic Material and Its Uses* (1923), was the result of long research and practical experience. He was also a member (1893-1901) of the string quartet of Theodore Spiering, in which he played viola. After 1900, he rarely played the violin in public, but he often appeared as an orchestral conductor, especially of his own compositions.

His long list of compositions include: while a student at Munich, a Symphony in C Minor and an overture, "Sappho," the latter performed by the Thomas Orchestra at the Columbian Exposition in Chicago, 1893; the songcycle "The Buccaneer;" numerous pieces for piano, violin and chorus; three string quartets (in D minor, A, and C minor); a string quintet; a piano trio; a suite for violin and piano; *Opus 21*, Romanza for the cello, *Opus 14*; and Serenade for strings, *Opus 16*. His large orchestral works are: "Semiramis," *Opus 33* (first performance, 1906), a symphonic fantasy based on a poem by Edwin Markham; "Drei Episoden," *Opus 38* (1908), based on Clarchen's song from Goethe's Egmont; Symphonic Suite in three movements (1914); and "Concert Overture," *Opus 65* (1919). The Chicago Symphony Orchestra gave first performances of all these except the "Concert Overture," which was played by the Minneapolis Symphony Orchestra with Weidig conducting. In the winter and spring of 1909 Weidig visited Germany and conducted several of his orchestral works, mainly the "Drei Episoden," in Berlin, Hamburg, Frankfort, and Wiesbaden.

On June 29, 1896, he was married to Helen Ridgway, of Hinsdale, Illinois, who survived him at the time of his death at Hinsdale in 1931.

WEST, ROY OWEN

(1868-1958) — Secretary of the interior and Republican party leader, was born on October 27, 1868, in Georgetown, Illinois, the son of Pleasant West and Helen Anna West. He received his early education in

Georgetown, and then attended DePauw University, where he received a B.A. and an LL.B. in 1890. He was awarded an M.A. from DePauw three years later. Upon completing his education, West moved to Chicago, Illinois, to practice law. There he met Charles S. Deneen, a lawyer and future leader of the Deneen (later Deneen-West) faction of the Illinois Republican Party.

In 1894, West became assistant county attorney, and from 1895 to 1897, he was city attorney for Chicago. On June 11, 1898, he married Louisa Augustus; they had one son. Also in 1898, he commenced five consecutive terms, lasting to 1914, as a member of the Cook County Board of Review. In 1902, West formed a law partnership with Percy B. Eckhart.

His wife died in 1901, and on June 8, 1904, West married Louise McWilliams; they had one daughter. In the gubernatorial campaign of 1904, West acted as Deneen's campaign manager. Deneen won the nomination and the election. (He was governor of Illinois from 1905 to 1913.) West then became chairman of the Republican State Central Committee, serving until 1914.

West's influence in the Republican national organization grew steadily. In 1908, 1912, 1916, and 1928, he was a delegate to the Republican National Convention. He succeeded Frank Lowden as the Illinois member of the Republican National Committee in 1912, holding this position until 1916 and again from 1928 to 1932. After Lowden became governor of Illinois in 1917, West became his consultant, and when Lowden aspired to the Republican presidential nomination in 1920, West traveled through New England at his own expense, seeking support for him. However, in 1928, when Lowden again sought the nomination, West was an enthusiastic supporter of Herbert Hoover.

In 1924, West directed the primary campaign that resulted in the election of Deneen to the U.S. Senate. That same year, West became secretary of the Republican National Committee, administering a budget system instituted by President Calvin Coolidge, with whom he worked closely. On July 20, 1928, Coolidge appointed West secretary of the interior to succeed Hubert Work, who had resigned in order to become chairman of the Republican National Committee.

West's term expired with the end of the Coolidge administration. President Herbert Hoover offered him the ambassadorship to Japan, but he declined. On Deneen's death in 1940, West became chief of the faction known as the National Republican Party. During World War II, West acted as special assistant to the U.S.

attorney general, and heard the cases of conscientious objectors until 1952.

From 1914 to 1950, he was a trustee of DePauw University, serving as board president from 1924 to 1950. He was instrumental in securing more than $10 million in gifts for his alma mater. He died in Chicago, Illinois, on November 29, 1958.

WESTERMANN, WILLIAM LINN

(1873-1954) — Papyrologist and ancient historian, was born on September 15, 1873, in Belleville, Illinois, the son of Louis and Emma Hilgard Tyndale Westermann. After completing his secondary education in Decatur, Illinois, he entered the University of Nebraska in 1890, receiving his B.A. in 1894 and M.A. in 1896. Westermann next taught Latin at Decatur High School for three years. In 1899, he went to Germany to study at the University of Berlin. He remained there, with the exception of half a year spent at Heidelberg, until 1902, when he received the Ph.D. after defending a dissertation entitled *De Hippocratis in Galeno memoria quaestiones*, done primarily under the direction of Ulrich von Wilamowitz-Moellendorff and Hermann Diels.

After returning to the United States in 1902, Westermann moved steadily up the academic ladder. Beginning as instructor at the University of Missouri, he became an assistant professor in 1904. In 1906, he moved to the University of Minnesota, and in 1908, he became an associate professor at the University of Wisconsin. On June 15, 1912, he married Avrina Davies; they had one son. Two years later he was promoted to professor. In 1920, Westermann accepted a professorship at Cornell University, which he held until he moved to Columbia University, where he spent the rest of his academic career, in 1923. While at Columbia, he was appointed professor in charge at the School of Classical Studies in Rome (1926-1927). In 1944, he served as president of the American Historical Association. After his retirement in 1948, Westermann twice accepted appointments in Egypt: in 1949 at Farouk I University and in 1953-1954 as lecturer in ancient history at the University of Alexandria.

Although also renowned as an editor of the *Zenon papyri* (in part) and other collections at Cornell and Columbia, Westermann made his greatest contribution in the field of economic history, following guidelines already set up by Eduard Meyer and K.J.B. Beloch. Michael Rostovtzeff persuaded Wilhelm Kroll, then editor of the *Real-Encyclopadie der classischen Altertumswissenschaft*, to commission

Westermann to do an article entitled "Sklaverei." The book-length article was published in 1935; twenty years later, just after Westermann's death, his *Slave Systems of Greek and Roman Antiquity* appeared, covering the same material in English, but with added material and some changes in emphasis.

Westermann served the United States as an expert on the Near East at the Paris peace conference in 1918-1919. During the Nazi period and afterward, he also helped Columbia to attract and retain such European scholars in exile as Kurt von Fritz Rafael Taubenschlag. He died in 1954.

WESTON, EDWARD HENRY

(1886-1958) — Photographer, was born March 24, 1886, in Highland Park, Illinois, the son of Edward Burbank Weston and Alice Jeanette Brett. His mother died before he was five. Weston dropped out of high school in 1903, the worked for Marshall Field & Company. In 1906, moved to Southern California, and after working as a railroad surveyor,

Edward Henry Weston

he bought an old postcard camera to take door to door, offering his services as an all-purpose family photographer.

Weston attended the Illinois College of Photography in 1908; he finished the course in six months, but because of a technicality, did not receive his diploma. Returning to California, he worked as a printer for other portrait photographers. On January 30, 1909, he married Flora May Chandler. They had four sons: Edward Chandler, Theodore Brett, Laurence Neil, and Cole.

In 1911, Weston built and opened his own studio in Tropico (now Glendale), California. From 1914 to 1917, his spontaneous, soft-focus, outdoor portraits of children and dancers won many awards. He gave many demonstrations of his "high-key" techniques, and in 1917, was elected to the London Salon, pictorial photography's highest honor.

In 1919 to 1921, Weston became dissatisfied with his work, and destroyed many of his earlier photographs in a bonfire. His new work involved experiments with semiabstract fragments of nudes or natural forms. In March 1922, Tina Modotti took some of Weston's new, sharp-focus contact prints to Mexico City, where they were enthusiastically received. In October of that year, Weston went east, taking his first industrial photographs of the Armco Steel plant in Ohio, before going on to New York in November to meet Alfred Stieglitz, Paul Strand, and Charles Sheeler, the leading exponents of "straight" photography.

In August 1923, Weston went to live in Mexico with Modotti. He opened a studio first in Tacubaya and then in Mexico City, where he met the leaders of the Mexican Renaissance, including Diego Rivera, David Alfaro Siqueiros, and Jose Clemente Orozco. After several months in 1925, when he shared a studio in San Francisco, California, Weston went back to Mexico for another year, traveling with Modotti while photographing marketplaces, bars, sculpture, landscapes, and clouds. He returned to Glendale, California, in November 1926.

Weston then began a series of extreme close-up studies of shells and vegetables, sharing a studio with his son Theodore Brett in Carmel, California (1929-1934). He was invited to help organize the American section of the Deutsche Werkbund "Film und Foto" exhibition held in Stuttgart, Germany, in 1929; he was given his first one-man show in New York (1930) and then in San Francisco (1931). Together with Ansel Adams and Willard Van Dyck, he was a leading member of the Group f64, an informal association founded in 1932 and disbanded in 1935 that promoted the principles of "pure" photography.

Having turned his attention from small details to larger forms and broader vistas in the early 1930s, Weston made his famous series of nudes and sand dunes at Oceano, California, in 1936. The following year, he was the first photographer to be awarded a Guggenheim Fellowship.

After divorcing his wife, Flora, in 1938, Weston married Charis Wilson on April 24, 1939. In 1946, a major retrospective of Weston's work was held at the Museum of Modern Art in New York City. Stricken with Parkinson's disease, Weston took his last negative at Point Lobos in 1948. Thereafter, he supervised his sons, Brett and Cole, and his darkroom assistant Dody Warren, as they produced several sets of prints from 1,000 selected negatives. He died on January 1, 1958, in Carmel, California.

WESTON, NATHAN AUSTIN

(1868-1933) — Economist, was born at Champaign, Illinois, the son of Nathan and Jane (Cloyd) Weston. He prepared for college in the local high school and in 1889 received a B.L. from the University of Illinois. The next four years were spent in teaching in the public schools, and he became an instructor in the academy of the University in 1893. On

September 4, 1894, he was married to Angelina Gayman of Champaign. They had two children. While teaching he carried on graduate study in economics and history, was awarded a fellowship in the University of Wisconsin, and received an M.L. from the University of Illinois in 1898. He was a fellow at Cornell University and in 1899-1990 an assistant in political economy there. He received a Ph.D. from Cornell in 1901. In 1910-11 he studied at the University of Berlin. He was called to the University of Illinois in 1900, where he became professor in 1919. In 1908 he was made assistant director of the courses in business administration and in 1915 acting dean of the College of Commerce. At his own request he was relieved of these administrative duties in 1919 and devoted himself entirely to his teaching, after 1920 to the teaching of graduate students only. He continued, however, to serve on numerous important committees, and his sound judgment and tolerance were highly valued by his colleagues.

His great work was teaching. His students found him a wise counselor and inspiring teacher, who insisted on a broad and rigorous training and stimulated them not only to acquire a wide knowledge of their fields but also to sharpen their ability to analyze data critically and to think logically. His influence on the study of economics was widespread and important, carried by the large number of those who studied under him. He was himself a man of wide reading, professional and cultural, and unusually well acquainted with the literature of economics. His own library was notable for its size and the range of its economic subjects. One of his special interests was the development of the quantity theory of money. His knowledge of the history of economic thought was profound, and he is to be regarded as one of the foremost American students of orthodox classical economic doctrine. He steadfastly refused to write in his field, holding that its existing literature was already unnecessarily voluminous and much of it superficial and repetitious. A follower of the ideas of Alfred Marshall, he thought that little that was new had been added to the field of economic theory in the past forty years, and that much of that was unimportant. His published papers in the field of economics were only three in number: a statistical inquiry into *The Cost of Production of Corn in Illinois in 1896* (1898); "The Study of the National Monetary Commission" in the *Annals of the American Academy of Political and Social Science* of January 1922; and "The Ricardian Epoch in American Economics," a masterly analysis in the *American Economic Review* of March 1933. He died in 1933.

WEYERHAEUSER, FREDERICK EDWARD

(1872-1945) — Lumberman and financier, was born on November 4, 1872, in Rock Island, Illinois, the son of Frederick Weyerhaeuser and Elizabeth Sarah (Bloedel) Weyerhaeuser. In 1891, the family moved to St. Paul, Minnesota, where his father led numerous family groups in investing in timberlands and sawmills located in Louisiana, Arkansas, Idaho, Oregon, and Washington. These ventures were soon represented by such corporations as the Southern Lumber Company, Boise Payette Lumber Company, Potlatch Lumber Company, and Weyerhaeuser Timber Company, their well-known successors being Boise Cascade Corporation, Potlatch Forests, Inc., and the Weyerhaeuser Company.

Frederick E. Weyerhaeuser attended public schools in Rock Island, Phillips Academy at Andover, Massachusetts, and Yale University, where he received a B.A. in 1896. After spending four years learning the various functions of the lumber business, in 1900, he became president of Southern Lumber Company in Warren, Arkansas. There he and others built saw mills, a railroad, and facilities for manufacturing and marketing lumber. In 1903, he entered his father's office in St. Paul. He gradually assumed responsibility for the coordination of family investments, as well as the financial supervision of the numerous lumber firms in which the family held an interest, taking complete charge after his father's death in 1914.

Early in his career, Weyerhaeuser instituted an auditing system that resulted in standardized financial reporting and more effective comparative analysis of the performance of the numerous companies with which he was concerned. Noting that many of the family's associated mills competed with each other in the same markets and utilized a variety of wholesaling outlets, he suggested that the wholesaling function be performed by a new, common agency. Beginning informally in 1916, the Weyerhaeuser Sales Company was incorporated three years later. The corporation became a nationwide wholesaler and remained active until the Weyerhaeuser Company absorbed its operations and properties in the 1960s.

Weyerhaeuser held directorships in the Edward Hines Lumber Company, Boise Payette Lumber Company, Northwest Paper Company in Virginia, Rainy Lake Lumber Company, and Weyerhaeuser Timber Company, as well as in the Great Northern Railway Company, the Merchants National and First National banks of St. Paul, and the Illinois Bank & Trust and Continental Illinois National Bank & Trust companies of Chicago. He served as treasurer of the Weyerhaeuser Timber

Company, the most important single firm among the Weyerhaeuser associated enterprises, from 1906 to 19Z8 and as president from 1934 until his death in 1945.

He headed the St. Paul Community Chest in 1922, and served for twenty-four years on the board of directors of the St. Paul Young Men's Christian Association, and for a time, as a member of the International Committee of the YMCA. An elder of the House of Hope Presbyterian Church in St. Paul, he was for a number of years president and a vigorous supporter of the Union Gospel Mission.

Weyerhaeuser married Harriette Louise Davis on December 3, 1902; they had three children: Virginia, Frederick, and Charles Davis. He died of leukemia on October 18, 1945, in St. Paul, Minnesota, and was buried there in Oakland Cemetery.

WILCZYNSKI, ERNEST JULIUS

(1876-1932) — Mathematician, educator, was born on November 13, 1876, in Hamburg, Germany, the son of Max and Friederike (Hurwitz) Wilczynski. His family immigrated to America while he was still quite young, and settled in Chicago, Illinois. He attended elementary school and high school in Chicago and, with the assistance of an uncle, returned to Germany to enter the University of Berlin, where he received a Ph.D. in 1897. He was then in his twenty-first year. After his return to the United States he was a computer in the office of the *Nautical Almanac* in 1898, and then he was appointed instructor in mathematics at the University of California. Here he remained as assistant and associate professor until 1907, with the exception of the period from 1903 to 1905 when he was in Europe as a research associate of the Carnegie Institution of Washington. He was associate professor of mathematics at the University of Illinois from 1907 to 1910 and at the University of Chicago from 1910 to 1914. He was made professor of mathematics at Chicago in 1914 and, after his health failed, professor emeritus in 1926. He died on September 14, 1932 in Denver, Colorado. Although the illness kept him in bed most of the time, he never gave up hope of some day returning to his academic duties.

He began his scientific career as a mathematical astronomer and his interest then turned to differential equations, but he attained eminence as a projective differential geometer. He largely created this field of geometry. He invented a new method in geometry and established himself as the leader of a new school of geometers. Various scientific honors and recognitions were conferred upon him. He was lecturer at the

New Haven Colloquium of the American Mathematical Society in 1906 with E. H. Moore and Max Mason. He was vice-president of the American Mathematical Society, and a member of the council of the Mathematical Association of America. In 1909 he won a prize of the Royal Belgian Academy of Sciences for an original paper in geometry, and he was elected a member of the National Academy of Sciences in 1919. He was also a fellow of the American Association for the Advancement of Science.

One of Wilczynski's primary accomplishments was his mastery of the difficult art of lucid mathematical exposition. He possessed a fine and polished style both in spoken and written English and in German, his native language. He was familiar with French and Italian. His lectures, clear and concise, were greatly admired by his students. His genius and enthusiasm for mathematics attracted many people around him and placed him early in a position of great influence in American mathematical education. His college texts, as well as various labors entirely disconnected with the classroom, contributed to this end. A complete bibliography of Wilczynski's publications numbers more than seventy-five. He was married to Countess Inez Macola of Verona, Italy, on August 9, 1906. She with their three daughters survived him.

WILLARD, FRANCES ELIZABETH CAROLINE

(1839-1898) — Educator, reformer and founder of the World Woman's Christian Temperance Union; she was born near Rochester, New York, on September 28, 1839, the daughter of Josiah Willard, a businessman and farmer, and Mary Thompson Hill, a schoolteacher. When she was two, her father sold the large farm and business interests and they moved to Ohio, where both parents studied at Oberlin College. Frances had a brother, five years older; her sister was born while the family lived in Oberlin, Ohio. In April 1846, the family moved to Janesville, Wisconsin, where she spent the remainder of her childhood on their large frontier farm at Forest Home, near Janesville. She was a strong-willed, independent child; her friends called her "Frank." She had brief stints at the rural public schools, but was mainly tutored by her mother. In 1857, she studied for one year at Milwaukee Female College (later named Milwaukee-downer College) and then at North Western Female College in Evanston, Illinois. Later, this became a part of Northwestern University. Willard graduated, receiving a "Laureatte of Science" in 1859. She was valedictorian. In 1861, she became engaged to Christ Fowler, who became a prominent Methodist minister and educator, but they never married. Willard had several serious relationships with men but her primary emotional ties were apparently with women, although they seem not to be homosexual in nature; including her mother and several colleagues and friends, especially Anna Gordon, her secretary and lifelong companion, and Lady Henry Somerset, a British temperance leader.

She taught school as a very young woman for several years in spite of a disapproving father. This included several Illinois academies and rural schools. Her sister died of Tuberculosis in 1862; Willard wrote a book as eulogy for her that year. In

Frances Elizabeth Caroline Willard

1868, she and her friend Kate Jackson made an extended tour of the world until 1870, which included some study at universities in Paris and Berlin, which completed her education. Upon her return she settled in Evanston. She became president of Evanston College for Ladies, dean of the women's department of Northwestern and professor of English and Art. She might have pursued an academic career had not her former fiancé, Charles Fowler, become Northwestern's president in 1871. Unable to share authority with him, she resigned in 1873.

The temperance movement, or the so-called "Woman's crusade," which was a flood of antiliquor sentiment among women, was gathering steam and it provided Willard with a new career. A group of Chicago women invited Willard to become president of their temperance organization (1874). She perceptively foresaw that the movement and women's concerns found real focus in the crusade of 1873 and the organization of the Woman's Christian Temperance Union (WCTU) the next year. She also recognized that temperance was about to be the reform cause most attractive to women in the public life and that there was enough room in the movement for creative leadership. She was elected secretary of the national WCTU at its organizational meeting in 1874 and transformed the position into the life force of the organization. She was a talented speaker and writer, and following an organized, effective campaign on behalf of temperance.

She resigned as president of the Chicago WCTU in 1877 and worked briefly as director of women's meetings for evangelist Dwight L. Moody. Later that year she left the national WCTU, partly because of the resistance president Annie Wittenmeyer to combine suffrage and liquor prohibition, which was Willard's idea. Willard lectured far and wide on suffrage for a year before she was elected president of the Illinois WCTU in 1878. She obtained more than one hundred thousand signatures on a petition, assisted by her friend and secretary Anna Gordon, requesting the Illinois legislature to grant women the vote in matters pertaining to the liquor industry. However, in March 1879, the petition died in committee. At the national WCTU convention (1879), Willard succeeded Wittenmeyer s president of the WCTU, a post she held the rest of her life. Willard therefore was elected president of the largest women's organization in the country, with twenty-seven thousand regular members and another twenty-five thousand junior auxiliaries. For the next twenty years, the WCTU grew both in number and in range of concerns. Under Willard's presidency the union endorsed and promoted woman suffrage, the kindergarten movement, prison reform, the eight-hour workday, model facilities for handicapped children, federal aid to education, and vocational training. Willard became both a highly respected and visible national leader.

Under her direction, the WCTU quickly evolved into a well-organized group able to campaign for public education and political pressure on many fields. She traveled constantly and spoke frequently (in 1883 she lectured in every state in the Union) and was a regular at the summer Lake Chautauqua meetings in New York. Lectures fees were her means of income until the WCTU voted her a salary in 1886. In 1883, efforts on an international scale began with the mission of Mary C. Leavitt and others and the circulation of the "Polyglot Petition" against the international drug trade. In 1888, she joined May Wright Sewall at the international Council of Women meeting in Washington, D.C. and laid the groundwork for a permanent National Council of Women, of which she was its first president in 1888-90. Willard also helped organize the General Federation of Women's Clubs (1889) and in 1891 was elected president of the World WCTU. However, Willard's attempt to persuade the WCTU to take an active role in politics ultimately failed. She organized a short-lived merger of the "Home Protection Party," regarding women voting on liquor laws, with the Prohibition Party in 1882-84, but the prohibitionists ultimately objected to a woman suffrage platform. Trying to organize this third political "People's Party" was a goal she never relinquished. After 1892, she spent much time in England on the international scene as world WCTU president and because of her close friendship with Lady Henry Somerset. Willard was in poor health in the 1890s, which limited her activity. She died in New York City on February 17, 1898, from pernicious anemia.

She was a leader of the first mass organization of American women; Frances Willard made an unparalleled contribution toward the movement of women into public life, combining leadership, social vision, and sharp intelligence with virtues of the nineteenth century. She raised temperance advocates' awareness of bigger issues and the possible impact of women in a modern society. Over the years, Willard wrote frequently for periodicals and WCTU publications. Her autobiography, Glimpses of Fifty Years, was published in 1889. In 1905, a statue of Willard became one of Illinois' two submissions to Statuary Hall in the United States Capitol.

WILLARD, FRANK HENRY

(1893-1958) — Comic artist, was born on September 21, 1893, in Anna, Illinois, the son of Francis William Willard and Laura Kirkham. After being "tossed out of the local high school for something or other," he had a similar experience at the Union Academy of Southern Illinois, also in Anna. He tried a run of odd jobs that included working at a mental hospital and operating a sandwich stand at county fairs. In 1909, his father moved to Chicago. Later the family followed, and Willard was a claim tracer in a department store. He attended night classes at the Illinois Academy of Fine Arts in 1913.

In the summer of 1914 Willard noted that the outbreak of World War I caught the Chicago Tribune temporarily lacking the services of a political cartoonist. He drew a caricature of the God of War as a chauffeur touring the battlefields with Death and Devastation as passengers. He entitled it "Touring Europe" and sold it to the managing editor of the Tribune for $15. His cartoon appeared prominently on the front page, four columns wide.

Willard continued as a freelance cartoonist while seeking a steady position. Since there was no full-time opening on the Tribune, he applied at the Chicago Herald, only to be rejected as lacking in education and experience. Willard then proposed drawing a comic strip, and it was accepted. Employed in 1914 at $20 a week, he produced "City Life," "Mrs. Pippin's Husband," and a children's attraction, "Tom, Dick and Harry." He stayed with the Herald until he was drafted into the army in

October 1917. Assigned to the Eighty-sixth Division as an infantryman, he was transferred in May 1918 to its road-building engineers, and served with the Allied Expeditionary Forces from September 1918 to July 1919.

After settling in New York City, Willard drew a strip called "The Outta Luck Club," the "Penny Ante" series, and an occasional cartoon for the King Features Syndicate (1920-1923). Joseph M. Patterson, of the *New York Daily News*, which begun in 1919, wanted a different comic strip for his new readership, and met up with Willard for its conception. After discussing the chief figure, a tough fellow utterly without manners that they named Moon Mullins, Willard developed the popular comic series. Moon Mullins made his bow on June 14, 1923, and Willard then joined the *Chicago Tribune-New York News Syndicate*.

In 1923, he married Priscilla Mangold; they had two children. He died in 1958.

Daniel Hale Williams

WILLIAMS, DANIEL HALE

(1856-1931) — Surgeon and hospital administrator; biracial physician known today for pioneer surgery on the pericardium, repairing a knife wound with the use of stitches; he is credited with the first successful heart surgery; he was born in Hollidaysburg, south central Pennsylvania on January 18, 1856, the son of Daniel Williams, Jr. and Sarah Price. He was fifth of seven children; Daniel's father was a barber who moved the family to Annapolis, Maryland but died shortly afterwards of tuberculosis. Daniel's mother sent some of the children to live with relatives, realizing she could not manage them all. Daniel was apprentices to a shoemaker in Baltimore, but ran away to rejoin his mother in Rockford, Illinois. Later, he moved to Edgerton, Wisconsin, where he joined his sister and opened his own barbershop. When he moved to Janesville, he began noticing a local physician and became enamored with the work, deciding to follow that career route. He apprenticed to Dr. Henry Palmer for two years and in 1880 entered a school now known as Northwestern University Medical School. He graduated in 1883 and opened his own medical practice in Chicago, Illinois.

The school he graduated from was called Chicago Medical College; he served as surgeon for the South Side Dispensary (1884-1892) and was physician for the Protestant Orphan Asylum (1884-1893). During this era, there were many primitive social and medical situations that existed and much of his early medical practice necessitated that he treat patients in their homes, including occasional emergency surgeries on kitchen tables. Because of that, Williams was able to utilize many of the new antiseptic sterilization procedures of the day; he thereby gained a great reputation for his professionalism. He was appointed surgeon on the staff of the South Side Dispensary and then became a clinical instructor in anatomy at Northwestern. In 1889, he was appointed to the Illinois State Board of Health and a year later decided to create an interracial hospital.

In April 1889, Williams married Alice Johnson in Washington, D.C.

In response to the opportunities lacking for minorities, African Americans in particular, Williams founded in 1891 the first interracial hospital, named Provident, to provide training for black interns and the first school for black nurses in the United States. He was a surgeon on staff there from 1892-1893, 1898-1912, and surgeon-in-chief of Freedmen's Hospital, in Washington, D.C. where he also established a school for African American nurses.

On July 10, 1893, Williams performed some brave and innovative heart surgery at Provident. Though conventional wisdom and contemporary medical opinion disapproved of surgical treatment for heart wounds, Williams opened the thoracic cavity of a patient (James Cornish, who had been stabbed by knife) without the benefit of transfusion, modern anesthetics, or antibiotics. He examined the patient's heart during surgery, sutured the pericardium of the wound (the sac around the heart) and closed his chest. Following surgery, the patient lived another twenty years or more. This procedure is often credited as the first heart surgery; critics argue that the pericardium is "not" the heart itself; other sources say that a similar operation was performed in 1891 by H.C. Dalton of St. Louis.

Williams served later on the staffs of Cook County Hospital (1903-1909) and St. Luke's Hospital, both Chicago. From 1899, he was professor of clinical surgery at Meharry Medical College in Nashville, Tennessee and was member of the Illinois State Board of Health (1889-

1891). He published numerous articles on surgery in medical journals. Williams became the only African American charter member of the American College of Surgeons in 1913.

In 1895, Dr. Williams co-founded the National Medical Association for black doctors. On August 4, 1931, Dr. Daniel Hale Williams died of a stroke in his home on Lake Idlewild, Yates Township in Lake County, Michigan.

WILLIAMS, FANNIE BARRIER

(1855-1944) — African American social reform lecturer and women's organizations leader, was born on February 12, 1855, in Brockport, New York, the daughter of Anthony J. and Harriet Prince Barrier. She attended local public schools, and graduated from the State Normal School at Brockport in 1870. She then taught at freemen's schools in the South and in Washington, D.C. While teaching, she also studied at the New England Conservatory of Music in Boston, Massachusetts, and the School of Fine Arts in D.C. In 1887, she retired from teaching and married S. Laing Williams, an attorney from Georgia. Shortly thereafter, they moved to Chicago, Illinois, where she helped her husband set up his law practice.

Williams became active in social reform and welfare, and in 1891, she helped Daniel Hale Williams establish Provident Hospital and its associated training facility for nurses. In 1983, she convinced to include African Americans in the World's Columbian Exposition in Chicago, and with her address, "The Intellectual Progress of the Colored Women of the United States Since the Emancipation Proclamation," given before the World's Congress of Representative Women at the exhibition, gained her a national reputation as a public speaker. In September of that same year, she addressed the World's Parliament of Religions. She was an instrumental figure in the founding of the National League of Colored Women, which in 1896 joined the National Federation of Afro-American Woman to form the National Association of Colored Women. She was also active in the Illinois Women's Alliance. In 1895, Williams was admitted as the first African American into the Chicago Women's Club. The African American Council elected her as corresponding secretary for their 1902 convention in Saint Paul, Minnesota.

An early supporter of Frederick Douglass' reform ideology, Williams became a strong supporter of conservative leader Booker T. Washington in the early 1900s, then supported W. E. B. Du Bois with the formation of the National Association for the Advancement of Colored People. Throughout the years, she contributed regularly to the *Woman's Era* (the first newspaper published by an African American Woman in the United States), *A New Negro for a New Century*, *New York Age*, and the *Record-Herald*, writing about religious duty, suffrage, race problems, and women's activities. After her husband's death in 1921, she became less active in social reform; however, from 1924 to 1926, was the first African American and first woman to serve on the Library Board of Chicago. She died on March 4, 1944, from arteriosclerosis. She had no children.

WILSON, HUGH ROBERT

(1885-1946) — Diplomat, was born on January 29, 1885, in Evanston, Illinois, the son of Hugh Robert Wilson and Alice (Tousey) Wilson. The father was a founder and partner of Wilson Brothers, a Chicago wholesale house dealing in men's furnishings. Wilson was educated at the Hill School in Pottstown, Pennsylvania, and at Yale, where he received a B.A. in 1906. After a year traveling around the world, he entered the family business. Wilson then looked to diplomatic service.

After studying at the École Libre des Sciences Politiques in Paris, France (1910-1911), and serving briefly as private secretary to Edwin Morgan, the American minister in Lisbon, Wilson returned to the United States and passed the Foreign Service examination. The following year, he was appointed secretary of the American legation in Guatemala. A similar post followed in Buenos Aires (1914-1916), and after other brief assignments, he became first secretary in Berne, Switzerland (1917-1919). Meanwhile, on April 25, 1914, he had married Katherine Bogle. They had one child, Hugh Robert, born in 1918.

Wilson was counselor of the American embassies in Berlin (1920-1921) and Tokyo (1921-1923), and chief of the Division of Current Information in the State Department (1924-1927). In the controversy over the administration of the Rogers Act of 1924, which amalgamated the diplomatic and consular branches into a single foreign service, he served as chairman of the Foreign Service Personnel Board. In 1927, President Calvin Coolidge appointed Wilson minister to Switzerland.

During Wilson's ten years in Switzerland, he reported on European events, channeled information to Washington on League of Nations affairs in Geneva, and represented the United States at conferences. During the Manchurian crisis of 1931-1932, he helped secure League of Nations adoption of the non-recognition doctrine of Secretary of State Henry L. Stimson. He also served as a delegate to the World Disarmament Conference of 1932-1934.

Wilson returned to Washington, D.C., as assistant secretary of state in August 1937. The following January, President Franklin D. Roosevelt named him to succeed William E. Dodd as ambassador to Germany. Wilson hoped to encourage reintegration of Germany into the political and economic mainstream of Europe. President Roosevelt recalled Wilson in November 1938 to protest the Nazi pogrom against the Jews, and he resigned at the end of August 1939.

Wilson next became an administrative officer in the state department assigned to handle war-related problems. In January 1940, he was appointed vice-chairman of the department's Advisory Committee on Problems of Foreign Relations, dealing with peace plans, disarmament, and international economics. He resigned from the Foreign Service at the end of 1940.

During World War II, he served (1941-1945) in the Office of Strategic Services, an agency for espionage and counter-intelligence. A Republican, Wilson also acted during the war as a liaison between his party and the Roosevelt administration. In 1945, he became chief of the foreign affairs section of the Republican National Committee. The next year, on December 29, 1946, Wilson died of a heart attack. He was buried in Rosehill Cemetery, Chicago, Illinois.

WILSON, JAMES HARRISON

(1837-1925) — Engineer, cavalryman, and author, was born near Shawneetown, Illinois, the son of Harrison and Katharine (Schneyder) Wilson. He attended school, and completed one academic year at McKendree College. He entered the U.S. Military Academy on July 1, 1855. Graduating in the class of 1860, he was commissioned second lieutenant of topographical engineers and assigned to duty at Fort Vancouver until ordered east in the summer of 1861. He was chief topographical engineer with General Thomas W. Sherman on the Port Royal expedition, and with General David Hunter, took part in the reduction of Fort Pulaski. Then, as volunteer aid to General George McClellan, he served in the battles of South Mountain and Antietam.

A few weeks later, Wilson joined General Ulysses S. Grant's headquarters, and early in 1863, was named inspector general, Army of the Tennessee. He was engaged in the action at Port Gibson; the capture of Jackson, Mississippi; the battles of Champion's Hill and Big Black

Bridge; and in the siege and capture of Vicksburg. He was advanced on October 31, 1863, to brigadier general of volunteers. He participated in the battle of Missionary Ridge, was chief engineer on the expedition for the relief of Knoxville, and in January 1864, was appointed chief of the cavalry bureau at Washington, D.C.

James Harrison Wilson

At the opening of the spring campaign, Wilson was assigned to command the third division in General Philip Sheridan's cavalry corps, Army of the Potomac. The division was in the combat of Yellow Tavern, covered Grant's passage to the Chickahominy, and formed part of Sheridan's first Richmond expedition. After a few days in front of Petersburg, Wilson was sent to Sheridan in the Shenandoah Valley, and took part in the Battle of the Opequon (Winchester) on September 19, 1864. In October, he was appointed chief of cavalry, Military Division of the Mississippi, with brevet rank of major general.

Encountering Confederate Nathan Forrest's cavalry at Franklin on November 30, 1864, Wilson drove it back across the Harpeth River, enabling General John Schofield to repulse Confederate General John Hood and withdraw to Nashville, Tennessee. With greater numbers present and better equipment, Wilson defeated Forrest at Ebenezer Church on April 1, 1865, and the next day, broke through and surmounted the fortifications of Selma, Alabama. He entered Montgomery without resistance, and took Columbus, Georgia, by assault. On April 20, 1865, he reached Macon, and there ceased hostilities, but kept military control. Detachments from his command intercepted Jefferson Davis and brought him to Macon.

In the army reorganization after the war, Wilson was appointed lieutenant colonel of the Thirty-fifth Infantry on July 28, 1866, but reassigned to the engineers. For four years, he superintended navigation improvements, mainly on the Mississippi, resigning from the army on December 31, 1870, to engage in railway construction and management. He settled in Wilmington, Delaware, in 1883, pursuing business enterprises, public affairs, travel, and writing.

Wilson volunteered for the Spanish-American War and was designated to command the VI Corps, which, however, was not organized. In July 1898, he conducted part of the I Corps to Puerto Rico, and was appointed military governor of the city and province of Ponce; while marching toward the interior, he was ordered back to the United States. He prepared the I Corps for Cuba, took one division to Matanzas, and in the military occupation was assigned the Matanzas department and later the Santa Clara department and the city of Cienfuegos. Knowing something of China from nearly a year's investigation in 1885-1886 of possible railway developments there, he was appointed second in command to General Adna R. Chaffee of forces sent to cooperate in suppressing the Boxer uprising; he reached Peking after the allies had rescued the legations, but led the American British contingent against the Boxers at the Eight Temples. Returning to the United States in December 1900, he was placed by special Act of Congress upon the retired list as brigadier general in the regular service. On March 4, 1915, he was advanced to major general. By presidential appointment, he represented the army at the coronation of King Edward VII in 1902.

Among his more significant publications were a number of military biographies, beginning with *The Life of Ulysses S. Grant* (1868), edited somewhat by Charles A. Dana, and including lives of *Andrew J. Alexander* (1887), *William Farrar Smith* (1904), his friend *John A. Rawlins* (1916), as well as articles for the Association of Graduates of the U.S. Military Academy on *Philip H. Sheridan* (1889) and *A. McDowell McCook* (1904). He contributed "The Union Cavalry in the Hood Campaign" to *Battles and Leaders of the Civil War* (1888). After his first trip to China, he published *China; Travels and Investigations in the "Middle Kingdom"* (1887), of which a third edition was issued in 1901 and extended to include an account of the Boxer episode. His own recollections of service in the Civil War, the war with Spain, and the Boxer trouble are included in *Under the Old Flag* (1912).

On January 3, 1866, Wilson married Ella Andrews, who was fatally burned at Matanzas, Cuba, on April 28, 1900; three daughters were born to them. He died in 1925 in Wilmington, Delaware.

WILSON, MARGARET WILHEMINA

(1882-1973) — Author and missionary, was born in Traer, Iowa, on January 16, 1882, the daughter of West Wilson and Agnes (McCornack) Wilson. The family moved from Traer to Ames, Iowa, then to Chicago,

Illinois, in 1897. Wilson attended Englewood High School in Chicago. From there, she went to the University of Chicago, receiving an associate's degree in 1903, and a bachelor's degree in philosophy in 1904. Wilson's first poem was published when she was twelve under the pseudonym Elizabeth West, entitled "Pain."

In the fall of 1904, just after graduating from University of Chicago, Wilson enlisted as a missionary in the *J* service of the United Presbyterian Church of North America. Her service was confined to the Punjab region in northern India, where she performed a variety of tasks including teacher and supervisor in the Gujranwala Girls School. It was from these experiences that she drew upon for two of her later novels, *Daughters of India* (1928) and *Trousers of Taffeta* (1929). Due to ill health, the result of a bout with typhoid, and the strain of the mission work, Wilson returned to the United States in 1910, and officially resigned in 1916.

Wilson entered the divinity school of the University of Chicago in 1912, as a degree student and completed the academic year. For the next five years, she taught at Pullman High School and worked on her short stories, written under the name An Elderly Spinster. She returned to divinity school in 1917, but remained only two quarters. Her father's health was failing and much of her time was spent caring for him and the rest spent on writing. It was during this period that she wrote several short stories and two novels, *The Able McLaughlins* (1923), for which she won the 1924 Pulitzer Prize, and the *Kenworthys* (1925). Her father died in 1923, and Wilson traveled to Europe, where she married George Douglas Turner in Paris on Christmas Eve 1923. The Two had met in India, where Turner had been secretary of the Young Men's Christian Association in Lahore.

During her early years of marriage, settled in England, Wilson wrote *The Painted Room* (1926), and her two novels based on India. Turner's views on the penal system, crime and prison began to influence Wilson and her writing; Turner had held a number of positions in British prisons, and maintained that often laws make the criminal and prisons are generally ineffective in producing rehabilitation.

With ill-health plaguing Turner, he retired in 1938, but continued his cause through writing and public appearances. In the meantime, Wilson wrote a nonfiction piece, *The Crime of Punishment* (1931), and three novels, *The Dark Duty* (1931), The *Valiant Wife* (1933) and *The Law and the McLaughlins* (1936).

During World War II, the British government called upon

Turner for a number of duties. Their home was often the site of shelter for a number of soldiers and refugees. Wilson's final novel, a children's story, *The Devon Treasure Mystery* (1939) was written to pay for the installation of central heat in their country home. Tuner died in 1946, and Wilson never resumed writing. She died on October 6, 1973, in Droitwichm Worcester, England.

WOLFE, HARRY KIRKE

(1858-1918) — Psychologist and educator, was born in Bloomington, Illinois, the son of Jacob Vance and Ellen B. Wolfe, descendants of ancestors prominent in Virginia and Kentucky. His father, a graduate of Indiana University, served for fifteen years as high school principal, lawyer, and legislator in Indiana, and then in 1871 settled on a farm in Nebraska, near Lincoln. There the parents maintained a cultured home, reared and educated a large family, and supported educational and political institutions. Harry Kirke, the eldest son, took his A.B. at the University of Nebraska in 1880. He then went in 1883 to the University of Berlin to win a doctorate in the classics. The next year, however, he transferred to the University of Leipzig, Germany, and became one of the early American students in psychology with Wilhelm Wundt. In 1886 he received a Ph.D. at Leipzig and returned to Nebraska as a high school teacher. In 1888 he went to a school position in San Luis Obispo, California. There he married Katherine H. Brandt of Philadelphia, Pennsylvania, on December 19, 1888. Wolfe returned to the University of Nebraska in 1889, commissioned to organize work in philosophy and psychology. At first designated lecturer, he became in 1890 associate professor and in 1891 professor and head of department. He at once began to prepare a laboratory for experimental psychology, one of the earliest to be established in America. The work was immediately successful. In a half dozen years he had sent forward into eastern graduate schools such men as Walter B. Pillsbury, Madison Bentley, Hartley Alexander, and several others of professional note, while students were crowding his classrooms and laboratories.

In the spring of 1897, certain administrative problems hung over the University of Nebraska. The effort of Wolfe to bear some hand in their solution proved unfortunate, and resulted in action by the Board of Regents on March 29, 1897, to discontinue his services. It seems clear that both sides to that controversy used less than sound judgment. But its effects upon the professional career of Wolfe were disastrous. He was indeed offered other posts in psychology. But hoping still and always to serve the people of the West he rejected offers from distant universities and threw himself rather into the work of modernizing the secondary schools. From 1897 to 1901 he was superintendent of schools in South Omaha, Nebraska, and from 1902 to 1905 principal of the Lincoln High School. In 1905 he went to the University of Montana as professor of philosophy and education, but returned to the University of Nebraska in 1906 as professor of educational psychology. Three years later he was shifted back to his old position and became professor of philosophy, his own portion of the work lying then, however, entirely in psychology. But his sudden death from angina pectoris came too soon to permit his new career in pure science to attain its full fruition.

WOLFSOHN, CARL

(1834-1907) — Musician, was born on December 14, 1834, in Alzey, Hesse, Germany, the son of Benjamin and Sara (Belmont) Wolfsohn. He began piano lessons at the age of seven, and was soon placed under the guidance of Aloys Schmitt at Frankfort, with whom he studied two years. Here he made his debut as a pianist in the Beethoven piano quintet in December 1848. He then studied two years with Vincenz Lachner, made successful concert tours through Rhenish Bavaria, and went to London, where he lived two years before coming to America in 1854. He settled in Philadelphia, Pennsylvania, and for nearly twenty years, wielded a wide influence through his varied activities as pianist, teacher, and conductor. During this period, he gave annual series of chamber-music concerts and for two seasons gave symphony concerts with a Philadelphia orchestra.

In 1863, he attracted nationwide attention by presenting all of the Beethoven piano sonatas in a series of recitals, first in Philadelphia, then in Steinway Hall, New York City. The series was repeated the following year in both cities with notable success. Soon after this, he gave the entire piano works of Schumann, then of Chopin, in a similar series of concerts. In 1869, he founded the Beethoven Society, and four years later, moved to Chicago, Illinois, to conduct a similar society organized especially for him. Its first concert took place on January 15, 1874, and the society soon attained an active membership of about two hundred. Wolfsohn directed its activities until 1884, when interest waned and it was disbanded. In addition, he gave monthly chamber music and piano recitals. In the spring of 1874, he repeated the series of ten Beethoven sonata recitals; in the next spring, the piano works of Schumann; and in 1876, those of Chopin. In 1877, he planned a series of historical recitals covering the whole literature of the piano. The project was abandoned after the fifteenth recital.

From 1856 on, Wolfsohn was closely associated with Theodore Thomas in chamber music in Philadelphia and Chicago and on tour. He died on July 30, 1907. He was never married.

WOOD, JOHN

(1798-1880) — Twelfth governor of Illinois (1860-1861), was born in New York, the son of Daniel and Catherine (Crouse) Wood. He arrived in Shawneetown, Illinois, in 1819, after leaving home with the intention of settling in Tennessee or northern Alabama.

Wood decided to stay at a farm in Pike County, Illinois, however, and lived there for two years before building the first cabin at what is now Quincy. He and Willard Keyes established claims there, and Wood became a leader in a settlement called "The Bluffs." He helped defeat those who pushed for a state constitution recognizing slavery in 1824, and his anti-slavery beliefs prevented him from moving to Missouri.

Wood was a private in the Black Hawk War. In 1825, he petitioned the state legislature to create Adams County, and was successful in retaining Quincy as the county seat. Throughout his lifetime, Woods continued to direct the city situated on the Mississippi as its trustee and mayor.

Wood was elected to the state senate in 1850, and in 1856, he was elected lieutenant governor of the state. This position led him to the gubernatorial chair when William Bissell died in 1860. A year later his successor, Richard Yates, appointed him one of the five delegates to the Peace Convention in Washington. But when war broke out, he was appointed quartermaster of the state, and then colonel of the 137th Illinois Volunteers in 1864. Later that year, he retired and returned to his business in Quincy.

He died in 1880 and was buried at Quincy.

WRIGHT, FRANK LLOYD

(1869-1959) — Architect, was born Frank Lincoln Wright on June 8, 1869, in Richland Center, Wisconsin, the son of William C. Wright, an itinerant musician and preacher, and his second wife, schoolteacher Anna Lloyd-James. (Wright later changed his middle name to Lloyd.) The family moved to Iowa in 1869, and then on to Rhode Island and Weymouth, Massachusetts, eventually settling back in Wisconsin.

Wright studied civil engineering at the University of Wisconsin from 1884 to 1887, while working for the dean of engineering to supplement the family income. He set out for Chicago, Illinois, in the latter year. He began working as a draftsman on residential plans, and one year later, he signed on with the Adler & Sullivan architectural firm. There he designed houses using characteristic horizontality and cubic ideas. This trend became known as the "Prairie School" of architecture, and by 1900, the style had matured, with Wright being its main practitioner. Between 1900 and 1910, Wright designed approximately fifty Prairie houses.

Frank Lloyd Wright

In June 1889, Wright married Catherine Tobin. They eventually had six children, but by 1909 the marriage was over and Wright was having an affair with Mamah Cheney, the wife of one of his former clients. Around this time, he began work on his own house near Spring Green, Wisconsin, which he called "Taliesin." By 1911, still married and unable to get a divorce, Wright was living with Cheney at Taliesin. In 1913, he had gained sufficient fame for his works that he was being considered as architect for a new hotel in Tokyo, Japan, as well as other notable buildings in Europe and the United States. In 1914, while Wright was in Chicago supervising the construction of Midway Gardens, a houseman at Taliesin killed Cheney and her children, and the house was set afire. Although devastated, Wright began to rebuild his home and was soon joined by a sculptress named Miriam Noel. Wright and Noel eventually moved to Japan in 1916, and lived there for five years. During that time, Wright was commissioned to design the Imperial Hotel in Tokyo, Japan. Although it was dismantled in 1967, this building was considered one of Wright's most significant works. Though shunned by conventional Victorian-gothic architects, he gained renown in the 1925 Paris Exposition, and was asked to give a series of lectures on modern architecture at Princeton University. He wrote an autobiography in 1932. His insistence on functionalism produced a revolutionary plan for a church in Kansas City (1940), which was air-conditioned, with pillars of light instead of the traditional tower. A triple-decker parking lot was an integral part of the plan, because Wright believed it would be "unethical" not to provide for traffic to the church. Wright's homes are scattered throughout Chicago's suburbs, and drawings and photographs of his works have been presented at the Museum of Modern Art in New York. He wrote *Modern Architecture* (1930), *Organic Architecture* (1940), *Genius and the Mobocracy* (1949), and *Natural House* (1954). He died on April 9, 1959, in Phoenix, Arizona.

Y

YANCEY, JAMES EDWARD, "JIMMY"

(1898-1951) — Musician credited with originating the "boogie-woogie" piano style, was born on February 20, 1898, in Chicago, Illinois. At the age of six, Yancey began touring with a vaudeville troupe as a singer and tap dancer, an occupation he continued into adolescence. He was a member of the Bert Earle, Cozy Smith, and Jeanette Adler organizations; traveled the Orpheum circuit; and worked under the direction of the Theater Owners' Booking Association. In 1910, during one of several trips to Europe, he appeared before the British royal family.

In 1913, Yancey returned to Chicago, where he became interested in baseball, and for several years, played with a team known as the All Americans. At the same time, he continued his musical activities, and as a self-taught pianist, began to perform regularly at "rent parties" and in barrelhouses on the city's south side. It was during this period that he married a vocalist named Estella, better known as "Mama"; they had one son.

Yancey specialized in the blues, playing the piano as if it was a percussion instrument capable of producing both melody and rhythm. His first number to gain wide acceptance, "Five O'Clock Blues" (better known as "The Fives"), dates from 1913. Although it was not then called boogie-woogie, the piece had the characteristic slow-rolling bass patterns that later came to be associated with this piano style. In addition to his jobs at private parties, Yancey played at such Chicago clubs as Bear Trap No. 1 and Moonlight Inn. In 1925, however, he ceased trying to earn a living from music and became a grounds keeper for the Chicago White Sox baseball club at Comiskey Park, a position he held for twenty-five years.

Although no longer active as a performing musician, Yancey did teach his piano style to his friends, Meade Lux Lewis and Albert Ammons, both of whom achieved fame as boogie-woogie players. He suffered a stroke in the mid-1930s that partially paralyzed his fingers and made playing temporarily impossible. Lewis made his mentor's name known, however, with a 1936 recording of "Yancey Special" and the Bob Crosby band recorded another version of the number. These, together with records by Ammons, Lewis, and other stars of the boogie-woogie idiom, were responsible for the pre-World War II interest in this musical form.

With the rise in popularity of boogie-woogie, Yancey was sought out and induced to record for the first time. In 1939 and 1940, his output included the piano solo "The Fives" and two vocals, "Death Letter Blues" and "Cryin' in My Sleep." Although he recorded periodically throughout the decade, it was in February 1948 that Yancey began his first steady playing job in twenty-five years, as featured soloist at the Beehive in Chicago. He and Mama also performed together at Carnegie Hall in New York as part of a concert tour by jazz trombonist Edward ("Kid") Ory in April of that year.

Toward the end of his life, Yancey's activities were seriously impeded by diabetes. Yancey died on September 17, 1951, in Chicago, Illinois.

Richard Yates

YATES, RICHARD

(1815?18-1873) — Thirteenth governor of Illinois (1861-1865), was born in Kentucky, the son of Henry and Millicent Yates. He moved to Sangamon County, Illinois, in 1831. He was educated at Miami University in Ohio, Georgetown College in Kentucky, and was a graduate of the first class of Illinois College in 1835.

After graduation, Yates moved back to Kentucky to study law at Transylvania University. In 1837, he returned to Illinois to begin a law practice. In 1842, he began a career in public life as a member of the state legislature, holding his seat until 1845, and again in 1848-1849.

Yates also served as a Whig in the U.S. House of Representatives for four years, beginning in 1851. Although unsuccessful in his attempts for reelection in 1854, he became a delegate to the Republican State Convention that year, and was also a delegate to the Republican National Convention in 1860. During that time, he also practiced law and controlled the interests of a new railroad company, the Tonica and Petersburg, later renamed the Chicago and Alton.

In 1860, Yates won the gubernatorial race on the Republican

ticket. In his inauguration speech, he stood against any concession or compromise with the South, thereby establishing his loyalty to newly elected President Abraham Lincoln and the Union. He declared that "the whole material of the government, moral, political, and physical, if need be, must be employed to preserve, protect, and defend the constitution of the United States." When Lincoln called for troops, Yates sent more than double the state's quota for volunteers. Yates also appointed West Point-educated Ulysses S. Grant as Mustering Officer for Illinois, which gave him the reputation of being the state's "war governor."

The state legislature, usually in opposition to the governor, passed a resolution to compromise with the seceded states, but Yates delayed the legislature until a Republican majority came into power a year later. He actively supported emancipation of African slaves, recommending to Lincoln that "loyal blacks" be enlisted in the Union cause. After his governorship, he was elected to the U. S. Senate, where he continued to fight against "Southern sympathizers," as well as for reconstruction efforts.

In 1871, Yates retired from public life, except for a position as U. S. Commissioner to inspect land subsidy railroads. He continued his law practice until his death in St. Louis, Missouri, in 1873.

YATES, RICHARD

(1860-1936) — Twenty-fourth governor of Illinois (1901-1905), was born in Jacksonville, Illinois, the son of Catherine Geers and former governor Richard Yates. The junior Yates was the first native-born Illinoisan to become governor.

In 1880, Yates received a Bachelor of Arts degree from Illinois College, and three years later, he earned a master's degree from that institution. Following the example of his father, Yates won honors for his oratory skills in college, and afterwards studied the law. He graduated from the law school at the University of Michigan in 1884, and was admitted to the bar that year.

From 1885 to 1890, Yates served as City Attorney of Jacksonville. After losing as the Republican candidate for U. S. Congress in 1892, he was elected Judge of Morgan County. He resigned that post five years later when President William McKinley appointed him U. S. Collector of Internal Revenue for the Central District of the state, based at Springfield.

Yates political connections soon gained him the nomination for governor, and he defeated the Democratic candidate. His nomination came on the fortieth anniversary of his father's nomination for the same office. While in office, Yates strove for more thrifty administration of public funds. He vetoed a bill for improvements on the executive mansion, as well as legislation to allow racetracks in the state. Yates also protected blacks with state troops when race riots broke out in Saline County.

Yates lost the re-nomination for governor at the Republican convention in 1894, however, and the next year he left office. He was also unsuccessful in gaining the nomination in 1908 and 1912. From 1914 to 1917, he was a member of the State Public Utilities Commission, and was elected to the U. S. House of Representatives in 1918, where he served until 1933. After losing a reelection in 1932, he retired from politics.

He died at Jacksonville and was buried at his birthplace in 1926.

YOUNG, ARTHUR HENRY, "ART"

(1866-1943) — Cartoonist, author, and Socialist, was born on January 14, 1866, in Stephenson County, Illinois, near Orangeville, the son of Daniel Stephen Young and Amanda Wagner. When he was a year old, the family moved to nearby Monroe, Wisconsin, where he attended the district school. While working as a photographer's helper, he sold a comic "boy-and-dog" drawing that poked fun at "literary Bostonese" to *Judge.*

At the age of eighteen, he went to Chicago, Illinois, enrolled in the Academy of Design, and began to support himself as a freelance illustrator. He published his first cartoon in 1884 in a grocer's magazine, the *Nimble Nickel.* After short hitches on the *Evening Mail*, the *Daily News*, and the *Tribune*, he moved on to New York City in 1888 to enroll at the Art Student's League. The next year, he tackled Paris, France, and the Academic Julian, only to be stricken in six months by pleurisy and an operation that nearly cost his life. Following a long convalescence in Monroe, in 1892, he signed up to draw daily political cartoons on the *Chicago Inter-Ocean.* He also participated in the *Inter-Ocean's* Sunday supplement for African Americans launched in 1892. Young was married on January 1, 1895, to Elizabeth North. They had two sons, North and Donald Minot, and separated after eight years. In 1896, he served briefly as cartoonist for the *Times* in Denver.

Foreseeing his future in New York, Young moved to Washington Square and prepared comic drawings for *Judge, Life,* and *Puck.* At the invitation of Arthur Brisbane, he drew cartoon illustrations for editorials in Hearst's *Evening Journal* and *Sunday American*. He volunteered his talents in 1902 for the reelection campaign of Governor Robert M. LaFollette of Wisconsin.

As he approached forty, Young undertook serious debate of public issues at Cooper Union, came under the influence of the muckraking journalists, and steeped himself in radical literature. Young now refused to draw cartoons whose ideas he did not support, and by 1910, concluded that he belonged in the Socialist "war on capitalism." He was a frequent contributor to the *Masses*, beginning with its first issue in January 1911. For much of this period, Young was also the Washington correspondent (1912-1917) for *Metropolitan* magazine. The Newspaper Enterprise Association syndicated his political cartoons in the election year of 1916.

His *Masses* cartoons were twice involved in prosecutions. In November 1913, he was indicted, along with Max Eastman, editor of the *Masses*, on a charge of criminal libel filed by the Associated Press. The offending cartoon, "Poisoned at the Source," showed a man personifying the Associated Press pouring into a reservoir labeled "The News" the dark contents of bottles of "Lies, Suppressed Facts, Prejudice, Slander, and Hatred of Labor Organizations." The case was dropped after a year. In April 1918, Young, with several colleagues, was charged with "conspiracy to obstruct enlistment." A cited cartoon, "Having Their Fling," presented an editor, capitalist, politician, and minister doing a wild dance before a war-munitions orchestra led by Satan. The defendants were tried twice and released because the juries disagreed.

When the *Masses* was suppressed in 1918, Young joined in establishing the *Liberator*, to which he contributed steadily. From 1919 to 1921, he published his own weekly, *Good Morning*. During the early 1930s, he contributed occasional cartoons and some prose to the *New Yorker*.

Young's first book, *Hades up to Date* (1892), self-illustrated as were all the others, appeared in Chicago when he was twenty-six. Other titles included *Author's Readings* (1897), *Through Hell with Hiprah Hunt* (1901), *Trees at Night* (1927), *On My Way* (1928), *Art Young's Inferno* (1934), and *Thomas Rowlandson* (1938). John N. Beffel edited the autobiographical *Art Young: His Life and Times* (1939). A harvest of his drawings, *The Best of Art Young*, appeared in 1936.

Young died of a heart attack on December 29, 1943.

YOUNG, MURAT BERNARD, "CHIC"

(1901-1973) — Cartoonist and creator of the popular "Blondie" cartoon strip, was born on January 9, 1901, in Chicago, Illinois, the son of James Luther and Martha (Techen) Young. He attended public schools in Chicago and St. Louis, Illinois, and then took classes in art schools in New York, Chicago, and Cleveland, Ohio. He got his first job as a cartoonist working at the Newspaper Enterprise Association in 1920. He switched to Bell Syndicate a year later. In 1923, he went back to King Features Syndicate where he stayed for the rest of his career. Early on, Young specialized in cartoons about "ditzy" women, including "Beautiful Babs," "Dumb Dora," and "Colonel Potterby and the Duchess." "Dumb Dora" was his most successful early strip, which ran from 1924 to 1930. Young had married Athel L. Lindorff in October 1927, and they eventually had three children. He created "Blondie" in 1930, as a gold-digging flapper named Blondie Boopadoop, who had her heart set on rich playboy Dagwood Bumstead, son of J. Bolling Bumstead, a foul-tempered railroad tycoon. The cartoon saw little success until King Features manager Joseph V. Connolly suggested that Young make the cartoon more domestic. "Why don't you have them marry?" he said to Young. "You know more about married life then you do about flighty dames anyway."

Taking his suggestion, Young had the newlywed Bumsteads settle down. Eventually they left Dagwood's blue blood behind and they became typical suburbanites. The cast of characters grew to include neighbors, Herb and Tootsie Woodley; Daisy the dog; Dagwood's short-tempered boss, J.C. Dithers, and his wife, Cora; not to mention the postman, the newspaper boy, and thousands of door-to-door salesmen. On April 15, 1934, the Bumsteads had a son, first known as Baby Dumpling, later named Alexander. They also had a daughter, Cookie. Dagwood was the typical harried husband and father, always trying to make more money that his wife spent as fast as he brought it home. He also had the typical refuges: the bed, the sofa for naps, and the hot bath, not to mention mile-high Dagwood sandwiches he made on nights he could not sleep. The strip and the couple became immensely popular, syndicated in 1,600 newspapers worldwide. In the 1930s and 1940s, there were movies and radio programs based on "Blondie," and in the early 1950s, she was the subject of a television series.

Young continued to draw the cartoon himself until he was seventy-one years old, when he passed it on to his son, Dean, and Jim

Raymond. He died a year later on March 14, 1973, in Clearwater, Florida.

YOUNG, RICHARD MONTGOMERY

(1798-1861) Senator from Illinois; Senate Years of Service: 1837-1843; born in Fayette County, Ky., February 20, 1798; attended the country schools and Forest Hill Academy, Jessamine County, Ky.; studied law and was admitted to the bar in Kentucky in 1816; member of the Kentucky Militia; moved to Illinois in 1817 and commenced the practice of law in Jonesboro; appointed captain in the Illinois Militia; member, State house of representatives 1820-1822; circuit judge of the fifth circuit 1825-1837, when he resigned, having been elected to the United States Senate; elected as a Democrat to the United States Senate and served from March 4, 1837, to March 3, 1843; chairman, Committee on Roads and Canals (Twenty-fifth and Twenty-sixth Congresses); member of the mission to England to negotiate a loan for the State of Illinois in 1839; associate justice of the State supreme court 1843-1847, when he resigned; appointed by President James Polk as Commissioner of the General Land Office 1847-1849; Clerk of the United States House of Representatives 1850-1851; resumed the practice of law in Washington, D.C., where he died November 28, 1861; interment in the Congressional Cemetery.

Richard Montgomery Young

Z

ZEISLER, SIGMUND

(1860-1931) — Lawyer, was born on April 11, 1860, in Bielitz, Silesia, Austria (later Poland), the son of Isaac L. and Anna (Kanner) Zeisler. Graduating in 1878 from the Imperial College in Bielitz, he began the study of law and political science at the University of Vienna, receiving a J.D. in 1883. He then immigrated to America, and in 1884, after a year's study at Northwestern University, was granted an LL.B. He was also awarded a prize for the best essay on an original thesis, "Rights and Liabilities of the Finder of Chattels Casually Lost on Land." Very shortly after entering upon the practice of law in Chicago, Illinois, 1884, he became associate counsel in a *cause celebre*, the Chicago Anarchists Case. His efforts on behalf of the defendants in that case, though unsuccessful in acquitting them of the charge of murder, identified him as a political liberal and as one with the courage to espouse unpopular causes that he thought to be just.

During the years that Zeisler engaged in general practice in Chicago, he was assistant corporation counsel for Chicago (1893-1894), master in chancery for Cook County Circuit Court (1904-1920), lecturer on Roman law at Northwestern University (1884-1886 and 1892-1893), and lecturer on constitutional law at John Marshall Law School (1901-1904). For many years he was active in the Municipal Voters League, and from 1925 until his death, was its president. He was also a member of the executive committee of the Civil Service Reform Association and of the advisory committee of the American Judicature Society.

Zeisler wrote or lectured frequently in the fields of art, music, literature, and science. He paid his way through Northwestern University in part by writing music criticisms for a German newspaper in Chicago. He was an earnest advocate of the abolition of the requirement of unanimity in the verdict of a jury, of a non-partisan system for the selection of judges, and of other reforms in the judicial system.

Zeisler's first wife, whom he married on October 18, 1885, was Fannie (Bloomfield) Zeisler, an internationally famous concert pianist. They had three sons, all of whom survived their parents. After Fannie Zeisler's death, he married Amelia Spielman on January 23, 1930. He died on June 4, 1931, in Chicago, Illinois.

ZIEGFELD, FLORENZ, "FLO"

(1867-1932) — Theatrical producer, was born on March 21, 1867, in Chicago, Illinois, the son of Florenz Ziegfeld, founder of the Chicago Musical College, and Rosalie (De Hez) Ziegfeld. He attended the Chicago public schools, and for the World's Fair of 1893, was involved in organizing entertainment, including bands and other musical features. He then became manager for Eugene Sandow, the strong man, exhibiting him at the fair, and later around the country. The first play he managed was *A Parlor Match* (1896), in which he introduced a young player he had seen in Paris, France, Anna Held. She appeared successively in *Papa's Wife*, *The Little Duchess*, *The Parisian Model*, and *Mlle Napoleon*. Ziegfeld, in 1907, began to experiment with a type of production rather new to America, the so-called "review." He called it "The Follies of 1901," and it was so favorably received that it was followed by a successor each season for more than twenty years.

The Ziegfeld Follies became noted all over the country for the lavish beauty of costumes, scenery, and stage tableaux, for the pulchritude of the chorus girls, and also for the liberal display of their charms. At the same time, the real beauty of his settings and ensemble effects raised the production standards of musical comedy. The humor of the librettos was generally turned over to such comedians as Will Rogers, Bert Williams, Eddie Cantor, and Leon Errol, who sometimes improvised their own skits.

In 1914, Ziegfeld produced *The Midnight Frolic* on top of the New Amsterdam Theatre, which continued until the advent of prohibition. In 1916, with Charles Dillingham, he took over for a time the ill-fated Century Theatre. Among his most successful productions, in addition to the *Follies* were *Sally*, with Marilyn Miller (1920), *Show Boat* (1927), *Bitter Sweet* (1929), and *Rio Rita*, with which he opened the Ziegfeld Theater on February 2, 1927. This theater, on Sixth Avenue near Central Park, New York, was designed for him by Joseph Urban especially to house his type of spectacular musical comedy.

Two years later, however, came the Great Depression. Ziegfeld's productions, mounted at great cost, and necessarily exacting a high tariff of the public, did not survive the depression. His fortunes ebbed, and he died in Hollywood, California, on July 22, 1932. His theater became a movie house.

Ziegfeld married Anna Held in Paris in 1897; they separated in 1908 and were divorced in 1913. On April 11, 1914, he married actress Billie Burke, who with a daughter survived him.

ZIEHN, BERNHARD

(1845-1912) — Musical theorist and teacher, was born on January 20, 1845, at Erfurt in Prussian Saxony, Germany. After graduating from a seminary for teachers, Ziehn received an appointment as teacher at Muhlhausen, where he remained for three years. He then immigrated to America to teach at a German Lutheran school in Chicago, Illinois, arriving in November 1868. For two years, he taught German, history, higher mathematics, and musical theory. He then devoted himself completely to the study and teaching of musical theory. All the musical literature he possessed was destroyed in the Chicago fire of 1871, save his collection of Beethoven sonatas. With these as a cornerstone, he resumed his researches into the nature of musical grammar and syntax. He became one of the greatest of autodidacts.

By 1886, the manuscript of Ziehn's great treatise on harmony was completed. It was published at Berlin in 1888 as *Harmonie-und Modulationslehre*. It was an epoch-making work on harmonic analysis, with hundreds of examples from musical literature. In 1907, he published the first volume of a completely recast English version of this work as *Manual of Harmony*. The second volume was never published, but presumably is preserved in manuscript. In the year 1911, he brought out his treatise on *Five and Six-Point Harmonies*, with eight hundred examples and five masterly harmonizations of German chorales. His noteworthy contribution to contrapuntal technique, published as *Canonical Studies-a New Technic in Composition* (1912), went to press as he lay on his deathbed. The development of the idea of symmetrical inversion of melodic phrases constitutes one of his most brilliant achievements. In his earliest publications, *System der Uebungen fur Clavierspieler* and *Ein Lehrgang fur den ersten Unterricht*, (Hamburg, 1881), he invented finger exercises in contrary motion so as to insure the symmetrical development of both hands.

An outstanding achievement was his solution of the unfinished final fugue in Sebastian Bach's *Art of the Fugue*. Gustav Nottebohm arrived independently at practically the same solution, but to Ziehn belongs the priority. Ziehn was also known for his monographic demonstration of the spuriousness of the St. Lucas Passion, a choral work traditionally attributed to Bach. He was a constant contributor to the German music journal, *Die Allgemeine Musik-zeitung*. Most of Ziehn's musicological writings were reprinted in 1927 by the German-American Historical Society of Illinois in a volume of "Gesammelte Aufsatze zur Geschichte und Theorie der Musik," *Jahrbuch der Deutsch-*

Amerikanischen Historischen Gesellschaft von Illinois, vols. XXVI-XXVII (1927).

Ziehn was married to Emma Trabing, of Chicago, who, with a son, survived him, upon his death on September 8, 1912. A daughter died in infancy.

ZIFF, WILLIAM BERNARD

(1898-1953) — Publisher, author, and editor, was born on August 1, 1898, in Chicago, Illinois, the son of David Ziff and Libby Mary Semco Ziff. He attended Crane Technical High School in Chicago, where he was chosen class artist. He then studied for two years (1915-1917) at the Art Institute of Chicago. After he left school, he set himself up as a commercial artist and worked briefly as a cartoonist for the *Chicago Daily News*. During World War I, Ziff served with the U.S. Army's 202nd Aero Observation Squadron.

At the age of twenty-two, Ziff organized an advertising agency in Chicago, which dealt principally with newspaper advertising. In 1923, Ziff became the head of E. C. Auld Company, a Chicago publishing house. *Ziff's Magazine*, a humorous periodical, was his first venture in magazine publishing. The name of the new magazine, which at first was written and illustrated almost entirely by Ziff, was subsequently changed to *America's Humor*. He continued as its editor for several years.

From 1931 to 1933, Ziff was editor and publisher of *Aeronautics*, a magazine that printed a number of General William ("Billy") Mitchell's controversial articles calling for the reformation of American air policy and a unified U.S. Air Force. A strong believer in Mitchell's doctrines, Ziff wrote many articles on military subjects.

In 1931, Ziff unsuccessfully sought the Republican nomination for congressman in the Second District of Illinois. In 1933, he organized the corporation that eventually became Ziff-Davis Publishing. By 1946, the firm was publishing a dozen magazines including: the semi-technical *Flying, Popular Photography, Radio News, and Plastics*, and the successful "pulps" *Amazing Stories, Air Adventures, Fantastic Adventures*, and *Mammoth Detective*. The company added a book publishing division in 1942 by buying Alliance Book Corporation, and was soon issuing some sixty titles a year. In 1949, the book publishing division was sold to Prentice-Hall.

Ziff's first book, *The Rape of Palestine* (1938), was a bitter criticism of Great Britain's acts and policies in the administration of the Palestine mandate and the treatment of Jews. His next book, *The Coming*

Battle of Germany (1942), urging the immediate Allied recognition that air power was the single weapon by which victory over Germany could be achieved, became a bestseller. In *The Gentlemen Talk of Peace* (1944), Ziff surveyed the problems of peacemaking. *Two Worlds* (1946) was a closely reasoned discussion of world power politics, a disillusioned analysis of the problems of keeping the peace. His last book, *He, the Maker* (1949), a short, episodic book of poetry, received little critical notice.

On July 25, 1923, Ziff married Denea Fischer; they had one daughter. The marriage ended in divorce; and on April 27, 1929, Ziff then married Amelia Mary Morton; they had three children. Ziff died on December 20, 1953, in New York City. His son William Bernard Ziff, Jr., eventually became the head of the publishing firm.

ZUPPKE, ROBERT CARL

(1879-1957) — Football coach, was born on July 2, 1879, in Berlin, Germany, the son of Franz Simon Zuppke and Hermine Bocksbaum. In 1881, the Zuppkes migrated to Milwaukee, Wisconsin, where he attended public school, and for two years, Milwaukee Normal School. Skilled at drawing and painting, he was a member of the art staff of the Milwaukee Normal yearbook in 1901. Zuppke then entered the University of Wisconsin at Madison, where he earned the Ph.B. After graduating in 1905, Zuppke spent a year doing commercial artwork in New York City. He then took a position as athletic director and football coach at Muskegon High School (1906-1910) in Michigan, where he also taught history.

He next served at the high school in Oak Park, Illinois, and three years later, the athletic directors of Northwestern, Purdue, and the University of Illinois all made Zuppke offers. Impressed by its athletic director, George Huff, he accepted a position at the University of Illinois as head football coach. In his second season (1914), Zuppke's team won the conference championship. Illinois captured a second conference title in 1915. What went into the record books as "the little Dutchman's" team scored one of the biggest upsets in football history in 1918. Minnesota, which had defeated Chicago 49-0, Wisconsin 54-0, and Iowa 67-0, was turned back by Illinois, 14-9. Zuppke teams also won conference championships in 1918, 1919, 1923, 1927, and 1928.

A persistent innovator, Zuppke either devised or contributed to the development of the huddle, the screen pass, the spiral pass from center, the "flea flicker" pass, and other plays and strategies. He was also credited with originating spring practice. Coaches throughout the country watched Illinois to see what its coach would come up with next.

Zuppke's last years as coach were controversial ones. Championships eluded his teams. A plan to remove him took form in 1938. He survived, but the athletic director, Wendell S. Wilson, was dismissed. In 1941, his team lost all its conference games. Just before the final game, Zuppke announced his retirement. His twenty-nine-year record was 131 victories, 81 defeats, and 12 ties. His teams were recognized as national champions in 1914, 1919, 1923, and 1927.

Zuppke often filled positions such as commissioner of sports programs at the Century of Progress Exposition at Chicago (1933-1934) and the New York World's Fair (1939-1940). He chaired the $2 million campaign for the University of Illinois War Memorial Stadium (1922-1923), and was president of the American Football Coaches Association (1924-1925). In 1942, he coached the All-Star Football Team. In 1951, Zuppke was elected to the National Football Hall of Fame.

Continuing to paint throughout his life, Zuppke's landscapes and other works were exhibited in New York, New York; Chicago, Illinois; Milwaukee, Wisconsin; Toledo, Ohio; Davenport, Iowa; and elsewhere. Arizona was a favorite setting.

He was married twice: on June 27, 1908, to Fanny Tillotson Erwin, who died in 1936; and on September 10, 1956, to Leona Rav. Zuppke died on December 22, 1957, in Champaign, Illinois.

Place Index

Albion
EMMERSON, LOUIS LINCOLN – (1863-1941) – Governor of Illinois
FLOWER, BENJAMIN ORANGE – (1858-1918) – Editor and social reformer
KOHLSAAT, HERMAN HENRY – (1853-1924) – Restauranteur and editor
PENTECOST, GEORGE FREDERICK – (1842-1920) – Clergyman and author

Alton
DAVIS, MILES DEWEY – (1926-1991) – Jazz trumpeter, composer

Anna
WILLARD, FRANK HENRY – (1893-1958) – Comic artist

Aurora
GALE, HENRY GORDON – (1874-1942) – Physicist
PARRINGTON, VERNON LOUIS – (1871-1929) – Teacher, philologist, and historian

Austin
BARRETT, ALBERT MOORE – (1871-1936) – Psychiatrist and neuropathologist

Beardstown
McLAUGHLIN, ANDREW CUNNINGHAM – (1861-1947) – Historian

Belleville
BAKER, JAMES – (1818-1898) – Trapper, guide, and pioneer settler
BLACK BEAVER – (1806-1880) – Native American of the Delaware tribe
DIXON, ALAN JOHN – (1927-) – Senator
KEMPFF, LOUIS – (1841-1920) – Naval officer
WESTERMANN, WILLIAM LINN – (1873-1954) – Papyrologist and ancient historian

Bloomingdale
LILLIE, GORDON WILLIAM, "PAWNEE BILL" – (1860-1942) – Frontiersman and Wild West showman

Bloomington
CROTHERS, RACHEL – (1878-1958) – Playwright
DAVISSON, CLINTON JOSEPH – (1881-1958) – Physicist
GOUDY, FREDERIC WILLIAM – (1865-1947) – Lettering artist, type designer, and printer
HARBORD, JAMES GUTHRIE – (1866-1947) – Army officer and corporation executive
HUBBARD, ELBERT – (1856-1915) – Writer
ILLINGTON, MARGARET – (1879-1934) – Actress
MOWRER, PAUL SCOTT – (1887-1971) – War correspondent
ROBINSON, BENJAMIN LINCOLN – (1864-1935) – Botanist
WOLFE, HARRY KIRKE – (1858-1918) – Psychologist and educator

Braidwood
MITCHELL, JOHN – (1870-1919) – Labor leader

Brocton
GARD, SANFORD WAYNE – (1899-1986) – Historian, educator, journalist and author

Bushnell
NEWELL, PETER SHEAF MERSEY – (1862-1924) – Cartoonist and illustrator

Byron
SPALDING, "A. G." ALBERT GOODWILL, "AL" – (1850-1915) – Sportsman and merchant

Cairo
HART, GEORGE OVERBURY – (1868-1933) – Painter and etcher

Canton
DURYEA, CHARLES EDGAR – (1861-1938) – Inventor and automobile manufacturer

Place Index

Carbondale
AYRES, AGNES – (1898-1940) – Screen star

Carlinville
AUSTIN, MARY (HUNTER) – (1868-1934) – Author
BORING, WILLIAM ALCIPHRON – (1859-1937) – Architect and educational administrator

Carlyle
SLADE, (JOSEPH ALFRED), "JACK" – (1824-1864) – Gunfighter, murderer

Carrollton
RAINEY, HENRY THOMAS – (1860-1934) – Speaker of the House

Cedarville
ADDAMS, (LAURA) JANE – (1860-1935) – Social reformer, peace activist

Champaign
WESTON, NATHAN AUSTIN – (1868-1933) – Economist

Chandlerville
LUCAS, SCOTT WIKE – (1892-1968) – Representative and Senator

Charleston
EDGAR, JAMES – (1946-) – Governor of Illinois

Chicago
ADAMS, FRANKLIN PIERCE – (1881-1860) – Author, editor, humorist, lyricist, and translator
AGER, MILTON – (1893-1979) – Song composer and pianist
ALINSKY, SAUL DAVID – (1909-1972) – Social activist
ALLISON, SAMUEL KING – (1900-1965) – Physicist
BALABAN, BARNEY – (1887-1971) – Motion picture executive
BARNES, MARGARET AYER – (1886-1967) – Author and critic
BELLAMY, RALPH – (1904-1991) – Actor
BELUSHI, JOHN – (1949-1982) – Comedian and actor
BENNY, JACK – (1894-1974) – Comedian, actor, and violinist
BERGEN, EDGAR – (1903-1978) – Ventriloquist comic

Place Index

BEVAN, ARTHUR DEAN – (1861-1943) – Surgeon

BLACKSTONE, HARRY – (1885-1965) – Magician

BLAGOJEVICH, ROD R. – (1956-) – Governor of Illinois

BLISS, GILBERT AMES – (1876-1951) – Mathematician and educator

BLOCK, HERBERT LAWRENCE – (1909-2001) – Editorial cartoonist

BOHROD, AARON – (1907-1992) – Artist and teacher

BOWEN, LOUISE DeKOVEN – (1859-1953) – Philanthropist and reformer

BRECKINRIDGE, HENRY SKILLMAN – (1886-1960) – Lawyer and government official

BURROUGHS, EDGAR RICE – (1875-1950) – Author

CAMERON, ANDREW CARR – (1834-1890) – Labor leader and publisher

CHALMERS, WILLIAM JAMES – (1852-1938) – Manufacturer

CHANCELLOR, JOHN WILLIAM – (1927-1996) – Broadcast journalist

CHANDLER, RAYMOND THORNTON – (1888-1959) – Author

COLLYER, ROBERT – (1823-1912) – Clergyman, Unitarian minister

COMISKEY, GRACE ELIZABETH REIDY – (1893-1956) – White Sox baseball team owner

COPPENS, CHARLES – (1835-1920) – Roman Catholic priest and educator

COSTIGAN, GEORGE PURCELL – (1870-1934) – Professor of law

COZZENS, JAMES GOULD – (1903-1978) – Author

CRANE, CHARLES RICHARD – (1858-1939) – Businessman and philanthropist

CURTIS, CHARLOTTE – (1928-1987) – Journalist and author

DALEY, RICHARD JOSEPH – (1902-1976) – Mayor

DANENHOWER, JOHN WILSON – (1849-1887) – Arctic explorer

DIAL, MORSE GRAN – (1895-1982) – President of Union Carbide and Carbon Corporation

DISNEY, WALTER ELIAS "WALT" – (1901-1966) – Creator of animated films

DOS PASSOS, JOHN RODERIGO – (1896-1970) – Author

DOUBLEDAY, NELTJE DeGRAFF, (NELTJE BLANCHAN) – (1865-1918) – Naturalist and author

DOUGLAS, EMILY TAFT – (1899-1994) – Congresswoman

DUNBAR, (HELEN) FLANDERS – (1902-1959) – Psychoanalyst

DUNHAM, KATHERINE – (1909-2006) – Dancer, choreographer, and anthropologist

DUNNE, FINLEY PETER – (1867-1936) – Humorist and author

Place Index

EDDY, MANTON SPRAGUE – (1892-1962) – Army officer in World War II

EDWARDS, INDIA (MOFFETT) – (1895-1990) – Journalist and political executive

FIELD, MARSHALL, III – (1893-1956) – Publisher and business executive

FOSSE, ROBERT LOUIS, "BOB" – (1927-1987) – Choreographer and director

FRANKENSTEIN, ALFRED VICTOR – (1906-1981) – Author, educator

FRANKFURTER, ALFRED MORITZ – (1906-1965) – Art critic and connoisseur

GARDNER, GILSON – (1869-1935) – Journalist

GATES, CALEB FRANK – (1857-1946) – Missionary and college president

GEIS, BERNARD J. – (1909-2001) – Publisher and editor

GOBEL, GEORGE LESLIE – (1920-1991) – Television comedian

GOLDBERG, ARTHUR JOSEPH – (1908-1990) – Supreme Court justice, secretary of labor

GOLDMAN, JAMES A. – (1927-1998) – Playwright, screenwriter, author, and lyricist

GOODMAN, BENJAMIN DAVID, "BENNY" – (1909-1986) – Clarinetist and orchestra leader

GRAHAM, EVARTS AMBROSE – (1883-1957) – Surgeon

GRAHAM, VIRGINIA – (1912?13-1998) – Journalist and radio and television personality

GROTH, JOHN AUGUST – (1908-1988) – Artist, illustrator and journalist

HALE, LOUISE CLOSSER – (1872-1933) – Actress and author

HANSBERRY, LORRAINE – (1930-1965) – Playwright

HAPGOOD, HUTCHINS – (1869-1944) – Newspaperman and author

HELMER, BESSIE BRADWELL – (1858-1927) – Lawyer, editor, and publisher

HORNER, HENRY – (1879-1940) – Governor of Illinois

KERNER, OTTO, JR. – (1908-1976) – Governor of Illinois

JORDAN, MICHAEL JEFFREY – (1963-) – Professional basketball player

KILEY, RICHARD PAUL – (1922-1999) – Musical and dramatic actor

KILGALLEN, DOROTHY MAE – (1913-1965) – Newspaperwoman, television and radio personality

KOCH, FRED CONRAD – (1876-1948) – Biochemist

LARDNER, JOHN ABBOTT – (1912-1960) – Journalist

Place Index

LAWSON, VICTOR FREEMONT – (1850-1925) – Journalist

LEIBER, FRITZ – (1882-1949) – Actor and theatrical producer

LEITER, JOSEPH – (1868-1932) – Capitalist

LENZ, SIDNEY SAMUEL – (1873-1960) – Authority on contract bridge

MAYER, OSCAR GOTTFRIED – (1888-1965) – Meat packer

McCORMICK, JOSEPH MEDILL – (1877-1925) – Representative and Senator

McCORMICK, ROBERT RUTHERFORD – (1880-1955) – Newspaper publisher

MILLER, PERRY GILBERT EDDY – (1905-1963) – Teacher and scholar

MONROE, HARRIET – (1860-1936) – Poet and editor

MOONEY, THOMAS JOSEPH – (1882-1942) – Labor radical

MOSELEY BRAUN, CAROL – (1947-) – Senator

MOTLEY, WILLARD FRANCIS – (1909-1965) – Novelist

NORRIS, CHARLES GILMAN SMITH – (1881-1945) – Novelist

NORRIS, FRANKLIN, "FRANK" – (1870-1902) – Author

NOVY, FREDERICK GEORGE – (1864-1957) – Microbiologist

PALEY, WILLIAM SAMUEL – (1901-1990) – Owner and president of CBS

PATTERSON, ELEANOR MEDILL, "CISSY" – (1881-1948) – Newspaper editor and publisher

PATTERSON, JOSEPH MEDILL – (1879-1946) – Newspaper publisher

PEATTIE, DONALD CULROSS – (1898-1964) – Naturalist and historian

PERKINS, GEORGE WALBRIDGE – (1862-1920) – Banker

POOLE, ERNEST COOK – (1880-1950) – Novelist and journalist

REDFIELD, ROBERT – (1897-1958) – Anthropologist and educator

REVELL, FLEMING HEWITT – (1849-1931) – Publisher

RUBY, JACK L. – (1911-1967) – Night Club owner, assassin of Lee Harvey Oswald

SILLS, MILTON (GEORGE GUSTAVUS) – (1882-1930) – Actor

SLATTERY, JAMES MICHAEL – (1878-1948) – Senator

SPALDING, ALBERT – (1888-1953) – Violinist

STETTINIUS, EDWARD REILLY – (1900-1949) – Corporate executive and U.S. secretary of state

STEVENSON, ADLAI EWING III – (1930-) – Senator

SWANSON, GLORIA MAY JOSEPHINE SVENSSON – (1899-1983) – Actress

SYMONS, (GEORGE) GARDNER – (1865-1930) – Landscape painter

TANNER, EDWARD EVERETT, III – (1921-1976) – Author

THOMPSON, ("BIG JIM") JAMES ROBERT – (1936-) – Governor of Illinois

THURSTONE, LOUIS LEON – (1887-1955) – Psychologist

TORME, MELVIN HOWARD – (1925-1996) – Singer, songwriter, film & television entertainer

WACKER, CHARLES HENRY – (1856-1929) – Brewer, executive and city planner

WASHINGTON, HAROLD – (1922-1987) – Mayor

YANCEY, JAMES EDWARD, "JIMMY" – (1898-1951) – Musician

YOUNG, MURAT BERNARD, "CHIC" – (1901-1973) – Cartoonist

ZIEGFELD, FLORENZ, "FLO" – (1867-1932) – Theatrical producer

ZIFF, WILLIAM BERNARD – (1898-1953) – Publisher, author, and editor

Cooperstown

DIETERICH, WILLIAM HENRY – (1876-1940) – Representative and Senator

Cortland

HOPKINS, ALBERT JARVIS – (1846-1922) – Representative and Senator

TALBOT, ARTHUR NEWELL – (1857-1942) – Civil engineer and engineering educator

Crete

McCUMBER, PORTER JAMES – (1858-1933) – Lawyer and politician

Danville

MORGAN, HELEN RIGGINS – (1900-1941) – Singer and actress

Davis

MEINZER, OSCAR EDWARD – (1876-1948) – Geologist

Decatur

DRESSEN, CHARLES WALTER, "CHUCK" – (1898-1966) – Baseball manager

Place Index

Dixon
BESTOR, ARTHUR EUGENE – (1879-1944) – Educator
DILLE, JOHN FLINT – (1884-1957) – Newspaper syndicator

Earlville
CRISLER, HERBERT ORIN, "FRITZ" – (1899-1982) – Football coach

East Haddam
BAKER, DAVID JEWETT – (1792-1869) – Senator

East St. Louis
DURBIN, RICHARD JOSEPH – (1944-) – Representative and Senator

Edwardsville
DENEEN, CHARLES S. – (1863-1940) – Governor of Illinois

El Paso
SHEEN, Bishop FULTON JOHN – (1895-1979) – Roman Catholic priest, writer, and educator

Elgin
BOSWORTH, EDWARD INCREASE – (1861-1927) – Congregational clergyman, educator
FITZGERALD, PETER G. – (1960-) – Senator
POWELL, ALMA WEBSTER – (1874-1930) – Singer and voice teacher
SHARP, KATHARINE LUCINDA – (1865-1914) – Librarian, library-school director

Elmwood
TAFT, LORADO ZADOC – (1860-1936) – Sculptor

Evanston
DOWNES, OLIN – (1886-1955) – Music critic
HARNWELL, GAYLORD PROBASCO – (1903-1982) – Physicist, educator, business executive, author
WILSON, HUGH ROBERT – (1885-1946) – Diplomat

Place Index

Fillmore
SHORT, WALTER CAMPBELL – (1880-1949) – U.S. Army officer

Flora
GREENLAW, EDWIN ALMIRON – (1874-1931) – Educator

Freeland Corners
PATTEN, JAMES A. – (1852-1928) – Grain merchant, capitalist, and philanthropist

Freeport
BENTLEY, ARTHUR FISHER – (1870-1957) – Political scientist, philosopher, and sociologist
THAYER, TIFFANY ELLSWORTH – (1902-1959) – Novelist, actor, and advertising scriptwriter

Galena
SCHWATKA, FREDERICK – (1849-1892) – Explorer

Galesburg
BANCROFT, EDGAR ADDISON – (1857-1925) – Lawyer, orator, and diplomat
BANCROFT, FREDERIC – (1860-1945) – Historian and philanthropist
CONGER, EDWIN HURD – (1843-1907) – Soldier, congressman, and diplomat
FERRIS, GEORGE WASHINGTON GALE – (1859-1896) – Civil engineer and inventor
HURLEY, EDWARD NASH – (1864-1933) – Industrialist and U.S. Shipping Board official
SANDBURG, CARL (AUGUST) – (1878-1967) – Author, poet, and biographer
WALGREEN, CHARLES RUDOLPH – (1873-1939) – Pharmacist and drugstore chain founder

Geneseo
CALKINS, EARNEST ELMO – (1868-1964) – Advertising executive and author

Place Index

Geneva
CHAMPION, GOWER – (1921-1980) – Choreographer, dancer, director

Georgetown
WEST, ROY OWEN – (1868-1958) – Secretary of the interior, party leader

Golconda
HODGE, JOHN REED – (1893-1963) – Army officer

Goodings Grove
BROPHY, TRUMAN WILLIAM – (1848-1928) – Oral surgeon

Grand Ridge
FINLEY, JOHN HUSTON – (1863-1940) – Editor, educator, and author

Granite City
SMITH, RALPH TYLER – (1915-1972) – Senator

Granville
SCHNEIDER, ALBERT – (1863-1928) – Bacteriologist

Greenup
WARMAN, CY – (1855-1914) – Journalist and author

Groveland
DUNIWAY, ABIGAIL JANE SCOTT – (1834-1915) – Suffragette and social historian
SCOTT, HARVEY WHITEFIELD – (1838-1910) – Editor

Harvey
BOUDREAU, LOUIS, "LOU" – (1917-2001) – Baseball player, manager, and baseball announcer

Highland Park
WESTON, EDWARD HENRY – (1886-1958) – Photographer

Place Index

Hillsboro
HUNTINGTON, WILLIAM EDWARDS – (1844-1930) – Clergyman and university president

Hope
VAN DOREN, CARL CLINTON – (1884-1950) – Literary critic and biographer

Hudson
STONE, MELVILLE ELIJAH – (1848-1929) – Journalist

Humboldt
BRANN, WILLIAM COWPER – (1855-1898) – Editor, reformer, and "iconoclast"

Hume
DOISY, EDWARD ADELBERT, Sr. – (1893-1986) – Biochemist and educator

Hunt Township
IVES, BURL – (1909-1995) – Folk singer and actor

Ingleside
STRATTON, WILLIAM G. – (1914-2001) – Governor of Illinois

Irwin
WARD, ARCH BURDETTE – (1896-1955) – Sportswriter and promoter

Jacksonville
BOVARD, OLIVER KIRBY – (1872-1945) – Newspaper editor
CAPPS, EDWARD – (1866-1950) – Classicist, instructor, and educator
JAMES, EDMUND JANES – (1855-1925) – Economist and university president
MARTIN, EVERETT DEAN – (1880-1941) – Social psychologist and educator
YATES, RICHARD – (1860-1936) – Governor of Illinois

Joliet
HIGINBOTHAM, HARLOW NILES – (1838-1919) – Merchant and

Mannheim
BRENTANO, LORENZ – (1813-1891) – Statesman and journalist

Mattoon
CHAMBERLIN, THOMAS CHROWDER – (1843-1928) – Scientist
GLENN, OTIS FERGUSON – (1879-1959) – Senator
McCLURE, ROBERT ALEXIS – (1897-1957) – Army officer, chief of psychological warfare

Maystown
McROBERTS, SAMUEL – (1799-1843) – Senator

McLeansboro
STELLE, JOHN H. – (1891-1962) – Governor of Illinois

Mendota
BETTENDORF, WILLIAM PETER – (1857-1910) – Inventor and manufacturer
HOKINSON, HELEN ELNA – (1893-1949) – Artist
GRAY, GLEN ("SPIKE") – (1900-1963) – Saxophonist and orchestra leader

Metropolis
MICHEAUX, OSCAR – (1884-1951) – Film producer and author

Moline
HARTZELL, JOSEPH CRANE – (1842-1929) – Missionary bishop

Morris
KINGSBURY, ALBERT – (1862-1943) – Mechanical engineer

Morrison
BROWN, GERTRUDE FOSTER – (1867-1956) – Suffragette and musician

Morrison
MILLIKAN, ROBERT ANDREWS – (1868-1953) – Physicist and educator

Place Index

Mounds
BURNETT, CORDAS CHRIS – (1917-1975) – Educator

Murphysboro
LOGAN, JOHN ALEXANDER – (1826-1886) – Representative and Senator
WALLER, WILLARD WALTER – (1899-1945) – Sociologist

Naperville
ADAMS, CYRUS CORNELIUS – (1849-1928) – Geographical writer and editor
STRONG, JOSIAH – (1847-1916) – Clergyman, social reformer, and author

Nashville
BLACKMUN, HARRY ANDREW – (1908-1999) – U.S. Supreme Court justice
EWING, WILLIAM LEE D. – (1795-1846) – Governor of Illinois

Normal
HOVEY, RICHARD – (1864-1900) – Poet

Norwood Park
REED, MYRTLE – (1874-1911) – Author

Oak Park
ENRIGHT, ELIZABETH – (1909-1968) – Artist and author
FEARING, KENNETH FLEXNER – (1902-1961) – Author and poet
HEMINGWAY, ERNEST – (1899-1961) – Author
HUMPHREY, DORIS – (1895-1958) – Dancer and choreographer

Orangeville
YOUNG, ARTHUR HENRY, "ART" – (1866-1943) – Cartoonist, author, and Socialist

Oswego
CROTHERS, SAMUEL McCHORD – (1857-1927) – Clergyman, essayist

Place Index

Oswego Township
BEAUPRE, ARTHUR MATTHIAS – (1853-1919) – Diplomat

Ottawa
CUSHMAN, VERA CHARLOTTE SCOTT – (1876-1946) – Organizer and leader in YWCA
STRAWN, SILAS HARDY – (1866-1946) – Lawyer and businessman

Otterville
McADAMS, CLARK – (1874-1935) – Editor, and newspaper

Park Ridge
CARPENTER, JOHN ALDEN – (1876-1951) – Composer

Pekin
BUMSTEAD, HENRY ANDREWS – (1870-1920) – Teacher, physicist
DIRKSEN, EVERETT MCKINLEY – (1896-1969) – Politician
STONE, ORMOND – (1847-1933) – Astronomer

Peoria
FRIEDAN, BETTY NAOMI (GOLDSTEIN) – (1921-2006) – Author and feminist leader
HOERR, NORMAND LOUIS – (1902-1958) – Histologist, neuroanatomist, and medical teacher
PRYOR, RICHARD – (1940-2005) – Actor, comedian

Peru
BRENNEMANN, JOSEPH – (1872-1944) – Pediatrician

Petersburg
McKINLEY, WILLIAM BROWN – (1856-1926) – Representative and Senator

Polo
PEEK, GEORGE NELSON – (1873-1943) – Businessman, farm leader

Prairie du Pont
SNYDER, JOHN FRANCIS – (1830-1921) – Physician, soldier, archaeologist, author

Princeton
BRYANT, RALPH CLEMENT – (1877-1939) – Forester and educator
ELLIOTT, JOHN LOVEJOY – (1868-1942) – Social worker and Ethical Culture leader
FOX, VIRGIL KEEL – (1912-1980) – Organist

Quincy
TURNER, AVERY – (1851-1933) – Railroad executive
TURNER, GEORGE KIBBE – (1869-1952) – Journalist, editor, and author

Ravenswood
BARROWS, DAVID PRESCOTT – (1873-1954) – Anthropologist, political scientist, journalist

Ridott
BODE, BOYD HENRY – (1873-1953) – Philosopher and educator

Rochelle
CORT, EDWIN CHARLES – (1879-1950) – Presbyterian medical missionary

Rock Island
ALBERT, EDDIE – (1906-2005) – Actor
ALMOND, GABRIEL ABRAHAM – (1911-2002) – Professor of political science and author
WALLACE, HENRY CANTWELL – (1866-1924) – Agricultural journalist, secretary of agriculture
WEYERHAEUSER, FREDERICK EDWARD – (1872-1945) – Lumberman and financier

Rockford
BREASTED, JAMES HENRY – (1865-1933) – Archaeologist and historian
GARST, ROSWELL – (1898-1977) – Agriculturist and businessman
LATHROP, JULIA CLIFFORD – (1858-1932) – Social worker

Rushville
DRAKE, FRANCIS MARION – (1830-1903) – Veteran, railroad builder, governor of Iowa

Place Index

SCRIPPS, EDWARD WYLLIS – (1854-1926) – Newspaper publisher

Salem
BRYAN, WILLIAM JENNINGS – (1860-1925) – Lawyer and political leader

Sandwich Township
PATTEN, SIMON NELSON – (1852-1922) – Economist

Saukenuk
KEOKUK – (1780-1848) – Native American Indian chief of the Sauk

Savanna
WAYMACK, WILLIAM WESLEY – (1888-1960) – Journalist and government official

Shabbona
HUSK, CHARLES ELLSWORTH – (1872-1916) – Physician

Sharpsburg
NEIHARDT, JOHN GNEISENAU – (1881-1973) – Author and poet

Shawneetown
WILSON, JAMES HARRISON – (1837-1925) – Engineer, cavalryman, and author

Silver Creek
FORBES, STEPHEN ALFRED – (1844-1930) – Entomologist, naturalist, ecologist

Springfield
BARROW, EDWARD GRANT – (1868-1953) – Baseball executive
COOLBRITH, INA DONNA – (1841-1928) – Poet
JOHNSON, ALBERT – (1869-1957) – Newspaper editor and politician
LINCOLN, ROBERT TODD – (1843-1926) – Secretary of war and minister to England
LINDSAY, (NICHOLAS) VACHEL – (1879-1931) – Poet
NICHOLSON, SETH BARNES – (1891-1963) – Astronomer
REVELL, NELLIE MacALENEY – (1872-1958) – Journalist, publicist, and radio personality

Place Index

ROSENWALD, JULIUS – (1862-1932) – Merchant and philanthropist

Streator
MULFORD, CLARENCE EDWARD – (1883-1956) – Writer
TOMBAUGH, CLYDE WILLIAM – (1906-1997) – Astronomer

Sublette
BARTON, WILLIAM ELEAZAR – (1861-1930) – Clergyman and author

Tampico
REAGAN, RONALD WILSON – (1911-2004) – President of the United States
REEVES, JOSEPH MASON – (1872-1948) – Naval officer

Tiskilwa
SIMPSON, CHARLES TORREY – (1846-1932) – Scientist

Troy Grove
HICKOK, JAMES BUTLER, "WILD BILL" – (1837-1876) – Soldier, scout, gunslinger and U.S. marshal

Turner Junction
GATES, JOHN WARNE – (1855-1911) – Financier

Tuscola
PEARSON, THOMAS GILBERT – (1873-1943) – Ornithologist and wildlife conservationist

Urbana
CRANE, FRANK – (1861-1928) – Methodist, Congregational clergyman and journalist

Vandalia
HUNT, HAROLDSON LAFAYETTE "H. L." – (1889-1974) – Industrialist

Virden
SIMONS, HENRY CALVERT – (1899-1946) – Economist